# Individual Decisions for Health

Although economics is a relative newcomer to research into the determinants of good health, its significance should not be underestimated. *Individual Decisions for Health* poses the important question of whether economic theory can be developed to explain why people engage in activities that are obviously a danger to their long-term health.

In looking first at the individual's own decisions that affect his or her health, and then at the impact of other agents' decisions for the individual's health, the authors provide an exhaustive account of the important issues to be faced to ensure the best future for public health. With contributions from such experts as Peter Zweifel, Donald S. Kenkel and Mark V. Pauly this book is a significant addition to the current debate and takes in such themes as:

- rationality and nicotine dependence
- cost-benefit analysis of screening for cancer
- insurers versus governments as complementary agents
- the role of patient expectations.

Of great interest to advanced students of health economics, *Individual Decisions for Health* will also be extremely useful to students, academics, and professionals involved in the sphere of public health.

**Björn Lindgren** is Professor of Health Economics at Lund University, Sweden, and Director of Lund University Centre for Health Economics (LUCHE).

**Routledge International Studies in Health Economics**

Edited by Charles Normand, *London School of Hygiene and Tropical Medicine*, and Richard M. Scheffler, *School of Public Health, University of California*

**1 Individual Decisions for Health**
  *Edited by Björn Lindgren*

# Individual Decisions for Health

Edited by Björn Lindgren

London and New York

First published 2002
by Routledge
11 New Fetter Lane, London EC4P 4EE

Simultaneously published in the USA and Canada
by Routledge
29 West 35th Street, New York, NY 10001

*Routledge is an imprint of the Taylor & Francis Group*

Typeset in Times by
Integra Software Services Pvt. Ltd, Pondicherry, India
Printed and bound in Great Britain by
The Cromwell Press, Trowbridge, Wiltshire

*British Library Cataloguing in Publication Data*
A catalogue record for this book is available
from the British Library

*Library of Congress Cataloging in Publication Data*
A catalog record for this book has been requested

ISBN 0–415–27393–5

# Contents

# Figures

# Tables

# Contributors

**Fredrik Andersson** is Associate Professor of Economics at Lund University, Sweden. His major research interests are public economics and the economics of organization. He has published on labour and insurance contracts, optimum taxation, and fiscal competition in the *Journal of Public Economics* and the *Journal of Labor Economics*.

**Kristian Bolin** is a Research Fellow at Lund University Centre for Health Economics (LUCHE), Sweden. His main research interests concern theoretical extensions and empirical applications of the demand-for-health framework, and he has published several papers within this area in the *Journal of Health Economics*.

**Paul Contoyannis** is a Research Fellow at the University of York, UK. His main research interests are in microeconometric methods and applications in health economics. He has published articles in *Health Economics*, *Journal of Health Economics*, and *Empirical Economics*.

**Louis Eeckhoudt** is Professor of Economics at the Catholic Faculties of Mons, Belgium, and Lille, France. The analysis of decisions under risk represents his major research interest. He has published on this topic in the *American Economic Review*, *Econometrica*, the *Journal of Economic Theory*, the *Journal of Health Economics*, *Management Science*, and *Social Science and Medicine*.

**Ulf-G. Gerdtham** is Professor of Health Economics at Lund University, Sweden. His main research interest concerns the microeconometric analysis of the determinants of health and the utilization of health care. He has published in a variety of journals, including *Health Economics*, the *Journal of Health Economics, and Social Science and Medicine*. He has written on international comparisons of health-care expenditures in the *Handbook of Health Economics*.

**Hugh Gravelle** is Professor of Economics at the University of York, UK. He specializes in the theoretical and empirical analysis of health and health care and has published in a wide variety of journals from the *Economic Journal* to the *British Medical Journal*.

**Dorte Gyrd-Hansen** is Associate Professor at the Institute of Public Health, University of Southern Denmark, Odense, Denmark. Her main research interests concern methodological issues in the economic evaluation of technologies for health. Her publications include articles in *Medical Decision Making* and the *International Journal of Health Care Finance and Economics*.

**Tor Iversen** is Professor of Health Economics at the University of Oslo and Scientific Adviser at the Ragnar Frisch Centre of Economic Research, Oslo, Norway. His main research interests are economic incentives and provider behaviour in health-care systems. His publications include articles in the *Journal of Health Economics* and the *Journal of Economic Behavior and Organization*.

**Lena Jacobson** is Outcomes Research Manager at Pfizer AB, Stockholm, Sweden, where she is responsible for health economic studies and projects within the CNS and respiratory disease areas. Major research interests are health-related behaviour, economic evaluation, and cost of illness. She has published several papers in the *Journal of Health Economics*.

**Magnus Johannesson** is Associate Professor of Health Economics at the Stockholm School of Economics, Sweden. His main areas of research are health economics, experimental economics, and behavioural economics. His work includes publications in the *Journal of Health Economics*, the *Journal of Public Economics*, the *Journal of Risk and Uncertainty*, and the *New England Journal of Medicine*.

**Andrew M. Jones** is Professor of Economics at the University of York, UK, where he directs the graduate programme in health economics. He researches in the area of microeconometrics and health economics, and his publications include articles in *Health Economics*, the *Journal of Applied Economics*, and the *Journal of Public Economics*. He has written on health econometrics in the *Handbook of Health Economics*.

**Bengt Jönsson** is Professor of Health Economics and Director of the Centre for Health Economics at the Stockholm School of Economics, Sweden. He has published extensively on the economic evaluation of technologies for health in economic and medical journals, including articles in the *Journal of Health Economics* and the *New England Journal of Medicine*. He has written on international comparisons of health-care expenditures in the *Handbook of Health Economics*.

**Donald S. Kenkel** is on the faculty in the Department of Policy Analysis and Management at Cornell University, USA. He is interested in the economics of health promotion and disease prevention and in the cost-benefit analysis of health policies. He has contributed to the *Journal of Health Economics* and to the *Journal of Political Economy*, and he has written on prevention in the *Handbook of Health Economics*.

**Hansjörg Lehmann** is a Research Assistant in Health and Insurance Economics at the Socioeconomic Institute of the University of Zürich, Switzerland. His main research interest is health economics, in particular the economic analysis of health insurance.

**Bengt Liljas** works as a Market Access Director at AstraZeneca in Lund, Sweden, but is also affiliated with Lund University and with Harvard School of Public Health. His major research interests include the demand for health and the theory and methods of economic evaluation. His publications include articles in *Applied Economics*, the *Journal of Health Economics*, the *Journal of Risk and Uncertainty*, and *Medical Care*.

**Björn Lindgren** is Professor of Health Economics at Lund University, Sweden, and Director of Lund University Centre for Health Economics (LUCHE). His main research interests are the economic analysis of individual health behaviour, medical decision making, and methodological issues in the economic evaluation of technologies for health. Recent journal publications include theoretical and empirical analyses of the allocation of health and health investment in families.

**Hilde Lurås** is a Research Economist at the University of Oslo, Norway. Her main research interest is the economic analysis of individuals' lifestyle choices and GP behaviour. Her publications include articles in *Health Economics* and the *Journal of Economic Behavior and Organization*.

**Carl Hampus Lyttkens** is Professor of Economics at Lund University, Sweden. His two major current research interests are health economics and institutional change in ancient Greece. He has published on health-related behaviour, equity, diffusion of medical technology, and discounting of health as well as on taxation in archaic and classical Greece.

**Giuliano Masiero** is a Research Fellow in the Dipartimento di Economia Politica e Aziendale at the University of Milan, Italy. His research interests include the investigation of markets with switching costs and experience goods, in particular the regulation of primary care, and patient movements between general practitioners. He has published in the *Journal of Health Economics*.

**Mark V. Pauly** is Bendheim Professor of Health Care Systems at the Wharton School, University of Pennsylvania, USA. He is co-editor in chief of the *International Journal of Health Care Finance and Economics* and past president of the International Health Economics Association. He is author of *Health Benefits at Work: An Economic and Political Analysis of Employment-based Health Insurance* (1997) and *Pooling Health Insurance Risk* (1999).

**Tomas Philipson** is a Professor in the Irving B. Harris Graduate School of Public Policy Studies and a faculty member of the Department of Economics and the Law School at the University of Chicago, USA. He has published on the economics of health care and longevity, including *Private Choices and Public*

*Health: An Economic Interpretation of the AIDS Epidemic* (with Richard Posner) and *Old-Age Longevity and Mortality Contingent Claims* (with Gary S. Becker).

**Jes Søgaard** is Professor of Health Economics and Director of the Danish Institute for Health Services Research, Copenhagen, Denmark. His main research interests include health services research, medical technology assessment, and comparative health economics. He has published in a variety of economic and medical journals, including *Health Economics*, the *British Journal of General Practice*, and the *Scandinavian Journal of Primary Health Care*.

**Lukas Steinmann** is a Research Assistant in Health Economics at the Socioeconomic Institute of the University of Zürich. His main research interest is health economics, in particular efficiency analysis.

**George Zanjani** is an economist at the Federal Reserve Bank of New York, USA. He specializes in the economics of insurance. His recent publications include *Pricing and Capital Allocation in Catastrophe Insurance*. The views expressed are those of the author and do not necessarily represent those of the Federal Reserve Bank of New York or the Federal Reserve System.

**Peter Zweifel** is Professor of Economics at the University of Zürich, Switzerland. He serves on the Swiss Competition Commission and is co-editor of the *International Journal of Health Care Finance and Economics*. Besides health economics, his major research interests include insurance economics and energy economics. He is co-author (with Friedrich Breyer) of *Health Economics* (a widely used text-book).

# Preface

This volume contains a selection of the papers presented at the 19th Arne Ryde Symposium – Individual Decisions for Health – held on 27–28 August 1999 at the Lund University, School of Economics and Management. During two beautiful summer days, some 70 economists met to discuss 23 papers in this rapidly expanding area of international health economics research. I want to thank all the participants for their contributions to the lively discussions that took place during the sessions. Special thanks are due to the appointed discussants. Together with selected peer reviewers they also helped to improve the papers of this volume by way of constructive criticism, for which I (and the authors) are most grateful.

I also wish to express my gratitude to the Arne Ryde Foundation for financing the Symposium. Arne Ryde was a promising doctoral student in Economics at Lund University, when he died after a road traffic accident in spring 1968 he was only 23 years old. In his memory, his parents Valborg and Sven Ryde established the Arne Ryde Foundation for the advancement of economic research at Lund University. Since 1973, the Foundation has generously supported international symposia, workshops, and lectures in pure theory as well as in a number of different areas of applied economic research.

Several people have contributed to the planning and realization of the Symposium and of this volume: Björn Thalberg (Chairman of the Board of the Arne Ryde Foundation), Carl Hampus Lyttkens, Katarina Steen Carlsson, Ingemar Ståhl, and Lars Söderström as members of the organizing committee; Kristian Bolin as assistant editor during the process of producing the final manuscript; and Inger Lindgren as administrative assistant during the whole process from the planning stages of the Symposium to the completion of this publication. Heartfelt thanks to you all!

Björn Lindgren
Lund, December 2001

# Acknowledgements

All chapters were peer-reviewed. Special thanks go to:

*Fredrik Andersson*, Lund University, Lund, Sweden.
*Fredrik Berggren*, AstraZeneca, Lund, Sweden.
*Han Bleichrodt*, Erasmus University, Rotterdam, The Netherlands.
*Åke Blomqvist*, University of Western Ontario, London, Ontario, Canada.
*Kristian Bolin*, Lund University, Lund, Sweden.
*Anders Borglin*, Lund University, Lund, Sweden.
*John Cairns*, University of Aberdeen, Aberdeen, UK.
*Paul Contoyannis*, University of York, York, UK.
*Louis Eeckhoudt*, Catholic University of Mons, Mons, Belgium.
*Ulrika Enemark*, University of Southern Denmark, Odense, Denmark.
*Susan Ettner*, University of California at Los Angeles, Los Angeles, CA, USA.
*Ulf-G. Gerdtham*, Lund University, Lund, Sweden.
*Hugh Gravelle*, University of York, York, UK.
*Michael Grossman*, City University of New York, New York, USA.
*Håkan Holm*, Lund University, Lund, Sweden.
*Tor Iversen*, Oslo University, Oslo, Norway.
*Magnus Johannesson*, Stockholm School of Economics, Stockholm, Sweden.
*Andrew M. Jones*, University of York, York, UK.
*Hans Keiding*, University of Copenhagen, Copenhagen, Denmark.
*Donald S. Kenkel*, Cornell University, Ithaca, NY, USA.
*Bengt Liljas*, AstraZeneca, Lund, Sweden.
*Petter Lundborg*, Lund University, Lund, Sweden.
*Mattias Lundbäck*, Lund University, Lund, Sweden.
*Carl Hampus Lyttkens*, Lund University, Lund, Sweden.
*Mark V. Pauly*, University of Pennsylvania, Philadelphia, USA.
*Markku Pekurinen*, STAKES, Helsinki, Finland.
*Tomas Philipson*, University of Chicago, Chicago, IL, USA.
*Carol Propper*, University of Bristol, Bristol, UK.
*Lise Rochaix-Ranson*, University of the Mediterranean, Marseille, France.
*Christopher Ruhm*, University of North Carolina at Greensboro, Greensboro, NC, USA.

*Mandy Ryan*, University of Aberdeen, Aberdeen, UK.

*Thomas Selden*, Agency for Healthcare Research and Quality, Rockville, MD, USA.

*Gun Sundberg*, Uppsala University, Uppsala, Sweden.

*Lars Söderström*, Lund University, Lund, Sweden.

*Jes Søgaard*, Danish Healthcare Institute, Copenhagen, Denmark.

*Curt Wells*, Lund University, Lund, Sweden.

*Peter Zweifel*, University of Zürich, Zürich, Switzerland.

# Introduction

*Björn Lindgren*

Research on the determinants of (good) health belongs to several disciplines – biology, medicine, epidemiology, public health, psychology, and sociology to name some of the most important and influential ones with a long history in the field. Economics is a relative newcomer. On the public health policy scene, health economics has often been considered as the provider of costing exercises (if considered at all), while the answers to the challenges of high costs of illness are to be looked for elsewhere, to those disciplines that have traditionally provided the information for public health interventions. The presence of health economists in government committees on public health issues is an exception.

This is unfortunate, since economics has much more to offer. Other disciplines may contribute to an understanding of which factors are important and which biological or social mechanisms that may explain the role of these factors. The contribution of health economics, however, consists mainly of a better understanding of the causes of individual variation in health-related behaviour. To the economist, observed individual behaviour is explained by a process in which the individual makes trade-offs between current psychic, time, and financial costs on one hand and future health benefits in the form of reductions in the probability of morbidity and mortality on the other. The contributions of health economics are sometimes complementing the analyses of the traditional public health disciplines but from a different analytical angle, sometimes challenging prevailing public health truths and myths.

So, even though an individual's health status is determined by the genes that the individual inherits at birth, by the environmental risk factors that the individual faces during his or her lifetime, by chance in the form of accidents and illness, and by the present state of health care technologies, the individual's own behaviour is an essential determinant. The health-related behaviour of an individual is an integrated part of his or her life style and living habits. It is affected by family relations and income but also by the structure of society at large and the incentives for a more or less healthy living created by institutions and regulations. Individual behaviour and changes in behaviour as a response to changes in the incentives structure often have long-term consequences for the individual's health status.

Individual health-related behaviour is also a challenge to the economist. Uncertainties in health abound, for instance. First, there is uncertainty about the individual's present health status. Second, there is uncertainty about if and when the individual will be struck by an illness or an accident. Third, there is uncertainty about the relationship between the inputs of various health interventions and changes in the individual's health status. All three types may, obviously, require some attention, when formulating economic models of individual decisions for health. There is the individual consumption of goods that are potentially addictive and/or harmful. Can economic theory – with its strong emphasis on 'rational behaviour' – be developed in order to explain why people engage in such activities, even though they may be well aware of the risks? Family and other relations matter, and there are also other agents, such as the employer, the GP, the insurance company, and the government that may care for the individual's health status. Strategic behaviour as well as imperfect and asymmetric information make these relations rather complex and call for further development of economic theory. Large sets of individual panel data covering many years are required in order to estimate and/or test empirical counterparts of the theoretical models.

This book presents a selection of topical research issues regarding 'Individual Decisions for Health'. So doing, it provides an account both of the challenge of some vital public health issues to the economist and of health economics as a challenge to the traditional public health debate. The book is divided into two parts. Part I consists of seven chapters devoted to the individual's own decisions for his or her health. Four of the chapters deal with theoretical issues. The remaining three chapters report on empirical studies. Part II contains six chapters dealing with the impact of other agents' decisions for an individual's health. Five of them are devoted to theoretical issues and one reports on an empirical study.

## Part I: The individual's own decisions for his or her health

Donald S. Kenkel develops a conceptual framework to measure individuals' investments in health, when chosen activities not only produce health but also direct utility. His focus is on consumers' revealed preferences for a health-related good that is an input into the individual health production function, and his aim is to show how national health accounts can be extended by including such individual investments in health which are not normally covered, i.e. investments through decisions outside the healthcare sector. His point of departure is a highly simplified one-period version of Grossman's demand-for-health model. Thus, he implicitly assumes that all returns on health investments are immediate and abstracts from the more complex issues of the optimal path of health investments and health capital over the individual's lifecycle.

Kenkel derives the monetary equivalent of the utility foregone when people make adjustments in their way of living in order to improve health. He shows that the information required is the magnitude of the change in consumption of the health-related good and the own-price elasticity of demand for that good. To illustrate his framework, Kenkel makes an estimate of the utility foregone in monetary terms when people reduced their tobacco consumption to improve health as a result of the anti-smoking campaign in the U.S. Former estimates indicate that the campaign meant an annual reduction of 1831 cigarettes per U.S. adult. Since the price elasticity has been estimated at $-0.4$, the virtual price change that would be equal to the anti-smoking campaign is \$0.20 and the investment worth \$700 per adult in 1995 prices. Neglecting just this aspect of prevention understates health investments as represented in conventional national health accounts by at least 20 per cent.

Bengt Liljas explores the effects of allowing for imperfect financial markets in Grossman's formal theoretical demand-for-health model. As compared to the original model, in which the individual could save and borrow money at the same constant interest rate without any restrictions or transactions costs, he or she can here save but not borrow. The individual's income is assumed first to increase and then to decrease over time. At some point in time, when current income is higher than average lifetime income, the individual starts to save money in order to even out income over the remainder of his or her life.

The main changes in results as compared to Grossman's original model are that the interest rate disappears from the solution of the optimization problem and that the marginal utility of income becomes time dependent. The net effect of these changes is shown to depend at a large extent on the level of individual income and the rate of change of income over time. However, even though the number of effects going in opposite directions are quite high, there are some intuitively appealing results to be found in the chapter. Thus, in time-periods when income is low but increasing, the demand for health at optimum is smaller than in Grossman's original model; the individual will postpone his or her investments in health as long as he or she knows that his or her income will increase over time. When income is constantly high (in later periods of life), the demand for health at optimum is likely to be higher than in Grossman's original model. Timing has important policy implications, and the paper certainly explores some of the complex issues involved in individual decision-making regarding when to undertake an investment in health.

Andersson and Lyttkens develop a theoretical one-period model of health behaviour in the presence of genuine uncertainty, i.e. uncertainty with unknown probabilistic properties. This is a new line of research; previous work on uncertainty and health has examined the implications of risk, i.e. uncertainty with known probabilistic properties. In the Andersson and Lyttkens model, individuals hold firm beliefs over one set of health states, whereas they do not know the probabilities of the remaining health states. They are risk and uncertainty averse; they are pessimistic in the sense that they prefer states of the world with no genuine uncertainty (i.e. with known probabilities) rather than the presence of genuine uncertainty; and they may be more or less confident regarding their information about probabilities. They spend their budgets on information, prevention, and consumption. By gathering information, the individual can reduce the relative importance of uncertainty, and by prevention he or she can increase the probabilities of better health states.

Among their results, Andersson and Lyttkens stress the fundamental complementarity which they find between information gathering and preventive activities. Under plausible assumptions, reduced pessimism, for instance, will decrease both information gathering and prevention; and increased confidence will increase not only prevention but also information gathering. Thus, if the individual is provided with information without any cost through a government campaign (exogenous information) and if this exogenous information is complementary with own information, both personal information gathering and prevention will increase; if own information gathering and exogenous information are substitutes, however, the effect is ambiguous. The effects of exogenous preventive activities by government are analogous. The presence of this fundamental complementarity suggests that there may be a natural tendency for health differentials to widen, a tendency which may easily be exacerbated by public health policy.

Contoyannis and Jones critically survey the economics of addiction. They first consider how economists have characterized addiction, noting the relationship between these specifications and the characterizations offered by physiology and psychology. A number of issues regarding individual health-related decisions are covered: the incorporation of the notions of tolerance, withdrawal, and reinforcement in economic models of addictive, but rational behaviour; inconsistent preferences over time; precommitment and multiple selves; non-convexities in tastes and technology; regret and learning; addiction asymmetry; adjustment costs; and bounded rationality.

Contoyannis and Jones then outline the implications of alternative economic models of addictive consumption for the empirical analysis of the determinants of quitting, without relating to the empirical work already done in the area. Although they focus on the problem of nicotine dependence, the general approaches and issues outlined are also applicable to other harmful (but also to beneficial) addictions.

Bolin, Jacobson, and Lindgren present an empirical estimation of the Grossman model. They first develop a theoretical family-as-producer-of-health framework, in which the cost of adjusting from initial to desired stock of health is explicitly taken into account. The presence of adjustment costs creates an incentive for the family to reach desired levels of health gradually rather than instantaneously. An empirical model is then derived; it is shown that, in order to make unbiased estimates, individual panel data from at least three different time periods are required. Finally, they make the empirical estimation using a Swedish data set, which satisfies the data requirements of the model. Self-assessed health is used as an indicator of health capital and physical exercise as an indicator of health investment.

The results support the assumption of adjustment costs. Among other statistically significant results: health capital and health investment both decrease with age; health capital increases with higher wage rates, better education, larger wealth, being married (or cohabiting), and being male; and health investment increases with better education, larger wealth, and being male, while it decreases with having children. Having experienced divorce shows no statistically significant effect, neither for health capital, nor for health investment.

Gerdtham, Johannesson, and Jönsson provide some estimates of the determinants of individual health, using pooled cross-section data from annual interviews conducted in Sweden 1980–1986. They use self-assessed health as an indicator of the unobserved dependent variable. Several indicators of determining factors are included as independent variables, the choice of variables being based on previous theoretical and empirical studies on the determinants of health in the health economics and public health literature. Four different income measures are used in order to test the sensitivity of results for the choice of alternative indicators.

Estimated effects of income on health are all positive, irrespective of income measure. Net wealth, education, and the number of children are positively correlated with health, whereas age, unemployment, immigration, and being single are negatively associated with health. The estimated effect of gender certainly depends on the income measure used, but the authors conclude that their results suggest that being male has a positive effect on health. There also seems to be a significant cohort effect; individual health is significantly higher in 1982–1986 than in 1980.

Gyrd-Hansen and Søgaard estimate individual preferences for participation in alternative screening programmes for breast and colorectal cancer. Interviews are made, using an iterative discrete choice design, with a random sample of Danish men and women. The design provides a ranking for each interviewee among four screening options. One option is not to participate at all; the remaining three options are participation in screening programmes with different values of four separate attributes – reduction in cancer specific mortality rate, probability of a false positive test outcome, number of screening tests, and out-of-pocket expenditures, all relating to the individual's remaining lifetime.

Sample size is 764 men and women; the primary drop-out rate is 19 per cent; and another 20 per cent is lost due to lack of understanding the hypothetical choice set-up or to unwillingness to state ranks. The estimation sample is, hence, reduced to 483 individuals: 155 women for the breast cancer screening programme, and 179 women and 149 men for the colorectal cancer screening programme. Gyrd-Hansen and Søgaard find that the utility from screening participation is positively correlated with cancer mortality risk reduction and negatively with out-of-pocket payments and – for the 78 per cent of the sample with some professional education – also to the probability of false positive test outcomes. Some differences appear between men and women regarding the size of these effects, and for women between the two cancer diseases.

## Part II: Other agents' decisions for an individual's health

Eeckhoudt extends the theoretical analysis of diagnostic risks by using some new concepts, notably the notion of prudence, developed in the framework of expected utility theory. The background is that there is no perfect diagnostic test available. Thus, after consulting his or her physician, the patient has to make the irreversible decision to be treated or not, while there is only suspicion that a single well-defined illness might be present. In his chapter, Eeckhoudt assumes that the decision is formally taken either by the patient or by the physician as a perfect agent for his or her patient. It is further assumed that the benefits and costs of the potential treatment are known with certainty.

It is shown that risk aversion makes the individual more often prefer treatment to non-treatment. This may seem a surprising result, but since the only source of risk in the model is the diagnostic risk, treatment is, in fact, a risk reducing strategy. Prudence indicates by how much the individual is willing to act when he or she faces risk, i.e. a prudent individual will choose a higher treatment intensity to compensate for the uncertainty that surrounds his or her health state if sick. The introduction of a new risk, for instance a comorbidity, will induce the prudent individual to better control the risk he or she can manage, i.e. the diagnostic risk, and to choose a higher treatment intensity. In addition, the greater the degree of prudence, the more value will an individual put on lifeyears gained.

Gravelle and Masiero analyse incentives for quality in a market for primary care in which general practitioners (GPs) are paid a tax financed capitation fee for each registered patient. One rationale behind a capitated system is to provide an incentive to GPs to compete via quality for additional patients. Patients may, however, be imperfectly informed about the quality of their doctors and, hence, make errors when choosing a particular GP. Moreover, even though some aspects of the service can be judged by patients once they have experienced them, switching to another GP is costly. In addition to the time and trouble involved in changing registrations, switching imposes costs due to the fact that a new GP will initially be less informed about his or her newly registered patients. The chapter focuses the extent to which imperfect information and switching costs interact to blunt incentives to improve quality when capitation fees are increased.

Gravelle and Masiero show that the capitation fee is a valid instrument for raising quality even when patients can make mistakes and have biased perceptions of quality. They further conclude that a reduction in the dispersion of the error distribution will make some patients better off and none worse off. On average patients will gain from a reduction in switching costs, but patients who then switch because they overestimate the quality of the other GP will be made worse off. The more patients are aware of the fact that they may initially be mistaken and the more they are prepared to act upon their experience, the higher will be the quality in primary care. Policy makers can reduce patient uncertainty by collecting and publishing information on practices; this will increase quality and reduce the number of patient errors.

Iversen and Lurås demonstrate the importance of micro data for the empirical analysis of income-motivated behaviour (supplier-induced demand) among general practitioners (GPs). A GP who experiences a shortage of registered patients in a mixed capitation and fee-for-service payment system is likely to have a more service-intensive practice style than his or her colleagues. The argument for this is: if the GP cannot obtain his or her desired number of registered patients, the second best alternative would be to increase the number of services per patient as long as the income received per time unit of providing services is greater than the marginal valuation of leisure. Annual data from 109 GPs participating in the capitation experiment in four Norwegian municipalities in 1994 and 1995 was used for the analysis.

The estimated effect of a patient shortage on a GP's income from fees per patient is positive and statistically significant. Only the municipality with the lowest GP density has a (statistically significant) negative effect. Thus, if only macro data on GP density would have been available, it might have been erroneously concluded that income-motivated behaviour among GPs cannot be detected. Aggregate data miss the intra-municipality variation in the actual number of patients registered with a GP relative to his or her desired number, since the effect of better access would not be distinguishable from the effect of GP-initiated services.

Philipson and Zanjani challenge the common qualitative argument that non-proprietary insurance organizations should be able to produce higher quality (health) insurance than stock firms because of the absence of conflicts of interest between owners and consumers. Yet, it could be observed that non-proprietary organizations are the minority players in, for instance, the U.S. insurance market and that they appear to be declining in importance. The objective of the paper is to contribute to the understanding of why stock firms are able to compete with non-profit and mutual firms in controlling opportunistic behaviour. While the literature has paid much attention to asymmetric information and opportunistic behaviour in claims-handling, this chapter emphasizes the importance of solvency concerns in the production of insurance.

Philipson and Zanjani argue that bonding, i.e. posting a bond (a surplus fund) that would be used to pay claims if the for-profit insurance firm misbehaves, is a close substitute to non-proprietary organizations in limiting opportunism. They demonstrate first the equivalence between public enforcement of bonding in for-profit firms and non-distribution constraints in non-profit insurance production. Then they show that the holding of a surplus can be a solution to opportunistic behaviour, even without the direct involvement of regulation. Philipson and Zanjani claim that the ability of for-profit firms to limit opportunism through bonding, combined with better access to the capital market, enables these firms to produce insurance of quality compared to, or even better than, that offered by non-proprietary organizations. The cost of capital is essential for the argument, though. The comparative advantage of the proprietary organization increases, when capital is cheap, and decreases, when capital is expensive.

Zweifel, Lehmann, and Steinmann analyse the choice of a complementary agent as a designer (or negotiator) of incentives for physicians (primary agents) to act in accordance with the interest of their patients (the principals). Thus, the patient–physician relationship is assumed to be one of imperfect agency. Devising an optimal payment scheme requires information about the relationship between the likelihood of observing some specific health outcome and the physician's unobserved effort. Since patients and physicians may describe and evaluate outcomes differently, this likelihood is not defined. The failure creates a demand for a complementary agent. The interaction between the complementary agent and the physicians may produce results that differ depending on the choice of complementary agent. There are several available options, of which two are analysed here: private insurers and governments. A consumer's choice of complementary agent is here based on a performance indicator comprising the quantity and quality of medical services as well as payments to the system.

Zweifel, Lehmann, and Steinmann conclude inter alia that government as the complementary agent means higher payment to physicians and higher quality but less quantity of medical services than the private insurer alternative. Technological change seem to favourably affect the performance of government compared to the private insurer as a complementary agent, while increased competition among physicians should cause consumers to switch their preferred choice from government to the private insurer. Increasing levels of consumer information and income also favour the private insurer alternative.

Pauly touches the same ground as Zweifel *et al.* but in a more general way, as he explores expected variations in the choice of institutional arrangements for rationing of health care under differing assumptions about the characteristics of populations. Rationing is inevitable in all modern societies, because of the existence of moral hazard caused by health insurance. Rationing, however, requires an agent. A person can choose his or her agent either individually through the market or collectively through the political process. This choice is made behind a veil of ignorance. Four cases representing differing characteristics of populations are analysed.

Pauly concludes that in a (non-existing) world of identical individuals, individual or collective choice should yield the same outcome, given that public management would be equally efficient as market behaviour with competing firms. If, on the other hand, people's preferences differ, there is a case for the market; the greater the variation in tastes, the greater the a priori advantage of market arrangements over collective choice. If the primary variation among people is due to substantial variation in income, the preference for markets is weaker, and if it is due to substantial variation in risk, collective choice may be better. It is a fact that different countries have chosen different mixes of individual and collective choice of rationing agents, but there is, unfortunately, too little empirical evidence in order to test whether observed differences are due to differences in the demand for health and rationing of health care, given levels of income and risk. According to Pauly, one should, hence, be slow to judge another country's health care system.

# Part I

# The individual's own decisions for his or her health

# 1 Investments in prevention

## Health economics and healthy people

*Donald S. Kenkel*

## Introduction

Over twenty-five years ago, health economics research had begun laying the foundation for now-familiar arguments about the importance of prevention in the health economy. After his compelling 'tale of two states' comparing mortality rates in Utah and Nevada, Victor Fuchs (1974, pp. 54–5) concluded: 'The greatest current potential for improving the health of the American people is to be found in what they do and don't do to and for themselves. Individual decisions about diet, exercise, and smoking are of critical importance....' Michael Grossman's (1972) model provided a theoretical framework for the argument. Diet, exercise, and smoking could be considered as inputs, on par with curative medical care, used by households to produce increments of health capital. Kenkel (2000) provides an up-to-date survey of health economics research on prevention.

Research from a variety of disciplinary bases has also made prevention a prominent part of health policy. In 1990 the US Public Health Service published *Healthy People 2000* setting out national health promotion and disease prevention objectives in eight areas: (i) physical activity and fitness; (ii) nutrition; (iii) tobacco; (iv) alcohol and other drugs; (v) family planning; (vi) mental health and mental disorders; (vii) violent and abusive behaviour; and (viii) educational and community-based programmes. Similarly, the OECD (1994) argues for 'a broader approach to health policy, an approach which emphasizes the promotion of healthy lifestyles and the active consideration of the health consequences of government policies across a range of policy sectors'.

The goal of this chapter is to develop and begin to implement an accounting framework to summarize individual investments in prevention. National health accounts conventionally focus on 'expenditures on activities whose *primary* intention (regardless of effect) is to improve health' (Griffiths and Mills, 1993). In practice, national health accounts often focus even more narrowly on the health care sector, and as a result are dominated by expenditures on curative medical care such as physician services and hospitalizations. A study for the Centers for Disease Control and Prevention (CDC) is an important attempt to extend health accounts to include national expenditures on health promotion and disease prevention activities (Brown *et al.*, 1991; CDC, 1992). They estimate that total spending on prevention in the US in 1988 was \$32.8 billion, or 0.7 per cent of the GNP.[1] The proportion of total national health expenditures spent on prevention was estimated to be 3.4 per cent. Proposals to further standardize national health accounts advocate classifying expenditures according to functions, which if adopted will make possible comparative cross-country studies of curative versus preventive care. As an example of this approach, national health accounts by function show that prevention accounts for nine per cent of India's total health spending (Berman, 1997).

However, individuals invest in prevention not only by purchasing preventive medical care, but probably more importantly through their decisions made outside the health care sector to reduce their consumption of tasty but unhealthy foods, to spend time exercising, to refrain from the presumably enjoyable but unhealthy habit of smoking, and so on. The OECD Health Data System's national health accounts include some information on 'non-medical determinants of health' such as expenditures on fats and oils, tobacco and alcohol. The conceptual challenge is to use expenditure estimates like these to develop measures of investment in prevention. These expenditures are not primarily intended to improve health. Instead, fatty foods, tobacco, alcohol, and many other goods and activities jointly produce direct utility for the consumer as well as positive or negative increments to health.

Below I develop a conceptual framework to measure investments when prevention choices jointly produce direct utility and health. To illustrate the framework, I use consumers' surplus calculations to estimate the investments in prevention due to the anti-smoking campaign in the US. Previous studies estimate that the anti-smoking campaign substantially reduced US tobacco consumption, making it a major prevention effort (e.g. Warner, 1977, 1981, 1989). My framework estimates the value of the utility foregone when people reduce tobacco consumption to improve their health. In this way, I account for investments in prevention by focusing on consumers' revealed preferences for a health-related good.

Accounting frameworks are used for a variety of purposes. In his essay advocating an accepted set of professional standards for cost-benefit analysis, Harberger (1971) observes that national income accounts measure societal welfare, although only under certain assumptions and to a first approximation. In a similar way, cost-benefit studies of the health care system combine national health accounts with data on health outcomes to explore whether spending less on health care (often called 'cost containment') could improve societal welfare. Anderson (1997) uses the OECD health care accounts to conduct a descriptive comparison of the recent performance of the US health care system with systems in other countries. Cutler and Richardson (1997, 1998) estimate the value of the US health capital stock and its growth between 1970 and 1990. Their evidence suggests that the health stock is growing faster than medical expenditures, leading them to cautiously conclude that 'the rate of return to medical care is not obviously of such low value that people should clearly spend less on it than they do now'. This chapter begins to fill in an important missing piece of the puzzle – the amount of non-medical investments in health. Because of new information about the importance of diet, exercise, smoking, and other lifestyles, people now make many healthier prevention choices than in 1970. These investments must be factored in, when trying to estimate the rate of return to medical care.

The next section provides an overview of the major categories of consumer expenditures on health-related goods. The section on Accounting for health investments: a framework outlines the framework for accounting for health investments. The section on Investments in prevention: an illustrative exercise presents the empirical estimates of per capita and national investments in prevention through reduced tobacco consumption. The final section discusses the possible uses of the estimates, and makes suggestions for future work.

## An overview of health-related consumption

How much do individual consumption choices matter for health and safety? And how much does health and safety matter for consumption choices? Much of the influential research that addresses the first of these questions comes from epidemiology, not economics.[2] McGinnis and Foege (1993) review evidence on the relative contributions of various external factors linked to the leading causes of death in the US. They conclude that the three most prominent contributors to mortality in 1990 were tobacco, diet and activity patterns, and alcohol, which together accounted for almost 40 per cent of all deaths.

As will be discussed in more detail below, some economics research addresses how much health and safety matter for specific consumption choices. Apparently, there has not yet been a complete accounting of this. To set the stage for such an accounting, Table 1.1 shows total consumer expenditures on a variety of health-related goods and activities. The National Income and Product Accounts provide measures of broad categories of personal consumption expenditures. Broad categories where health and safety concerns play some role include expenditures on food (8.9 per cent of the GDP), housing (10.3 per cent of the GDP), household operation (7.7 per cent of the GDP), vehicle purchases (3 per cent of the GDP), alcoholic beverages (1.1 per cent of the GDP), and tobacco products (0.7 per cent of the GDP). Expenditures on exercise, calculated by multiplying the average time spent exercising by the median wage rate as a measure of the value of time, amount to another 2.5 per cent of the GDP. All told, personal consumption expenditures on these broad categories of health-related goods accounted for about one-third of the GDP. Expenditures on medical care were another 12 per cent of the GDP.

The accounts in Table 1.1 could be extended to develop sub-categories of consumer expenditures where the health and safety issues are more directly relevant. For example, consumer expenditures on housing and housing services include the purchase of smoke detectors, which an industry source identifies as involving annual expenditures of $100 million. Home radon measurement and abatement are additional examples of housing expenditures directly motivated by

*Table 1.1* Personal consumption expenditures by the type of product (billions of dollars)

| Item | Total expenditure in 1995 | Expenditure as a % of GDP |
|---|---|---|
| Personal consumption expenditures | 4953.9 | 68.15[a] |
| Food | 649.1[b] | 8.93 |
| Fruits and vegetables | 57.96[c] | 0.79 |
| Fats and oils | 10.70[d] | 0.15 |
| Butter | 1.91[e] | 0.026 |
| Housing | 750.4 | 10.32 |
| Household operation | 559.4 | 7.69 |
| Vehicle purchase | 219.3[f] | 3.02 |
| Medical care | 875.0 | 12.04 |
| Alcohol beverages | 82.7 | 1.14 |
| Tobacco products | 48.6 | 0.67 |
| Physical activity | 183.789[g] | 2.53 |

Source: US Bureau of Economic Analysis, Survey of Current Business, August 1998.

Notes
a  The GDP is $7269.6 billion in 1995.
b  Food expenditure excludes tobacco products and alcoholic beverages.
c  Source: US Bureau of Economic Analysis, unpublished data.
d  Source: US Bureau of Economic Analysis, unpublished data.
e  In 1995, per capita consumption of butter is 4.5 pounds and the average retail price for butter is $1.61 per pound. Also, the total population in 1995 is 263.168 million. All these figures are from ERS data set (http://usda.mannlib.cornell.edu).
f  Consists of new autos, net purchase of used autos and other motor vehicles.
g  The formula we use to calculate the average time spent on physical activity for individuals is as follows: $[(0.25 \times 0) + (0.22 \times 150) + (0.15 \times 60) + (0.38 \times 75)]/60 = 1.175$ hours per week. Related information is from the 1996 Report of the Surgeon General. According to the date of US Bureau of Labor Statistics, the average hourly earnings is $11.43 in 1995. The total population in 1995 is 263.168 million according to the date of US Bureau of Census.

health concerns. Ford *et al.*'s (1999) report estimates that a long-term radon test costs about $40, while the average cost of radon abatement is almost $2000. Based on these estimates, a universal radon screening and abatement programme is estimated to cost $18.8 million.[3] Some of the expenditures on vehicle purchases are also explicitly safety-related. Boulding and Purohit (1996) estimate that the presence of a drivers-side airbag increases the price of a midsize car by about $2300, while an antilock brake system is valued at $870. A set of accounts of consumer expenditures outside the health care sector that directly improve health could be built up from estimates like these, although it would be very difficult to make such an accounting comprehensive. The more fundamental problem is that such an accounting would omit health investments that involve joint production of health and direct utility.

As documented in Table 1.1, the consumer expenditures on goods and activities related to health and safety suggest that health and safety concerns have some influence on a large part of the economy. However, most of these expenditures are not primarily intended to improve health, and many are actually detrimental to health. The next section develops a revealed-preference approach to measure prevention investments. The material in Table 1.1 lays a foundation for this by showing that consumers spend a great deal on health-related goods.[4]

Although consumers spend a great deal on health-related goods, health and safety concerns may have little influence on consumer choices. An extreme example is when consumers are totally ignorant of the health consequences of their choices. This example suggests an economic approach grounded in revealed preferences to determine the role health concerns play in consumer choices. The choices of uninformed consumers do not reflect health concerns, while the choices of informed consumers reflect their health concerns. Therefore, the impact of health information on consumer choices reveals the preferences of the informed consumers over their health.

Results from studies of the impact of health information on smoking behaviour are used below in the section on Investments in prevention: an illustrative exercise. As a more general overview, two lines of economics research estimate the impact of health information on consumer choices. One line of research exploits 'information shocks' that lead to fairly immediate changes in consumer behaviour. Information shocks such as the 1964 surgeon general's report on the hazards of smoking and required cigarette warning labels are estimated to have significantly decreased the demand for cigarettes (Hamilton, 1972; Lewit *et al.*, 1981; Schneider *et al.*, 1981; Warner, 1977, 1981, 1989). In the mid-1980s, changes in the regulatory environment that made it easier for firms to advertise the link between diet and disease created additional health information shocks. In the cereals market, producer's claims about the health benefits of adding dietary fibre appear to have been an important information source for consumers, leading to substantial dietary improvements (Ippolito and Mathios, 1990). Similarly, individual food consumption data and food production data show that the consumption of fats, saturated fats, and cholesterol fell from 1977 to 1985 but fell more rapidly between 1985 and 1990 after producer health claims became more common (Chern *et al.*, 1995; Ippolito and Mathios, 1995, 1996).

Another line of research estimates consumer demand for health-related goods using cross-sectional data with direct measures of consumer information. In a sense, this line of research also exploits information shocks: because consumers learn at different rates, the extent of health information varies in the cross-section long after the initial shocks. For example, Viscusi (1990) and Kenkel (1991) find that information is an important determinant of cigarette demand, confirming the earlier findings based on information shocks. Kenkel (1991) also extends previous research by exploring the impact of health information on the demand for exercise and alcohol.

## Accounting for health investments: a framework

There are several possible approaches to accounting for health investments. Previous empirical work has focused on health outcomes – the outputs of the

health production function such as mortality rates (Fuchs, 1974) or the mone-
tized value of the health capital stock (Cutler and Richardson, 1997, 1998). In a
closely related approach, there is increasing attention to the cost-effectiveness
of prevention policies for improving health outcomes (Haddix *et al.*, 1996). For
example, the USDHHS (1999) recently published a second edition of 'An Ounce
of Prevention.... What Are the Returns?'

In contrast to the prevailing focus on health outcomes, this chapter takes
a revealed preference approach to health investments and examines consumer
choices about the health-related goods that are the inputs into the health production
function. The simplest accounting approach of measuring consumer expenditures
on health-related goods, like those presented above, immediately runs into
conceptual problems. Investing in health often means spending *less* on unhealthy
goods such as butter and cigarettes. When a person consumes less dietary fat or
quits smoking, even though he/she may spend less money, he/she still gives
up something of value in order to improve his/her health. Conversely, when a
person consumes more fruit and vegetables to improve his/her health, he/she
enjoys direct utility gains as well as health gains. A suitable accounting framework
must incorporate such joint production to measure the net sacrifice consumers
make to invest in prevention.

### The framework

The accounting framework to be implemented is based on the economic model of
consumer behaviour and methods from applied welfare economics. The model is
a highly simplified one-period version of Grossman's (1972) model of the demand
for health capital, where the consumer's choices of health-related goods determine
his/her gross investment in health, and hence his/her health capital stock, according to a household health production function. By focusing on one period the
model assumes that all returns on health investments are immediate and abstracts
from the more complex issues surrounding optimal health capital over the life
cycle. As in Grossman's (1972) original model, the model also abstracts from
uncertainty and assumes that consumer choices lead deterministically to health
outcomes. A more complete treatment would allow consumer choices to change
the probabilities associated with different health outcomes. However, the focus
here is on health input choices, where the consumer foregoes utility with certainty,
so it seems reasonable to abstract from the uncertainty around health outcomes.

To simplify notation and to allow a partly graphical exposition, consider the
case where there are only two consumption goods, a health-related good $x_1$ and a
numeraire good $x_2$. The consumer's utility is assumed to be a separable function of
utility from consumption of goods and utility from health $h$: utility $= u(x_1, x_2) +
w(h_0)$.[5] Let $h_0$ be the exogenously given baseline health status the consumer
achieves if he/she makes no investments in health. Setting health investments to
zero, the consumer's optimization problem is to:

$$\max_{x_1, x_2} \quad u(x_1, x_2) + w(h_0) \tag{1.1}$$

subject to a standard budget constraint

$$Y = p_1 x_1 + p_2 x_2.$$

Call the optimizing choices of goods that solve this problem $x_1^*$ and $x_2^*$. The consumer can invest in health by changing the consumption of $x_1$. Health status is therefore the sum of baseline health and the investments in health produced according to a household production function:

$$h = h_0 + i(x_1).$$

The consumer's maximization problem that takes into account both the direct utility and health consequences of goods consumption is to solve:

$$\max_{x_1,\, x_2} \quad u(x_1, x_2) + w(h_0 + i(x_1)). \tag{1.2}$$

Calling the optimizing choices of goods that solve this problem $x_1^{**}$ and $x_2^{**}$, then measured in physical units (quantities of goods), the consumer's investments in health are the differences $\Delta x_1 = x_1^{**} - x_1^*$. (When $\Delta x_1 = 0$, it is ignored as an uninteresting special case because it means that there are no investments in health.)

Figure 1.1 shows the case where $x_1$ is an unhealthy good. With zero health investment the consumer is at point A and consumes $(x_1^*, x_2^*)$. Investing in prevention means reducing his/her consumption of the unhealthy good to the level $x_1^{**}$ and choosing point B. Following Schelling (1980, 1984), one interpretation is

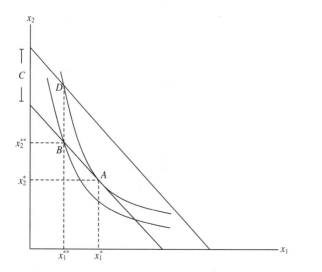

*Figure 1.1* Investing in health – the case of an unhealthy good ($x_1$).

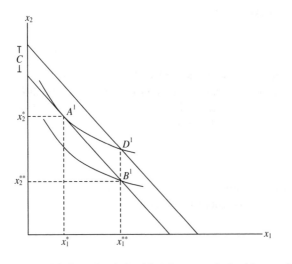

*Figure 1.2* Investing in health – the case of a healthy good ($x_1$).

that the consumer is made up of two selves: one self just enjoys goods and solves equation (1.1) to maximize utility from goods consumption; the other self is health-minded and solves equation (1.2) to maximize the sum of utility from goods consumption and utility from health. The health-minded self puts the consumption-oriented self on a diet and rations him/her to consume no more than $x_1^{**}$.

As is clear from Figure 1.1, the reduced consumption of the unhealthy good $x_1$ leads to a lower level of utility from goods, even though the consumption of the numeraire good $x_2$ increases. Figure 1.2 shows the case when $x_1$ is a health-enhancing good. Rationing consumption to some amount other than $x_1^*$ again reduces utility: the utility gained from the extra consumption of $x_1$ is not worth the utility lost from reducing the consumption of $x_2$. That is, the consumer's direct utility from goods consumption is lower because of the health investments:

$$\Delta u = u(x_1^{**}, x_2^{**}) - u(x_1^*, x_2^*) < 0. \tag{1.3}$$

Measured in utility units, $\Delta u$ is the utility from goods consumption foregone in order to invest in health. But it should be stressed that with health investments the consumer's total utility from goods consumption plus health is greater than total utility when health investments are zero:

$$u(x_1^{**}, x_2^{**}) + w(h_0 + i(x_1^{**})) > u(x_1^*, x_2^*) + w(h_0). \tag{1.4}$$

The ability to invest in health expands the consumer's opportunity set and so cannot make him/her worse off and, ignoring the special case when the consumer optimally chooses zero health investments, necessarily makes him/her better off. Rearranging expression (1.4) yields

$$\Delta u < \Delta w = w(h_0 + i(x_1^{**})) - w(h_0). \tag{1.5}$$

The accounting exercise is about what is given up to invest in health, so it focuses on the loss in consumption utility. This loss is given by the left-hand side of expression (1.5). The ultimate goal of the accounting framework is to measure prevention investments in monetary units. As will be shown below, the dollar value of prevention investments is measured by Harberger's (1971) triangles of lost consumer's surplus from changing patterns of consumption of health-related goods. As shown in expression (1.5), focusing on health inputs provides a measure that is a lower bound to the total value of health produced by prevention. This follows because the gain in health utility (given by the right-hand side of equation (1.5)) is greater than the loss in consumption utility.

An alternative approach to accounting for prevention investments would be to focus on the increase in utility from improved health, given by the right-hand side of expression (1.5). Similar to Cutler and Richardson's (1997, 1998) approach, the first step to implement this alternative accounting approach would be to estimate the improvements in health due to prevention. Combining this estimate with an estimate of the dollar value of the health improvements would yield a measure of the total value of health outcomes due to prevention. Although in principle the results from the two accounting exercises should be related to each other according to expression (1.5), in practice the results might diverge for several reasons. First, the implementation of either accounting approach will be imprecise and sensitive to the validity of the approximating assumptions required along the way. There is also a second, more fundamental conceptual reason the approaches could yield divergent results. The revealed preference approach yields an estimate of the investments in prevention *as perceived by the individual*. The health outcomes' approach would ultimately rest on experts' judgements about what improvements in health have resulted from prevention. Whenever individuals and experts disagree, investments in health as measured by the individual will be different than investments in health as measured by the experts.

### Placing a value on investments in prevention

Standard methods from applied welfare economics allow the development of a precise definition of the value of the utility from goods consumption foregone in order to invest in health. To account for the dollar value of this utility loss, the framework can be restated in terms of a special version of an indirect utility function. The standard indirect utility function from the consumer's problem described above would be based on the consumer's total utility from both goods consumption and health. Instead, I focus here on an indirect utility function for goods consumption only, termed $v(p, Y)$. Given prices $p_1^0$, $p_2^0$ and income $Y^0$, define the consumer's indirect utility from goods consumption when health investment is zero, and the consumer chooses $x_1^*$, $x_2^*$ as $v^* = v(p_1^0, p_2^0, Y^0)$. Given the same prices and income, but rationing the consumer to consume $x_1^{**}$, let his/her indirect utility be given by $v^{**} = v(p_1^0, p_2^0, Y^0; x_1^{**})$. A dollar-valued measure of the utility from goods consumption foregone to invest in health is $C$, the compensating variation in income implicitly defined by:

$$v(p_1^0, p_2^0, Y^0) = v(p_1^0, p_2^0, Y^0 + C; x_1^{**}). \tag{1.6}$$

This compensating variation is the amount the consumer would have to be paid when he/she invests in health to give him/her just as much utility from goods consumption as he/she would receive if his/her health investments were zero. Or using the 'two selves' interpretation, this is the amount the health-minded self would have to bribe the consumption-oriented self for the health investment. (Unlike Schelling's analysis, however, I ignore self-control problems and assume the health-minded self actually makes decisions.) The amount $C$ will be the operable definition of the dollar value of the consumer's health investments. In Figure 1.1, the compensating variation in income $C$ is given by the vertical distance DB. In Figure 1.2 when $x_1$ is a health-enhancing good, the compensating variation for the net change in utility from goods consumption is given by $D'B'$.

From the dual approach to the theory of the consumer, the compensating variation can also be expressed in terms of a special version of the consumer's expenditure function.[6] Let the value of the expenditure function corresponding to the solution of the consumer's optimization problem given by equation (1.1) (when health investments are zero) be defined as:

$$e(p_1^0, p_2^0, v^*) = \min_{x_1, x_2} [p_1^0 x_1 + p_2^0 x_2 : u(x_1, x_2) >= v^*]. \tag{1.7}$$

This will be termed the unconstrained expenditure function, in the sense that the consumer's choices of goods are not constrained by any health concerns.[7] The solution of the consumer's optimization problem given by equation (1.2) means that because of health concerns the consumption of $x_1$ is rationed or constrained to be $x_1^{**}$, so the value of the corresponding constrained expenditure function is:

$$e(p_1^0, p_2^0, v^*; x_1^{**}) = \min_{x_2} [p_1^0 x_1^{**} + p_2^0 x_2 : u(x_1, x_2) >= v^*]. \tag{1.8}$$

The compensating variation in income for the utility from goods consumption lost because of health investments is given by the difference between the value of the unconstrained and the constrained expenditure functions:

$$C = e(p_1^0, p_2^0, v^*) - e(p_1^0, p_2^0, v^*; x_1^{**}). \tag{1.9}$$

Following Neary and Roberts (1980), let $p_1^|$ be the virtual price vector such that the solution to equation (1.1) when health investments are zero yields $x_1^{**}$, the same consumption choice that solves equation (1.2) when health investment is nonzero. As Neary and Roberts (1980) show, the constrained expenditure function can be related to the unconstrained expenditure function evaluated at the virtual price:

$$e(p_1^0, p_2^0, v^*; x_1^{**}) = e(p_1^1, p_2^0, v^*) + (p_1^0 - p_1^1) x_1^{**} \qquad (1.10)$$

So the compensating variation in income for the utility from goods consumption lost because of health investments can be rewritten as:

$$C = [e(p_1^0, p_2^0, v^0) - e(p_1^1, p_2^0, v^0)] - (p_1^0 - p_1^1) x_1^{**}. \qquad (1.11)$$

This formulation is useful for applied welfare economics because the difference in expenditure functions given by the term in brackets [ ] in equation (1.11) is the compensating variation in income for the change in price of $x_1$ from $p_1^0$ to $p_1^1$. A standard result (Deaton and Muellbauer, 1980; Varian, 1978) is that this also corresponds to the consumerD's surplus area measured to the left of a compensated (utility-held-constant or Hicksian) demand curve for $x_1$:

$$CS = [e(p_1^0, p_2^0, v^*) - e(p_1^1, p_2^0, v^*)] = \int_{p_0}^{p_1} g_1(p_1, p_2, v^*) \, dp_1. \qquad (1.12)$$

where $g_1(\ )$ is the compensated demand curve for $x_1$. This means that the compensating variation in income for the utility from goods consumption lost because of health investments is given by:

$$C = CS - (p_1^0 - p_1^1) x_1^{**}. \qquad (1.13)$$

Figure 1.3 shows the areas of interest when the health-related good $x_1$ is unhealthy, while Figure 1.4 holds when $x_1$ is health-enhancing. As shown in these Figures, graphically $C$ is measured by Harberger's triangles of dead weight loss. This suggests an analogy between the approach here and the standard approach to measuring the welfare costs of price distortions. When the consumer perceives a health cost to consuming the good $x_1$, he/she acts as if there is a tax imposed on the good equal to the dollar value he/she places on the health consequences. The value of the decreased consumption of $x_1$ is given by the area under the demand curve. But consuming less $x_1$ also reduces the consumer's expenditures on $x_1$ by the rectangle $p_1^0 \Delta x_1$, yielding a partially offsetting increase in utility from consuming more of all other goods. This leaves the net loss given by the shaded triangle in Figure 1.3. When the consumer perceives a health benefit to the good $x_1$, he/she acts as if there is a subsidy to consuming $x_1$, financed by reducing his/her expenditures on all other goods. The value of the increased consumption of the health-enhancing good $x_1$ is given by the area under the demand curve, but this is less than his/her increased expenditures on $x_1$, yielding a net loss again given by a triangle (Figure 1.4).

When the demand curve for $x_1$ is approximately linear, the area of the triangle that measures $C$ is:

$$C = \tfrac{1}{2} \Delta x_1 \Delta p_1. \qquad (1.14)$$

As shown in equation (1.14), the proposed approach to accounting for investments in prevention only requires two pieces of information: $\Delta x_1$ and $\Delta p_1$. The

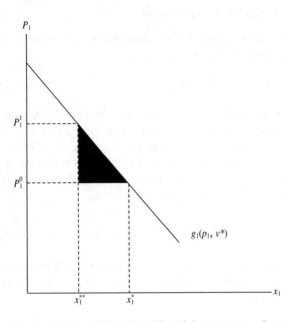

*Figure 1.3* The dollar value of health investments – the case of an unhealthy good.

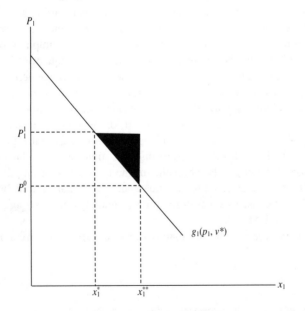

*Figure 1.4* The dollar value of health investments – the case of a healthy good.

first piece of information, $\Delta x_1$, is the extent to which the consumption of $x_1$ is changed because of health investment motives. This change can be inferred from studies of the impact of new health information on the demand for health-related goods. To illustrate, suppose that initially consumers do not perceive any health consequences from the consumption of $x_1$, but new information convinces them that there are significant health hazards. The consumer demand function $g_1$ prior to the new health information corresponds to demand for $x_1$ with zero health investments. The quantity demanded at a given price $p_1^0$ is $x_1^*$. The quantity demanded at the same price $p_1^0$ after the new information reflects health investment motives and so corresponds to $x_1^{**}$. The change in quantity demanded $\Delta x_1 = x_1^{**} - x_1^*$ is the extent to which the consumption of $x_1$ is changed because of health investment motives.

The next step is to calculate $p_1^1$, which is the virtual price that has an impact on the demand for $x_1$, the same as the impact of the health investment motives. In addition to an estimate of $\Delta x_1$, calculating $p_1^1$ also requires an estimate of $\epsilon_1$, the price elasticity of the demand for $x_1$. By definition,

$$\epsilon_1 = \frac{[\Delta x_1/x_1]}{[\Delta p_1/p_1]}.$$ (1.15)

Rearranging yields

$$\frac{\Delta p_1}{p_1} = [1/\epsilon_1][\Delta x_1/x_1].$$ (1.16)

So the virtual price change can be calculated with information about the percentage change in the quantity consumed of $x_1$ due to health concerns and the price elasticity of the demand for $x_1$. In practice, available price elasticity estimates correspond to ordinary rather than compensated demand curves. However, the area $C$ measured with an ordinary demand curve can be considered an approximation to the exact measure of compensating variation in income for the lost utility due to health investments (Willig, 1976). The size of the approximation error depends on the magnitude of income effects.

Using this framework also allows accounting for investments in health that do not involve joint production. Examples include not only the purchase of medical care but also vitamins, herbal supplements, and safety equipment, as long as these goods are perceived by the consumer to affect health and safety but do not provide direct utility. Call such a good $x_3$. Because total utility is separable in goods consumption ($x_1$ and $x_2$) and health, the consumer's optimization problem can be solved in two stages. Consumption of both $x_1$ and $x_2$ is rationed to allow the purchase of the optimal amount of medical care $x_3^{**}$. As before, the amount $C$, the dollar value of the utility from consumption foregone to purchase medical care as an investment in health, is implicitly defined by

$$v(p_1^0, p_2^0, Y^0) = v(p_1^0, p_2^0, Y^0 - x_3^{**}p_3 + C).$$ (1.17)

By inspection, to equalize utilities so that equation (1.17) holds requires that $C = x_3^{**}p_3$. Because the increase in consumption of medical care does not provide any offsetting direct utility gain, the dollar value of the utility loss is exactly the consumer's expenditures on medical care. This provides justification for conventional accounts of personal health care expenditures as a partial measure of health investments.

## Investments in prevention: an illustrative exercise

In this section I begin to implement the accounting framework to summarize individual investments in prevention. As shown above (pp. 21–2), the consumers' surplus estimate approximates the dollar value of the utility from goods consumption foregone in order to invest in health. To illustrate the framework, I calculate the value of the utility foregone from reductions in tobacco consumption due to the anti-smoking campaign. This example is chosen for two reasons. First, the anti-smoking campaign has been a major public health prevention effort. Second, on a practical level the empirical estimates needed to implement the framework are readily available for the case of tobacco.

A key step in the calculations is to use estimates of the impact of health information on consumer choices to estimate the extent to which consumption is changed because of health investment motives. Warner (1989) estimates that adult per capita cigarette consumption would have been 79 per cent higher in the absence of the anti-smoking campaign. This translates into a reduction of 1831 cigarettes per US adult (Tobacco Institute, 1997). The next step is to calculate $p_1^1$, which is the virtual price that has an impact on the demand for $x$, the same as the impact of the health investment motives. Assuming that the price elasticity of the demand for tobacco is $-0.4$ (Manning *et al.*, 1991; Chaloupka and Warner, 2000), at the average price of cigarettes in 1995, the virtual price change that is equivalent to the anti-smoking campaign is $0.20.

Calculated as in equation (1.14), these estimates imply that in 1995 US consumers' investments in prevention through reduced tobacco consumption totalled $179 billion, or almost $700 per adult. From conventional national health accounts, total expenditures in 1995 on medical care were $875 billion, suggesting that neglecting just this aspect of prevention understates investments in health by at least 20 per cent. As another comparison, the CDC (1992) estimates explicit prevention expenditures of $32.8 billion in 1988. Even updated to 1995, explicit prevention expenditures as calculated by the CDC are much lower than the estimate of investments in prevention based on consumers' revealed preferences for tobacco as a health-related good.

Smoking has been called the leading preventable cause of death in the US, so it may not seem surprising that refraining from smoking is a substantial individual investment in prevention. It is important to note that this investment is estimated to be so large for two reasons. First, health concerns appear to have substantially reduced tobacco consumption. Since the 1964 surgeon general's report on the health consequences of smoking, the prevalence of smoking among adults has decreased from 40 per cent to about 25 per cent (USDHHS, 1999). But according to Warner's estimates, this observed decrease substantially understates the impact of health information because pre-1964 trends are not accounted for. Until 1964, per capita tobacco consumption in the US steadily rose over time, and even after 1964, smoking prevalence among women increased. Comparing actual tobacco consumption with that predicted if pre-1964 trends had continued leads Warner (1989) to conclude that adult per capita cigarette consumption in 1987 would have been an estimated 79 per cent higher in the absence of the anti-smoking campaign.

The second reason that the estimated value of the utility foregone is so large is because reducing tobacco consumption appears to be very difficult for consumers. The lack of economic substitutes means that tobacco demand is relatively price inelastic. Convincing people to give up a substantial amount of consumers' surplus from tobacco products should therefore be seen as a major public health success. Of course, it could be argued that the reduction in tobacco consumption should be viewed as a success only if the health benefits are worth the costs. It follows automatically by revealed preference that consumers perceive net benefits from the observed reduction in tobacco consumption. Many observers feel that further reductions are in consumers' and society's best interest, although it could be argued that this is not necessarily the case.[8]

## Discussion

Attention is increasingly focusing on whether the health improvements gained from specific health interventions or even entire health care systems are worth the costs. This chapter focuses on accounting for costs that are frequently overlooked – the losses people experience when they change their consumption of health-related goods. An illustrative calculation suggests that the net value of foregone tobacco consumption amounts to almost $700 per adult.

The accounting framework could be extended to consider investments in prevention through changes in other consumer health-related behaviours. For example, Chern et al. (1995) estimate the impact of information on butter consumption, while Kenkel (1991) estimates the impact of information on alcohol consumption and exercise. Combined with price elasticity estimates, it is straightforward to calculate the consumers' surplus foregone for these examples of prevention. However, for many examples of health behaviours, consumer changes have been much less dramatic than for tobacco consumption. For example, although there have been some changes towards diets lower in fat and higher in fibre, the typical US diet does not meet nutrition guidelines. Physical activity levels do not seem to have changed much, and the prevalence of obesity in the US is actually increasing. Understanding why consumers are relatively unwilling to make health investments through nutrition and physical activity is an interesting avenue for future research.

An accounting framework that summarizes individual investments in prevention provides a more complete picture of a nation's health system than is possible using conventional health accounts. The illustrative exercise presented above, and the extensions just discussed, can help document the increased investments in prevention in the US over the past 40 years. The framework could also be used to shed light on national objectives for future improvements in health behaviours, such as those set out for the US in *Healthy People 2000* and *Healthy People 2010*. Similarly, different investments in prevention through healthy behaviours are a potentially important part of international comparisons of health care systems.

However, it may not make sense to complete a total accounting of investments in prevention that could be compared with total expenditures on curative care. At some level, almost all goods and services are 'health related', obscuring the point of the accounting exercise. For example, adequate food and housing are clearly necessary for good physical health, and it could even be argued that entertainment expenditures and the like are necessary for good mental health. The majority of national expenditures could thus be classified as prevention, under a sufficiently broad definition. The point of the accounting exercise is to allow quantifiable statements such as made in the section on Investments in prevention: an illustrative exercise (p. 24): the US invests \$179 billion more in prevention because of the anti-smoking campaign than it did in 1964. Even this incomplete accounting of investments in prevention shows the importance of prevention in the health economy.

## Notes

Paper prepared for the 19th Arne Ryde Symposium: Individual Decisions for Health, Lund, Sweden, August 27–28, 1999. Tsui-Fang Lin provided valuable research assistance. I would like to thank Bengt Jönsson, participants at the Arne Ryde Symposium, and an anonymous reviewer for helpful comments.

1 Brown *et al.* (1991) use a broad concept of prevention and include expenditures on a fairly wide range of prevention activities in the following major funding sectors: federal, state, and local governments, voluntary organizations, worksite health promotion programmes, and personal prevention services. However, important categories of prevention are excluded, such as personal expenditures on exercise and vitamins and health foods (p. 5). In addition, the report does not attempt to account for the value of time used to produce prevention, or for the value of consumption or activities foregone to improve health.

2 Although as Kenkel (1995) argues, economists who estimate health production functions use an economic framework to address many of the same relationships that epidemiologists study.

3 Akerman *et al.* (1991) estimate that in Sweden the actual average costs of radon mitigation are between \$215 and \$575 per house, depending upon the mitigation method used.

4 It should be noted that expenditures on environmental quality and workplace safety are intentionally excluded from Table 1.1. Consumers and workers demand environmental quality and workplace safety, but current levels of these goods are driven to a large extent by public policy instead of individual choices. So while expenditures on the environment and workplace safety reflect societal investments in prevention, it is difficult to incorporate them into the revealed-preference approach developed below.

5 This model is what Grossman calls a consumption model of health, and ignores the possibility that health improvements lead to more time available for productive purposes (what Grossman calls the investment motive). In the more general Grossman model, people invest in health as a consumption good and for motives related to time available for productivity.

6 The standard expenditure function is defined based on the consumer's total utility from both goods consumption and health. Instead, I focus here on expenditure functions that correspond to the indirect utility function for goods consumption only.

7 Because health investments are set at zero in equation (1.1), the expenditure function given by equation (1.7) corresponds to a model where the consumer's objective function only reflects utility from goods consumption.

8 For example, estimates of the external costs of smoking call into question the claim that externalities justify higher cigarette taxes (Manning *et al.*, 1991). Viscusi (1992) provides estimates that many people overestimate the health risks of smoking, suggesting that observed reductions in tobacco consumption may have gone too far.

# References

Akerman, J.F., Johnson, R. and Bergman, L. (1991). 'Paying for Safety: Voluntary Reduction of Residential Radon Risks'. *Land Economics* 67 (4): 435–46.

Anderson, G.F. (1997). 'In Search of Value: An International Comparison of Cost, Access, and Outcomes'. *Health Affairs* 16 (6): 163–71.

Berman, P.A. (1997). 'National Health Accounts in Developing Countries: Appropriate Methods and Recent Applications'. *Health Economics* 6: 11–30.

Boulding, W. and Purohit, D. (1996). 'The Price of Safety'. *Journal of Consumer Research* 23 (June): 12–25.

Brown, R.E., Elixhauser, A., Corea, J., Luce, B.R. and Sheingold, S. (1991). *National Expenditures for Health Promotion and Disease Prevention Activities in the United States*. Washington DC: The Medical Technology Assessment and Policy Research Center, Battelle.

Centers for Disease Control and Prevention (1992). 'Estimated National Spending on Prevention – United States, 1988'. *Mortality and Morbidity Weekly Review* 41 (29): 529–31.

Chaloupka, F.J. and Warner, K. (2000). 'The Economics of Smoking'. In: Newhouse, J.P. and Culyer, A. (eds), *Handbook of Health Economics*. Elsevier Science B.V., pp. 1539–1627.

Chern, W.S., Loehman, E.T. and Yen, S.T. (1995). 'Information, Health Risk Beliefs, and the Demand for Fats and Oils'. *The Review of Economics and Statistics* 77: 555–64.

Cutler, D. and Richardson, E. (1997). 'Measuring the Health of the United States Population'. *Brookings Papers on Economic Activity: Microeconomics*, 217–71.

Cutler, D. and Richardson, E. (1998). 'The Value of Health: 1970–1990'. *American Economic Review Papers and Proceedings* 88 (2): 97–100.

Deaton, A. and Muellbauer, J. (1980). *Economics and Consumer Behavior*. Cambridge: Cambridge University Press.

Ford, E.S., Kelly, A.E., Teutsch, S.M., Thacker, S.B. and Garbe, P.L. (1999). 'Radon and Lung Cancer: A Cost-Effectiveness Analysis'. *American Journal of Public Health* 89 (3): 351–57.

Fuchs, V.R. (1974). *Who Shall Live? Health, Economics, and Social Choice*. New York: Basic Books.

Griffiths, A. and Mills, A. (1993). 'Health Sector Financing and Expenditure Surveys', In: Lee, K. and Mills, A. (eds), *The Economics of Health in Developing Countries*. Oxford: Oxford University Press.

Grossman, M. (1972). 'On the Concept of Health Capital and the Demand for Health'. *Journal of Political Economy* 80 (2): 223–55.

Haddix, A.C., Teutsch, S.M., Shaffer, P.A. and Dunet, D.O. editors (1996). *Prevention Effectiveness: A Guide to Decision Analysis and Economic Evaluation*. New York: Oxford University Press.

Hamilton, J.L. (1972). 'The Demand for Cigarettes: Advertising, the Health Scare, and the Cigarette Advertising Ban'. *Review of Economics and Statistics* 54: 401–11.

Harberger, A.C. (1971). 'Three Basic Postulates for Applied Welfare Economics: An Interpretive Essay'. *Journal of Economic Literature* 9 (3): 785–97.

Ippolito, P. and Mathios, A. (1990). 'Information, Advertising and Health: A Study of the Cereal Market'. *Rand Journal of Economics* 21 (3): 459–80.

Ippolito, P. and Mathios, A. (1995). 'Information and Advertising: The Case of Fat Consumption in the United States'. *American Economic Review: Papers and Proceedings* 85 (2): 91–5.

Ippolito, P. and Mathios, A. (1996). *Information and Advertising Policy: A Study of Fat and Cholesterol Consumption in the United States, 1977–1990*. Bureau of Economics Staff Report, Federal Trade Commission, Washington D.C.

Kenkel, D.S. (1991). 'Health Behavior, Health Knowledge, and Schooling'. *Journal of Political Economy* 99 (21): 287–305.

Kenkel, D.S. (1995). 'Should You Eat Breakfast? Estimates from Health Production Functions'. *Health Economics* 4 (1): 15–29.

Kenkel, D.S. (2000). 'Prevention'. In: Newhouse, J.P. and Culyer, A. (eds), *Handbook of Health Economics*. Elsevier Science B.V., pp. 1675–720.

Lewit, E., Coate, D. and Grossman, M. (1981). 'The Effects of Government Regulation on Teenage Smoking'. *Journal of Law and Economics* 24: 545–73.

McGinnis, J.M. and Foege, W.H. (1993). 'Actual Causes of Death in the United States'. *JAMA* 270 (18): 2207–12.

Manning, W., Keeler, E.B., Newhouse, J.P., Sloss, E.M. and Wasserman, J. (1991). *The Costs of Poor Health Habits*. Cambridge Mass: Harvard University Press.

Neary, J.P. and Roberts, K.W.S. (1980). 'The Theory of Household Behavior Under Rationing'. *European Economic Review* 13: 25–42.

Organization for Economic Cooperation and Development [OECD] (1994). *New Orientations for Social Policy*. OECD Social Policy Studies No. 12. Paris, France: OECD Publications.

Schelling, T.C. (1980). 'The Intimate Contest for Self-command'. *The Public Interest* 60: 94–113.

Schelling T.C. (1984). 'Self-command in practice, in policy, and in a theory of rational choice'. *American Economic Review* 74: 1–11.

Schneider, L., Klein, B. and Murphy, K.M. (1981). 'Governmental Regulation of Cigarette Health Information'. *Journal of Law and Economics* 24: 575–612.

Tobacco Institute (1997). 'The tax burden on tobacco'. *Historical Compilation*, Vol. 32. Washington, DC: The Tobacco Institute.

U.S. Department of Health & Human Services (USDHHS) (1999). *An Ounce of Prevention.... What Are the Returns?* Atlanta Georgia: Centers for Disease Control and Prevention.

Varian, H.R. (1978). *Microeconomic Analysis*. New York: W.W. Norton & Co. Inc.

Viscusi, W.K. (1990). 'Do smokers underestimate risks?' *Journal of Political Economy* 98(5): 1253–69.

Viscusi, W.K. (1992). *Smoking: Making the Risky Decision*. New York: Oxford University Press.

Warner, K.E. (1977). 'The Effects of the Anti-Smoking Campaign on Cigarette Consumption'. *American Journal of Public Health* 67: 645–50.

Warner, K.E. (1981). 'Cigarette Smoking in the 1970s: The Impact of the Antismoking Campaign on Consumption'. *Science* 211: 729–31.

Warner, K.E. (1989). 'Effects of the Antismoking Campaign: An Update'. *American Journal of Public Health* 79 (2): 144–51.

Willig, R.D. (1976). 'Consumer's surplus without apology'. *American Economic Review* 66: 589–97.

# 2 An exploratory study on the demand for health, lifetime income, and imperfect financial markets

*Bengt Liljas*

## Introduction

Even if health is but one factor influencing the utility of the individual, it may though be an especially important one. Yet, economic models describing the individual's optimal demand for health and factors that affect the individual's health-related behaviour (from which the individual's demand for health care, etc., could be derived) are relatively few. This is, though, one of the fundamental issues in the area of health economics, and such knowledge is vital in order both to understand risk behaviour, such as smoking and illicit drug abuse, and to create a basis for normative evaluation of health care programmes based on individual preferences.

The groundbreaking work in the area of individuals' demand for health was done by Michael Grossman and was published in the early 1970s, building on Gary Becker's work on human capital theory (Becker, 1965). In his seminal article on the individual's demand for health (Grossman, 1972), Grossman treated the demand for health in a dynamic setting where the individual was born with a certain level of health that depreciated over time, unless the individual invested in health through various activities. A decade after his original paper was published, Grossman pointed out a number of directions in which his original model could be further developed (Grossman, 1982). However, even though his original model has been used for empirical applications a number of times, the theoretical contributions have been limited. Some of the perhaps most notably theoretical contributions to the original model so far have been the introduction of uncertainty (see, e.g. Cropper, 1977. Dardanoni and Wagstaff, 1990; Liljas, 1998; Picone *et al.*, 1998; Zweifel and Breyer, 1997), insurance (Liljas, 1998, 2000; Tabata and Ohkusa, 2000), and the family as a producer of health (Bolin *et al.*, 2001; Jacobson, 2000). For a good overview of many of these developments, see Grossman (2000).

Another simplifying assumption made in the original model was to allow the individuals to borrow and save money at the same (constant) interest rate without any restrictions or transaction costs, i.e. implicitly making the constrained maximization problem an isoperimetric problem (i.e. when there are integral restrictions, an assumption also made by Grossman's successors[1]). Thus, by applying an integral constraint, Grossman thereby assumed that the budget only had to be binding over the individual's entire lifespan. This was a very convenient assumption since, among other things, the Lagrange multipliers could be regarded as constants in the optimization problem (Chiang, 1992). Imperfections in the financial markets, however, would change the budget constraint and, hence, the optimization problem of the individual.

Several alternative constraints with imperfect financial markets are possible, for example: (1) neither saving, nor borrowing, money is possible (i.e. the individual is consuming his or her entire income in every time-period); (2) saving, but not borrowing, money is possible, i.e. the budget has to be exactly binding in every time-period (differential equation equality constraints); and (3) both borrowing and saving money are possible, but at different interest rates (which, for example, could depend on the financial institution's estimate and forecast of the individual's level of health). The first case was treated in Liljas (2000), and I will in this chapter focus on the second case. Even though this may seem to represent a fairly extreme case (as compared to the third case, which is more general), it will clearly illustrate some of the complex effects of imperfect financial markets on the optimal demand for health.

The chapter starts with a brief description of Grossman's demand-for-health model including the original budget constraint, and is then followed by the developments of the case without borrowing money. The next section holds a comparison of the optimal demand for health in Grossman's original model and in the case without borrowing money. A discussion ends the chapter.

## The original Grossman model

The individual is assumed to derive utility ($u$) according to the function $u(\phi_t H_t, Z_t)$, where $\phi_t$ is defined as the number of healthy days yielded by a unit health ($H_t$) (so $h_t = \phi_t H_t$ is the total number of healthy days in a given time-period), $Z_t$ is a vector of other goods, and $t$ is the time notation. It is assumed that utility increases in both arguments, but at a decreasing rate, and that the utility function is jointly concave in its arguments. Health capital can be increased by investments ($I_t$) through inputs of time and/or medicine in the household's production function.[2] If the individual does not invest in his or her health, the level of the health capital will not remain at a constant level, due to the depreciation of health ($\delta_t$): $dH_t/dt = \dot{H}_t = I_t - \delta_t H_t$ where $\dot{H}_t$ is the time derivative with respect to health capital.[3] The more the individual invests in his or her health the longer he or she will live, ceteris paribus.

The budget that the individual has to take into consideration ($R$) is equal to his or her initial assets ($A_0$) plus the present value of all future income if the individual will spend all his or her time working ($W_t \Omega_t$), where $W_t$ is the wage rate and $\Omega_t$ is the total disposable time per period. Part of this wealth is spent on non-market production time (i.e. on the restoration and production of health), part of it is spent on consumption of market goods, and part of it is lost due to illness. This reads: $\pi_t \delta_t H_t + \pi_t \dot{H}_t + q_t Z_t + W_t TL_t$, where $\pi_t$ is the price-vector for the inputs in the production of health capital, $q_t$ is the price-vector for the inputs in the production of other goods, and $TL_t$ is the time loss from market and non-market activities due to illness or injury (see Grossman (1972) for a derivation of the budget constraint).

The individual seeks to maximize his or her lifetime utility, subject to the budget constraint and some terminal conditions:

$$\text{Max.}U = \int_0^T u(\phi_t H_t, Z_t)e^{-\theta t}dt, \tag{2.1}$$

$$s.t.R = \int_0^T (\pi_t \delta_t H_t + \pi_t \dot{H}_t + q_t Z_t + W_t TL_t)e^{-rt}dt, \tag{2.2}$$

$$H(0) = H_0; \qquad t = 0, \tag{2.3a}$$

$$H(T) = H_{min}; \qquad T \text{ free}, \tag{2.3b}$$

$$H_t > H_{min}; \qquad t < T, \tag{2.3c}$$

where $\theta$ is the individual's subjective rate of time preferences, $r$ is a constant interest rate, $H_{min}$ is the level of the health stock when the individual dies, 0 is the present time, and $T$ is the time of death, which depends on the level of health, defined by:

$$T = \min\{t:H_t \le H_{min}\}. \tag{2.4}$$

Since the budget constraint here only requires that the present value of lifetime income (wealth) must equal the present value of lifetime expenditures, the budget constraint obviously allows for both borrowing and saving. Moreover, this dynamic optimization problem has a variable terminal-point (i.e. the individual's time of death depends on his or her earlier investments in health capital). Thus, we also need a transversality condition for the missing boundary condition (i.e. a condition that determines the individual's time of death), see Forster (1989), Erlich and Chuma (1990), Liljas (1998), Reid (1998), and Grossman (1998, 2000), for derivations.[4] According to the equations (2.1–2.4), the Lagrange function reads:

$$L = \int_0^T \left[ u(\phi_t H_t, Z_t)e^{-\theta t} - \lambda(\pi_t \delta_t H_t + \pi_t \dot{H}_t + q_t Z_t + W_t TL_t)e^{-rt} \right]dt. \tag{2.5}$$

The Euler equation for the optimal trajectory of the stock of health capital reads:

$$\frac{\partial h_t}{\partial H_t}\left[ W_t + \frac{\partial u}{\partial h_t}e^{(r-\theta)t}/\lambda \right] = \pi_t(r + \delta_t) - \dot{\pi}_t, \tag{2.6}$$

and can be graphically illustrated as in Figure 2.1.

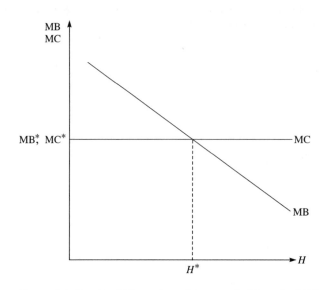

*Figure 2.1* Graphical illustration of the marginal benefit (MB) curve and the marginal cost (MC) curve of health investments in Grossman's original model, the marginal valuation (MB*) and marginal cost (MC*) evaluated at optimum, and the demanded level of health (*H**) at optimum.

The left-hand side of (2.6) is the marginal benefit (MB) of an investment in health capital, which consists of the increase in labour income and of the monetary value of the increase in utility due to a unit's increase in healthy time. The right-hand side of (2.6) is the marginal cost (MC) of holding an additional unit of health capital, where $r\pi_t$ is interest forgone, $\dot{\pi}_t$ is the price change of the additional unit of health capital for the time the individual is holding it, and $\pi_t\delta_t$ is the cost of the depreciation of health capital.

## A demand for health model with savings, but without borrowing

If borrowing money is not possible, the budget constraints have to be exactly binding in every time-period. As the individual's budget (*R*) is likely to vary over time, this variable will here be time-dependent ($R_t$). Obviously, the Lagrange multiplier ($\lambda$) can then also vary over time. For example, in a time-period when the individual does not have very much money, i.e. a very tight budget constraint, the marginal utility of money ($\lambda_t$) is higher (Zweifel and Breyer, 1997).

Another change as compared to Grossman's original model (as well as in the model presented in Liljas, 2000) is that we here assume that savings ($S_t$) is an explicit component of the model in every time-period (so the individual can save and consume old savings in each time-period).[5] The amount of savings in each time-period depends (by assumption – see above) on the individual's level of health, since the better health the individual has, the less time and money he or she will have to spend on improving it, as well as on the interest rate (i.e. $S_t = S_t (H_t, r)$, where: $\partial S_t / \partial H_t > 0$ and $\partial S_t / \partial r$ could be either larger or smaller than zero, depending on whether the substitution or income effect of an increase in $r$ is dominant). In this case the budget constraint reads:

$$R_t = W_t \Omega_t + A_t = \pi_t \delta_t H_t + \pi_t \dot{H}_t + q_t Z_t + W_t TL_t + S_t (H_t, r); \quad \forall t, \quad (2.7)$$

where $A_t$ are the financial assets, or the accumulated net savings (including interest), up until time $t$ (where obviously $A_t \geq 0$; $\forall t$, even though $\Delta S_t < 0$ for some $t$).

It can be shown that the using of (2.7) instead of (2.2) gives the following Euler equation for the optimal trajectory of $H_t$:

$$\frac{\partial h_t}{\partial H_t} \left[ W_t + \frac{\partial u}{\partial h_t} e^{-\theta t} / \lambda_t \right] = \pi_t (\delta_t - \dot{\lambda}_t / \lambda_t) - \dot{\pi}_t + \frac{\partial S_t}{\partial H_t}. \quad (2.8)$$

Thus, compared to the Euler equation for $H_t$ in Grossman's original maximization problem (2.6), there are five changes in (2.8): (1) the discount factor on the left-hand side has changed from $e^{(r-\theta)t}$ to $e^{-\theta t}$; (2) the marginal utility of income on the left-hand side has changed from $\lambda$ to $\lambda_t$; (3) the discount-rate term, $r$, on the right-hand side has disappeared; (4) an additional term, $-\pi_t \dot{\lambda}_t / \lambda_t$, has appeared on the right-hand side, where $\dot{\lambda}_t$ is the time-change of how binding the budget constraint is; (5) the component $\partial S_t / \partial H_t$ is added to the right-hand side.

Since $r$ is positive, the first and third change decreases both the marginal benefit and the marginal cost of (2.8). The sign of the second change depends on the level of the individual's budget, $R_t$, which in turn determines $\lambda_t$. For the fourth change it is valid that: sign $(-\pi_t \dot{\lambda}_t / \lambda_t) = $ sign $(-\dot{\lambda}_t)$, since both $\pi_t$ (the price-vector for the inputs in the production of health capital) and $\lambda_t$ (the marginal utility of income) are positive per definition. The fifth change is also positive by definition.

## The demand for health with the original versus the new budget constraint

To be able to conclude how the alternative budget constraint affects the level of health demanded at optimum as compared to the original budget constraint, we need to know the size of $\lambda_t$ and the sign of $\dot{\lambda}_t$. We know that $d\lambda / dR_t < 0$ and that $(dR_t / dt = \dot{R}_t > 0; d^2 R_t / dt^2 < 0) \rightarrow (d\lambda_t / dt = \dot{\lambda}_t < 0; d^2 \lambda_t / dt^2 < 0)$, i.e. if $R_t$ is concave then $\lambda_t$ is convex. Obviously, to be able to compare (2.6) and (2.8) we need to know the size of $R_t$ and how it develops over time. With the original budget constraint, the individual could borrow money when his or her income was low and save money when it was high, as to even out the life cycle income at the level $R$. In Liljas (2000), where neither borrowing nor saving money was possible, $R_t$ was a concave function over time, and would at certain time-periods lie above $R$, twice equal $R$, but otherwise lie below $R$ (see Figure 2.2). The present model (with the possibility of saving money) has some similarities and some

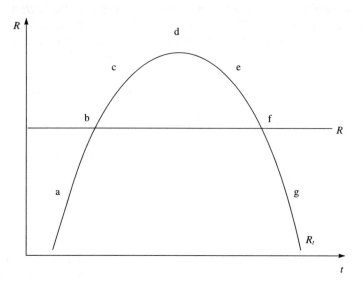

*Figure* 2.2 Graphical illustration of a concave function of income over time ($R_t$) and the average lifetime income ($R$).

differences as compared with the model in Liljas (2000). We will return to these shortly.

The reasons why $R_t$ is concave over time could, of course, be many. A reasonable explanation within the current framework, though, could be that the stock of educational capital (see Grossman, 1972) increases with time. It can then be argued that this increase will positively affect the individual's productivity at work, which in turn will increase the exogenously determined wage-rate ($W_t$). However, the increase in the stock of educational capital might be partly offset at an older age if, for example, the individual's 'general productivity' per unit of time, or learning capability, decreases. Thus, the reason why $R_t$ follows the pattern in Figure 2.2 is that $W_t$ follows a similar pattern. Since this hypothesis includes most of the possible combination of values for $\lambda_t$ and $\dot{\lambda}_t$, it will be the frame of reference for my analysis.

In Figure 2.2 it can be seen that there are seven different cases (a–g) where changes *2* and *4*, above, affect the differences between (2.6) and (2.8). However, in the case with savings, but without borrowing, the individual's budget does not exactly follow the pattern of Figure 2.2 anymore. For cases a, b, and up to c, $R_t^*$ (which is the individual's budget for the case when saving, but not borrowing, money is possible) follows the pattern of Figure 2.2, but approximately at c, $R_t^*$ becomes a horizontal line above $R$ (so for cases c–g, $R_t^* > R$ ), see Figure 2.3. This is so because the individual saves a part of his or her income when it is higher than the lifetime average income ($R$) in order to 'even out' his or her remaining lifetime income (and thereby resembling Grossman's original model, where both saving and borrowing are allowed).[6] Obviously, $R_t^*$ is here no longer

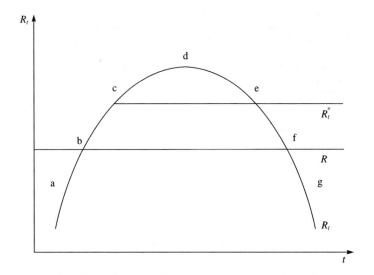

*Figure 2.3* Graphical illustration of a concave function of income over time ($R_t$),
a concave function of income over time without the possibility of
borrowing money ($R_t^*$), and the average lifetime income ($R$).

a strictly concave function over time. Thus, when $R_t$ is decreasing (in cases e, f,
and g), the individual will have a negative net-saving (i.e. $\Delta S_t < 0$). This means
that $\dot{\lambda}_t = 0$ and that $\lambda_t < \lambda$ for cases c–g (contingent upon that the financial
assets, and savings in the current period, are viewed as untouchable by the individual until later time-periods when they are needed, e.g. pension funds, so that
they do not affect the marginal utility of money).

Furthermore, in the case when borrowing money is not allowed (2.8), the
MC-curve in Figure 2.1 slopes upwards. This is because the opportunity cost of
investing in health has increased in every time-period since the individual now can
earn interest on his or her savings. Comparing (2.8) with (2.6) is obviously very
difficult since we have three changes affecting the MC-curve, and two changes
affecting the MB-curve in Figure 2.1. Some of the conclusion presented below will
therefore have to rest on the rather strong (and perhaps somewhat arbitrary)
assumption that two changes in opposite direction within either the MC- or
MB-curve cancel out. See Table 2.1 for a summary of the effects in these cases.

Hence, as compared to Grossman's original model the following holds; for
(a): $R_t^* < R, \dot{R}_t^* > 0, \lambda_t > \lambda, \dot{\lambda}_t < 0$; for (b): $R_t^* = R, \dot{R}_t^* > 0, \lambda_t = \lambda, \dot{\lambda}_t < 0$;
whereas for all other cases: $R_t^* > R, \dot{R}_t^* = 0, \lambda_t < \lambda, \dot{\lambda}_t = 0$. The marginal valua-
tion of health at optimum for cases a and b has increased, whereas the demanded
level of health at optimum has decreased. Thus, as long as $R_t^* \leq R$ and $\dot{R}_t^* > 0$,
the demanded level of health at optimum tends to decrease with this budget
constraint. For cases c–g the effects on the marginal valuation of health at
optimum and the demanded level of health at optimum are zero (or perhaps
indeterminate). However, as the individual's income in these cases is higher in

*Table 2.1* A summary of the five changes (*1* and *2* affecting the marginal benefit, and *3*, *4*, and *5* affecting the marginal cost) and their effect on *MV* (marginal valuation of health) and *H*. This is shown for the case when borrowing money is not allowed, as compared to Grossman's original model, for the seven different cases shown in Figure 2.3. A minus denotes a negative effect, plus a positive effect, and zero no effect

| | *1* | *2* | *3* | *4* | *5* | *MV* | *H* |
|---|---|---|---|---|---|---|---|
| | $e^{(r-\theta)t} \rightarrow e^{-\theta t}$ | $\lambda \rightarrow \lambda_t$ | *No r* | Add: $-\pi_t\lambda_t/\lambda_t$ | Add: $\partial S_t/\partial H_t$ | | |
| a | − | − | − | + | + | + | − |
| b | − | 0 | − | + | + | + | − |
| c | − | + | − | 0 | + | 0 | 0 |
| d | − | + | − | 0 | + | 0 | 0 |
| e | − | + | − | 0 | + | 0 | 0 |
| f | − | + | − | 0 | + | 0 | 0 |
| g | − | + | − | 0 | + | 0 | 0 |

this new setting, it does not seem unreasonable that his or her optimal demand for health would also be higher.

These results are intuitively reasonable; as long as the individual's income is low ($R_t^* < R$) and he or she knows that his or her income will increase in future time-periods ($\dot{R}_t^* > 0$), his or her opportunity cost of making investments in health is relatively high in this time-period. Thus, he or she will postpone these investments, and the demanded level of health at optimum will be lower with this budget constraint. Consequently, when the individual's income is high ($R_t^* > R$) and he or she knows that his or her income will not increase (i.e. decrease or remain constant) in future time-periods ($\dot{R}_t^* \leq 0$), his or her opportunity cost of making investments in health is relatively small in these time-periods. Thus, in these cases the demanded level of health at optimum will be larger with this budget constraint. The result following from this reasoning does not seem unreasonable: at early stages in an individual's life, he or she does not invest in health as heavily as at later stages in his or her life.

## Discussion

The number of theoretical contributions to the important area of individuals' demand for health, which (of course) is one of the central topics within health economics, have been relatively few. In Michael Grossman's classic demand-for-health model, the budget constraint only had to be binding over the individual's entire lifespan, an assumption which implies a perfect market for loans and savings, with equal and constant interest rates on deposits and loans, and no restrictions and/or transaction costs. This assumption was relaxed in this chapter, and a setting with imperfect financial markets was tested. Here, saving but not borrowing was possible (the individual's expenditures could at least not be larger than his or her income plus total financial assets for that time-period).

A perhaps more realistic budget constraint would allow the individual to both save and borrow money but at different interest rates. This is, however, a fairly complex analysis within the current framework but could be an interesting topic for further research.

As the new extension of the model affected the solution to the optimization problems in several directions, it was very difficult to make *any* comparison to the original model. However, in order to understand the effects of imperfect financial markets, some comparisons still had to be made. A rather heroic assumption about cancelling of two effects in opposite directions (within either the MB- or the MC-curve) was therefore applied. This assumption is, of course, rather arbitrary (as was the assumption on the individual's savings as being a 'rest-product' instead of a choice variable) but do give some quite plausible results, and definitely shows how complex the model quickly becomes when taking these important aspects into account.

The main effects of the new budget constraint without borrowing (as compared to Grossman's original model) were that the interest rate disappeared from the solution of the optimization problem, and that the marginal utility of income became time dependent. The fact that the interest rate disappeared implies that the opportunity cost of investing in health capital in the current rather than in future time-periods has decreased. The change in the marginal utility of income has to do with the fact that the individual's income, in this setting, and hence how binding the budget constraint is, varies over time. The net effect of these changes was shown to depend to a large extent on the level of income, and the change of income over time. Making any direct comparisons were, however, difficult (and resulted in many indeterminate solutions) since the number of effects going in opposite directions were high.

However, some intuitive appealing results were found. The two different scenarios described in this chapter (Grossman's original budget constraint, and the new extension) basically differ in how much the individual can equate the lifetime income over the different time-periods. For the individual, it was assumed to be optimal to 'even out' the income over the lifecycle, and therefore also optimal to save whenever the current time-period's income is higher than the average lifetime income, and use these savings otherwise. However, if the total lifetime income for both cases is fairly similar, the investments in health might be more related to *when* they are being made rather than *if* they are being made. Thus, in the time-periods when income is low but increasing, the demand for health at optimum is smaller with the new budget constraint. In these cases, the individual will postpone his or her investments in health as long as he or she knows that his or her income will increase over time (since the opportunity cost of investments in health then will decrease over time). When income is high (and in this case constant), the demand for health at optimum is *likely* to be higher (even though that could not be firmly established in the model because of the many effects going in different directions). The individual would in these cases invest more in his or her health during the later parts of his or her life.

Obviously, the timing of these investments could be of great importance, e.g. an investment in health prevention might have a vastly different lifetime effect on health than an equally large investment in health restoration (for example, by its indirect effects on the depreciation rate of health). This is, however, not explicitly studied here. Furthermore, these aspects of timing could imply that empirical formulations of the original model might overstate the individual's preventive actions (or early investments in health), and thus have important welfare implications. If the market imperfection is large, and the health policy implications hold true, this might call for more governmental interventions than implied by the original Grossman model, e.g. aimed at supporting preventive investments in health. Empirically, however, the measurability of health, health inputs, and the relative productivity of these inputs is difficult, and it will be hard to determine with any accuracy whether individuals are investing too much or too little in health at a specific point in time. Furthermore, because of the number of assumptions that had to be made in the analysis, the results are tentative at most, and any policy implications should therefore be interpreted with great caution.

Moreover, as with investments in health, it is of course also possible that substitutions of consumption goods occur over the individual's lifespan in this new setting. Even though this is not explicitly studied here, it seems clear that the pattern of lifetime consumption of other goods than health will be affected by these changes. This could then, naturally, also be of interest to analyse in this context. Further, if the time-period when a young individual may start his or her use of tobacco and/or alcohol might be postponed, this will then indirectly affect the individual's level of health in the model. Other elaborations with the Grossman model, such as how the equation for investments in health should be formulated, could also be of great interest to study. For example, contrary to the idea behind the original model, many activities an individual can undertake will actually save money and increase health at the same time (e.g. the decisions of not to smoke, to keep a healthy weight and a balanced diet, and to avoid excessive consumption of alcohol). These decisions are, in fact, probably related to some of the most important investments in health that (especially) younger individuals can make. Still, many individuals are not making these investments (perhaps in part because of issues related to rational addiction, see, e.g. Becker and Murphy, 1988), and this fact should perhaps be further investigated and incorporated into the model. Since the Grossman model is a fundamental part of the area of health economics, and is the basis for many empirical applications (with the possibility of resulting in important policy implications), further theoretical developments of the model as well as competing models for the individual's demand for health are indeed important areas for future research.

## Notes

I would like to thank Fredrik Andersson and Björn Lindgren (Lund University), John Cairns (University of Aberdeen), Michael Grossman (City University of New York Graduate School), Mark Pauly (University of Pennsylvania), Adam Wagstaff (University of Sussex), participants of the 2nd World Conference in Health Economics (Rotterdam, The Netherlands), the 19th annual Arne Ryde symposium (Lund, Sweden), and two anonymous referees for their comments on earlier versions of this chapter.

1 See, for example, Muurinen (1982), Wagstaff (1986), Erlich and Chuma (1990), Ried (1996), Liljas (1998), and Reid (1998).
2 See Grossman (1972) for a closer description of the model.
3 See, e.g. Muurinen (1982), Reid (1996), and Liljas (1998) for different treatments of the depreciation factor of health.
4 Dynamic utility theoretic models investigating the individual's demand for consumption over time have, naturally, existed for a long time (see, e.g. Kamien and Schwartz, 1991). More general models where the lifetime of the individual is uncertain also exist and have been shown to affect the amount of consumption, savings, and borrowing (Yaari, 1965; Leung, 1994).
5 Obviously, in reality the individual should be able to choose the amount of savings in each time-period, i.e. $S_t$ should be a choice variable (such as investments in health and consumption). However, a simplifying assumption is invoked here by making the amount of savings in each time-period more of a 'rest-product', i.e. the individual is assumed to save whatever he or she is *not* spending on investments in health and/or on consumption. Future research should attempt at relaxing this strong assumption, and instead investigate the effects of the possibility of savings when the optimal paths of these three choice variables are *jointly* determined.
6 Obviously, this depends on the individual's rate of time preferences (i.e. how much he or she will reduce his or her savings in each time-period) – it is here assumed that the individual as far as possible will try to 'even out' his or her income in the remaining time-periods. Even though this might be regarded as a 'tough' assumption, it recapitulates some of the ideas behind the well-known lifecycle hypothesis, where it is assumed that the individual strives toward a smooth consumption-path over the lifecycle (Ando and Modigliani, 1963).

# References

Ando, A. and Modigliani, F., 1963. The life cycle hypothesis of saving: aggregate implications and tests. *American Economic Review* 53, 55–84.

Becker, G.S., 1965. A theory of the allocation of time. *The Economic Journal* 75, 493–517.

Becker, G.S. and Murphy, K.M., 1988. A theory of rational addiction. *Journal of Political Economy* 96, 675–700.

Bolin, K., Jacobson, L. and Lindgren, B., 2001. The family as the health producer – when spouses are Nash-bargainers. *Journal of Health Economics* 20, 349–62.

Chiang, A.C., 1992. *Elements of dynamic optimization.* McGraw-Hill International Editions, Singapore.

Cropper, M.L., 1977. Health, investment in health, and occupational choice. *Journal of Political Economy* 85, 1273–94.

Dardanoni, V. and Wagstaff, A., 1990. Uncertainty and the demand for medical care. *Journal of Health Economics* 9, 23–38.

Erlich, I. and Chuma, H., 1990. A model of the demand for longevity and the value of life extension. *Journal of Political Economy* 98, 761–82.

Forster, B.A., 1989. Optimal health investment strategies. *Bulletin of Economic Research* 41, 45–57.

Grossman, M., 1972. On the concept of health capital and the demand for health. *Journal of Political Economy* 80, 223–55.

Grossman, M., 1982. The demand for health after a decade. *Journal of Health Economics* 1, 1–3.

Grossman, M., 1998. On optimal length of life. *Journal of Health Economics* 17, 499–509.

Grossman, M., 2000. The human capital model of the demand for health. In: Culyer, A.J. and Newhouse, J.P. (eds), *Handbook of Health Economics*, pp. 347–408.

Jacobson, L., 2000. The family as producer of health – an extension of the Grossman model. *Journal of Health Economics* 19, 611–38.

Kamien, M. and Schwartz, N., 1991. *Dynamic optimization: the calculus of variations and optimal control theory in economics and management*. Elsevier, New York.

Leung, S.F., 1994. Uncertain lifetime, the theory of the consumer, and the life cycle hypothesis. *Econometrica* 62, 1233–9.

Liljas, B., 1998. The demand for health with uncertainty and insurance. *Journal of Health Economics* 17, 153–70.

Liljas, B., 2000. Insurance and imperfect financial markets in Grossman's demand for health model – a reply to Tabata and Ohkusa. *Journal of Health Economics* 19, 821–7.

Muurinen, J.-M., 1982. Demand for health, a generalized Grossman model. *Journal of Health Economics* 1, 5–28.

Picone, G., Uribe, M. and Wilson, R.M., 1998. The effect of uncertainty on the demand for medical care, health capital and wealth. *Journal of Health Economics* 17, 171–85.

Ried, W., 1996. Willingness to pay and cost of illness for changes in health capital depreciation. *Health Economics* 5, 447–68.

Ried, W., 1998. Comparative dynamic analysis of the full Grossman model. *Journal of Health Economics* 17, 383–425.

Tabata, K. and Ohkusa, Y., 2000. Correction note on 'The demand for health with uncertainty and insurance'. *Journal of Health Economics* 19, 811–20.

Wagstaff, A., 1986. The demand for health. Some new empirical evidence. *Journal of Health Economics* 5, 195–233.

Yaari, M., 1965. Uncertain lifetime, life insurance, and the theory of the consumer. *Review of Economic Studies* 32, 137–50.

Zweifel, P. and Breyer, F., 1997. *Health Economics*. Oxford University Press, Oxford.

# 3 Health, genuine uncertainty, and information

*Fredrik Andersson and*
*Carl Hampus Lyttkens*

## Introduction

Ever since the seminal article by Arrow (1963), it has been a commonplace to note that the presence of uncertainty is a particularly salient feature in decisions on health and health care. A number of studies have appeared that introduce probabilistic elements in the individual's demand for health, and there is a substantial literature that focuses on the value of changes in health risks. For example, in the so-called demand-for-health tradition – emanating from Grossman's (1972) well-known work – there are several probabilistic versions,[1] and the implications of risk in the health production function have been explored in a valuation context (Johansson, 1994).[2] There remains to introduce, however, the distinction between risk – i.e. uncertainty with known probabilistic properties – and genuine uncertainty – i.e. uncertainty with *unknown* probabilistic properties – in formal models of health-related behaviour.

In this chapter, we introduce genuine uncertainty as well as uncertainty aversion into a simple model of individual decision-making about health-related activities. This is potentially important, since, arguably, the conditions for many of the decisions an individual makes concerning his own health more closely resemble conditions of genuine uncertainty than pure risk. The individual is likely to be highly uncertain if not completely ignorant about the probabilities involved. For example, he may be vaguely aware that there is a serious disease called leukaemia while having no idea of whether he is likely to get it and no idea about his possibilities to affect the likelihood of getting it.

Within this format, we investigate the consequences for health-related behaviour of individual attitudes towards health and information as well as of exogenous changes in the individual's decision environment. In the section on Individual trade-offs and personality traits we show how health-related decisions are affected by the individual's degree of pessimism with respect to health states with unknown probabilities; we also consider the effects of the individual being confident or diffident about the accuracy of the information he possesses.

Furthermore, we analyse in the section on Individual trade-offs and exogenous changes in information, prevention, prices, and income, how different forms of health policy and other exogenous factors are likely to affect individual behaviour, in particular the individual's propensity to gather information and engage in own prevention. Specifically, we explore how the individual reacts when provided with information without cost (exogenous information), when there is a reduction in the health risks he faces (exogenous prevention), and finally when he learns something new about the welfare implications of a particular health state. We also make certain observations about the effects of changes in prices and income. In the section on Health policy and socio-economic differences in health and behaviour we discuss the implications of our results for differential behaviour across socio-economic groups, and for the effects of health policy on these cross-sectional clusters.

## The model

We now turn to constructing a model where an individual faces two sorts of health states – those to which he can assign probabilities and those which he is genuinely uncertain about. He can influence the relative importance of genuine uncertainty by collecting information.

### General specification

Individual utility depends on the anticipated health status, $h$, and on a vector, $a$, of activities. Health statuses are ranked in terms of *healthy days*, $h^s$, and they may equivalently be thought of as being characterized by a number of quality-adjusted healthy days, so that the ranking also takes account of quality-of-life aspects; the key requirement is that the individual is able to make an unambiguous ranking.

The utility function is

$$U(a) = \gamma(a) \cdot \sum_{s=1}^{s} \pi_s(a)u(h^s, a) + (1 - \gamma(a)) \cdot u_0(a). \tag{3.1}$$

It is a convex combination – weighted by $0 \leq \gamma(a) \leq 1$ – of two components, the first being an ordinary expected utility, and the second one being (a reduced form for) a generalized expected utility. We describe these in turn.

1   The first component is an expected utility over $S$ states of health whose outcomes are ranked from better to worse in terms of healthy days; i.e. $h^1 > \ldots > h^s$. (Note that we employ the convention that a state with a higher number is worse.) The individual assigns probabilities, $\pi_1(a), \ldots, \pi_S(a)$, to these health states, and $u$ is a von Neumann–Morgenstern utility function which is positive and increasing in $h$.

2   The second component is a reduced form, sharing a number of properties with a generalized expected utility exhibiting 'uncertainty aversion'.[3] To construct it, we assume the existence of a set of states $S + 1, \ldots, S + S'$, in addition to the states described under 1. These states are distinguished by the

individual not being able to assign firm probabilities to them. In the literature on genuine uncertainty and uncertainty aversion,[4] uncertainty is captured by the assumption that the individual assigns *generalized probabilities* to these in a fashion that is 'pessimistic'. The theory works in a way such that states are assigned generalized probabilities that need not sum to one (and that are not required to satisfy standard additivity properties). When expectations are computed these generalized probabilities are transformed into weights summing to 1. The result of this evaluation is a generalized expected utility $u_0(a) = \tilde{E}\{u(h; a) \mid S + 1, \ldots, S + S'\}$ where the tilde signifies that the evaluation is by the generalized probabilities. The generalized expectation is taken over the same von Neumann–Morgenstern utility function.[5] We will work directly with $u_0(a)$ which is a reduced form in that it captures *the effect* of both the genuine uncertainty and the uncertainty aversion (or pessimism) that the individual exhibits in evaluating the uncertainty.

Some of the activities, $a$, are costly in the individual's budget. The budget should be thought of as, somewhat roughly, capturing the objective costs of various activities – e.g. costs in terms of money and time – while the subjective costs would be captured by the utility function depending directly on $a$.

The probabilities, $\pi_1(a), \ldots, \pi_S(a)$, depend on $a$, and the cumulative distribution is denoted $F(h;a)$ (i.e. $F$ is the probability that the number of healthy days is less than or equal to $h$ given $a$).

We will call the states $1, \ldots, S$ to which the individual assigns ordinary probabilities the 'firm states', and the remaining states, $S + 1, \ldots, S + S'$, are called the 'uncertain states'.

Although one could work with a more general specification (with the individual's probabilistic frame of reference being specified completely in terms of generalized probabilities depending on activities), such a specification would be operationally very weak since there is no agreed notion of uncertainty and uncertainty aversion. Our specification has the significant advantage of providing a natural parameterization (through $\gamma$) of the uncertainty faced by the individual.[6] Moreover, it is possible to rank the degree of uncertainty aversion (being captured by $u_0$) and the probabilistic favourability of the firm states (through $\pi_1(a), \ldots, \pi_S(a)$) within this framework.

It is important to realize that the loss of generality that follows from the reduced form is only in terms of the flexibility of the utility function (the restriction is qualitatively very similar to imposing, e.g. separability restrictions on a utility function). There seems to be little conceptual loss of generality in this simplification. If for example an exogenous event – like the alarm about the mad cow disease in Britain in 1996 – simultaneously makes people more genuinely uncertain and more dismal regarding the probability of brain disease, this is captured perfectly well by a simultaneous shift in the degree of uncertainty ($\gamma$) and in the probabilities. Conversely, it is clear that conventional probability-based models are inherently incapable of capturing uncertainty. One may note that at this stage, the model is algebraically equivalent to a model with only risk present and with $u_0$ occurring with probability $\gamma$, but one should also note that the equivalence is upset as soon as one considers an exogenous change or behavioural implications; for example, preventive behaviour is assumed to have a known effect on the probabilities for the firm states but not on the assessment of the likelihood of uncertain states.

To recapitulate briefly, the individual utility function is given by a convex combination of a standard expected utility over the probability distribution $\pi_1(a),\dots,\pi_S(a)$ over the firm states $1,\dots,S$, (with $\Sigma\pi_s = 1$), and a reduced form of a generalized expected utility, $u_0$, over the uncertain states. He assigns weight $\gamma$ to the firm states. Hence $\gamma$ measures the degree of certainty or, as we shall phrase it later, the individual's degree of *confidence* in his information about the firm health states; $u_0$, on the other hand, measures the degree of uncertainty aversion – i.e. the utility loss from being uncertain.[7]

### Pessimism

The basic tenet of the literature on uncertainty aversion is one of pessimism, and basic pessimism with respect to genuine uncertainty will be the maintained assumption unless otherwise stated. We will take this to mean that the individual assigns higher expected utility to the firm states than to the uncertain states; i.e. that

$$u_0(a) < \sum_1^s \pi_s u(h^s; a) \tag{3.2}$$

for each $a$. In words, the utility of being completely uncertain ($\gamma = 0$) is always lower than the utility of facing no genuine uncertainty ($\gamma = 1$). For many health applications it seems reasonable to assume this to be the main case. It is clear, however, that the model can also capture fundamental optimism, and we will make a comment on that case in the subsection on Pessimism and confidence: basic analysis.

The *degree of pessimism* is arguably an important trait in an individual's personality. There is obviously scope for more or less pessimism, and this corresponds to the individual exhibiting more or less uncertainty aversion; it is modelled by allowing $u_0$ to vary. In our terminology, a person with a large $u_0$ is less pessimistic; such a person values relatively highly the health states that are surrounded by genuine uncertainty.

### Information and confidence

We will assume that the degree of certainty ($\gamma$) is affected by information. It seems intuitively very plausible that by gathering information the individual can reduce the relative importance of uncertainty in his life. Hence we assume that he may take an active decision to increase $\gamma$ by gathering information and can weigh the pros and cons of such a decision. The decision cannot be contingent on the expected direction of the information; i.e. while the individual may well find *ex post* that $\pi_S$ has changed in the light of new information, such changes cannot influence the decision to gather information. Assuming this seems natural in our case.[8] This part of the model is primarily intended to represent the acquisition of general information about health risks. This is in contrast to, for example, the health care setting of undergoing a diagnostic test to determine whether one has contracted a specific disease and submitting to treatment accordingly (individual-specific information); we do not model such a sequence of events – just the individual's propensity to seek information and engage in prevention.

A natural interpretation of the weight γ is that it is a measure of how much *confidence* the individual has regarding the information that he has about the probabilities of the firm health states. Henceforth we will say that a larger γ corresponds to the individual being more confident about the accuracy of his information. Conversely, a person who is diffident about his information (small γ) puts more weight on the uncertain states of the world.[9]

Confidence, notably, is not only a result of information gathering. Rather, just like pessimism, the degree of confidence is an important personality trait in itself, and the implications of this can be explored by allowing γ to vary.

### Prevention and risk

The final basic feature of the model is *conventional risk* – i.e. probabilities assigned to different health states as described by the distribution $F(h; a)$ (or, equivalently, $\pi_1(a), \ldots, \pi_S(a)$). This distribution may change as the result of health-promoting activities. Here we will make use of the fact that probability distributions over the states $1, \ldots, S$ are ordered by (first-order) stochastic dominance. One distribution *stochastically dominates* another if for each outcome, $h$, something smaller is less probable according to the dominating distribution; i.e. a distribution with cumulative distribution function $G$ dominates a distribution $F$ if for each $h$, $G(h) \leq F(h)$.[10] The activity $a_i$ makes the distribution more favourable if

$$F_{a_i}(h;a) = \frac{\partial F(h; a)}{\partial a_i} \leq 0;$$

i.e. if it induces a shift in the distribution in the direction of stochastic dominance.

We define prevention as an activity which shifts the distribution $F$ in the direction of stochastic dominance (an activity with the opposite effect would be hazardous).[11]

The interaction between the risk and uncertainty aspects of the model seems to capture an important element in decisions about health-related activities. Even when we are dealing with risk – so that an individual is implicitly thinking in terms of a probability for, say, lung cancer – it seems reasonable to argue that he is often unsure about whether he has in fact the correct probability ($\pi_s$) and about the effect of his actions on the probability of ill health ($\partial \pi_s / \partial a$), e.g. the effect of smoking on the probability of lung cancer. The size of γ reflects the degree to which the individual is confident about $\pi_s$ and $\partial \pi_s / \partial a$ (though we cannot separate the two attitudes).

Note that in this model, prevention has no effect on utility under the uncertain health states ($u_0$). Consequently, the individual will never engage in prevention in order to increase $u_0$. The reason for this is the sharp formal distinction in the utility function between the health states with probabilities attached and those where there is genuine uncertainty. (In relation to fully general uncertainty models, this assumption is analogous to assuming that the lower bound of the support – i.e. the worst outcome in terms of healthy days – cannot be affected by prevention.) As soon as the individual believes that it is possible to influence the probability of health outcomes – even if it is a very vague belief or hope – the probabilistic part of the utility function is involved.

## A specified set of individual activities

In the following, we will make an unambiguous distinction between information gathering and prevention, which are both distinguished from consumption. We will distinguish between three types of activities that enter the individual's decision problem: information gathering (generically denoted $a_1$), prevention ($a_2$), and consumption ($a_3$). This is not to say that these activities are always separable, but separability is very useful in order to keep the arguments transparent; it is also clear that the effects of an activity entailing both information gathering and prevention are the obvious 'sum' of the effects of the components adjusted for complementarities.

Hence we assume that the informative activity ($a_1$) affects $\gamma$ but not $F$, and conversely for the preventive activity ($a_2$). We will also assume that neither prevention nor information gathering enters the individual's utility function directly (doing so would simply add a cost component – direct negative effects on utility – and this is unlikely to change the results qualitatively); utility is thus a function of health and consumption ($a_3$). This is in line with the Grossman (1972) model with its basis in household production theory, where healthy days appear in the utility function together with consumption, and where the healthy days are ultimately produced by medical inputs and the like. Consumption is assumed not to influence health. We should note that with this kind of formulation, we cannot analyse strictly hazardous activities such as smoking or rock climbing, which are usually activities that have a positive direct effect on utility but a negative expected net effect on health.

## The budget and the maximization problem

We will assume that all our three activities are costly, i.e. have positive prices in the individual's budget. For simplicity, we take the individual's income $A$ to be exogenously given and not dependent on health. In terms of the Grossman (1972) model, one could say that we are investigating a consumption model of health. It seems intuitively clear that if health also had a positive effect on $A$, this would increase the attractiveness of health-promoting activities in our model.

The individual strives to maximize utility. In order to obtain more convenient expressions, we let $h^{s+1}$ denote a fictitious worst state (thus redefining $h^{s+1}$). With the convention that $u(h^{s+1}; a) = 0$, an equivalent representation of the problem (which follows from a manipulation of sums analogous to integration by parts) is

$$\max U(a_1, a_2, a_3) = \gamma(a_1)\sum_{i=1}^{s}(u(h^s, a_3) - u(h^{s+1}, a_3))(1 - F(h^{s+1}; a_2))$$
$$+ (1 - \gamma(a_1))u_0(a_3),$$

$$s.t. \sum_{i=1}^{3}p_i a_i \leq A, \quad a_i \geq 0, \quad i = 1, 2, 3.$$

We assume that information gathering increases the individual's degree of confidence, $\gamma'(a_i) > 0$, but at a decreasing rate, $\gamma''(a_i) < 0$. This amounts to assuming information acquisition to be a concave problem. We will also assume that choosing the preventive activity is a concave problem; this requires that $F$ is convex in $a$, i.e. that $F_{aa} > 0$, and that utility is concave in consumption. In addition, we assume that the objective function is jointly quasi-concave in $a$, and hence that first-order conditions define optimal choices. Finally, we assume that the marginal utility of consumption is independent of the health state. This seems to be a reasonable simplification, since it is equally possible to argue that the marginal utility of consumption is higher for a healthy individual as it is to argue that it is lower. In particular, we assume that the marginal utility of consumption is the same in the firm health states as in the uncertain ones.

## Individual trade-offs and personality traits

In this section, we will investigate how the individual's trade-off between activities is affected by his attitudes towards health in terms of pessimism and confidence.

### *Pessimism and confidence: basic analysis*

In order to illustrate our assumption of basic pessimism, we begin by looking at the first-order condition with respect to the information activity $a_1$; for an interior solution, it is

$$\frac{\partial \gamma}{\partial a_1}\left(\sum_{s=1}^{S}(u(h^s, a) - u(h^{s+1}, a))(1 - F(h^{s+1}; a_2) - u_0(a_3))\right) = \lambda p_1.$$

The derivative of $\gamma$ is positive by assumption, and the right-hand side is positive if the price of activity $a_1$ is positive. Hence, an interior solution exists only if the expression in the parenthesis is positive, i.e. if the utility from being completely certain is larger than the utility from being completely uncertain; if that is not the case, $a_1 = 0$. This has an interesting interpretation: the individual will invest in gathering information only if he – taking his attitude toward uncertainty into account – from the outset is better off in the firm states; i.e. if he is a basic uncertainty pessimist as we have assumed (cf. expression (3.2)). Conversely, if the individual is instead a basic uncertainty optimist (the opposite of expression (3.2) holding), he may prefer to engage in an activity which makes him more uncertain (e.g. seeking out conflicting information, or gathering information even if he believes it will confuse him).

The last observation has a direct correspondence in the welfare effects of exogenously provided information. Consider an impact, $g$, which the agent is exposed to exogenously. The natural interpretation of $g$ is information provided by the government, but other interpretations are possible. A complete welfare analysis would consider the trade-off between the positive effects of $g$ and the cost of providing it; we confine ourselves, however, to the simple case where it is costless, because the substantive point to be made stands out more clearly without costs.

**Proposition 3.1**    *Exogenous information is welfare-improving if the individual is a basic uncertainty pessimist; it has a* negative *welfare effect if the individual is a basic uncertainty optimist.* (See the Appendix for proof.)

Performing a similar analysis for exogenous prevention – i.e. an activity that improves the individual's health – it is clear from the proof that it is unambiguously welfare-improving. These results are not surprising but nevertheless important since they stress the significance of the assumption of pessimism. The welfare implications of interventions that entail changing prices of the individuals' own efforts are completely clear; lowering prices, and thereby expanding individuals' feasible sets, is always at least weakly beneficial.

It is worth noting that the result highlights a difference between our model and expected-utility models where individuals may gather pieces of information (typically called 'experiments') whose degree of informativeness differ.[12] In such a framework, basic consistency requirements imply that the expected utility *ex ante* be independent of the informativeness of the experiment performed in the absence of a behavioural response to the experiment (the purpose of the experiment being to adjust actions conditional on it). This difference illustrates the additional degree of freedom introduced by allowing for attitudes toward uncertainty. One virtue of allowing for such attitudes is, in our view, that intuitive notions of pessimism and optimism are captured in a more germane fashion.

We should note here that the case of basic uncertainty optimism does not seem altogether unrealistic. One may well imagine that, for example, certain individuals are better off not knowing that they may some day contract osteocarcinoma. Remember, however, that in the analysis to follow, the maintained assumption is that the individual is a basic pessimist with respect to uncertainty.

Given basic pessimism, we now focus on the individual's *degree* of pessimism, i.e. the effects of variations in $u_0$. We will employ the traditional approach of differentiating the first-order conditions (henceforth FOC) – which in our case include the FOC for $a_1$, $a_2$, and $a_3$ – and the budget constraint implicitly and then solving for the derivatives in question. The FOC are (where we denote derivatives of $\gamma$ with primes since it only depends on $a_1$)

$$\gamma' \cdot \left[ \Sigma(u^s - u^{s+1})(1 - F(h^{s+1}; a)) - u_0(a) \right] - \lambda p_1 = 0,$$

$$\gamma \cdot \Sigma(u^s - u^{s+1})(-F_a(h^{s+1};a)) - \lambda p_2 = 0,$$   (3.3)

$$\partial_{a_3} u - \lambda p_3 = 0,$$

$$A - p_1 a_1 - p_2 a_2 - p_3 a_3 = 0.$$

The differentiated FOC, letting $\Delta u^s = u^s - u^{s+1}$, take the form

$$
\begin{bmatrix}
\gamma''(\Sigma\Delta u^s F - u_0) & -\gamma'\Sigma\Delta u^s F_a & 0 & -p_1 \\
-\gamma'\Sigma\Delta u^s F_a & \gamma\Sigma\Delta u^s F_{aa} & 0 & -p_2 \\
0 & 0 & \partial^2_{a_3} u & -p_3 \\
-p_1 & -p_2 & -p_3 & 0
\end{bmatrix}
\cdot
\begin{bmatrix}
\partial a_1/\partial u_0 \\
\partial a_2/\partial u_0 \\
\partial a_3/\partial u_0 \\
\partial \lambda/\partial u_0
\end{bmatrix}
=
\begin{bmatrix}
\gamma' \\
0 \\
0 \\
0
\end{bmatrix},
$$   (3.4)

where the right-hand side is the negative of the derivative of the first-order conditions with respect to $u_0$. The first factor on the left-hand side is the Jacobian matrix for the FOC. Under the assumption that the individual's objective function is (strictly) quasi-concave, we know the FOC define the unique maximum; moreover, we know that the determinant, $D$, is negative (Simon and Blume, 1994).

The upper left corner of the inverse of the Jacobian matrix is $1/D$ times the following expression

$$
\begin{bmatrix}
-p_2^2 (\partial^2 u/\partial a_3^2) + p_3^2 \gamma \Sigma \Delta u^s F_{aa} \\
p_1 p_2 (\partial^2 u/\partial a_3^2) - p_3^2 \gamma' \Sigma \Delta u^s F_a \\
- p_3(p_1 \gamma \Sigma \Delta u^s \partial^2_a F - p_2 \gamma' \Sigma \Delta u^s F_a)
\end{bmatrix} .
$$

The derivative of $a_1$ with respect to $u_0$ is thus

$$\partial a_1/\partial u_0 = \frac{\gamma'}{D}\left( -p_2^2 (\partial^2 u/\partial a_3^2) + p_3^2 \gamma \Sigma \Delta u^s F_{aa} \right) < 0,$$

and we see that a less pessimistic assessment of the remaining number of healthy days in states that the individual cannot fully describe leads to less resources being spent on information gathering. This is natural since information in this model has the effect of reducing the weight placed on these uncertain states (increasing $\gamma$); to gather information is then less attractive, the more highly these uncertain states are valued. Inspection of the corresponding expression for $a_2$,

$$\frac{\partial a_2}{\partial u_0} = \frac{\gamma'}{D}\left(p_1 p_2 \frac{\partial^2 u}{\partial a_3^2} - p_3^2 \gamma' \Sigma \Delta u^s F_a\right),$$

shows that the effects on prevention are ambiguous; more specifically, $a_2$ decreases along with $a_1$ if marginal utility of consumption ($a_3$) is constant, and it is substituted for $a_1$ if $u$ is sufficiently concave in consumption. The magnitude of changes in the marginal utility of consumption is positively related to the magnitude of *income effects*; this will be discussed in the next subsection. Similar inspection of the derivative of $a_3$ shows that consumption unambiguously increases.

**Proposition 3.2**    *Reduced pessimism will divert resources from information gathering, and shift some resources toward consumption; prevention will decrease if income effects are small, and it will increase if income effects are large.*

We now turn to the difference in behaviour between individuals who are inherently confident and individuals who are diffident about the information that they possess. In our model, this corresponds to a shift in the parameter $\gamma$. The following statement is a corollary of Proposition 3.2 (and Table 3.2 ), and it is therefore stated without proof.

**Proposition 3.3**    *Confidence will increase prevention; information gathering will increase if income effects are small, and decrease if income effects are large.*

This proposition introduces a fundamental *complementarity* which we will encounter repeatedly, and which will be discussed in more details below. This is the complementarity between confidence on the one hand, and a favourable distribution over firm states on the other; in this instance, increasing confidence increases the marginal returns to prevention. The effect on information gathering depends on whether the individual is willing to substitute it for consumption, which in turn depends on income effects to which we now turn.

### *Income effects*

As we have just indicated, several of our results depend on the magnitude of *income effects* of $a_1$ and $a_2$; i.e. on the extent to which the demand for $a_1$ and $a_2$ depends on $A$. Income effects are small if this dependence is weak; in particular, income effects are zero if $a_1$ and $a_2$ are independent of $A$. In terms of the utility function, income effects are zero if marginal utility of consumption, $\partial u /\partial a_3$, is independent of $(a_1, a_2, a_3)$; since we have ruled out $\partial u /\partial a_3$ depending on $(a_1, a_2)$, only the dependence on $a_3$ shows up in our expressions.[13] Throughout the chapter, we will sort out the two obvious cases; the main case will be that they are small, and we will then consider the case where they are large. (Our encountering this problem is not novel. Consumer-surplus analysis and the Coase theorem are significant examples of modes of analysis that depend on income effects being small.)

At a fundamental level, the most convincing reason for income effects being small is that the objects affected directly by an exogenous change constitute a small share of the budget; marginal utilities of other goods will then be affected only negligibly. Consequently, the income effect will be negligible. Thus, attention should be concentrated on the case with small income effects in the context of changes that do not affect an individual's total consumption of other goods too much.

This suggests that the nature of the individual's budget is important in this context. Consider first the case when the budget is thought of only in monetary terms. It then seems quite plausible that income effects are small. An individual's outlays on information and prevention is usually only a small part of his budget. This is particularly the case since unhealthy behaviour is implicitly subsidized by (social and private) health insurance when premiums are not differentiated with respect to preventive or hazardous behaviour (Kenkel, 2000, Sec. 3).

The situation is somewhat different in the case when the budget also includes time costs. Gathering information often takes more time than money. Furthermore, physical exercise is a preventive activity that often seems to entail significant time costs; jogging or going to the gym four times a week seems to be good cases in point. Hence, even if leisure is valued less than working time, it does not seem inconceivable that one could encounter cases where income effects are significant.

## Individual trade-offs and exogenous changes in information, prevention, prices, and income

This section is devoted to analysing exogenous changes in the individuals' decision environment. The discussion will mostly be phrased in terms of public programmes, but the analysis covers several other possible mechanisms, such as when a person unexpectedly learns that he suffers from diabetes.

We will proceed by invoking the assumption that income effects are small. In formal terms, the first two columns of the inverse of the Jacobian matrix of expression (3.4) are as follows, where the factor $1/|D|$ is omitted, and thus the sign of the determinant taken into account; for the last row, we only state the signs.

$$
\begin{bmatrix}
p_2^2(\partial^2 u/\partial a_3^2) - p_3^2\gamma\Sigma\Delta u^s F_{aa} & -p_1 p_2(\partial^2 u/\partial a_3^2) + p_3^2\gamma'\Sigma\Delta u^s F_a \\
-p_1 p_2(\partial^2 u/\partial a_3^2) + p_3^2\gamma'\Sigma\Delta u^s F_a & p_1^2(\partial^2 u/\partial a_3^2) + p_3^2\gamma''(\Sigma\Delta u^2 F - u_0) \\
p_3(p_1\gamma\Sigma\Delta u^2\partial_a^2 - p_2\gamma'\Sigma\Delta u^s F_a) & -p_3(p_2\gamma''(\Sigma\Delta u^s \cdot F u_0) + p_1\gamma'\Sigma\Delta u^s F_a) \\
\underline{\phantom{-}} & \underline{\phantom{-}}
\end{bmatrix}
$$

All terms involving the income effect are underlined, and by income effects being *small*, we mean that these terms are small enough not to determine signs. The sign pattern of the above matrix is then

$$
\begin{bmatrix}
- & -* \\
-* & - \\
+ & + \\
- & -
\end{bmatrix},
\tag{3.5}
$$

where the asterisks indicate which signs depend on income effects being small.

We explore three sets of exogenous changes directly related to health. First, we look at exogenous information that affects the individual's degree of confidence ($\gamma$). Second, we investigate the effects of exogenous prevention, which changes the probability distribution for known health states ($F$); exogenous information and exogenous prevention may be either a complement or a substitute to one's own corresponding activities. Third, the individual may learn something new about the implications of a specific (firm) health state ($h^t$ changes for some $t$). We also make certain brief observations about changes in prices and income; these are mostly obvious but also serve as a consistency check on the model.

We will deal with changes in $\gamma$, $F$, and $h^t$ separately. To keep the presentation short, we will phrase the analysis in this section in terms of changes that increase $\gamma$, shift $F$ in a favourable direction, and suggest that $h^t$ is better than previous thought. We will discuss unfavourable information and the consequent implications in the section on health policy.

Obviously, exogenous changes may also affect the individual's degree of health-pessimism. For example, $u_0$ may shift downwards or upwards as news spread about AIDS or about innovations in transplantation technology. This kind of change has already been dealt with analytically in the previous section, and does not require any treatment here.

### *Exogenous information affects the degree of information-confidence ($\gamma$)*

Consider some exogenous information on health received by the individual which increases $\gamma$, e.g. as a result of health campaigns organized by the government or someone else. Since the purpose of the individual's own informative activity is to increase $\gamma$, it is useful analytically to treat the new information as a costless activity ($g_1$) which increases $\gamma$ and which may or may not be complementary with the individual's own informative efforts. The costless information activity does not enter the utility function directly.

Formally, the degree of certainty is a function $\gamma(a_1, g_1)$, where $g_1$ is *complementary* with the individual's own information gathering if

$$\frac{\partial^2 \gamma}{\partial a_1 \partial g_1} \geq 0;$$

i.e. if $g_1$ increases the marginal returns to the individual's own information gathering. If the opposite inequality holds, $a_1$ and $g_1$ are *substitutes*.

The negative of the derivative of the FOC with respect to $g_1$ – i.e. the relevant right-hand side of the expression corresponding to expression (3.4) but with $g_1$ being the exogenous change – is

$$\left[ -\frac{\partial^2 \gamma}{\partial a_1 \partial g_1} \cdot \left[ \Sigma \Delta u^s (1 - F) - u_0 \right] \quad \frac{\partial \gamma}{\partial g_1} \cdot \Sigma \Delta u^s \frac{\partial F}{\partial a_2} \quad 0 \quad 0 \right]^T. \tag{3.6}$$

The expression in square brackets in the first element is positive by our assumption of basic pessimism in expression (3.2), and hence the sign pattern is $(-/+,-,$ 0, 0) in case of complements/substitutes. Evoking the sign pattern in expression (3.5), we thus have for complements

$$\frac{\partial a_1}{\partial g_1} > 0, \quad \frac{\partial a_2}{\partial g_1} > 0, \quad \frac{\partial a_3}{\partial g_1} < 0,$$

whereas, for substitutes, all effects are ambiguous.

It is important to note, however, that for the above sign pattern to be broken, $a_1$ and $g_1$ have to be *sufficiently strong* substitutes; for the case of a zero or slightly negative cross derivative, the direct effect on $\gamma$ through $g_1$ is certain to dominate.

**Proposition 3.4**   *If exogenous information is complementary with own information gathering, it will shift resources from consumption towards information gathering and prevention; if it is a substitute, the effect is ambiguous.*

The first part of Proposition 3.3 is easily derived from the above; a shift in confidence (a shift in $\gamma$) corresponds to the case where the cross-partial derivative is zero.

Another way of expressing the above is to say that information is *inherently complementary* with prevention; information increases the marginal returns from prevention and vice versa. (Information increases confidence and thus the weight on the set of firm health states; the purpose of prevention is to improve the prospects in these firm states.) In the absence of income effects, the marginal utility of consumption remains constant; exogenous information increases $\gamma$ and thereby the marginal returns from prevention, which, in turn, increases the marginal benefit from own information. For this virtuous circle to be broken, exogenous and own information must be substitutes.

While it is fairly obvious that exogenous information can be a substitute to your own informative activity (you get information for free without having to look for it), it may be worth pointing out that the case of complementarity is realistic in many cases. By providing general information on health – in the form of, say, pamphlets – the government can facilitate individuals' collection of specific information since they now know what to look for and where; if you are made aware of the particular high-risk groups to which you belong, this may increase the expected return to your own information gathering.

Some readers, surprised by the complementarity between information and prevention, have objected that prevention is often a response to 'uncertainty' and to a lack of confidence in the precision of one's information. This seems to be true when more information means *less variance*. (In a setting where there is only risk, a reduction in variance seems likely to reduce prevention.)[14] Our results show, however, that when more information means *less genuine uncertainty*, a force working in the opposite direction is present. As will be clear below, this force may be quite powerful in explaining some cross-sectional patterns.

A related observation is that information on specific aspects of health obtained prior to the making of preventive decisions may or may not be complementary with prevention.[15] This stresses the fact that our model captures trade-offs involving the acquisition of general information (see subsection on Information and confidence, p. 44).

### Exogenous prevention affects the probability of known health states (F)

Government activity in areas such as workplace safety, traffic safety and air pollution can, from the individual's point of view, be seen as exogenous prevention; i.e. as exogenous activities that shift the probability distribution for known health states $(F)$ in a favourable direction (in the direction of stochastic dominance). While we will use the term 'exogenous prevention' for such exogenous shifts in $F$, it is obvious that the analysis covers any exogenous occurrence that causes favourable shifts in the probability distribution for known health states. For example, public information on existing health risks may suggest that the probability of ill health is less than the individual previously has reckoned with.

As in the previous case, it is useful to treat exogenous prevention as a costless activity $g_2$ which may or may not be complementary with the individual's own preventive efforts (and which does not enter the individual's utility function directly). The negative of the derivative of the FOC with respect to such an activity, $g_2$, is

$$\left[ \gamma' \cdot \Sigma \Delta u^s \frac{\partial F}{\partial g_2} \quad \gamma \Sigma \Delta u^s \frac{\partial^2 F}{\partial a_2 \partial g_2} \quad 0 \quad 0 \right]^T. \tag{3.7}$$

The exogenous activity is complementary with own prevention if the second derivative of $F$ is *negative*, since a better distribution corresponds to a smaller value of $F$. The sign pattern is $(-, -/+, 0, 0)$ for complements/substitutes and – analogously to the case with the exogenous information affecting certainty – we have a clean result for complementary activities,

$$\frac{\partial a_1}{\partial g_2} > 0, \quad \frac{\partial a_2}{\partial g_2} > 0, \quad \frac{\partial a_3}{\partial g_2} < 0,$$

whereas for the case where $g_2$ and $a_2$ are substitutes, all are ambiguous.

**Proposition 3.5** *If exogenous prevention is complementary with own prevention, it will shift resources from consumption towards information gathering and prevention; if it is a substitute, the effect is ambiguous.*

Again, prevention and information gathering are inherently complementary, and with small income effects, such a positive feedback circle is broken only if $g_2$ and $a_2$ are sufficiently strong substitutes. Analogously to the above, it is not hard to think of exogenous prevention that is strongly complementary with individuals' own efforts. For example, information on proper lifting techniques will help people avoid lower back pain and thereby also enable them to engage in preventive physical activities.

### New knowledge about the implications of a firm health state ($h^t$)

We will now consider the impact of new knowledge about the implications of a firm health state in terms of the number of healthy days, quality-adjusted healthy days, etc. Formally, we will investigate what happens when $h^t$ changes slightly for some state $t$; we confine our analysis to changes that are small enough not to change the *ranking* of states.

This covers a great deal of cases of public information on the availability of new medical technologies; for example, the fact that laparoscopic surgery may now be used instead of conventional cholecystectomy, making the operation less dramatic for the patient with consequently shorter convalescence, or that stenoses of the coronary arteries nowadays are often treatable with balloon dilatation (PTCA) rather than with open heart surgery. This may also be the relevant framework for information on the existence of 'hospital infections', which makes inpatient care more hazardous, or new forms of tuberculosis which do not respond to existing therapies.

In order to structure this part of the analysis, we will distinguish two categories of preventive activities. Activity $a_2$ is said to be *bottom-end* preventive if

$$\frac{\partial F(h; a)}{\partial a_2}$$

is increasing in $h$; i.e. if $F(h; a)$ is *more decreasing* for small $h$. Thus a bottom-end preventive activity has a larger effect on the probabilities of the worst realizations of $h$ (e.g. to stay out of the sun to reduce the risk of malignant melanoma). Correspondingly, a *top-end* preventive activity has the derivative $F_a$ decreasing with $h$, and has its largest impact on the best realizations of $h$ since it is most negative there (e.g. to avoid standing close to someone with a cold). Note that these are local properties that cannot generally be satisfied globally.[16]

Since $F(h; a)$ is piece-wise constant in $h$ and hence independent of $h$ in the interval considered, the negative of the derivative of the first-order condition with respect to $h^t$ is

$$\left[ -\gamma' u'(h^t)(F(h^t; a) - (F(h^{t+1}; a)) - \gamma' u'(h^t)\left( \frac{\partial F}{\partial a}(h^t; a) - \frac{\partial F}{\partial a}(h^{t+1}; a) \right) 0 \; 0 \right]^T \quad (3.8)$$

The sign pattern is $(-, -/+, 0, 0)$ for a bottom-end/top-end preventive activity, and for a bottom-end activity, the derivatives then satisfy

$$\frac{\partial a_1}{\partial h} > 0, \quad \frac{\partial a_2}{\partial h} > 0, \quad \frac{\partial a_3}{\partial h} < 0.$$

For a top-end activity, on the other hand, the result is ambiguous.

**Proposition 3.6** *If the preventive activity is bottom-end, a favourable shock will shift resources from consumption towards information gathering and prevention; if the preventive activity is top-end, the effects of a favourable shock are ambiguous.*

These results may be surprising at first sight – information to the individual that something is not as bad as he thought may induce him to increase his own prevention. Comparison with previous results suggests that favourable information is *complementary* with own prevention if prevention is bottom-end. That is actually the case. Consider a state $h^t$ and an activity that is bottom-end preventive in the neighbourhood of $h^t$. A favourable change in $h^t$ is complementary with own prevention since own prevention reduces the likelihood of the next worse state $h^{t+1}$ (note the ordering conventions) rather than $h^t$, relatively more than it reduces the likelihood of $h^t$ rather than $h^{t-1}$. Thus, when $h^t$ shifts upwards (as illustrated in Figure 3.1), the marginal return (in terms of $h$) to the bottom-end preventive activity increases.

In conclusion, an increase in $h^t$ increases the marginal returns from bottom-end prevention. When several states, $h^t$, are perturbed, the reasoning applies if prevention is bottom-end over the whole range of outcomes.[17] Along similar lines, a top-end preventive activity can be interpreted as a substitute for favourable information about some states, $h^t$. The fact that the effect on own information gathering takes the same sign as that of the effect on prevention is to be expected, given the earlier observed complementarity between prevention and information gathering.[18]

### Changes in prices and income

Let us now turn to the effects of income, $A$, and prices. The calculations then require the entire top of the inverse of the matrix of derivatives, which is

$$
\begin{bmatrix}
- & -* & + & -(0) \\
-* & - & + & -(0) \\
+ & + & - & - \\
-(0) & -(0) & - & +(0)
\end{bmatrix},
\tag{3.9}
$$

where the asterisks denote signs that depend on the income effect being small, and where the zeros in parentheses indicate terms that vanish if the income effect vanishes.

The corresponding right-hand sides, i.e. the negative of the derivatives with respect to income and the three prices are

$$
\begin{bmatrix} 0 \\ 0 \\ 0 \\ -1 \end{bmatrix}, \quad
\begin{bmatrix} \lambda \\ 0 \\ 0 \\ a_1 \end{bmatrix}, \quad
\begin{bmatrix} 0 \\ \lambda \\ 0 \\ a_2 \end{bmatrix}, \quad
\begin{bmatrix} 0 \\ 0 \\ \lambda \\ a_3 \end{bmatrix}.
$$

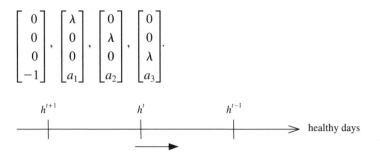

*Figure 3.1* An improvement in the state $h^t$.

It is easily seen that the effects of increases in income are positive for both information gathering and prevention; i.e. both $a_1$ and $a_2$ are increasing in $A$. This is true unless the income effect is indeed zero; the very meaning of zero income effects is that all extra consumption is allocated to one good, the consumption good in our case. Further, the own price effects are the expected ones, i.e. $\partial a_i/\partial p_i < 0$. Perhaps less expectedly, the cross price effects are also negative. Once again, this reflects the inherent complementarity between information gathering and prevention; it depends, however, on the income effect being small (this fact is stressed by asterisks in Table 3.1 below). Finally, the effect of an increase in the price of consumption is to shift resources toward prevention as well as information gathering; this is subject to the qualifications that the income effect be small enough, and this is indicated by asterisks in Table 3.1 which gives a summary of income and price effects.

### Large income effects

We will now turn to the case where income effects are large in the sense that they dominate the expressions marked with asterisks in the sign table of the two first columns of the inverse of the Jacobian matrix; the table for this case is

$$
\begin{bmatrix}
- & +* \\
+* & - \\
+ & + \\
- & -
\end{bmatrix},
\tag{3.10}
$$

and we will now provide a set of statements about this case.

Consider first exogenous information, $g_1$. The sign pattern of the right-hand side of the matrix equation is given by expression (3.6) and it is $(-/+, -, 0, 0)$ for exogenous information and own information being complements/substitutes. This implies that for substitutes we have an unambiguous result for prevention and information gathering,

$$
\frac{\partial a_1}{\partial g_1} < 0, \quad \frac{\partial a_2}{\partial g_1} > 0.
$$

For complements, on the other hand, the only unambiguous implication is that consumption decreases. Consider now exogenous prevention, $g_2$. The sign pattern

*Table 3.1* Effects of income and price changes

|       | $A$    | $p_1$ | $p_2$ | $p_3$ |
|-------|--------|-------|-------|-------|
| $a_1$ | $+(0)$ | $-$   | $-*$  | $+*$  |
| $a_2$ | $+(0)$ | $-*$  | $-$   | $+*$  |
| $a_3$ | $+$    | $?$   | $?$   | $-$   |

*Table 3.2* Large income effects

| Substitutes | | | Complements | | |
|---|---|---|---|---|---|
| | $g_1$ | $g_2$ | | $g_1$ | $g_2$ |
| $a_1$ | − | + | $a_1$ | ? | ? |
| $a_2$ | + | − | $a_2$ | ? | ? |
| $a_3$ | ? | ? | $a_3$ | − | − |

is $(−,−/+, 0, 0)$ for $a_2$ and $g_2$ being complements/substitutes. For the case of substitutes, the derivatives satisfy

$$\frac{\partial a_1}{\partial g_2} > 0, \quad \frac{\partial a_2}{\partial g_2} < 0.$$

The exogenous activity substitutes the own one, and resources are shifted towards information gathering. For complements, consumption decreases. These results are summarized in Table 3.2.

These results are intuitive. When income effects are large, a small change in consumption has a large effect on the marginal utility of consumption; if the individual increases consumption, the marginal utility of other activities must fall sharply, and vice versa. This amounts to the individual being *reluctant* to change his consumption, and as a consequence he is likely to substitute information gathering for prevention, or vice versa, in the face of exogenous impulses related to health. This pattern is seen most clearly if the impact, $g_i$, is a substitute for the individual's corresponding own activity, $a_i$; then there is an unambiguous case for substitution. If the activities are complementary, there are opposing forces, and there are no clear-cut conclusions for prevention and information gathering. However, since consumption decreases, it is clear that the total spending of resources on $a_1$ and $a_2$ *combined* increases; once again, this reflects the fundamental complementarity lurking in the background.

Now, let us turn to local changes in the health states, i.e. changes in $h^t$ for some $t$. The sign pattern of the right-hand side derivatives is $(−, −/+, 0, 0)$ for a bottom-end/top-end preventive activity, and we see that for a top-end activity, we have

$$\frac{\partial a_1}{\partial h} > 0, \quad \frac{\partial a_2}{\partial h} < 0;$$

that is, it has similar effects as an exogenous preventive activity that is a substitute for own prevention. This is unsurprising in the light of our arguments, above that a top-end preventive activity is in effect, a substitute for favourable perturbations to the states. Indeed, for a bottom-end preventive activity, the pattern of the second half of Table 3.2 applies.

For price changes, the only change is that the effects on information gathering and prevention from changes in other prices become ambiguous; the details are set out by asterisks in Table 3.1 above.

## Health policy and socio-economic differences in health and behaviour

### *Aspects of health policy in the model*

In our analysis of exogenous shocks to the individual's decision, we have implicitly covered much of the effects of health policy. First, one important aspect of health policy is the attempt to directly influence individual health-related decisions. This is accomplished by (i) price changes of various goods, e.g. taxation of tobacco or subsidies to athletic associations (physical exercise); (ii) regulations, e.g. age-limits for the purchase of alcohol; and (iii) dissemination of information. Effects of price changes have been dealt with, and several aspects of the effects of new information on the individual's informative and preventive activities have also been analysed. Note also that regulations can be seen to a certain extent as price changes (you can always choose not to comply, if you accept the expected penalty).

Second, the model allowed us to analyse the effects on individual behaviour of general preventive measures that can be treated as exogenous from the individual's point of view, such as workplace safety, product safety and environmental regulation.

Third, a common form of health policy is public support of R&D in the health area. The output from this process may change the individual's decision environment, as well as his basic attitudes. Several of the possible effects fall within the categories we have analysed above, but obviously research can also have effects that are difficult to capture in our model, such as the identification of a new disease.

### *Differential behaviour across socio-economic groups*

In this section, we will explore the implications of our results for differences in behaviour across population groups as defined by health-prospects, age, income, and education. In all cases except when we discuss income, we will assume that income effects are small. Several of the differences in behaviour relate to differential reactions to health policy, which is our reason for treating them here.

It is readily apparent that different individuals face different probabilities for ill health; for example, because of genetic factors. In our context, a difference in health prospects across individuals can be modelled as a pure shift in $F$, i.e. without effects on the marginal effect on individual prevention ($\partial F/\partial a_2$ is unaffected). (It seems equally possible to argue that the level of health risks has a positive or a negative effect on the perceived marginal effect of prevention on health risks.) It is easily seen from expressions (3.5) and (3.7) above that someone with worse health prospects will spend less on prevention (and information gathering).

Ageing is a process whereby an individual's health prospects tend to deteriorate over time. Our results therefore suggest that the older you get, the less you will engage in prevention (and information gathering), unless this has at the same time a sufficiently strong positive impact on the marginal effect of your own preventive efforts. It is interesting to compare this result with the result in the demand-for-health literature, where ageing individuals may choose to increase their spending on medical care in order to counteract the increasingly rapid depreciation of their stocks of health.[19] The mechanism in our model is quite different; it is due to the presence of genuine uncertainty, where a deterioration of health prospects in the probabilistic world reduces the return to information gathering which in turn reduces the marginal return to prevention. Clearly, there are reasons for old people to invest less in prevention from a lifecycle perspective as well; one fundamental reason is that their payoff period is shorter (Cropper, 1977).[20]

Health policy will also affect the individual's health prospects. We focused above on the case where the exogenous activity $g_2$ has a favourable effect on $F$. However, remembering that $g_2$ may represent *any* exogenous occurrence that shifts $F$, it is obvious that the opposite may happen. For example, a person may learn through public information that his health prospects are worse (instead of better) than he thought.

Consider the case where there are shifts in $F$ as a consequence of a government action, $g_2$, but where $F$ shifts in different directions for different individuals; some receive good news about their health prospects and some receive bad news. One can either imagine that a particular piece of information affects different individuals differently, or that certain information only affects a part of the population. (For example, news that a storage of nuclear waste is moved from one locality to another, or news that those who have acquired artificial suntans in solariums have increased their risk of malignant melanoma.) *Ceteris paribus* – i.e. assuming that the marginal effect of individual preventive activity ($\partial F/\partial a_2$) is unaffected – it is clear from expressions (3.5) and (3.7) that those who receive bad news reduce their prevention (and information gathering), while the opposite is true for those who receive good news.

**Proposition 3.7** *An exogenous unfavourable shift in F (worsening health prospects) will lead to a reduction in the individual's preventive activity $a_2$, ceteris paribus, while a favourable shift will have the opposite effect. This implies that there is a natural tendency for health differentials in the population to widen, unless those who receive good news about their health tend to be in relatively bad health and vice versa.*

If we allow $\partial^2 F/\partial a_2 \partial g_2 \neq 0$, there are four configurations of signs (combinations of $F$ and $\partial F/\partial a_2$ being increasing or decreasing in $g_2$), all of which are perfectly plausible since it is possible that the same information is a complement to their own prevention for some individuals while it is a substitute for others, for example because their level of health differs. In three out of four of these cases, health differentials will tend to widen. (The exception is the case where those who receive bad news experience a positive shift in $\partial F/\partial a_2$ and those who receive good news experience a negative shift in $\partial F/\partial a_2$.) In a much different model of life cycle investments in health under certainty, Ehrlich and Chuma (1990) also find that health differentials have a natural tendency to widen in the sense that a higher initial endowment of health increases the demand for health investment and attained longevity.

The implication in the second part of the proposition is interesting not least because social differences in health are a major policy concern in many countries;[21] moreover, the results suggest that the problem is quite fundamental and that government policy might easily contribute to such differences.

This result is also in accordance with the results in the literature on complementarities. It has, for example, been shown that the evolution of modern manufacturing can be understood as driven by exogenous technological change, and that with complementarities, the result will be that modes of organization will exhibit *clustering* in the sense that technologies will evolve – in their model jump – in several dimensions simultaneously (Milgrom and Roberts, 1990).

It is worth making a short digression to consider the likely health status of those who receive good and bad news, even though considering the *ex ante* health status of individuals takes us outside the scope of our model. It is interesting to compare the effects of three different kinds of government action which all serve to shift $F$: (i) dissemination of information on existing health probabilities; (ii) dissemination of information on the effects of the individual's preventive behaviour; and (iii) preventive activities undertaken by the government. While all three of these government actions can be represented by our $g_2$, their properties differ in the specific respect of who gets what kind of news. For concreteness, suppose the individual learns that: (i) 'contrary to previous beliefs, people with blue and brown eyes do not face identical health risks, rather, it has been discovered that all blue-eyed persons face low risk of ill health and all brown-eyed persons face high risks'; or (ii) 'while it was believed that eating carrots and eating broccoli were equally good for your health, we now know that eating carrots is more beneficial than previously thought but eating broccoli does not have any effect on your health'; or (iii) 'new and reduced speed limits for cars will reduce air pollution and this will reduce sickness in densely populated areas'.

In the first of these cases, it is those in good health who receive the good news, and vice versa. Those with blue eyes are on average healthier than those with brown eyes (without previously having known why), and the information tends to increase health differentials. Similarly, assume in the second case a random *ex ante* distribution of the population into carrot and broccoli eaters. The carrot eaters receive good news and have on average better health than the broccoli eaters (because they have happened to have made the correct choice). The information tends to widen the health differentials. In the third case, however, we get the opposite tendency. A preventive action by the government will be beneficial to those who have been exposed to the health risk and who *ipso facto* are likely to be in relatively bad health compared to the unexposed part of the population, *ceteris paribus*. (The *ceteris paribus* condition is important here. It is of course possible that the government strives primarily to reduce those health risks that affect the healthier part of the population.)

The general conclusion is that the effect of a particular government action on social differences in health will depend on which specific form the action takes. In particular, information about the effect of individual preventive behaviour seems likely to widen health differentials whereas preventive activities seem likely to reduce them.

The fact that differences in health are related to differences in economic resources is a major concern of policy makers. There are two sources of such differences in our model. The first one is quite simply the size of the individual's budget. Since health does not affect the budget constraint in our model, we have, as noted above, a consumption model of health, and the effect of an expansion of the budget was to unambiguously increase prevention (unless income effects are zero). Hence wealthier people end up healthier, just as in the consumption part of Grossman's (1972) original demand-for-health model. (In stochastic investment models of health, on the other hand, the effect of an increase in wealth on the demand for health has been found to be ambiguous.[22])

In addition, however, we have seen that the size of income effects are potentially important for behaviour in our model. Moreover income effects are likely to vary across income groups. If we assume that the budget is of a purely monetary nature, we have a case where income effects are likely to be greater among low-income groups (given decreasing marginal utility of consumption and money). Now, we have seen that there is a basic complementarity between information gathering and prevention. We have also seen that as long as income effects are small, this complementarity is only upset if the exogenous impact, $g_i$, is a sufficiently strong substitute for the corresponding own activity, $a_i$. This implies that as long as income effects are small, the effect of providing individuals with information or prevention will often be to increase their own efforts; people will 'match the contribution'. This effect is much less likely if income effects are large, the reason being that an individual with a large income effect is much less prone to give up consumption in the face of a more favourable payoff from caring about his health. (Similarly, in the case of unfavourable information, the general tendency is that information gathering and own prevention will fall, but to a lesser extent the larger the income effects.)

Hence if the budget constraint is of a mainly monetary character, this is likely to imply that rich people will take advantage of health policy by 'matching the contribution' to a larger extent than will poor people. Note that this does not mean that poor people do not take advantage of health policy. However, since they are poor, they are less likely to sacrifice consumption and thereby in a sense fail to exploit the complementarity fully. Correspondingly, several of our results seem roughly consistent with the common argument that high-income people are relatively more prone to change their health-related behaviour in response to health information. One may note, for example, that if public information is complementary with the own informative activity, this unambiguously increases prevention among high-income earners (small-income effects), whereas the effect is ambiguous for low-income earners (large-income effects). Moreover, favourable information on a specific health state is certain to increase bottom-end prevention among high-income people and to reduce top-end prevention among those with low incomes.

Education, finally, can of course have many different effects.[23] If, for example, education raises efficiency in the household production of health as in Grossman (1972), this would in our model have the same kind of effect as exogenous prevention; i.e. it would act as a complement to the individual's own prevention. However, in this context it seems particularly relevant to explore the possibility that it affects the individual's confidence in the information that he possesses and perhaps also the effects of new information on his level of confidence. If one believes that education makes an individual more confident about the information that he possesses (larger $\gamma$), this implies that those with more education will engage more in prevention and information gathering. In general, it is obvious that the effect of $g_1$ on $\gamma$ is not necessarily positive; the individual's degree of confidence does not necessarily increase as, e.g. new results of medical research are published. Furthermore, one could hypothesize that those with high education will become more confident by receiving public information while those with little education are likely to become less confident. If this happens to be the case, the information will cause increasing information differentials, *ceteris paribus*. (That is, assuming that $\partial \gamma / \partial a_1$ is unaffected; if not, the situation is parallel to the one with health differentials: allowing for $\partial^2 \gamma / \partial a_1 \partial g_1 \neq 0$ gives four cases, and in three of these differentials tend to widen.)

## Concluding remarks

We have introduced uncertainty and uncertainty aversion into a simple model of health-related behaviour. We have thereby made a first attempt at filling a gap that has potentially important consequences. Indeed, some of the positive conclusions of our analysis – in particular the fundamental complementarity – indicate that the presence of uncertainty unveils forces that were previously hard to identify.

The model employed seems to capture several interesting features of these health-related decisions. The model allows the individual to experience an element of genuine uncertainty in the way he thinks about his health and also to reduce the importance of this element by information gathering. The individual may also engage in a preventive activity with respect to the health states that he knows something about, and conceptually this may also include consumption of medical care.

We have explored how individuals react to changes in their decision environment. These changes include exogenous information and prevention, such as health education campaigns or safety regulations undertaken by the government, as well as new knowledge about the properties of a particular state of ill health. While of course not being exhaustive, the analysis seems to cover a great deal of the possible effects of new information and health policy. The significance of some personality traits (confidence and pessimism) was also explored.

Perhaps the most interesting analytical result was the fundamental complementarity found between prevention and information gathering, and the implications that this may have for individual behaviour and the effects of health policy. For example, the presence of this mechanism suggests that there may be a natural tendency for health differentials to widen, a tendency which may easily be exacerbated by health policy.

It seems to us that we have far from exhausted the potential for this line of inquiry. For example, we have analysed each activity and each exogenous influence separately, but obviously there will in practice often be interactions between different activities, and public policy will also have mixed effects. Our investigation provides some preliminary indications that analyses of more complex situations can produce interesting results. For instance, we have seen that exogenous prevention such as safety regulation may increase the individual's own preventive efforts. If, however, the public regulatory activity simultaneously makes the individual more diffident about the information he possesses, the result could be reversed.

For empirical applications of the theoretical framework presented above, the most promising avenue – and a reasonable first step – would be to investigate the relationship between the individual's confidence in his probabilistic information and health-related behaviour.[24] Results from a qualitative study suggest that such general attitudes towards genuine uncertainty are discernible. The general attitude seems particularly evident when a person, on the subject of health risk information, states that: 'It doesn't matter what you do. . . . The day after you will read that you shouldn't have done it. [. . .] I think that I used to trust things more before. Nowadays they seem to be finding just too much shit'.[25] In a qualitative setting, the individual's position in the confidence dimension can be compared with statements about behaviour. Furthermore, based on this kind of qualitative research, it seems possible in the future to insert questions on this confidence attitude in questionnaires on health behaviour and to make the concept amenable to quantitative research.[26] A challenge for the future is to find ways of varying the relative importance of genuine uncertainty in an experimental setting, so that the effect on hypothetical choices can be observed, paralleling the efforts to find individual parameter values for risk aversion and time preferences (Barsky *et al.*, 1997). It seems somewhat less obvious that one can elicit the individual's relative (health) pessimism, though a viable tentative hypothesis is that individuals in lower social positions are relatively more likely to feel at home in situations where probabilities are unknown (more favourably disposed to genuine uncertainty), as a corollary to the fact that they are less accustomed to making probabilistic choices.[27]

# Appendix

The welfare effects of an intervention, $g$, that affects utility directly as well as behaviour, is, generally,

$$\frac{\partial U}{dg} = \frac{\partial U}{\partial g} + \frac{\partial U}{\partial a_1}\frac{\partial a_1}{\partial g} + \frac{\partial U}{\partial a_2}\frac{\partial a_2}{\partial g} + \frac{\partial U}{\partial a_3}\frac{\partial a_3}{\partial g},$$

but since $\partial U/\partial a_i = \lambda p_i$, and $p_1 a_1 + p_2 a_2 + p_3 a_3$ is constant, the marginal welfare effect is given by the partial derivative $\partial U / \partial g$. It is thus clear that exogenous information – a favourable intervention affecting only $\gamma$ – will be beneficial only for basically pessimistic individuals

$$\frac{\partial U}{\partial g} = \frac{\partial \gamma}{\partial g} \cdot \left( \Sigma \Delta u^s (1 - F) - u_0 \right),$$

while prevention – a favourable intervention affecting only $F$ – is always welfare improving,

$$\frac{\partial U}{\partial g} = \left( \gamma \cdot \Sigma \Delta u^s \frac{-\partial F}{\partial g} \right).$$

# Notes

Financial support from the Swedish Medical Research Council (grant no. 27P-10737) and the Bank of Sweden Tercentenary Foundation is gratefully acknowledged. The paper was presented at the 19th Arne Ryde symposium on Individual Decisions for Health in Lund, August 1999, and we are most grateful for insightful comments and suggestions from our discussant, Louis Eeckhoudt. We also appreciate comments from Tomas Philipson and the audience at the seminar. In addition, we have received helpful comments from Dan Anderberg, John Hey, Håkan J. Holm, Bengt Liljas, Björn Lindgren, and two anonymous referees. Any remaining errors are the sole responsibility of the authors.

1 Examples include Chang (1996), Cropper (1977), Dardanoni and Wagstaff (1987, 1990), Liljas (1998), Picone *et al.* (1998), and Selden (1993).
2 Significant contributions with deterministic models are still appearing in the demand-for-health tradition (Grossman, 1998; Ried, 1998), as well as in other areas.
3 In fact, Eichberger and Kelsey (1999) have provided axiomatic foundations for a utility function which is similar to (3.1); i.e. which is a convex combination of an expected utility and a generalized expected utility.
4 See, e.g. Schmeidler (1989). The notion of genuine uncertainty was introduced by Knight (1921); it is sometimes referred to as 'Knightian uncertainty'.
5 The generalized probabilities generate weights, $v_s$, by means of which the modified expectation is computed: $u_0(a) = \Sigma v_s u(h^s, a)$.
6 A framework employing a utility function similar to ours is employed by Mukerji (1998) in an exploration of the effect of uncertainty on contractual incompleteness.
7 Note that it may be the case that the outcomes ($h$) of a firm state and an uncertain state coincide; increasing $\gamma$ then leads to a change in the expectation only due to better knowledge of the probability of this outcome.

8 Clearly, there are cases where information gathering reduces variance rather than uncertainty; we do not consider such information. We will comment on information in the form of 'more informative experiments' in Pessimism and confidence: basic analysis.

9 In the context of understanding the choice between systematic and rule-of-thumb (heuristic) information processing, it has been suggested that the motivation for expending efforts in systematic processing is to attain a certain level of confidence that one's knowledge about risks is sufficient, based on a desire to judge situations correctly. Cf. Griffin *et al.* (1999).

10 See, e.g. Mas-Colell *et al.* (1995).

11 These activities could also be thought of as medical care in the sense that the essence of medical treatment is to improve the probability distribution with respect to future health states. However, health-production possibilities could be dependent on whether the individual is healthy or sick (Picone *et al.*, 1998; Zweifel and Breyer, 1997). Cf. Kenkel (2000), Sec. 2, for an overview of prevention in health economics models of individual health decisions.

12 See, e.g. Hirshleifer and Riley (1992, Sec. 5.2.3).

13 More generally, income effects are small if the second derivatives involving $a_3$ are small relative to the bordered Hessian of the utility-maximisation problem; see, e.g. Varian (1992, pp. 123–4).

14 Dardanoni and Wagstaff (1990), Liljas (1998), Lyttkens (1992) and Picone *et al.* (1998). In addition, some activities which we tend to think of as 'preventive' may in fact be undertaken in order to reduce the relative weight of genuine uncertainty, and not to affect probabilities. Such an activity would in our model by definition be termed an informational activity, just as anything that serves to shift the individual's $F$ by definition is termed prevention (which may include public information on health risks. Furthermore, if we leave the present framework, there can be other reasons to engage in 'preventive' behaviour. For example, the individual may engage in an activity without any known health consequences in order not to experience regret at some future date when such a relationship may have been discovered (cf., e.g. Loomes and Sugden (1982) on regret theory).

15 Louis Eeckhoudt provided an example along the following lines: an early diagnosis makes it possible to tailor the treatment decision to the actual health state. This possibility, however, undermines incentives for *ex ante* prevention. In such a case, acquiring information in the sense of obtaining the diagnosis reduces incentives for *ex ante* prevention. For a model relating to this example and dealing with the effect of information on environmental precaution, see Gollier *et al.* (2000).

16 We are grateful to Louis Eeckhout for calling our attention to the latter fact.

17 Note that the bottom-end property defines a class of preventive activities for which we can make clear predictions about the effect of very specific changes in the individual's environment.

18 There is an intriguing relationship between the bottom-end and top-end properties and the *Monotone Probability Ratio* order (MPR) introduced by Eeckhoudt and Gollier (1995). This order requires that ratios between values of the distribution function (for two different actions) satisfy a monotonicity property similar to the one imposed here on the derivative (and thus on differences). Eeckhoudt and Gollier explore the implications of MPR for the demand for a risky asset by a risk-averse individual.

19 Grossman (1972), Muurinen (1982).

20 Kenkel (1994) provides some empirical support for the notion that investments in prevention decline with age.

21 Health 21 (1999); Healthy People 2000 (1990); Healthy People 2010 (2000); Hälsa på lika villkor (1999).

22 Chang (1996), Dardanoni and Wagstaff (1987), Selden (1993).

23 Cf. Kenkel (2000), pp. 1680–82, for a brief overview of the relationship between schooling and health.

24 At present, it seems less useful to focus on exogenous shocks for hypothesis testing, both because the direction of influences is often open to question (e.g. information may either increase or decrease confidence) and because exogenous events are likely to have more mixed effects than we have assumed (e.g. a preventive activity may affect the degree of information confidence). Hence testing based on exogenous shocks will have to await more empirical information about the partial relationships (and possibly more theoretical work).

25 Lindbladh and Lyttkens (2000). Similarly, a tendency to perceive the health-related part of the world in terms closely akin to genuine uncertainty is suggested by the following reaction to posters about the health risks associated with smoking in a waiting room at the primary health care centre: 'I can be knocked down by a car when I cross the street, I can get other diseases if I do not smoke, so I don't think much about such things'. Note that the respondent in question is not arguing that the risk associated with smoking is *small*. He or she rather seems to express a fatalistic attitude, implying that there is a multitude of unknown risks and that therefore no point in trying to influence them.

26 The relationship between trust in information sources, regulatory agencies, etc. and risk perceptions has been investigated in a number of studies. Cf., e.g. Grobe *et al.* (1999) and Slovic (1999).

27 Lindbladh and Lyttkens (2000).

# References

Arrow, K., 1963. Uncertainty and the welfare economics of medical care, *American Economic Review* 53, 941–73.

Barsky, R.B. *et al.*, 1997. Preference parameters and behavioural heterogeneity: an experimental approach in the health and retirement study, *Quarterly Journal of Economics* 112, 537–79.

Chang, F.R., 1996. Uncertainty and investment in health, *Journal of Health Economics* 15, 369–76.

Cropper, M.L., 1977. Health, investment in health, and occupational choice, *Journal of Political Economy* 86, 1273–94.

Dardanoni, V. and Wagstaff, A., 1987. Uncertainty, inequalities in health and the demand for health, *Journal of Health Economics* 6, 283–90.

Dardanoni, V. and Wagstaff, A., 1990. Uncertainty and the demand for medical care. *Journal of Health Economics* 9, 23–38.

Eeckhoudt, L. and Gollier, C., 1995. Demand for risky assets and the monotone probability ratio order, *Journal of Risk and Uncertainty* 11, 113–22.

Ehrlich, I. and Chuma, H., 1990. A model of the demand for longevity and the value of life extensions, *Journal of Political Economy* 98, 761–82.

Eichberger, J. and Kelsey, D., 1999. E-capacities and the Ellsberg paradox, *Theory and Decision* 39, 107–40.

Gollier, C., Jullien, B. and Treich, N., 2000. Scientific progress and irreversibility: an economic interpretation of the 'Precautionary Principle,' *Journal of Public Economics* 75, 229–53.

Griffin, R.J., Dunwoody, S. and Neuwirth, K., 1999. Proposed model of the relationship of risk information seeking and processing to the development of preventive behaviours, *Environmental Research* 80, S230–45.

Grobe, D., Douthitt, R. and Zepeda, L., 1999. A model of consumers' risk perceptions toward recombinant bovine growth hormone (rbGH): the impact of risk characteristics, *Risk Analysis* 19, 661–73.

Grossman, M., 1972. On the concept of health capital and the demand for health, *Journal of Political Economy* 80, 223–55.

Grossman, M., 1998, On optimal length of life, *Journal of Health Economics* 17, 499–509.

Hälsa på lika villkor, 1999. *Delbetänkande av Nationella folkhälsokommittén*, SOU 37.

Health 21, 1999, *The health for all policy framework for the WHO European Region.* WHO, Regional Office for Europe, Copenhagen.

Healthy People 2000, 1990. (US Department of Health and Human Services, Washington, DC).

Healthy People 2010, 2000. (US Department of Health and Human Services, Washington, DC).

Hirshleifer, J. and Riley, J., 1992. The Analytics of Uncertainty and Information. Cambridge University Press, Cambridge.

Johansson, P.-O., 1994. Valuing changes in health: a production function approach, In: R. Pethig, ed., *Valuing the Environment: Methodological and Measurement Issues.* Kluwer Academic Publishers, Dordrecht, pp. 151–67.

Kenkel, D.S., 1994. The demand for preventive medical care, *Applied Economics* 26, 313–25.

Kenkel, D.S., 2000. Prevention, In: A.J. Culyer and J.P. Newhouse, eds., *Handbook of Health Economics.* Elsevier, Amsterdam, Vol. 1B, pp. 1675–720.

Knight, F., 1921. *Risk, Uncertainty, and Profit.* Houghton Mifflin, Boston.

Liljas, B., 1998. The demand for health with uncertainty and insurance, *Journal of Health Economics* 17, 153–70.

Lindbladh, E. and Lyttkens, C.H., 2000. Perceptions of risk information. A perspective on social differences in health-related behaviour, *Studies in Health Economics* 33, Department of Community Medicine, Lund University.

Loomes, G. and Sugden, R., 1982. Regret theory: an alternative theory of rational choice under uncertainty, *Economic Journal* 92, 805–24.

Lyttkens, C.H., 1992. A note on the economics of prevention. Individual behaviour and preventive information, *Actes du Colloque Européen 'De l'analyse économique aux politiques de santé'* Credes-Ces, Paris.

Mas-Colell, A., Whinston, M. and Green, J., 1995. *Microeconomic Theory.* Oxford University Press, New York.

Milgrom, P. and Roberts, J., 1990. The economics of modern manufacturing: technology, strategy, and organization, *American Economic Review* 80, 511–28.

Mukerji, S., 1998. Ambiguity aversion and incompleteness of contractual form, *American Economic Review* 88, 1207–31.

Muurinen, J.M., 1982. Demand for health: a generalized Grossman model, *Journal of Health Economics* 1, 5–28.

Picone, G., Uribe, M. and Wilson, M.R., 1998. The effect of uncertainty on the demand for medical care, health capital and wealth, *Journal of Health Economics* 17, 171–85.

Ried, W., 1998, Comparative dynamics of the full Grossman model, *Journal of Health Economics* 17, 383–425.

Schmeidler, D., 1989. Subjective probability and expected utility without additivity, *Econometrica* 57, 571–87.

Selden, T.S., 1993. Uncertainty and health care spending by the poor, *Journal of Health Economics* 12, 109–15.

Simon, C.P. and Blume, L., 1994. *Mathematics for Economists.* Norton, New York, pp. 529–30.

Slovic, P., 1999. Trust, emotion, sex, politics, and science: surveying the risk-assessment battlefield, *Risk Analysis* 19, 689–701.

Varian, H.R., 1992. *Microeconomic Analysis*. Norton, New York, pp. 123–4.

Zweifel, P. and Breyer, F., 1997. *Health Economics*. Oxford University Press, New York, Ch. 3.

# 4 Rationality, nicotine dependence, and adjustment costs

*Paul Contoyannis and Andrew M. Jones*

## Introduction

This chapter focuses on two related areas in the economics of addiction. First, it considers how economists have characterized addiction, noting the relationship between these specifications and the characterizations offered by pharmacology and psychology. Second, it outlines the implications of alternative addiction models for the empirical analysis of the determinants of quitting. It should be noted throughout that while our focus is the problem of nicotine dependence, the general approaches and issues outlined are also applicable to other harmful, and possibly beneficial, addictions.

To put the economic approach into perspective, it is important to be aware of the pharmacology and psychology of addiction. Useful sources are Ashton and Stepney (1982) and Kuhn *et al.* (1998). Kuhn *et al.* offer the following definition of addiction: 'addiction is the repetitive, compulsive use of a substance that occurs despite negative consequences of use'. From this perspective, physiological and psychological dependence entails not just the repetition of past behaviour, but also the compulsion to continue despite the harm that continued consumption inflicts on the drug user. Nicotine dependence is associated with three key features of addiction: reinforcement, tolerance, and withdrawal.

The desire for repetitive consumption can be understood in terms of the phenomenon of reinforcement: 'In the language of psychology a reinforcer is something that motivates an individual to work towards getting more' (Kuhn *et al.*, 1998, p. 154). In other words, experience of consumption means that the user will be willing to make sacrifices (for instance, be willing to pay) to repeat the experience. This process works through the basic reward circuit of the central nervous system which, in turn, controls the circulatory, respiratory, and reflex systems: 'Drugs that are truly addictive (stimulants, opiates, alcohol, nicotine) can actually substitute for food, sex or other primary reinforcers' (Kuhn *et al.*, 1998, p. 244). Furthermore, as everyone has this basic reward circuit, this is 'true of everyone who has a brain'.

Tolerance describes the way in which the body adapts to taking a drug. For most drugs, tolerance is more likely to develop the more frequently the drug is consumed and the higher the dose. In the case of nicotine, tolerance corresponds to the disappearance of the negative side effects, such as nausea and dizziness, that people experience when they start to smoke.

As the body adapts to taking a drug, these adaptations can become counterproductive when consumption stops, leading to withdrawal symptoms. Kuhn *et al.* (1998) suggest that, in this sense, withdrawal is the 'flip side of tolerance'. Withdrawal symptoms are different for different drugs. In the case of nicotine, they are generally characterized by craving and irritability. Gritz *et al.* (1991) (p. 57) report that studies of tobacco withdrawal syndrome have found the following components: 'the urge or desire to smoke ("craving") and a variety of symptoms including dysphoric emotions (irritability, anger, frustration, anxiety, tension, depression), restlessness, difficulty concentrating, drowsiness or fatigue, sleep disturbances, increased appetite or hunger and weight gain, and a variety of physiologic changes'.

While reinforcement, tolerance and withdrawal are the concepts most frequently referred to in justifications and interpretations of economic models of addiction, other concepts from pharmacology and psychology have been adopted by economists. Harris and Chan (1999) draw on the concept of a 'continuum of addiction', with the smoker progressing through trying the first cigarette, experimenting, regular smoking, and nicotine dependence. They note that 'at each stage symptoms of withdrawal become more pronounced and successful quitting becomes less likely'. This leads them to argue that the price responsiveness of smoking will decline with the stages of addiction. A similar concept of progression is the stages of change model (Prochaska *et al.*, 1992). This posits five stages of quitting; precontemplation, contemplation, preparation, action and maintenance. Suranovic *et al.* (1999) link this framework to the different styles of quitting predicted by their model. They also suggest that price responsiveness will vary across different types of individual, with those who are starting and those who are about to quit being more responsive than regular and dependent smokers who are not contemplating quitting.

The concept of addiction as repetitive, compulsive, and harmful behaviour characterized by reinforcement, tolerance and withdrawal can be used to consider the way in which economists have attempted to model the phenomenon. The following section outlines the pertinent assumptions of alternative economic models of smoking and addiction, and their implications for consumption and quitting behaviour. The final section is a short conclusion.

## Economic models of smoking and addiction

The consumption of addictive goods provides a challenge for economic analysis. It is a temptation to assume that the usual neoclassical analysis is inapplicable due to the inherent inseparability of addiction and irrationality; consumers cannot be expected to act rationally if they are addicted. However, economists have responded by modelling consumption and predicting responses to changes in economic conditions under addiction (e.g. Barthold and Hochman, 1988; Becker and Murphy, 1988; Orphanides and Zervos, 1995, 1998) and conceptualizing these responses as rational behaviour. Most of these models distinguish addictive consumption from the consumption of non-addictive goods by recognizing the fact that current consumption will depend explicitly on past consumption, and they attempt to incorporate the psychological and physiological concepts of tolerance, reinforcement, and withdrawal, outlined in the previous section. That is not to imply that the models are equivalent in their conceptual structure or predictions, and the distinctions between them are outlined below. In this section we review these models, with particular reference to their characterization of addiction, and their implications for the empirical analysis of rehabilitation, or quitting behaviour.

The simplest models of smoking behaviour are those based on decision theory in a static context. In their simplest, non-stochastic, form these models compare the utility in two alternative states, normally smoking and not smoking. This decision theoretic perspective is taken by Robbins and Kline (1991) who conceptualize tobacco smoking as a reasoned act based upon its subjective net worth to the individual. Factors which are expected to explain initiation, persistence, and cessation of smoking are: (i) an individual's beliefs about outcomes; (ii) their evaluation of the outcomes; (iii) beliefs about the expectations of others (social norms) and (iv) the desire to adhere, or otherwise, to these social norms. Robbins and Kline's chapter is presented from an anthropological perspective, and an economic model may well subsume (iii) and (iv) in (i) and (ii), respectively. In stochastic form, subjective expected utility theory has been used to explain the participation decision by Viscusi (1990) and the quitting decision by Jones (1994) and Hsieh (1998).

### Stock adjustment

Most attempts to model addiction have involved dynamic specifications in which current choices are influenced by past behaviour. There are two main elements in most dynamic economic models of habits and addiction. The first specifies how habits evolve over time, and the second specifies how habits affect preferences or the technology of household production. The literature shows considerable consensus on modelling the evolution of habits with most authors adopting the state adjustment approach introduced by Houthakker and Taylor (1966).[1]

The essential feature of the stock adjustment approach is that individuals have 'psychological stocks of habits' which evolve according to:

$$\dot{S} = C - \delta S, \tag{4.1}$$

where $\dot{S}$ is the rate of change of the (physical or psychological) stock $S$, and $C$ is the current consumption of the habit-forming good. Houthakker and Taylor adopted a declining balance specification where depreciation is at a constant proportional rate $\delta$ on the current stock $S$.

The presence of $C$ in (4.1) implies that habits are measurable in units of physical consumption, such as numbers of cigarettes, with current consumption representing a one-for-one addition to the stock. The assumption of a constant proportional rate of depreciation is, in principle, quite restrictive. It seems plausible that the intensity of the rate at which a particular habit decays could well be influenced by the consumer's behaviour.

It should be clear that equation (4.1) relates the habit stock for a particular commodity to the consumption of that commodity alone. However, it is sometimes argued that attention should also be paid to more general habit effects which permit some degree of substitution between the consumption of (say) tobacco and alcohol as means of satisfying a more deep-seated need. For example, Dockner and Feichtinger (1993) extend the rational addiction model to allow for multiple stocks, while Pacula (1997) redefines the stock to represent the cumulative influence of past consumption of two drugs, with an application to marijuana and alcohol.

## Alternative approaches to modelling preferences

### Tolerance, withdrawal, and reinforcement

The influence of habits on preferences is usually incorporated through an instantaneous utility function,

$$U = U[C,\ S,\ Y], \tag{4.2}$$

where $Y$ is the consumption of other (non-addictive) goods. This specification encompasses the models used in Barthold and Hochman (1988), Becker and Murphy (1988), Boyer (1983), Chaloupka (1991), Jones (1987), Orphanides and Zervos (1995), Pollak (1970), Spinnewyn (1981), and many others. More structure can be imposed by assuming that the utility function takes the form,

$$U = U[F(C,\ S),\ Y], \tag{4.3}$$

where $F(.)$ can be interpreted as an intermediate production function, and utility is assumed to be increasing and (quasi-)concave in $F(.)$ and $Y$. In this case, current consumption of cigarettes can be viewed as an input into the production of a fundamental commodity such as euphoria, relaxation, or smoking pleasure (e.g. Stigler and Becker, 1977; Jones, 1987; Barthold and Hochman, 1988; Chaloupka, 1991).

Most economic models of addiction have incorporated the notions of tolerance, withdrawal, and reinforcement by making assumptions about the shape of the utility and intermediate production functions. Typically, tolerance is modelled as a negative marginal utility of the addictive stock, $(U_S < 0)$. In models that use intermediate production functions, this is a consequence of the assumption that the marginal product of $S$ is negative, $(F_S < 0)$, sometimes coupled with the assumption that the addictive good is harmful and damages the individual's health and well-being. This definition of tolerance means that, as addiction grows, a greater level of current consumption is required to achieve a given level of utility. Becker and Murphy (1988) note that this definition captures 'a form of tolerance'.

However, it is not the only possibility. Another plausible interpretation of the phenomenon is that tolerance reduces the marginal product of current consumption ($F_{CS} < 0$). Then, as addiction grows, an extra dose of nicotine provides a smaller 'hit'. The implications of this additional aspect of tolerance are explored below.

Reinforcement is captured by the idea that an increase in current consumption will give rise to an increase in future consumption, all else remaining equal. In myopic models of habit formation a sufficient condition for reinforcement is that current and past consumption are complements ($U_{CS} > 0$). In rational addiction models it depends on the more general notion of adjacent complementarity (Becker and Murphy, 1988). Complementarity implies that an increase in the addictive stock increases the gratification from increased current consumption, relative to other activities. This is what drives reinforcement.

Reinforcement is sometimes viewed as an assumption to be imposed on the model (by assuming complementarity). But it is more satisfactory to regard the phenomenon as an implication of the interaction between individual preferences and the characteristics of the addictive good. With an intermediate production function,

$$U_{CS} = U_{FF}F_C F_S + U_F F_{CS}. \tag{4.4}$$

The first term on the right-hand side of (4.4) is positive. As the addictive stock grows, it reduces the individual's level of satisfaction from smoking ($F_S < 0$). Owing to diminishing marginal utility ($U_{FF} < 0$), the marginal utility associated with the pleasure of additional current consumption as ($F_C > 0$) increasing. So, the tolerance created by an increase in the addictive stock leads to a craving for more consumption.

The sign of the second term depends on $F_{CS}$. Chaloupka (1991) assumes that $F_{CS}$ is positive, which ensures that $U_{CS}$ is unambiguously positive. However, if one of the effects of tolerance is to reduce the marginal product of current consumption, then the sign and hence the scope for tolerance creating reinforcement will be ambiguous. By reducing the 'hit' from an extra dose of current consumption, tolerance makes current consumption less attractive relative to other activities. This trade-off is analogous to the trade-off between income and substitution effects, and tolerance will only lead to complementarity if the net effect is positive. So the addictive good may be a positive reinforcer for some individuals and not for others.

In the rational addiction model withdrawal is reflected by the fact that 'total utility falls if cigarette consumption is reduced' (Chaloupka, 1991). This is an implication of the positive marginal utility of current consumption, and complementarity ensures that this marginal utility grows as the addiction develops. An alternative view of withdrawal symptoms is to regard them as costs of adjustment, which are only incurred when consumption is reduced (e.g. Atkinson, 1974; Jones, 1987; Suranovic et al., 1999). This approach is explored in more detail below. One feature that the adjustment cost approach shares with others is the possibility that utility can be non-concave with respect to $C$ and $S$. In Barthold and Hochman (1988), Jones (1987, 1999) and Suranovic et al. (1999)

this arises from convexity in the intermediate production function $F(.)$. In Becker and Murphy it arises when the degree of complementarity between $C$ and $S$ is sufficiently strong. In all cases, it is this possibility that leads to predictions of quitting by cold-turkey. A diagrammatic representation of the alternative approaches to incorporating tolerance, withdrawal and reinforcement is provided in Table 4.1.

### Time inconsistency and multiple selves

Much of the discussion of alternative models of addiction has focused on the consistency of the evaluation of outcomes over time, or alternatively, the stability of preferences over time. One class of models describe individuals as having stable but *inconsistent* preferences over time. For example, an individual may choose a consumption path, but when the future arrives, they will desire an alternative consumption bundle, '...even though his original expectations of future desires and means of consumption are verified'. (Strotz, 1956). The time inconsistency problem arises in this model due to individuals having a non-exponential discount function. If this is replaced with one that takes an exponential form with a constant rate of discount the problem disappears. Strotz goes on to argue that individuals who recognize this time inconsistency may precommit themselves to a particular future consumption plan.

Schelling (1978) also notes the importance of precommitment as a way of overcoming another form of inconsistency, claiming that '...everybody behaves like two people, one who wants clean lungs and long life and another who adores tobacco'. Exemplifying this perspective is the work of Thaler and Shefrin (1981), which emphasizes the possibility of a multi-self individual. In their (non-addiction) model, the preferences of a far-sighted planner compete with those of a 'doer' which surfaces each period, and from whose consumption the individual derives utility. Unfortunately for the individual, the 'doers' are unlikely to implement what the planner perceived as optimal, and must be constrained by rules (pre-commitments) or manipulated by using an optimal combination of incentives.

A stochastic analysis which integrates features of an endogenous preference model with the type of time inconsistency recognized by Schelling is that of Winston (1980). He characterizes addiction as including withdrawal pain, loss of control and attempts to reverse behaviour as inherent features. He posits constant but unstable preferences where the individual switches between myopic and farsighted preference sets, while meta-preferences are assumed over preference sets. The manifestation of these alternatives also depends on a *random* shock and the capital effects of addiction. The individual then evaluates utility conditional on his current preference set and acts accordingly. Hence in some periods the individual behaves farsightedly and in others myopically, what Barthold and Hochman (1988) call 'Jekyll and Hyde' behaviour, recalling Schelling above. Unfortunately, whether an individual is myopic in several periods and is thereby labelled as an 'addict' depends only on random factors, and therefore as noted by Barthold and Hochman, the '...nebulous character of the switching mechanism

Table 4.1 Alternative representations of tolerance, withdrawal, and reinforcement

| | Jones (1987) | Becker and Murphy (1988) | Chaloupka (1991) | Barthold and Hochman (1988) | Orphanides and Zervos (1995) |
|---|---|---|---|---|---|
| Instantaneous utility | $U(F(C, S), Y)$ | $U(C, S, Y)$ | $U(C, S, Y) = U[R(C, S), H(M, S), Z(Y)]$ | $U(e(C, S), Y)$ | $U(C, Y) + aV(C, S)$ |
| Tolerance | $F_S < 0$ | $U_S < 0$ | $R_S < 0 \Rightarrow U_S = U_R R_S + U_H H_S < 0$ | $U_S < 0$ | |
| | 'Ashton and Stepney (1982) describe tolerance as "a decreased responsiveness to a previously administered drug". For the economist an obvious corollary is to define it as a negative marginal productivity of lagged consumption (or more generally of the relevant habit stock)' p. 62 | 'Tolerance means that given levels of consumption are less satisfying when past consumption has been greater. Rational harmful addictions...imply a form of tolerance because higher past consumption of the harmful good lowers the present utility from the same consumption level' p. 682 | 'Increased cigarette consumption has a positive effect on the production of relaxation, whereas past consumption has a negative effect. This assumption incorporates the notion of tolerance into the model' p. 721  'Tolerance is captured by the negative marginal utility of the addictive stock...' p. 722 | '...ever-higher levels of $C$ are required to sustain a specified level of utility, so long as $\delta > 0$, as the individual builds tolerance to the addictive good' p. 97 | 'Tolerance appears because a larger quantity of $C$ is required to achieve a fixed level of utility when the stock is larger' p. 743 |
| Withdrawal | $F = F^1 \text{ if } C_t < C_{t-1}$  $F = F^2 \text{ if } C_t \geq C_{t-1}$  $\lim F_C^1 > \lim F_C^2$ | | $U_C = U_R R_C > 0$ | | $V_{CS} > 0$ |

| | | | | |
|---|---|---|---|---|
| | '. . . an asymmetry in the effect of current consumption around the individual's previous level of consumption' p. 78 | '. . . describes withdrawal since total utility falls if cigarette consumption is reduced' | | 'Withdrawal appears because the utility loss from a reduction in the consumption of C is larger when the stock is larger' p. 743 |
| *Reinforcement* | $F_S < 0 \Rightarrow \partial C_t/\partial C_{t-1} > 0$ | $R_{CS} > 0 \Rightarrow U_{CS} = U_{RR} R_C R_S + U_R R_{CS} > 0$ | $U_{CS} > 0$ | $V_{CS} > 0$ |
| | 'Reinforcement means that greater current consumption . . . raises its future consumption. Reinforcement is closely related to the concept of adjacent complementarity' p. 682 | 'To capture reinforcement effects in consumption, the marginal productivity of cigarette consumption in the production of relaxation is assumed larger the larger the level of the addictive stock' p. 721 | | 'Complementarity is the key assumption required for describing addictive behaviour. It implies that past consumption raises the marginal utility of current consumption which as emphasized by Boyer (1978) and Becker and Murphy (1988) corresponds to the addiction characteristic of reinforcement' |
| *Non-convexity* | $F(.)$ convex | $U_{CC} U_{SS} < (U_{CS})^2$ | | $e(.)$ sufficiently convex |

limits its usefulness'. In this formulation, there are no predictions of the way that smoking behaviour will change in response to changes in economic variables: the individual is either myopic or farsighted, with the probability of observing a particular preference set depending on the capital effect of addictive consumption; a probabilistic endogeneity. In addition, the individual may have plans which turn out to be time inconsistent if the plans of 'Jekyll' are contradicted by the unforeseen appearance of the myopic 'Hyde'.

### Non-convexities in tastes and technology

Barthold and Hochman (1988) attempt to incorporate the idea that those prone to addictive behaviour differ in their innate characteristics and preferences.[2] As they note, the formulations of Stigler and Becker (1977), and those that account for addiction through endogenous preferences, or habit formation (Pollak, 1970; Spinnewyn, 1981)[3] allow for no basis for addiction except previous consumption. Barthold and Hochman present a modification of earlier approaches by claiming the possibility that, for some individuals and over some range of the consumption set, individuals may have concave indifference curves independent of previous behaviour. They show that this possibility may lead to 'extreme-seeking', where an individual seeks consumption bundles which approach corner solutions. Barthold and Hochman rely on the notion that 'addictive and compulsive acts are atypically unresponsive to incentives'. The core of their model revolves around the concepts of capital and threshold effects. Capital effects increase the consumption of the addictive good, similar to the effects of reinforcement and tolerance, while the effect of the 'threshold' is to limit consumption of the addictive good to within bounds that would not 'foreclose opportunities'. The concept of craving is introduced as an increase in the ratio of static marginal utilities between addictive and non-addictive goods. An implication of the model is that some individuals will respond discontinuously to price variation, while the 'continuous adjusters' will live up to their label. The possibility that some individuals will respond discontinuously contradicts models of habitual behaviour which predict smooth adjustment for all individuals (Pollak, 1970; Spinnewyn, 1981). With particular reference to quitting, Barthold and Hochman note that 'reversal may require a quantum increase in the price of the addictive good. The addict, while resisting withdrawal, may endure it if there is a strong enough movement against the addictive good in relative prices'. By implication, once an individual has moved to a corner solution, the imbalance is best reversed through changes in tastes or nonprice constraints. An example of the latter would be the alteration of perceived survival probabilities, leading consumption to reduce such that the threshold which 'forecloses opportunities' is not crossed.

Michaels (1988) also employs the constant taste approach, but allows addictive behaviour to be introduced through variation in the consumption technology, rather than by assuming non-convexity of indifference curves for some individuals. Addiction is treated as 'an increase in the productivity of the addictive activity as consumption cumulates'. This increased productivity is attributed to learning about the characteristics of the addictive good. The model generates explanations for such phenomena as habit acquisition, restarting, and the age and income distribution of addicts. For example, by deriving conditions under which drug consumption is an inferior activity, the model can explain the observation that the heaviest consumers of drugs are those with lower incomes. By postulating that the productivity of drug consumption relative to 'normal' activity in producing desirable attributes decreases with age, the age distribution of addicts can be explained. It also predicts corner solutions and discontinuous responses to relative price variation, or alternatively, 'cold-turkey' withdrawals and bingeing. In addition, and unlike the model of Barthold and Hochman, a drastic change in relative prices is not required to persuade an individual to break their habit; variation in the consumption technology or income can be sufficient. In particular, if cumulative consumption of the addictive activity causes further addictive consumption to be sufficiently unproductive at producing a fundamental commodity, while maintaining the level of another, the resultant pattern will be specialization in the non-addictive activity. However, with a short memory, the individual may relapse, thinking that the addictive activity is as productive as when it was initially consumed. Michaels claims that these potential cycles are likely to be damped. He also discusses the possibility of withdrawal pain (adjustment costs), noting that one interpretation is that the biased change in the consumption technology (as above) can lead the user to progressively lower indifference curves prior to ending the habit. However, the individual will not move to a higher indifference curve after consumption of the addictive activity ends; the 'withdrawal pain' is due to the degradation of productivity, leading to a contraction of the choice set, which leads to a reduction in consumption of the addictive good and a reduction of utility.

Michaels' also suggests the possibility of the emergence of a non-linear fundamental commodity frontier as a result of cumulative consumption of the addictive activity. However, as portrayed, this is a sufficient condition for a corner solution, not for specialization in the non-addictive activity. The specialization chosen will depend on the utility function. As with the model of Barthold and Hochman, a drastic price increase or an alteration of the perceived attributes of the activities may be necessary. Finally, and as recognized by Michaels, his model is not explicitly intertemporal and as such the explanations suggested may not be consistent with intertemporal utility maximization where an individual has '. . . some plausible foresight about the costs of withdrawal'.

### Forward-looking models

An early example of the constant and consistent taste approach is Stigler and Becker (1977), who use a household production framework, encompassing addiction through variation in the parameters of the production technology of the household.

A forward-looking model that employs the assumption of stable preferences, and which has been subjected to the majority of empirical testing, is that of Becker and Murphy (1988).[4] The model encompasses addiction by allowing past consumption to affect the full price of current consumption, while *maintaining* time consistency and stable preferences.[5, 6]

The model of Becker and Murphy is one of rational addiction in that it assumes that the individual considers the effects of present consumption on *optimal* future consumption, unlike addiction models assuming myopia. These ignore the dependence of *optimal* future consumption on current consumption when making current decisions, while recognizing the importance of past consumption for current consumption (Pollak, 1970).[7] Becker and Murphy model addiction in an intertemporal household production framework by introducing an addictive stock, or 'consumption capital'. We use Chaloupka's (1991) formulation of the model to illustrate the argument.

The rational addict maximizes an intertemporal utility function,

$$u = \int_0^\infty e^{-\sigma t} u \, [C, \ S, \ Y] \, dt, \tag{4.5}$$

where $Y$ is a vector including inputs into the production of a composite commodity and the individual's health, and the stock of the addictive good, $S$, evolves according to (4.1). This stock has a number of impacts on the utility of current cigarette consumption which are given interpretations in terms of reinforcement, tolerance, and withdrawal. First, it increases the marginal utility of current cigarette consumption (reinforcement). Second, it reduces the level of utility gained from a particular level of consumption of cigarettes and other goods (tolerance).

Chaloupka also introduces the concept of withdrawal[8] as, by assumption:

$$u_C = u_R R_C > 0, \tag{4.6}$$

where $R$ is the fundamental commodity 'relaxation' given by $R = R(C, S)$. Chaloupka argues that (4.6) 'describes withdrawal since total utility falls if cigarette consumption is reduced'. However condition (4.6) seems a weak way of modelling the phenomenon of withdrawal. The assumption that cigarette consumption has a positive marginal utility is something assumed for virtually all goods in most models of consumer choice.

Becker and Murphy (1988) show that potentially addictive goods must induce 'adjacent complementarity', a condition which implies an increase in future consumption when current consumption increases. In particular, they show that adjacent complementarity exists when

$$(\sigma + 2\delta) \, \alpha_{cs} > -\alpha_{ss} > 0, \tag{4.7}$$

where $\sigma$ is the rate of time preference, $\delta$ is the depreciation rate on consumption capital, $\alpha_{cs}$ is the change in the marginal utility of consumption as consumption capital changes, and $\alpha_{ss}$ is the change in the marginal benefit of $S$ as it increases.

Adjacent complementarity arises when the increase over time in the marginal utility of consumption exceeds the rise in the full price of consumption (Boyer, 1983). It can be seen from equation (4.7) that this depends on the extent of reinforcement but also on the rate of time preference, the rate of depreciation of consumption capital, and the impact of consumption capital on earnings. For given reinforcement and other determinants of adjacent complementarity, if the rate of time preference is higher, consumption now will add less to the full price of consumption in the future and so induce an increase in current consumption. An increase in the depreciation rate causes an equivalent effect, while an increase in the impact of an increase in consumption capital on earnings will reduce consumption. Additionally, for a given joint distribution of rates of time preference, marginal effects of consumption capital on earnings, and depreciation rates, more individuals will achieve the conditions for adjacent complementarity due to a rise in the characteristic of reinforcement. This can induce the distribution of consumption to be bimodal, as we observe with tobacco consumption. This suggests that tobacco is a highly addictive commodity. This bimodality also highlights the fact that goods are only potentially addictive; some individuals who recognize this complementarity choose not to consume. Becker and Murphy (1988) note (p. 682) 'Whether a potentially addictive person becomes addicted depends on his initial stock of capital and the location of his demand curve'. However, this is problematic given that consumption capital is measured in terms of the past consumption of the potentially addictive good. Although Becker and Murphy attempt to justify the assumption of non-zero and individual-specific initial stocks, the surreptitious introduction of preference variation, while crucial to their theoretical model, as it determines whether an individual will abstain, continuously increase consumption, or move to a steady state, is empirically unhelpful. This raises the issue of the meaning of addiction in Becker and Murphy's formulation. Given that the strength of a potential addiction is determined by the ratio of the left to the right-hand side of equation (4.7), an individual may be strongly *addictive* and consume zero, while another similarly addictive individual consumes at the unstable steady state, while an individual who is less addictive than both consumes more, still at a stable steady state. In terms of quantifying the degree of actual addiction, we are offered little guidance.

The existence of adjacent complementarity suggests a method by which to distinguish rational addiction from myopic habit formation or 'irrational' addiction models and models which assume rational neutrality (Strotz, 1956; Ippolito, 1981).[9] As Becker and Murphy (1988) note, '... adjacent complementarity is a necessary and sufficient condition for negative compensated cross-price effects'. In particular, if past prices increase, the effect on current consumption is due to the effect of current consumption capital, and we would expect this to be negative due to adjacent complementarity. However, a negative response would also occur due to irrational addiction which is not forward looking. If, however, future prices increase then the individual will recognize that optimal future consumption will be reduced and, due to adjacent complementarity, will respond optimally by reducing current consumption. This cannot be accounted for by models of irrational habit formation or addiction. However, individuals must be able to model perfectly the future price for Becker and Murphy's analysis to hold, or at least to hold rational expectations if the model is to hold on average.

The existence of future price and consumption effects are able to account for the demand functions resulting from the approach of Becker and Murphy being *observationally* distinct from those of myopic models,[10] which do not recognize the impact of present consumption on the future and where demand functions are derived from repeated instantaneous utility maximization.

Becker and Murphy's model also predicts a number of other observed features of addictions. In particular, given the importance of the extent of adjacent complementarity and, by implication, potential addiction, *ceteris paribus* we would expect those with a larger rate of time preference to be more likely to become addicted. If, as has been noted by Farrell and Fuchs (1982), the highly educated are more likely to have lower rates of time preference, the rational addiction model predicts an inverse relationship between consumption and education. It should also be the case, as noted by Becker *et al.* (1991) that the ratio of the short-run and long-run elasticities is greater for the less educated than the more educated due to the dependence of the long-run elasticity on the degree of adjacent complementarity and the above hypothesis concerning the relationship between adjacent complementarity and education. It also appears that Becker and Murphy predict that addiction will increase with age (with a finite time horizon), as the negative impact of an increase in current consumption on future utility is reduced. However, given that Becker and Murphy analyze the dynamic properties of their model assuming an infinite horizon, this implication is not produced explicitly.

### *Health, information, and quitting*

Becker and Murphy (1988) assume that new information enters their model through an increase in health knowledge, which, subject to qualifications, should increase the income elasticity of harmful addictions, and should, with the same qualifications, lead to a positive effect of information on earnings. Their model is also able to account for the existence of cold-turkey withdrawals and the phenomenon of instability with unstable steady states and large adjacent complementarity.[11] As noted above, other authors have also predicted such phenomena.[12] However, the model of Becker and Murphy does not rely on time inconsistency or imperfect foresight (Michaels, 1988), or concave indifference curves (Barthold and Hochman, 1988). Notwithstanding these characteristics, the model appears hard to reconcile with existing, albeit casual evidence. In particular, Schelling (1978) notes the extent of regret about the decision to consume an addictive good. In a model of addiction with perfect foresight and constant preferences this cannot be accommodated. In particular, the assumption that individuals know the degree of adjacent complementarity which their behaviour will exhibit before consuming the particular commodity is highly suspect, and appears to contradict the evidence of regret.

In addition, assuming knowledge of the impact of tolerance and withdrawal is questionable. It is also difficult to integrate new health information into this model, which does not model the parameters as random variables. Given that individuals have observed variations in health knowledge in the past, it would be irrational, or at least non-Bayesian to expect that the latest estimates of the health consequences of tobacco consumption would be definitive. As these health effects are also probabilistic at the individual level, the assumption of knowledge of personal health effects seems even more untenable. A possible extension is to incorporate these factors into the model by allowing new information concerning the distribution of health consequences to lead a prior distribution of beliefs to be updated. A Bayesian updating formula may be assumed, as in the non-addiction model of Ippolito (1981), and attitudes to risk would be likely to enter the model as determinants of the optimal consumption path. It should be noted that this criticism is not confined to the model of Becker and Murphy.

On rehabilitation, Becker and Murphy (1988) claim (p. 692) that 'a rational person decides to end his addiction if events lower either his demand for the addictive good sufficiently or his stock of consumption capital sufficiently'. They also note that claiming a desire to quit but to be unable to do so is merely a technological constraint; finding an acceptable quitting mechanism will allow individuals to overcome the pain of withdrawal (p. 693): 'What these claims mean is that a person will make certain changes...when he finds a way to raise long-term benefits sufficiently above the short-term costs of adjustment'. This conceptualization appears to be nebulous. If, in a model with perfect foresight and parametric knowledge, an individual recognizes that reduced consumption, either gradually or by cold-turkey, increases discounted utility, they will do so. It is impossible in the full information formulation of Becker and Murphy for an individual to claim a desire to quit and not do so. A fully informed rational addict cannot be 'unhappy'. They can only claim a conditional statement to the effect that, 'if events occur such that my total utility is higher from not smoking than smoking, I will quit'. To accomodate a desire to quit, but an inability to do so in the framework of Becker and Murphy, requires the relaxation of the full information assumption, with an explicit model of adjustment costs and the search for improved technology. It may then be rational for an individual not to quit while searching for alternative mechanisms which would reduce the costs of adjustment. Becker and Murphy recognize this possibility but present no factors which may affect adjustment costs other than those which influence adjacent complementarity.

Levy's (1994) model incorporates the impact of imperfect information by assuming the possibility of local but not global optimization. Of course, under some scenarios, the results will be equivalent. However, when individuals use an adjustment mechanism due to imperfect information (or bounded rationality) these may diverge. In particular, Levy shows that with non-convex isoquants for a fundamental commodity, it is possible to remain at a local optimum (addicted), while greater utility would be attained by not consuming the addictive good. Levy also shows how this model is able to predict the relative elasticity condition of the model of Becker and Murphy. He also shows that it is able to explain the apparent irrationality of joining Alcoholics Anonymous, which as Becker and Murphy correctly claim is inconsistent with rational addiction under global optimization. It may also be rational for addicts and altruists to vote to ban tobacco. However, Levy's model is not explicitly intertemporal, and he does not derive dynamic demand curves under local optimization, but the element of randomness in consumption due to bounded rationality does allow observed phenomena to be consistent with (boundedly) rational decision making.

Another attempt to incorporate imperfect foresight is the model of Orphanides and Zervos (1995). They introduce a model of rational addiction with learning and regret which resolves some of the criticisms of Becker and Murphy's (1988) rational addiction model outlined earlier.

The model incorporates learning by allowing for individuals to hold subjective prior beliefs regarding how harmful the potentially addictive good is. However, these may be incorrect, and their beliefs are updated using a Bayesian process as they learn through experimentation how dangerous the substance is. Under these conditions, those individuals who realize their tendency to addiction too late will be drawn or 'hooked' into addiction, and will regret their earlier consumption. However, behaviour will be rational and dynamically consistent. The authors claim that their model also offers a role for dissemination of health information, as the probability of experimentation is dependent on initial beliefs. However, as all learning is through consumption, it does not offer a role for information dissemination once addiction has ensued. Relatedly, the model is unable to explain a problem noted earlier, the inconsistency of joining Alcoholics Anonymous and rationality, as behaviour is modelled as *ex ante* rational and time consistent, even if regret ensues ex post. Reinforcement effects are introduced by assuming that the addictive good and the stock are complements. As noted in Table 4.1, the authors allow for the effects of tolerance by assuming that a '... larger quantity of the addictive good is required to achieve a given utility level when the stock is larger'. These definitions are equivalent to those of Becker and Murphy (1998), and Chaloupka (1991). Withdrawal effects are described as arising because '... the utility loss from a reduction in the consumption of the addictive good is larger when the stock is larger'. This definition relies on the sign of a second derivative rather than a first derivative of the utility function and is another implication of complementarity.

Irrespective of its relative sophistication, fundamentally this model attempts to explain rational initiation and addiction, and offers little for the analysis of rehabilitation. As Orphanides and Zervos (1995) note (p. 754), 'In present form, our theory cannot explicitly deal with the issues regarding rehabilitation decisions and the recurrence of addiction. Dealing with these issues within the rational framework requires abandoning the time invariance of preferences and opportunity sets we have imposed on the theory. Relaxation of this constraint, for example, by introducing a Markovian process for income, prices, or the marginal rate of substitution between the ordinary and addictive goods would provide a resolution'.

Orphanides and Zervos (1998) attempt to circumvent some of the problems outlined above by introducing probabilistically endogenous time preferences into a model of rational addiction. They characterize addiction by assuming that the cumulation of consumption capital increases the expected rate of time preference, allowing myopia to be a consequence rather than a cause of addiction. They also show that the expected intertemporal complementarity generated allows addictive behaviour to be described without assuming complementarity between past and present consumption in the instantaneous utility function. This leads to a reinforcement effect which differs from that assumed in previous models. First, this effect is probabilistic. Second, it works through increasing the rate of time preference rather than increasing the marginal utility of current addictive consumption relative to non-addictive consumption. Tolerance is introduced by allowing the stock to have a direct and negative effect on utility, hence requiring a larger level of consumption in the future to reach the same utility level. This is similar to the conceptualization of tolerance effects in previous rational addiction approaches. In the model of Orphanides and Zervos (1998), individuals take account of the likelihood of successful rehabilitation and the possibility of recurrence. However, the mechanism which induces quitting is opaque. In particular they claim that (p. 85) '. . . after an individual has become an addict, a favourable event in his life may provide him with a window to re-evaluate his addiction, become (temporarily perhaps) less myopic and decide to get rehabilitated', and (p. 88) 'Shifts in the marginal utility of ordinary consumption could easily be considered as the impetus for starting or stopping of a harmful addiction'. These probabilistic or exogenous preference shifts imply little for the empirical analysis of quitting behaviour. Further, like Becker and Murphy (1988), and Orphanides and Zervos (1995), an individual can want to quit but be unable to do so. They may regret starting, as a losing gambler regrets placing his stake, but they cannot desire their current consumption level to be other than it is.

### Addiction asymmetry and adjustment costs

It is generally accepted that withdrawal effects and the associated craving are important features of nicotine dependence. One interpretation of this phenomenon is as a cost of adjustment that must be overcome if an individual reduces his/her consumption of tobacco. Atkinson (1974) argues that the concept of adjustment costs offers an improvement on the conventional approach towards habit formation. His model introduces a cost of adjustment function to the utility function. The important feature of this model is that adjustment costs are asymmetric and only apply to reductions in consumption.

More recently, Jones (1987, 1999) argues that, for economists concerned with modelling addiction, two stylized features of withdrawal effects stand out. First, the effects are asymmetric and only occur when consumption falls below its previous level. Second, once a threshold has been passed the role of consumption is not simply to provide satisfaction but also to ward-off the unpleasant consequences of withdrawal. In this respect withdrawal can be thought of as increasing the efficiency of current consumption. From this perspective it seems appropriate to write the direct utility function in terms of an intermediate production function $\phi(C)$, and allow for an asymmetry in the 'marginal productivity' of current consumption around the individual's reference level of consumption, ($C^R$). The reference level of consumption could simply be consumption in the previous period. But an intuitive alternative would be to use the level of consumption that 'maintains the habit' by keeping the habit stock constant,

$$C^R = \delta S. \tag{4.8}$$

One possible specification of $\phi(.)$ is the linear form,

$$\phi^-(.) = C - a(Z) + b(Z) \cdot (C - C^R), \text{ if } C < C^R, \tag{4.9}$$

and

$$\phi^+(.) = C \text{ if } C \geq C^R. \tag{4.10}$$

In this case $a$ can be interpreted as the fixed effect of withdrawal, while $b$ can be interpreted as a constant marginal effect of withdrawal, with the levels of $a$ and $b$ determined by the vector of exogenous variables $Z$. For example, withdrawal effects could be an increasing function of past consumption.

The gist of the model is that, as a result of withdrawal effects, the marginal productivity of current consumption is asymmetric, implying a discontinuity in the slope of the indifference curves. With withdrawal effects defined by (4.9) and (4.10) the utility function will be non-differentiable at the reference level of consumption, and it is possible to establish the conditions under which the consumer's indifference curves are either kinked or non-convex. If $a = 0$, with a single addictive good and the linear specification (4.9, 4.10), the condition for kinked rather than non-convex indifference curves is simply $b > 0$.[13]

The existence of non-convex indifference curves due to $a \neq 0$, or $b < 0$, can lead to discontinuous responses to changes in exogenous variables such as prices or income. In particular they can lead to cold-turkey quitting from an interior solution at $C^R$ to a corner solution at $C = 0$. Non-convexities are central to the prediction of cold-turkey quitting in the models of Barthold and Hochman (1988), Becker and Murphy (1988), Michaels (1988), Yen and Jones (1996), and Suranovic *et al.* (1999).

Yen and Jones (1996) develop an empirical model of the simultaneous decisions of how many cigarettes to smoke and whether to quit smoking. This is based on the trade-off between the expected benefits of quitting for the smoker's health, wealth and self-esteem, and the fixed costs of quitting associated with nicotine dependence and withdrawal. The influence of nicotine dependence is modelled as a fixed cost of quitting. Yen and Jones (1996) assume that expected fixed costs ($A$) depend on a vector of variables, including past consumption, and a random error reflecting unobservable individual heterogeneity. The expected benefits of quitting ($B$), in terms of health, wealth, and self esteem, will depend on how much the individual would have smoked otherwise. These benefits are likely to be increasing in the individual's level of cigarette consumption. The decision to quit smoking depends on the expected net benefit of quitting, ($B-A$). By assuming that the fixed costs of adjustment, ($A$), and the individual's desired level of cigarette consumption are both functions of a set of explanatory variables and random error terms, Yen and Jones (1996) derive an econometric specification. This takes the form of a 'double-hurdle' model. A feature of this model is that variables that have no (or small) influence on the fixed costs of quitting are expected to have equal and opposite effects on quitting and on the level of smoking. This reflects the intuition that, conditional on overcoming the fixed costs of quitting, heavier smokers have the greatest incentive to quit. By the same reasoning, the econometric specification suggests that it would not be appropriate to assume independence of the error terms in the double-hurdle model, and that there will tend to be a negative correlation between the error terms.

A recent theoretical contribution by Suranovic *et al.* (1999) recognizes the withdrawal effects of quitting and the importance of the delayed health effects of smoking. Their approach follows the concept of addiction as repetitive, compulsive, and damaging, as described in the first section. For example, '... repetitive usage of a good is not sufficient to call consumption of that good an addiction.... Instead, addiction requires that someone would like to either cease of reduce habitual consumption but is unable to do so'.

This idea is incorporated into their model as asymmetric adjustment costs. Their model predicts that individuals will get 'hooked' and can be regarded as 'unhappy addicts'.[14] The model shows how different forms of adjustment costs will lead to gradual or cold-turkey quitting, while providing a rationale for smoking cessation programmes and nicotine replacement therapies, and showing how ageing can induce quitting.

Suranovic *et al.* use a specification of the utility function that is additively separable in smoking and other consumption. The utility associated with current smoking $(C)$ at age $\alpha$ is assumed to consist of three components,

$$U_\alpha(C) = B_\alpha(C) - L_\alpha(C) - A_\alpha(C). \tag{4.11}$$

$B_\alpha(.)$ represents the direct benefits of consumption and is assumed to be increasing and concave. $L_\alpha(.)$ represents future losses which are modelled as the impact of continued smoking on the present value of expected utility streams. $A_\alpha(.)$ represents the costs of adjustment associated with withdrawal. Rather than allowing for full intertemporal rationality, Suranovic *et al.* assume a form of bounded rationality in which the individual takes account of the impact of current consumption on future health but does not plan the optimal path of future consumption. In particular, $W_t$, the level of instantaneous utility at time $t$, is implicitly assumed independent of the decision to continue or quit smoking. The loss $L_\alpha(.)$ is related to the reduction in life expectancy from smoking, given the individual's history of smoking and is equal to;

$$L_\alpha(.) = V(S_\alpha, 0) - V(S_\alpha, C)$$

$$= \int_{T_a + \alpha - \beta(S_a + C)}^{T_a + \alpha - \beta S_\alpha} e^{-\sigma(t - \infty)} W_t \, dt, \tag{4.12}$$

where $W_t$ is instantaneous utility at time $t$, $\sigma$ is the rate of time preference, $T_\alpha$ is the life expectancy of a non-smoker at age $\alpha$ which is reduced by the stock of addiction, $S_\alpha$ and by current smoking $C$. For simplicity Suranovic *et al.* assume that the impact of smoking on life expectancy is linear and is indicated by the parameter $\beta$.

Under their assumptions, $L$ is increasing and convex in current consumption and increases with age; as death is brought forward a higher discount rate is applied to the final years of life. This further implies that the incentive to quit also increases with age. Smoking can become a net 'bad' with ageing, with the utility of consumption becoming negative as the impact on future health outweighs the direct benefits of consumption. Hence Suranovic *et al.* (1999) predict that consumption will decline with age. This contradicts the conclusion of Becker and Murphy (1988), which was noted earlier. In their model the impacts of addictive consumption are immediate and continual, leading to an increase in consumption as individuals age.

Individuals start smoking at an age when the anticipated health effects are heavily discounted. Also, although the model relies on bounded rationality and does not allow for forward planning of future consumption, Suranovic *et al.* speculate that the anticipated costs of quitting would also be heavily discounted. Once consumption ensues the addictive stock accumulates and costs of adjustment set in. Costs of adjustment are assumed to be asymmetric around the habitual level of consumption and to depend on the level of consumption and the addictive stock. Suranovic *et al.* show that different assumptions about the shape of the cost of adjustment function lead to different styles of quitting. Convex adjustment costs (giving kinked indifference curves) are associated with gradual quitting. Concave adjustment costs (giving non-convex indifference curves) are associated with cold-turkey quitting. A mixture of concave and convex portions leads to predictions that are consistent with the 'stages of change' view of addiction, where repetitive consumption is followed by gradual reduction and then cold-turkey quitting.[15]

As mentioned earlier, 'cold-turkey' quitting is predicted by other models; the role of non-convexities in inducing the decision to quit an addictive behaviour abruptly appears ubiquitous. Non-convexities are often necessary and sometimes sufficient to induce cold-turkey quitting. This is true of the fully rational, intertemporal framework of Becker and Murphy (1988), the myopic models of Michaels (1988), and Barthold and Hochman (1988), or the pragmatic, imperfect foresight models of Yen and Jones (1996), and Suranovic *et al.* (1999). Although we may be offered hints by previous work, Jones (1999) suggests that until a theoretical model is developed which is able to combine the possibilities of non-convexities and multiple optima with unbounded rationality, the theoretical and empirical implications of the simplification of imperfect foresight are difficult to judge. This requires a model which is able to tackle the mathematical complexities created by incorporating adjustment costs into a model assuming full intertemporal rationality.

## Conclusion

In this chapter we considered how addiction has been incorporated into economic models. We have also discussed the relationships between these specifications and the characterizations offered by pharmacology and psychology, and outlined the implications of alternative theoretical models of addictive consumption for the empirical analysis of the determinants of quitting. Our focus has been the problem of nicotine dependence, although the general approaches and issues outlined are also applicable to other harmful, and possibly beneficial, addictions. Further, while we have not focused on the empirical work in this area, it should be noted that this is not due to a paucity of research (see Chaloupka and Warner, 2000 for a recent survey of the economics of smoking). Other authors have considered economic issues related to other potentially addictive products such as alcohol (e.g. Cook and Moore, 2000). While these and other issues are beyond the scope of this chapter, it is hoped that it has introduced readers to the alternative economic approaches to modelling addictive consumption (and particularly nicotine dependence), and their relationships to the conceptual apparatus used in medicine.

## Notes

We are grateful for research funding from the ESRC award no. R000222492, and for comments from Tadashi Yamada and Peter Zweifel. We also thank participants at the Taipei International conference on Health Economics, the International Workshop on Nicotine Dependence, Lausanne, the Arne Ryde symposium, Lund, the IFS Health Economics seminar, and the York Seminars, and the York Seminars in Health Econometrics (YSHE).

1  While the vast majority of economic models of addiction have relied solely on past consumption to influence current behaviour, there are examples that do not (e.g. the addiction asymmetry model of Young (1983), and the 'extreme-seeking' model of Barthold and Hochman (1988)).

2  Geist and Herman (1990) compare the psychological characteristics of smokers, ex-smokers, and never-smokers using qualitative data. They find that ex-smokers have more self-control, order, and endurance than either smokers or never-smokers, and that smokers have less self-control than never-smokers. Zakela *et al.* (1990) find that smokers are also more likely to drink alcohol and coffee. Whether these characteristics are innate is a matter of debate, and may depend on both environment and behaviour. For example, observed psychological characteristics may be conditional on the consumption state in which they are measured. Ex-smokers may differ from smokers because they have quit, not because of an innate difference. Also, preferences for other goods may be dependent on the consumption of cigarettes, in which case the results of Zakela *et al.* (1990) do not inform our concern with *unconditional* preferences.

3  Dardanoni and Jones (1988) allow for the response to the habit 'stock' and the depreciation of the habit stock to be stochastic, but this joint distribution is assumed independent of personal characteristics.

4  Earlier 'rational' models include Lluch (1974), Klijn (1977), Boyer (1983), and Iannaccone (1984).

5  It is noticeable that Becker and Murphy use an exponential form of the discounting function in their model of rational addiction which avoids the problem of time inconsistency. As noted earlier, it is the use of a non-exponential form of the discount function attached to 'instantaneous' utility which causes time inconsistency in the formulation of Strotz (1956).

6  In this context, it should be noted that recent papers have analysed the empirical existence and welfare implications of 'intra-personal externalities' raised by hyperbolic or other forms of non-exponential discounting (see Gruber and Koszegi, 2000; Laux, 2000).

7  Spinnewyn (1981) models rational habit formation through endogenous preferences, assuming that the individual recognizes the impact of current consumption on future preferences. A similar approach is taken by Orphanides and Zervos (1998).

8  This is not characterized explicitly in Becker and Murphy's original formulation.

9  Myopia will be 'rational' if an individual has an infinite rate of time preference. Becker and Murphy also note that even if time preference was neutral (the future is undiscounted), older individuals would be expected to be more addicted assuming the implicit discount rate can be approximated by the inverse of the number of life years remaining. However, this contradicts the assumptions of the special case of the model which employs an infinite lifespan and a constant rate of time preference. The potentially misleading implications of assuming an infinite horizon for analyzing the dynamic properties of Becker and Murphy's model are discussed by Ferguson (1996).

10  In the formulation of Spinnewyn (1981: p. 108), 'Models with rational habit formation yield demand equations which for *estimation* purposes have a structure that is equivalent to those derived under naive habit formation'. In addition, Phlips and Spinnewyn (1982) show that, using the linear expenditure system, rational and myopic demands are equivalent under habit formation. Phlips and Spinnewyn (1982) also show that a model of rational habit formation can be made formally equivalent to one without it under certain separability conditions, and when the cost of consumption is redefined the wealth constraint takes the same form as those of non-habit models, as in Spinnewyn (1981).

11  In particular, Becker and Murphy show that a sufficiently strong degree of complementarity and potential addiction can lead to non-convex indifference curves. This can then lead to a discontinuity in the relationship between the stock of consumption capital and the optimal consumption level in each time-period. It is then possible for a small change in prices or consumption capital which crosses this critical stock value to lead to 'cold-turkey' quitting.

12  Dockner and Feichtinger (1993) show that cycling and bingeing are impossible in a rational addiction model with perfect foresight unless addictive consumption produces at least two stocks of consumption capital (e.g. a health and addictive stock). They also derive the analytical conditions for limit, damped, and explosive cycles, and demonstrate these alternatives using numerical simulations.

13  Jones (1989) uses a similar framework in incorporating the tolerance effects of addiction in the cost function, while maintaining constant preferences.

14  The potential for unhappy addiction appears to be borne out by the self-reported responses of current smokers in the longitudinal follow-up of the British Health and Lifestyle Survey. In particular 72 per cent of current smokers report that they want to quit. Of these 65 per cent claim that they would definitely quit if they could do so easily; a further 19 per cent say that they would probably quit, while only 16 per cent say that they would not.

15  The stages of change perspective also applies to the predicted price responsiveness in the model. Those who are just starting and those who are about to quit are expected to be price responsive, while those who are addicted will be unresponsive (Harris and Chan, 1999). An implication is that the analysis of aggregate price effects may be misleading if the tobacco consumer distribution changes as prices vary, and will also mask these different responses.

# References

Ashton, H. and Stepney, R. (1982). *Smoking, Psychology and Pharmacology*. Tavistock, London, first edition.

Atkinson, A. (1974). Smoking and the economics of government intervention. In: M. Perlman (ed.), *The Economics of Health and Medical Care*. Macmillan, pp. 428–41.

Barthold, T. and Hochman, H. (1988). Addiction as extreme seeking. *Economic Inquiry*, 26:89–106.

Becker, G., Grossman, M. and Murphy, K. (1991). Rational addiction and the effect of price on consumption. *American Economic Review*, 81:237–41.

Becker, G. and Murphy, K. (1988). A theory of rational addiction. *Journal of Political Economy*, 96:675–700.

Boyer, M. (1983). Rational demand and expenditures patterns under habit formation. *Journal of Economic Theory*, 31:27–53.

Chaloupka, F. (1991). Rational addictive behaviour and cigarette smoking. *Journal of Political Economy*, 99:722–42.

Chaloupka, F. and Warner, K. (2000). The Economics of Smoking. In: Culyer, A.J. and Newhouse, J.P. (eds), *Handbook of Health Economics*. Elsevier, ch. 29, pp. 1539–1627.

Cook, P. and Moore, M. (2000). Alcohol. In: Culyer, A.J. and Newhouse, J.P. (eds), *Handbook of Health Economics*. Elsevier, ch. 30, pp. 1629–73.

Dardanoni, V. and Jones, A. (1988). Stochastic habits and the consumption-savings decision. *Studi Economici*, 34.

Dockner, E. and Feichtinger, G. (1993). Cyclical consumption patterns and rational addiction. *American Economic Review*, 83:256–63.

Farrell, P. and Fuchs, V. (1982). Schooling and health: the cigarette connection. *Journal of Health Economics*, 1:217–30.

Ferguson, B. (1996). A note on the interpretation of the rational addiction model. Mimeo. University of Guelph, Canada.

Geist, C. and Herman, S. (1990). A comparison of the psychological characteristics of smokers, ex-smokers and non-smokers. *Journal of Clinical Psychology*, 46:102–5.

Gritz, E.R., Carr, C. and Marcus, A. (1991). The tobacco withdrawal syndrome in unaided quitters. *British Journal of Addiction*, 86:57–69.

Gruber, J. and Koszegi, B. (2000). Is addiction 'rational?' theory and evidence. NBER working paper no. 7507.

Harris, J. and Chan, S. (1999). The continuum of addiction: cigarette smoking in relation to price among Americans aged 15–29. *Health Economics*, 8:81–6.

Houthakker, H. and Taylor, L. (1966). *Consumer Demand in the United States: Analyses and Projections*. Harvard UP, Cambridge, MA, first edition.

Hsieh, C.-R. (1998). Health risk and the decision to quit smoking. *Applied Economics*, 30:795–804.

Iannaccone, L. (1984). *Consumption Capital and Habit Formation with an Application to Religious Participation*. Ph.D. thesis, University of Chicago.

Ippolito, P. (1981). Information and the life-cycle consumption of hazardous goods. *Economic Inquiry*, 19:529–58.

Jones, A. (1987). *A Theoretical and Empirical Investigation of the Demand for Addictive Goods*. Ph.D. thesis, University of York.

Jones, A. (1989). A systems approach to the demand for alcohol and tobacco. *Bulletin of Economic Research*, 41:85–105.

Jones, A. (1994). Health, addiction, social interaction and the decision to quit smoking. *Journal of Health Economics*, 13:93–110.

Jones, A. (1999). Adjustment costs, withdrawal effects, and cigarette addiction. *Journal of Health Economics*, 18:125–37.

Klijn, N. (1977). Expenditure, saving and habit formation: a comment. *International Economic Review*, 18:791–8.

Kuhn, C., Swartzwelder, S. and Wilson, W. (1998). *Buzzed*. W.W. Norton and Co., New York, first edition.

Laux, F. (2000). Addiction as a market failure: using rational addiction results to justify tobacco regulation. *Journal of Health Economics*, 19:421–37.

Levy, D. (1994). The fragile politics of addiction. *Public Choice*, 81:263–75.

Lluch, C. (1974). Expenditure, savings and habit formation. *International Economic Review*, 15:786–97.

Michaels, R. (1988). Addiction, compulsion, and the technology of consumption. *Economic Inquiry*, 26:74–88.

Orphanides, A. and Zervos, D. (1995). Rational addiction with learning and regret. *Journal of Political Economy*, 103:739–58.

Orphanides, A. and Zervos, D. (1998). Myopia and addictive behaviour. *Economic Journal*, 108:75–91.

Pacula, R. (1997). Economic modelling of the gateway effect. *Health Economics*, 6:521–4.

Phlips, L. and Spinnewyn, F. (1982). Rationality versus myopia in dynamic demand systems. In: Basmann, R.L. and Rhodes, G.F., Jr (eds), *Advances in Econometrics*. JAI, Greenwich, Connecticut, vol. 1.

Pollak, R. (1970). Habit formation and dynamic demand functions. *Journal of Political Economy*, 78:745–63.

Prochaska, J., DiClemente, C. and Norcross, J. (1992). In search of how people change: applications to addictive behaviours. *American Psychologist*, 47:1102–14.

Robbins, M. and Kline, A. (1991). To smoke or not to smoke: a decision theory perspective. *Social Science and Medicine*, 33:1343–7.

Schelling, T. (1978). Economics, or the art of self-management. *American Economic Review. A.E.A. Papers and Proceedings*, 68:290–4.

Spinnewyn, F. (1981). Rational habit formation. *European Economic Review*, 15:91–109.

Stigler, G. and Becker, G. (1977). De gustibus non est disputandum. *American Economic Review*, 67:76–90.

Strotz, R. (1956). Myopia and inconsistency in dynamic utility maximization. *Review of Economic Studies*, 23:165–80.

Suranovic, S., Goldfarb, R. and Leonard, T. (1999). An economic theory of cigarette addiction. *Journal of Health Economics*, 18:1–29.

Thaler, R. and Shefrin, H.M. (1981). An economic theory of self-control. *Journal of Political Economy*, 89:392–406.

Viscusi, W. (1990). Do smokers underestimate risks? *Journal of Political Economy*, 98:1253–69.

Winston, G. (1980). Addiction and backsliding: a theory of compulsive consumption. *Journal of Economic Behaviour and Organization*, 1:295–324.

Yen, S. and Jones, A. (1996). Individual cigarette consumption and addiction: a flexible limited dependent variable approach. *Health Economics*, 5:105–17.

Young, T. (1983). The demand for cigarettes: alternative specifications of Fujii's model. *Applied Economics*, 15:203–11.

Zakela, K. *et al.* (1990). Concurrent use of cigarettes, alcohol and coffee. *Journal of Applied Social Psychology*, 10:835–45.

# 5 The demand for health and health investments in Sweden 1980/81, 1988/89, and 1996/97

*Kristian Bolin, Lena Jacobson,
and Björn Lindgren*

## Background

The introduction of the demand-for-health model some 30 years ago (Grossman, 1972a,b) was a major contribution to economics, and it remains a central theoretical model for the economic analysis of individual health behaviour. It was built on traditional neoclassical capital theory, the human capital theory developed for educational investments by Becker (1964), the theory of the allocation of time (Becker, 1965), and Lancaster's new approach to consumer theory, which draws a sharp distinction between fundamental objects of choice – 'commodities' – and market goods (Lancaster, 1966). In his seminal paper, Grossman (1972a) emphasized (a) that health is a durable capital stock; (b) that health capital differs from other forms of human capital in that its main impact is on the total amount of time a person can spend producing money earnings and commodities rather than on his or her wage rate; and (c) that the demand for health care must be derived from the more fundamental demand for good health.

True, the demand-for-health model, as presented in Grossman's theoretical paper, relied by necessity on a number of simplifying assumptions, 'all of which should be relaxed in future work' (Grossman, 1972a, p. 247). However, the paper presented a completely new approach for the economic analysis of individual health behaviour and provided essential insights; the most important predictions being that, under certain conditions, (a) age would be negatively correlated with health capital but positively correlated with expenditures on health care; (b) the individual's wage rate would be positively correlated both with the demand for health and with the demand for health care; and (c) education would be positively correlated with health capital but negatively correlated with expenditures on health care. The demand-for-health model explains variations in health status (besides the exogenously given initial levels of health) and health care utilization among individuals.

Theoretical extensions and modifications of the Grossman model include the introduction of uncertainty, which *inter alia* implies that the individual no longer knows his or her age of death with certainty (Liljas, 1998); a 'use-related' deterioration of health capital influenced by, *inter alia*, education and other exogenous variables, and a health investment efficiency parameter declining with age, replacing the household production function framework used by Grossman (Muurinen, 1982b); the rate of depreciation of health capital being a negative function of the level of health and, hence, being endogenous instead of exogenous in the model (Liljas, 1998); imperfect instead of perfect financial markets (Liljas, 2000, 2002); and the family instead of the individual as producer of health – (Jacobson, 2000) for the case when the family has a common utility function; Bolin *et al.* (2001b) for the case when spouses are Nash-bargainers; Bolin *et al.* (2002a) for the case when spouses act strategically; and Bolin *et al.* (2002b) for the case when an employer has incentives for investing in the health of one family member. Ried (1998) applied comparative dynamic analysis to the Grossman model focusing on direct and indirect effects of marginal changes in the rate of health capital depreciation as well as the impact of the initial levels of wealth or health. Similar models for analysing individual health behaviour have been developed by Dowie (1975), Cropper (1977, 1981), Dardanoni and Wagstaff (1987, 1990), Selden (1993), Zweifel and Breyer (1997, pp. 62–88), Picone *et al.* (1998), all emphasizing uncertainty and health status as being governed by a stochastic process; Ehrlich and Chuma (1987, 1990) who applied optimal control techniques to determine the optimal length of life; Ehrlich (2000, 2001) who, building on his joint work with Chuma, provided a theory of the demand for life expectancy under uncertainty and analysed the impacts of specific personal characteristics and alternative insurance options; and Forster (2001), who investigated the impact of various terminal conditions on lifespan, pathways of health-related consumption, and health in a dynamic micro-simulation model.

Many empirical studies of the demand for health and the demand for health care certainly refer to Grossman's ideas, but few have actually been based on empirical counterparts to Grossman's formal model. Empirical estimations of the demand-for-health model include Grossman's own study (Grossman, 1972b) on American data, as well as Muurinen (1982a) on Finnish data, Wagstaff (1986, 1993) on Danish data, and Sundberg (1996) on Swedish data, all following Grossman's own empirical formulation and employing double logarithmic demand functions for health and health care, but providing conflicting evidence regarding the main predictions of the demand-for-health model.

Wagstaff (1993) claimed that this formulation is inappropriate since it fails to capture the inherently dynamic character of the model and proposed an alternative formulation apparently more consistent both with Grossman's theoretical model and with (Danish) data. However, Wagstaff introduced the cost of adjusting from initial to desired stock of health in a rather *ad hoc* manner, without any development of a formal, theoretical model, by estimating demand for health and demand for health investment functions in which the lagged stock of health is a determinant of the current stock of health. Since in a correct specification of the cost-of-adjustment model, current stock of health also depends on the future stock of health, his estimate was biased; at least three data points would be required in order to make unbiased estimates (Grossman, 2000).

It should be observed that while all previous empirical estimations of the demand-for-health model, including Grossman's own study (1972b), used medical care as the empirical counterpart to the concept of health investment, Grossman's theoretical model does not preclude other types of health investments. Housing, diet, recreation, cigarette smoking, alcohol use, and many other market goods and services influence health. Most of them, however, are not purchased primarily because of their effect on health (or, sometimes, rather despite their negative influence on health) but because they are inputs in the production of the consumption commodities which yield direct pleasure to the individual. Certainly, the joint production of health and consumption commodities was considered in Grossman (1972b), but in order to make the further analysis simpler such cases were ruled out from the model.

This chapter develops a theoretical family-as-producer-of-health framework in which the cost of adjusting from initial to desired stock of health is explicitly taken into account. An empirical model is derived and estimated using a set of individual panel data from three different time-periods in Sweden. Physical exercise will here be used as the indicator of health investments.[1] The chapter proceeds as follows: first, we will discuss the theoretical framework shortly, and from this the empirical model will be developed. Then the data will be discussed. Third, we shall move on to a description of the specific empirical method used in the chapter. Fourth, the empirical model will be specified in terms of the previously discussed method, and fifth, the model will be estimated. The chapter is concluded with a discussion of the results.

## Theoretical framework

In Grossman's original theoretical model (Grossman, 1972a,b) the individual is regarded as the producer of health and the sole receiver of the benefits accruing from good health. However, the seminal work by Becker (1973, 1974, 1991) suggests that also the family structure is important for the demand for health and health investment. Following this tradition, Jacobson (2000) argues that each family member produces not only own health but also the health of other family members. The rationale for this is that as other family members become healthier, the family's income increases which benefits everyone. Another rationale is that each family member might be 'consuming' other family members' health; each family member's utility increases from an increase in other family members' health per se.[2] We shall here use the Jacobson (2000) model of the family as producer of health as our theoretical framework.

Thus, formally, the *family's* preferences are represented by $U(H_t^h, H_t^w, H_t^c, Z_t)$ where $H_t^h$, $H_t^w$, and $H_t^c$ should be interpreted as health of respective spouse and the child (Jacobson, 2000) and $Z_t$ is the family's production of consumption commodities. The family acts so as to maximize its lifetime utility. That is, the family solves

$$\max U = \int_0^T e^{-\rho t} U(H_t^h, H_t^w, H_t^c, Z_t)\, dt, \tag{5.1}$$

where $\rho$ is the subjective rate of discounting, subject to certain restrictions: the two spouses and the child each inherit an initial stock of health capital, $H_0^h$, $H_0^w$, and $H_0^c$, and the stock of health capital evolves according to:

$$\dot{H}_t^i = I_t^i - \delta_t^i H_t^i, \quad i = h, w, c, \tag{5.2}$$

where $I_{t-1}$ is gross investment and $\delta_{t-1}$ is the rate of depreciation of the health capital at time $t - 1$. The development of family wealth follows:

$$\dot{W}_t = rW_t + y_t^h(H_t^h, H_t^c) + y_t^w(H_t^w, H_t^c) - p_t^I(I_t^h + I_t^w + I_t^c) - p_t^z Z_t$$

$$-p_t^A(I_t^h - \delta_t^h H_t^h) - p_t^A(I_t^w - \delta_t^w H_t^w) - p_t^A(I_t^c - \delta_t^c H_t^c), \tag{5.3}$$

where $p_t^I$ is the price of health investments at time $t$, $p_t^z$ is the price of consumption commodity at time $t$, y is income and $r$ is the rate of interest.[3] There is a cost of adjusting from actual to desired stock of health capital which is reflected by a price, $p_t^A$ (in monetary units), per unit of adjustment of the stock of health capital. Hence, the marginal cost of net investment in health is a positive function of the amount of investment. This makes the cost of gradual adjustment smaller than the cost of instantaneous adjustment, creating an incentive for the family to reach the desired stocks of health gradually rather than instantaneously.

One of the first-order conditions for a solution to the family's optimization problem says that the spouses invest in health up to the point where the condition that the marginal utility of an investment in health is equal to the marginal cost is satisfied for both spouses simultaneously. The marginal rate of substitution between the spouses' consumption and investment benefits of health is then equal to the ratio of *net* marginal costs of health investments. Another condition says that the family will allocate resources in order to equate the marginal utility of health that can be bought per dollar (or whatever money unit is used) for each family member. Further, this ratio shall be equal to the marginal utility of wealth. Somewhat simplified and attuned to account for the adjustment cost, the conditions that appear in Jacobson (2000) are:

$$\frac{\partial U(H_t^w, H_t^h, H_t^c, Z_t)/\partial H_t^i}{\partial U(H_t^h, H_t^w, H_t^c, Z_t)/\partial H_t^c} = \frac{\left(r + \delta_t^h - \dfrac{\dot{p}_t}{p_t}\right)p_t - \dfrac{\partial Y^i}{\partial H_t^i} - p_t^A \delta^i}{\left(r + \delta_t^w - \dfrac{\dot{p}_t}{p_t}\right)p_t - \dfrac{\partial Y^i}{\partial H_t^c} - p_t^A \delta^c}, \ (i = h, w), \tag{5.4}$$

and

$$\lambda_t^{H,h} = \lambda_t^{H,w} = \lambda_t^A p_t^I, \tag{5.5}$$

where $p_t = p_t^I + p_t^A$, $\lambda_t^A$ is the costate variable for the asset accumulation constraint, and the $\lambda^H$, s are the costate variables associated with the family's lifetime utility of investing in health.[4]

Among the variables that Grossman analyses in particular are age, wage, and education. Our model incorporates both the investment and the consumption aspects of health. Both these effects work in the same direction for age. That is, age increases the depreciation rate of the health capital, and hence, the net cost of health capital will also increase. That is, the demand for health will decrease with age. However, the change of gross investments over the life cycle also reflects the fact that a rise in the rate of depreciation reduces the amount of health capital that can be produced from a given amount of gross investments. That is, the change in demand may, or may not, exceed the change in supply of health capital. Thus, in general, the effect of a rise in the rate of depreciation on gross investments is ambiguous. However, if the elasticity of the marginal efficiency of health capital (MEC) curve is less than 1, gross investments will increase when the rate of depreciation increases. The relationship between health capital and productive time implies, as Grossman (2000) points out, that this elasticity is less than one.

The wage rate effects on family members' demand for health and health investments are more complicated since the effects differ between the investment model and the consumption model.[5] We begin with the investment aspects of health. First, a higher wage rate for one spouse implies that sick time becomes more expensive, which induces the household to increase the holdings of that spouse's health capital. Second, inasmuch as health investments are not time consuming this reinforces the incentive to hold health as an asset. On the other hand, if health investments are time consuming a higher wage rate means that the time supplied to investing in health becomes more expensive, which reduces the incentives to invest in health. However, if gross investments are not produced solely by time the first effect will outweigh the second and, hence, the demand for health will increase as the wage rate increases (Grossman, 2000). As the amount of health capital, which can be produced from a given amount of gross investments, does not depend on the wage rate, the gross investments will also increase. Next, consider the consumption effects on the demand for health of a wage rate increase. In this case, a rise in the wage rate will change the ratio of marginal costs for health capital and the consumption commodity. The effect of this on the demand for health and gross investments is, hence, ambiguous. Hence, the total effect of a wage rate increase on the demand for health and gross health investments is ambiguous (Grossman, 1972a).

The level of education affects market as well as nonmarket productivity. Thus, education is positively correlated to the wage rate, and higher education means that the production of a given quantity of health investment and a given quantity of the consumption commodities each requires less inputs. The first effect is the wage rate effect and has been discussed above. Keeping the wage rate constant, the investment model predicts that the demand for health increases as education increases. The effect of education on gross investments depends on how sensitive the production of gross health investments is to education. The consumption model predicts that if education affects the production of gross investments in health less than it affects the production of household commodities, health investments may increase or decrease as education increases. Hence, keeping the wage rate constant, our theoretical model predicts that the demand for health will increase while the effect on health investments is ambiguous from an increase in education (Grossman, 1972a).

In addition, the theory implies several hypotheses that link family structure to health-related behaviour. The last condition in the theoretical discussion, (5.5), says that the family invests in health of its members up to the point where the family's marginal lifetime utility of wealth is equal to the ratio of the family's marginal lifetime utility of investing in either family member's health to the price of health investments.[6] Hence, we have the following proposition concerning the relation between family wealth and the level of health capital: given that health is a normal good, the demand for health and gross health investments is positively linked to wealth.

The family structure is important for the time allocation decisions that, in turn, affect investments in all types of human capital. Becker's explanation for the existence of the family is the gains created by specialization according to comparative advantages. Thus, gains from specialization achieved in a two-person family's allocation of time and money create resources, in excess of those that would have been created by two single households. So, Becker's theory of the family predicts that individuals who live together are wealthier than those who live as singles. Bolin and Pålsson (2000) confirm this prediction for Swedish data. The theoretical model developed by Jacobson (2000) states that the marginal utility of wealth, $\lambda^A$, is equal to the marginal utilities of investing in the health of either spouse, $\lambda^{H,i}$. Consequently, our next testable proposition is: living together (either in cohabitation or in marriage) is associated with higher stocks of health capital. The effect on health investments is ambiguous, since the increase in the demand for health might be outweighed by increased productivity, induced by marriage, in the production of gross investments.

To achieve the gains from specialization it is necessary that family members cooperate. In case of strategic behaviour, those gains are diluted.[7] Bad previous experience of cooperation with other family members may create incentives to behave less cooperatively in the future. Individuals who are divorced may have such bad experience, or at least have such bad experience to a larger extent than those not divorced. Moreover, having gone through a divorce may also reflect that individual's ability of cooperation. Consequently, individuals who are divorced should be expected to behave less cooperatively, which creates fewer resources that could be spent on health investments, i.e. $\lambda^A$ increases. Thus, one further proposition is: family members in a family where one spouse has gone through a divorce have lower amounts of health capital and invest less in health than family members in families without such experience.

The presence of children affects the family's demand for health and health investments in two ways. First, given that investments in child health are time consuming, less time is available for investments in parental health. This decreases the demand for health capital and health investments. If, however, parental health and child health are complements, i.e. the healthier a given number of children are, the more utility each parent enjoys from a given amount of health capital. The total effect on the demand for health is, hence, ambiguous.

Our theoretical model gives no predictions concerning the difference in the demand for health and health investments between men and women.

*Table 5.1* Predictions concerning the effect on the demand for health and health investments from changes in explanatory variables[a]

| Variable | Health | Health investments |
|---|---|---|
| Age | H ↓ | I↑ ↓ |
| Wage | H ↑ ↓ | I↑ ↓ |
| Education | H ↑ | I↑ ↓ |
| Wealth | H ↑ | I↑ |
| Married or cohabiting | H ↑ | I↑ ↓ |
| Divorced | H ↓ | I↓ |
| Children | H ↑ ↓ | I↓ |
| Sex | H ↓ ↑ | I↑ ↓ |

Note
a It should be observed that our 'mixed' consumption and investment demand-for-health model
produces less powerful predictions for health investments (and for the wage effect on health capital) than the pure investment model, estimated, for instance, by Grossman (1972a).

In Table 5.1, we summarize our predictions concerning the effect on the
demand for health and health investments.

## The empirical model

In a first best empirical approach we would want to estimate a model that simultaneously reflects both spouses' health behaviour. Thus, we would like to estimate a
simultaneous equations system made up by one demand-for-health equation and
one health-investment equation for each spouse. Then it would be possible to model
the importance of different family structures for the decisions concerning health,
which are made within the family. However, the available data set do not allow this
approach, since it does not include any information on the health-related behaviour
of the respondent's spouse. Instead, we are restricted to model the health-related
behaviour of the respondent alone. This is not necessarily such a big disadvantage
compared to the first best approach, since we know from the first-order conditions,
(5.4), that the spouses' health levels are connected in a specific way.

Following Grossman (2000) and using our continuous-variable theoretical
model, we develop a discrete-variable empirical model. Grossman (2000) derives
a model with costs of adjustment of the stock of health capital, which implies an
empirical demand-for-health-equation of the following structure:

$$H_t = \alpha X_t + \beta H_{t-1} + \gamma H_{t+1} + u_t, \tag{5.6}$$

where $H_t$ is the desired stock of health capital, $H_{t-1}$ and $H_{t+1}$ are the stocks of health
capital in period $t-1$ and period $t+1$, respectively.[8] $X_t$ reflects the importance of
the variables appearing in the first-order conditions for a solution to the family's
optimization problem, (5.4) and (5.5). Since we expect the family structure to
influence the decisions that the respondent makes, $X_t$ will, for example, contain the
number of children and marital status. Grossman derives explicit expressions for

the parameters, $\alpha$, $\beta$, and $\gamma$, and shows that the effects of both the lagged and the future stock of health capital on the current stock of health capital are positive.

The investment equation is obtained by replacing $H_t$ in the discrete-time version of (5.2) with the right-hand side of expression (5.6). This yields:[9]

$$I_{t-1} = \alpha X_t + (\beta - 1 + \delta_t)H_{t-1} + \gamma H_{t+1} + u_t. \tag{5.7}$$

The coefficient of the future stock should be positive, while the coefficient of the past stock should be negative. Our empirical model consists of equations (5.6) and (5.7).

## The data

A set of individual panel data was created by using data from the Swedish biannual survey of living conditions, ULF (Undersökningar av levnadsförhållanden). In ULF, a sample of approximately 16 000 people, aged 16–84 years old, are interviewed about their living conditions; the response rate is normally 80–85 per cent. Every survey covers a number of areas: housing, leisure, health, employment, education, private financial situation, and social relations. Responses are supplemented with individual data on income, taxes, and various transfer payments from administrative registers. There is also a rolling schedule of extra coverage of some specific areas every eight years. Thus, there was a both broader and deeper coverage of health-related variables in 1980/81, 1988/89, and 1996/97. Furthermore, approximately 40 per cent of the respondents are part of a rotating panel in which respondents are interviewed every eight years. Thus, the data set that we use have health-related and background information for a panel consisting of 3800 individuals for the years 1980/81, 1988/89, and 1996/97.

The choice of year of observation for each variable must be consistent with the empirical model, which consists of the demand-for-health equation (5.6), and the health investment equation (5.7). The year 1988/89 will represent time point $t$, 1980/81 will represent time point $t - 1$ and 1996/97 will represent time point $t + 1$. That is, we are interested in indicators for health in 1980/81, 1988/89 and 1996/97, and indicators for health investments in 1980/81. The explanatory variables, $X_t$, are present in the equations only at time point $t$, i.e. 1988/89. The exception will be the explanatory variable AGE, which is observed in 1980/81, which, for obvious reasons, is no problem.

Chosen variables are described below; means and standard deviations are reported in Table 5.2.

### Dependent variables

- SRH1 is a discrete variable, which reflects the self-assessed health in 1988/89. The respondent is asked to report his or her health status as one of three categories: 1, 2 or 3, where 3 is the category with highest health status. (All dependent discrete variables are later rescaled so that the ordinal scale begins at 0.) The variable was chosen in order to be an indicator of the unobserved variable health.

*Table 5.2* Descriptive statistics of panel data[a]

| Variable | Mean | Standard deviation |
|---|---|---|
| *Dependent variables* | | |
| SRH1 | 2.76 | 0.49 |
| EXERCISE | 2.78 | 1.19 |
| *Explanatory variables* | | |
| SRH0 | 2.79 | 0.46 |
| SRH2 | 2.71 | 0.48 |
| AGE | 39.65 | 14.53 |
| WAGE (SEK/h) | 54.27 | 48.29 |
| EDU | 3.01 | 1.63 |
| WEALTH | 2200 | 100 |
| COHAB | 0.76 | 0.43 |
| DIVORCED | 0.02 | 0.15 |
| CHILD | 0.22 | 0.42 |
| SEX | 0.48 | 0.50 |

Note
a The explanatory variables are later rescaled in order to facilitate convergence in the numerical maximization of the likelihood function.

- EXERCISE is a discrete variable, which can take the values 1, 2, 3, 4 or 5, where 1 indicates that the respondent does not exercise at all; 5 indicates that the respondent exercises regularly at least twice a week; and 2, 3 and 4 indicate exercise levels in between. The exercise levels are for 1980–81. The variable was chosen in order to indicate the level of health investments.

### Explanatory variables

- SRH0 is the same as SRH1 but for the years 1980/81.
- SRH2 is the same as SRH1 but for the years 1996/97. However, the coding is different: the respondent is asked to report his or her health status as one of five categories: 1, 2, 3, 4 or 5, where 1 is the highest health status. This variable is rescaled in the following way: 1 corresponds to the highest health status, 2 and 3 correspond to the second highest health status and 4 and 5 correspond to the lowest health level.
- AGE is the respondent's age in years in the panel 1980/81.
- WAGE is a continuous variable for the respondent's wage rate in 1988/89.
- EDU is achieved level of education 1988/89. This variable is a discrete variable and gives an index used by Statistics Sweden to reflect the level of education.
- WEALTH is the respondent's income from capital in 1988/89. In hundreds of SEK.
- COHAB is a dummy variable, which takes the value 1, if the respondent was either married or cohabiting in 1988/1989 and 0 otherwise.
- DIVORCED is a dummy variable, which takes the value 1, if the respondent was cohabiting *and* had the marital status divorced in 1988/89 and 0 otherwise.

- CHILD is a dummy variable, which takes the value 1, if the respondent has children born between 1980 and 1989 and 0 otherwise.
- SEX reflects sex: 0 corresponds to the respondent being a female and 1 corresponds to the respondent being a male.

## The econometric method and model specification

As an indicator for the unobserved variable health, we chose self-assessed health. As health investments indicator we chose the level of exercise conducted by the respondent. Both indicators are reported as ordinal rankings, and we estimate an ordered probit model for each indicator. The ordered probit model is based on the following specification:

$$y_i^* = \eta' x_i + \varepsilon_i, \tag{5.8}$$

where $\mu'$ is the vector of parameters to be estimated and $\varepsilon_i \sim N(0, 1)$. $y_i^*$ is the unobservable dependent variable. The observed counterpart is denoted $y_i$ and specified as follows:

$$y_i = \begin{cases} 0 & \text{if} \quad y^* \le \mu_0 \\ 1 & \text{if} \quad \mu_0 < y^* \le \mu_1 \\ 2 & \text{if} \quad \mu_1 < y^* \le \mu_0, \\ \cdot \\ \cdot \\ \cdot \\ J & \text{if} \quad y^* > \mu_{J-1} \end{cases} \tag{5.9}$$

where the $\mu'$'s are threshold parameters. To calculate marginal effects, we first notice that in the ordered probit model there are several conditional mean functions. Hence, we consider the effect on the probability of achieving a particular value of the indicator variable from changes in the explanatory variables. These effects are:

$$\frac{\partial \text{prob}(y_i = 0)}{\partial x} = -\phi(\mu_0 - \eta' x)\eta$$

$$\frac{\partial \text{prob}(y_i = 1)}{\partial x} = (\phi(\mu_0 - \eta' x) - \phi(\mu_1 - \eta' x))\eta$$

$$\frac{\partial \text{prob}(y_i = 2)}{\partial x} = (\phi(\mu_1 - \eta' x) - \phi(\mu_2 - \eta' x))\eta$$

$$\cdot$$
$$\cdot$$

$$\frac{\partial \text{prob}(y_i = J)}{\partial x} = \phi(\mu_{J-1} - \eta' x)\eta, \tag{5.10}$$

where $\phi$ is the normal distribution function.[10]

## Empirical results and discussion

We begin this section by presenting our results and move on to a discussion in which we relate our results to results obtained in previous studies of the demand for health and health investments.

We present the results in Tables 5.3 and 5.4. The estimated marginal effects in the health equation are reported in Table 5.3 and the estimated marginal effects for the investment equation in Table 5.4.[11] The empirical results are summed up in Table 5.5.

Concerning the effects of age on health status the results are as expected: the probability of bad health increases with age. However, the demand for health investments decreases with age. The explanation for this may be that we use exercise and not health care as the indicator for health investments.

The estimated marginal effect on health investments from a change in the wage rate was not significant. However, the estimated marginal effect on the demand for health from changes in the wage rate was positive. This implies that the investment aspects of health capital outweighed the consumption aspects; a rise in the wage rate would decrease the net cost of health capital. This constitutes mixed evidence for or against a pure investment model. Grossman (1972b, pp. 42–3; 2000, pp. 379–80) offers two empirical procedures for assessing whether the

*Table 5.3* Marginal effects for ordered probit model of the health equation. Self-assessed health as indicator of health[a,b]

| Variable | Srh1 = 0 (low) | | Srh1 = 1 (medium) | | Srh1 = 2 (high) | |
|---|---|---|---|---|---|---|
| | Marginal effects | p-values | Marginal effects | p-values | Marginal effects | p-values |
| Constant | −2.0E−4 | (0.482) | 0.002 | (0.478) | −0.002 | (0.479) |
| Srh0 | **−0.018*** | (0.000) | **−0.160*** | (0.000) | **0.178*** | (0.000) |
| Srh2 | **−0.017*** | (0.000) | **− 0.148*** | (0.000) | **0.164*** | (0.000) |
| Age | **2.0E−4*** | (0.000) | 0.002 | (0.160) | **−0.002*** | (0.001) |
| Wage | **−2.464** | (0.069) | −21.726 | (0.311) | **24.190** | (0.066) |
| Education | **−0.019*** | (0.000) | **−0.164** | (0.076) | **0.183*** | (0.000) |
| Wealth | **−0.017*** | (0.041) | −0.153 | (0.283) | **0.170*** | (0.040) |
| Cohab | **−0.002** | (0.089) | −0.016 | (0.331) | **0.018*** | (0.090) |
| Divorced | 0.004 | (0.174) | 0.031 | (0.380) | −0.035 | (0.175) |
| Child | −0.002 | (0.140) | −0.018 | (0.357) | 0.020 | (0.132) |
| Sex | **−0.002** | (0.087) | −0.015 | (0.332) | **0.016** | (0.092) |

Notes
a Notice that in order for LIMDEP to work we had to rescale the dependent variables. 1 has been assigned the value 0, 2 has been assigned the value 1 and so on.
b Bold indicates that the estimated coefficient is significant at the 10 per cent level and bold and * indicate that the coefficient is significant at the 5 per cent level.

Table 5.4 Marginal effects for ordered probit model of the health investment equation. Exercise as indicator of health investments[a]

| Variable | Exercise = 0 (none) | | Exercise = 1 | | Exercise = 2 | | Exercise = 3 | | Exercise = 4 (regularly) | |
|---|---|---|---|---|---|---|---|---|---|---|
| | Marginal effect | p-value | Marginal effect | p-value | Marginal effect | p-value | Marginal effect | p-value | Marginal effect | p-value |
| Constant | **-0.126*** | (0.000) | **-0.182*** | (0.000) | **0.042*** | (0.000) | **0.108*** | (0.000) | **0.158*** | (0.000) |
| Srh0 | **-0.047*** | (0.000) | **-0.068*** | (0.000) | **0.016*** | (0.000) | **0.040*** | (0.000) | **0.059*** | (0.000) |
| Srh2 | **-0.020*** | (0.000) | **-0.029*** | (0.000) | **0.007*** | (0.000) | **0.017*** | (0.000) | **0.025*** | (0.000) |
| Age | **0.001*** | (0.000) | **0.002*** | (0.000) | **-4.0E-4*** | (0.000) | **-0.001*** | (0.000) | **-0.002*** | (0.000) |
| Wage | 0.951 | (0.434) | 1.380 | (0.434) | -0.317 | (0.443) | -0.814 | (0.357) | -1.201 | (0.434) |
| Education | **-0.139*** | (0.000) | **-0.202*** | (0.000) | **0.046*** | (0.000) | **0.120*** | (0.000) | **0.176*** | (0.000) |
| Wealth | -0.030 | (0.197) | -0.043 | (-0.197) | 0.010 | (0.232) | **0.026*** | (0.029) | 0.038 | (0.197) |
| Cohab | 0.002 | (0.389) | 0.003 | (0.388) | -6.0E-4 | (0.409) | -0.002 | (0.269) | -0.002 | (0.389) |
| Divorced | 0.010 | (0.282) | 0.015 | (0.283) | -0.003 | (0.311) | **-0.009** | (0.100) | -0.013 | (0.282) |
| Child | **0.026*** | (0.000) | **0.038*** | (0.000) | **-0.009*** | (0.002) | **-0.023*** | (0.000) | **-0.033*** | (0.000) |
| Sex | **-0.015*** | (0.006) | **-0.022*** | (0.006) | **0.005*** | (0.013) | **0.013*** | (0.000) | **0.019*** | (0.006) |

Note

a Bold indicates that the estimated coefficient is significant at the 10 per cent level and bold and * indicate that the coefficient is significant at the 5 per cent level.

*Table 5.5* Estimated effects on the demand for health and health investments from changes in independent variables

| Variable | Health | Health investments |
|---|---|---|
| Age | ↓ | ↓ |
| Wage | ↑ | n.s. |
| Education | ↑ | ↑ |
| Wealth | ↑ | ↑ |
| Married or cohabiting | ↑ | n.s. |
| Divorced | n.s. | n.s. |
| Children | n.s. | ↓ |
| Sex | ↑ | ↑ |

investment model gives a more adequate representation of people's health behaviour than the consumption model. *First*, the wage rate would have a positive effect on the demand for health. *Second*, health capital would have zero wealth elasticity in the pure investment model. Certainly, the wage rate had a positive effect on health capital, which is consistent with the first test, but also wealth had a significant, positive effect, so the second test failed in our estimations.[12]

The result concerning the effects of education on the demand for health was as expected: higher education decreased the probability of belonging to the lowest health status. A rise in education increased the probability that the respondent maintained a high level of exercise. That is, education and health investments were positively linked.

The prediction that wealth is positively linked to both demand for health and health investments is confirmed by the marginal effects on wealth at the lowest and the highest health levels in the demand for health equation and by the marginal effect on health investment at the second highest investment level. The signs imply that as wealth increases, the probability that the respondent belongs to the lowest health level decreases and the probability that the respondent belongs to the highest health and health investment level increases. Our result supports Ettner (1996), who found a significant and positive relationship between self-assessed health status and income.

In the theoretical discussion we predicted that those married or cohabiting have higher health status. This prediction was confirmed, as the marginal effects on the demand for health were significant (at the 10 per cent level). The prediction that the experience of divorce implies smaller amounts of health capital and health investments was only partly supported. The marginal effects associated with the demand for health equation were not significant. However, the marginal effects associated with the health investment equation were, at one level, significant, which imply that divorce decreases health investments. This is consistent with Fuchs (1974), who states that in all (developed) countries being married lowers death rates.[13] This result may also be explained by selection effects, i.e. that those marrying are healthier than the average.

The hypothesis concerning the effects on the demand for health and health investments of children predicted that the demand for health would increase or decrease and the demand for health investments would decrease. Certainly, the marginal effects associated with the demand for health equation were not significant, but the level of health investments decreased with the presence of children. Children enhancing the efficiency of the production of gross health investments may explain this. That is, in the presence of children it will take a smaller amount of inputs in the production of gross health investments in order to produce a given amount of gross health investments.

The probability of having a high self-assessed health status increased if the respondent was a man; the marginal effects of *sex* associated with the demand for health equation indicated that men are healthier than women. Also, the probability of maintaining a high exercise level increased, if the respondent was a man. The marginal effects on *sex* associated with the investment equation indicated that men invest more in their health than women do.

In Grossman's empirical formulation of his model, it was implicitly assumed that individuals adjust instantaneously to their desired health stock. Theoretically, this assumption is manifested in the coefficient of the lagged health stock, $Srh0$, being zero. That is, the health stock is both demanded and achieved at the same point in time, and it is perfectly determined by factors other than the health stock at previous points in time. The assumption of instantaneous adjustment was rejected, as the estimated marginal effects of the lagged stock of health capital were not zero.[14] This result confirms the result obtained by Wagstaff (1993).

Grossman (2000) derives a cost-of-adjustment model and shows that all coefficients are expected to be positive, besides the coefficient of the lagged stock of health capital in the investment equation, which should be negative. When we estimated our demand-for-health equation, we found a positive effect of both the lagged and the future stock of health capital. The estimated marginal effects in the investment equation were also positive for both the lagged and the future stock of health capital. There are at least three explanations for this difference between the theoretically predicted values and the empirically derived values of the coefficients in our estimation. First, the assumption of independent explanatory variables may not be fulfilled, i.e. we may experience multicollinearity in that the lagged stock of health capital and the future stock of health capital may be correlated. Second, lagged and future stocks of health capital may be endogenous and correlated with the disturbance term in the demand for health equation. The third explanation concerns the fact that the panel we use only allowed us to measure the stocks of health capital (and other variables) with an eight-year interval.

Let us briefly compare our results with previously obtained results on the demand for health and health investments in some of the most important studies.[15] Empirical studies can be roughly divided into two groups: those that used cross-sectional data and those that used longitudinal data. Of the first kind are, for example, Grossman (1972b) and Wagstaff (1986). Grossman used US data and Wagstaff the 1976 Danish welfare study. Grossman estimated reduced form demand functions for health and medical care using two-stage least square, while Wagstaff estimated both reduced form and structural form demand functions for health and health care using the MIMIC (multiple indicators–multiple causes) technique. Grossman (2000) argued that the most important result in his study (1972b) was that education and wage rates had positive and significant effects on the health demanded, and that health decreased and the demand for medical care increased with age.

Studies that used longitudinal data (or panel data) are, for example, Wagstaff (1993), Sundberg (1996), and Bolin *et al.* (2001a). Wagstaff used the Danish study, which was fitted to a MIMIC model. He did not include any wage rate variable, instead household income was used as an explanatory variable. The result was that household income had no significant effect on the demand for health investments, but had a positive and significant effect on the demand for health. In the same way, education was positively and significantly linked to the level of health and the demand for health investments. Regarding age, only the coefficient in the demand for health equation for those over 41 was significant, in which case the sign was negative. Regarding education, the coefficient in the demand for health equation for those under 41 and the coefficient in the investment equation were significant. Wagstaff's findings on the effects of wage rate, education, and age confirm the results obtained by Grossman. Our own results on the effect of age and education on the demand for health and health investments confirm these previously obtained results.

Health and health investments are unobservable variables. Thus, in order to estimate the empirical Grossman model, proxy variables for health and health investments have to be used. In this chapter, we utilized but one possible set of proxy variables. In order to examine the robustness of the empirical results of the demand-for-health model, Bolin *et al.* (2001a) made estimations for several different empirical representations of health capital and health investments. They found that the empirical results of the demand-for-health model were qualitatively similar regardless of indicators used.

## Summary and conclusion

In this chapter we estimated a dynamic cost-of-adjustment model of the demand for health and health investments within a household or family production framework. Our results confirm our predictions regarding age and education. Instantaneous adjustment between desired and actual stocks of health capital was rejected. This is certainly a result in line with Wagstaff (1993), but his estimates were biased, since his empirical model did not take into account the impact of future health stocks on present health and past investments. To the best of our knowledge, our empirical model is the first attempt to estimate a correctly specified cost-of-adjustment model, including three years of observation for each individual.

One main objective of this chapter was to examine the importance of the household or family structure for the demand for health and health investments. Married or cohabiting individuals were found to be healthier than single individuals. This is consistent with Becker's theory of the family, which asserts that one two-person household creates more resources than two one-person households do because of specialization according to comparative advantages. Our finding is also in line with most previous empirical studies.[16]

However, we found no significant difference in health investments when we have compared single individuals to those married or cohabiting. One tentative explanation for this result is that the presence of a family increases the productivity of gross health investments and that this outweighs the increase in the demand for health, i.e. the change on the supply side is larger than the change on the demand side. This is an important and interesting area for future research, since it might be the case that information on *both* spouses' health-related behaviour would produce different results.

In our theoretical discussion we argued that divorce might be positively correlated to strategic behaviour in a new family. If this is the case, gains accruing, as a result of specialization, will be diluted. Our results imply that those who are divorced invest less in health. This, on the other hand, can be interpreted as support for Becker's theory of the family, and corroborates the results of previous empirical studies.[17]

The presence of children was found to increase the demand for health and to decrease the demand for health investments, a result that implies that children shift the MEC schedule upwards. This means that children raise the marginal efficiency of a given amount of health capital. At the same time, household production may become more time consuming in the presence of children, i.e. the opportunity cost of making gross investments in health increases and, hence, lowers health investments. Our result implies that the change on the demand side is larger than the change on the supply side.

We found differences in the demand for health between men and women: Swedish men are healthier than Swedish women. Also, men were found to invest more in their health than women do. These results are rather surprising. One possible explanation for the result concerning the health investments is that men exercise more often than women do. In the pure investment model another explanation would be that, for a given level of health capital, a gross investment reduces sick time more for men than for women. This also implies that men hold more health capital than women do, something which is implied by our results.

## Notes

We are especially grateful to Michael Grossman and Jes Søgaard for comments on earlier versions of the paper, and to Peter Zweifel and other participants at the 19th Arne Ryde Symposium 'Individual Decisions for Health', Lund 27–28 August 1999. The financial support from the Vårdal Foundation to this project is gratefully acknowledged. The development and use of the database were facilitated by research grants to Björn Lindgren from the Swedish Social Research Council, the Vårdal Foundation, the Swedish National Institute of Public Health, and the Medical Faculty of Lund University.

1 The choice of empirical representations of health capital and health investments is constrained by the fact that health capital and health investments are latent variables. Bolin *et al.* (2001a) discussed different approaches to handle this problem and performed estimates of the empirical model developed in this chapter for different empirical representations of health capital and health investments. The empirical results appeared

qualitatively similar, irrespective of indicator used for health capital. However, different empirical representations of health investments reflect different inputs to the production of gross health investments. Thus, since the inputs are not perfect substitutes, empirical results were expected to be more sensitive to the choice of empirical representation of health investments, which they also were. In their study, Bolin *et al.* (2001a) argue that physical exercise probably is a better representation of inputs in the gross health investment production function than, for instance, medical care or days of absence from work.

2  Notice that this is analogous to altruism. Becker's famous rotten kid theorem states that even though a family member may be nonaltruistic, he will behave in the interest of the family. Hence, altruism or 'consumption' of other family members' health is by no means a necessary condition for the existence of incentives for producing health of other family members.

3  The price of health investments, $p_t^I$, is assumed to be decreasing in education since a more educated individual in general may utilize the investments more efficiently. In our model, however, we have assumed that the spouses have identical prices, and hence, the relation between the spouses' stocks of health is not dependent on the price.

4  Notice that the costate variables are very similar to the Lagrange variables. There are, however, differences: the costate variables are connected to the equations of movement of the state variable while the Lagrange multipliers are connected to the constraints.

5  The fact that one or both spouses supply time to the labour market implies that *both* the family and the employer(s) have incentives of investing in the health of the spouse(s). This is analysed in Bolin *et al.* (2002b).

6  Notice that this does not necessarily imply that the family equalizes the stock of health capital among family members. Rather, how the family values an investment in the health of a particular family member in relation to the same investment in another family member's health is dependent on relative wage rates, effectiveness of investments, and relative rates of depreciation.

7  The case when the family is the producer of health and the spouses act strategically is analysed in Bolin *et al.* (2002a).

8  In Grossman's (2000) formulation, both the equation for $H_t$ and $I_t$ depend also on $X_{t-1}$. However, we are not able to separate empirically between $X_t$ and $X_{t-1}$. Attempts to do so lead to problems with multicollinearity.

9  Notice that this produces an equation with the same disturbance term as in (5.6).

10  All calculations were performed using the LIMDEP computer program. For the ordered probit model, however, LIMDEP does not provide the covariance matrix for the marginal effects. So these matrices were calculated by us (one matrix for each column of marginal effects). In general, the covariance matrix for the marginal effects can be calculated according to:

$$\left[ \frac{\partial M}{\partial \hat{\gamma}} \right] H \left[ \frac{\partial M}{\partial \hat{\gamma}} \right]',$$

where $H$ is the covariance matrix of the estimated parameters, $M$ is the vector of marginal effects, and $\hat{\gamma} = (\hat{\eta}_1, \ldots, \hat{\eta}_N, \mu_1, \ldots, \mu_{J-1})$, where $\hat{\eta}_1, \ldots, \hat{\eta}_N$ are the estimated parameters, and $\mu_1, \ldots, \mu_{J-1}$ are the threshold values which are also estimated and, hence, contribute to the variance of the marginal effects. Thus the expressions for the marginal effects have to be differentiated not only subject to the estimated parameters but also subject to the threshold values.

11  Besides the empirical specifications discussed here, we tried to include also the wealth and wage of the respondent's spouse. In all cases, the estimated coefficients for these variables were close to zero and, hence, left out.

12  Health would also have a positive wealth effect in the pure investment model for people who are not in the labour force. This may be another explanation to our finding, since there were a substantial number of retired people in our data set. Grossman's own

empirical estimations, however, were confined to members of the labour force (Grossman, 1972b).

13 There are a number of studies that examine the interaction between marital status and health. For example, see Fuchs (1974), Taubman and Rosen (1982), Ellwood and Kane (1990), and Smith and Waitzman (1994).

14 The results in Bolin *et al.* (2001a) corroborate this result.

15 A comprehensive survey of empirical studies is provided by Grossman (2000).

16 See the studies referred to in note 13.

17 In addition to the studies referred to in note 13 there are several studies, which analyse the relationship between health and divorce, e.g. Gähler (1999). Bolin *et al.* (2002a) survey this literature.

# References

Becker, G.S., 1964. *Human Capital*. New York: Columbia University Press (for NBER).

Becker, G.S., 1965. A theory of the allocation of time. *Economic Journal* 75:493–517.

Becker, G.S., 1973. A theory of marriage: part 1. *Journal of Political Economy* 81:813–46.

Becker, G.S., 1974. A theory of marriage: part 2. *Journal of Political Economy*. 82(suppl.):S11–S26.

Becker, G.S., 1991. *A Treatise on the Family*. Enlarged edition. Cambridge MA: Harvard University Press.

Bolin, K. and Pålsson, A., 2000. Male and female net wealth – the importance of the family structure. Working paper, Department of Economics, Lund University.

Bolin, K., Jacobson, L. and Lindgren, B., 2001a. How stable are the empirical results of the Grossman model? Testing different indicators of health capital and health investments in Sweden 1980/81, 1988/89, and 1996/97. *Studies in Health Economics* 36. Lund University Centre for Health Economics (LUCHE), Lund University.

Bolin, K., Jacobson, L. and Lindgren, B., 2001b. The family as the producer of health – when spouses are Nash bargainers. *Journal of Health Economics* 20:349–62.

Bolin, K., Jacobson, L. and Lindgren, B., 2002a. The family as the producer of health – when spouses act strategically. *Journal of Health Economics* 21:475–95.

Bolin, K., Jacobson, L. and Lindgren, B., 2002b. Employer investments in employee health. Implications for the family as health producer. *Journal of Health Economics* 21:563–83.

Cropper, M.L., 1977. Health, investment in health, and occupational choice. *Journal of Political Economy* 85:1273–94.

Cropper, M.L., 1981. Measuring the benefits from reduced morbidity. *American Economic Review* 71:235–40.

Dardanoni, V. and Wagstaff, A., 1987. Uncertainty, inequalities in health, and the demand for health. *Journal of Health Economics* 6:283–90.

Dardanoni, V. and Wagstaff, A., 1990. Uncertainty and the demand for medical care. *Journal of Health Economics* 9:23–38.

Dowie, J., 1975. The portfolio approach to health behaviour. *Social Science and Medicine* 9:619–31.

Ehrlich, I., 2000. Uncertain lifetime, life protection, and the value of life saving. *Journal of Health Economics* 19:341–67.

Ehrlich, I., 2001. Erratum to 'Uncertain lifetime, life protection, and the value of life saving'. *Journal of Health Economics* 20:459–60.

Ehrlich, I. and Chuma, H., 1987. The demand for life: theory and applications. In: Radnizky, G. and Bernholtz, P. (eds), *Economic Imperialism*. New York: Paragon.

Ehrlich, I. and Chuma, H., 1990. A model of the demand for longevity and the value of life extensions. *Journal of Political Economy* 98:761–82.

Ellwood, D. and Kane, T., 1990. The American way of aging: an event history analysis. In: Wise, D. (ed.), *Issues in the Economics of Aging*. Chicago: University of Chicago Press.

Ettner, S., 1996. New evidence on the relationship between income and health. *Journal of Health Economics* 15:67–85.

Forster, M., 2001. The meaning of death: some simulations of a model of healthy and unhealthy behaviour. *Journal of Health Economics* 20:613–38.

Fuchs, V., 1974. *Who Shall Live? Health, Economics and Social Choice*. New York: Basic Books.

Gähler, M., 1999. Att skiljas är att dö en smula – skilsmässa och psykisk ohälsa hos svenska kvinnor och män. *Sociologisk forskning* 36:4–39.

Grossman, M., 1972a. On the concept of health capital and the demand for health. *Journal of Political Economy* 80:223–55.

Grossman, M., 1972b. *The Demand for Health: A Theoretical and Empirical Investigation*. New York: Columbia University Press for the National Bureau of Economic Research.

Grossman, M., 2000. The human capital model of the demand for health. In: Culyer, A.J. and Newhouse J.P. (eds), *Handbook of Health Economics*. Amsterdam: Elsevier, pp. 347–408.

Jacobson, L., 2000. The family as producer of health – an extension of the Grossman model. *Journal of Health Economics* 19:611–37.

Lancaster, K.J., 1966. A new approach to consumer theory. *Journal of Political Economy* 74:132–57.

Liljas, B., 1998. The demand for health with uncertainty and insurance. *Journal of Health Economics* 17:153–70.

Liljas, B., 2000. Insurance and imperfect financial markets in Grossman's demand for health model – a reply to Tabata and Ohkusa. *Journal of Health Economics* 19:821–7.

Liljas, B., 2002. An exploratory study on the demand for health, lifetime income, and imperfect financial markets. Chapter 2 in this volume.

Muurinen, J.M., 1982a. *An Economic Model of Health Behaviour – With Empirical Applications to Finnish Health Survey Data*. Department of Economics and Related Studies, University of York. (Ph.D. thesis)

Muurinen, J.M., 1982b. Demand for health: a generalised Grossman model. *Journal of Health Economics* 1:5–28.

Picone, G., Uribe, M. and Wilson, R.M., 1998. The effect of uncertainty on the demand for medical care, health capital, and wealth. *Journal of Health Economics* 17:171–85.

Ried, M., 1998. Comparative dynamic analysis of the full Grossman model. *Journal of Health Economics* 17:383–425.

Selden, T., 1993. Uncertainty and health care spending by the poor: the health capital model revisited. *Journal of Health Economics* 12:109–15.

Smith, K. and N. Waitzman, 1994. Double jeopardy: interaction effects of marital and poverty status on the risk of mortality. *Demography* 31:487–93.

Sundberg, G., 1996. The demand for health and medical care in Sweden. In: Sundberg, G. (ed.), *Essays on Health Economics*. Economic Studies 26. Uppsala University: Department of Economics, 13–77. (Ph.D. thesis)

Taubman, P. and Rosen, S., 1982. Healthiness, education and marital status. In: Fuchs, V. (ed.), *Economic Aspects of Health*. Chicago: University of Chicago Press.

Wagstaff, A., 1986. The demand for health: some new empirical evidence. *Journal of Health Economics* 5:195–233.

Wagstaff, A., 1993. The demand for health: an empirical reformulation of the Grossman model. *Health Economics* 2:189–98.

Zweifel, P. and Breyer, F., 1997. *Health Economics*. New York: Oxford University Press.

# 6  The determinants of health in Sweden

*Ulf-G. Gerdtham, Magnus Johannesson,
and Bengt Jönsson*

## Introduction

The demand-for-health model by Grossman (1972a,b) has become a cornerstone in the field of health economics.[1] The model has been tested in a number of empirical applications (Grossman, 1972a; Cropper, 1981; Wagstaff, 1986, 1993; van Doorslaer, 1987; Leu and Gerfin, 1992; Erbsland *et al.*, 1995; Nocera and Zweifel, 1998). An important problem in the empirical analyses has been the unobservability of health capital (health status). Measures of health status have been constructed based on various health indicators, e.g. various health problems and symptoms. This has led to problems in interpreting the resulting health measure and the size of the regression coefficients in the estimated demand for health equations.

To overcome these problems Gerdtham *et al.* (1999) recently carried out an analysis with some direct measures of overall health status from a dataset from Uppsala County in Sweden. Two continuous measures of health status based on the rating scale method and the time trade-off method were used.[2] A categorical measure of overall health status was also used that divided health status into five categories: poor health, fair health, good health, very good health and excellent health.[3] The demand for health was estimated as a function of age, gender, income, education, being single, the distance to the health care provider, unemployment, overweight, smoking, alcohol consumption, and sporting activities. Especially the categorical health measure yielded results consistent with theoretical predictions. In the regression equation with the categorical health measure the effects of all variables were in the expected direction, with the exception of alcohol consumption that had a positive effect on health. The effect of gender and unemployment did not reach statistical significance.

Gerdtham and Johannesson (1999) carried out a further study based on a categorical health measure that divided health status into three categories. That study was based on data from a random sample of the Swedish population, the Level of Living Survey (LNU) from 1991. The demand for health was estimated as a function of age, gender, income, being single, unemployment, overweight, living in big cities, and the initial inherited stock of health. According to the results the demand for health increased with income, education and the initial inherited stock of health and decreased with age, male gender, overweight, living in big cities, and being single. The effect of unemployment did not reach statistical significance. The results were thus consistent with the results of Gerdtham *et al.* (1999), with the exception that gender had a significant effect.

In this chapter we provide some new results on the determinants of health in Sweden. The analysis is based on pooled data from Statistics Sweden's Survey of Living Conditions (the ULF survey), and the data set contains over 40,000 individuals. Health status is measured by a categorical measure of overall health status, and an ordered probit model is used to econometrically estimate the demand-for-health equation. In the next section we describe the data and the variables used, and in the following section the estimation methods are outlined. The penultimate section reports the results. In the final section we compare the results to our two previous studies in Sweden and provide some concluding remarks.

## Data and hypotheses

The analysis is based on data from Statistic Sweden's Survey of Living Conditions (the ULF survey) (Statistics Sweden, 1997) which have been linked to income data from the National Income Tax Statistics. Every year, Statistics Sweden conducts systematic surveys of living conditions, in the form of one-hour personal interviews with randomly selected adults aged 16–84 years. We use pooled data from the annual interviews conducted in 1980–1986 for all the subjects aged 20–84 years at the time of the interview. We exclude subjects younger than 20 years of age, to avoid having subjects that are still in high school (most people finish high school when they are 19 in Sweden). The total sample consists of 43,898 individuals. After correcting for missing values, the sample is reduced to 41,024 individuals. In Table 6.1, the variables used are defined and in Table 6.2 summary statistics for the variables are given.

### *Dependent variable*

The dependent variable is the stock of health (the health status) which is measured by a categorical health measure. In the categorical health rating question the individuals rated their own current health status on a three-point scale (0 = poor health, 1 = fair health, 2 = good health). This type of categorical health measure has been shown to capture important information about the individual's health and to be an important predictor of mortality (Connelly *et al.*, 1989; Wannamethee and Shaper, 1991; Kaplan and Camacho, 1983; Idler and Kasl, 1991).

### *Independent variables*[4]

#### *Income*

We use four different income measures in four separate regression analyses to test the sensitivity of the results to different income measures. The source of the income data is the National Income Tax Statistics, linked to the ULF data. All

| Variable | Definition |
|---|---|
| *Dependent variables* | |
| HEALTH | Assessment of own health on a three point scale (0 = poor health, 1 = fair health, 2 = good health) |
| *Independent variables* | |
| MALE | = 1 if male |
| AGE1 | = 1 if age is 20–34 years |
| AGE2 | = 1 if age is 35–49 years |
| AGE3 | = 1 if age is 50–64 years |
| AGE4 | = 1 if age is 65–74 years |
| AGE5 | = 1 if age is 75–84 years |
| CHILD1 | = 1 if no children in the household |
| CHILD2 | = 1 if 1 child in the household |
| CHILD3 | = 1 if 2 children in the household |
| CHILD4 | = 1 if ≥3 children in the household |
| IM1 | = 1 if born in Sweden and the parents are Swedish citizens |
| IM2 | = 1 if born abroad and the parents are current or previous foreign citizens |
| IM3 | = 1 if born in Sweden and the parents are current or previous foreign citizens |
| SINGLE | = 1 if the individual is not married or cohabiting |
| EDUC1 | = 1 if less than high school education |
| EDUC2 | = 1 if high school education |
| EDUC3 | = 1 if university education |
| UNEMP | = 1 if unemployed |
| PINC1–5 | = five dummy variables for the quintiles of the distribution of gross annual personal income (SEK 62,664; 112,714; 155,400; 196,474). |
| HINC1–5 | = five dummy variables for the quintiles of the distribution of the annual disposable household income per adult person in the household (SEK 72,177; 92,806; 110,720; 131,461) |
| FINC1–5 | = five dummy variables for the quintiles of the distribution of the disposable househould income per adult person in the household and the annuity of household net wealth per adult person in the household (SEK 84,367; 104,537; 121,908; 145,994) |
| LINC1–5 | = five dummy variables for the quintiles of the distribution of the annuity of lifetime dispos-able income and the annuity of household net wealth per adult person in the household (SEK 85,233; 106,056; 124,190; 147,557) |
| PPROP1–5 | = five dummy variables for taxable personal net wealth. The dummy variables correspond to zero net wealth and the four quartiles of the distribution of positive net wealth (SEK 49,022; 135,680; 305,274) |
| PROP1–5 | = five dummy variables for taxable household net wealth per adult person in the household. The dummy variables correspond to zero net wealth and the quartiles of the distribution of net wealth (SEK 51,112; 129,120; 252,400) |
| Y80–86 | = 1 if interviewed in 1980–1986 |

*Table 6.2* Sample descriptive statistics (N = Number of observations)

| Variables | Mean | Sd | Min | Max | N |
|---|---|---|---|---|---|
| HEALTH | 1.690 | 0.578 | 0 | 2 | 41,024 |
| MALE | 0.495 | 0.500 | 0 | 1 | 41,024 |
| AGE2 | 0.280 | 0.449 | 0 | 1 | 41,024 |
| AGE3 | 0.225 | 0.418 | 0 | 1 | 41,024 |
| AGE4 | 0.138 | 0.345 | 0 | 1 | 41,024 |
| AGE5 | 0.058 | 0.233 | 0 | 1 | 41,024 |
| CHILD2 | 0.150 | 0.357 | 0 | 1 | 41,024 |
| CHILD3 | 0.159 | 0.366 | 0 | 1 | 41,024 |
| CHILD4 | 0.056 | 0.230 | 0 | 1 | 41,024 |
| IM2 | 0.080 | 0.271 | 0 | 1 | 41,024 |
| IM3 | 0.007 | 0.086 | 0 | 1 | 41,024 |
| SINGLE | 0.310 | 0.463 | 0 | 1 | 41,024 |
| PINC2 | 0.196 | 0.397 | 0 | 1 | 41,024 |
| PINC3 | 0.206 | 0.404 | 0 | 1 | 41,024 |
| PINC4 | 0.210 | 0.407 | 0 | 1 | 41,024 |
| PINC5 | 0.209 | 0.407 | 0 | 1 | 41,024 |
| PPROP2 | 0.150 | 0.357 | 0 | 1 | 41,024 |
| PPROP3 | 0.146 | 0.353 | 0 | 1 | 41,024 |
| PPROP4 | 0.146 | 0.353 | 0 | 1 | 41,024 |
| PPROP5 | 0.148 | 0.355 | 0 | 1 | 41,024 |
| HINC2 | 0.194 | 0.395 | 0 | 1 | 41,024 |
| HINC3 | 0.207 | 0.405 | 0 | 1 | 41,024 |
| HINC4 | 0.210 | 0.408 | 0 | 1 | 41,024 |
| HINC5 | 0.211 | 0.408 | 0 | 1 | 41,024 |
| PROP2 | 0.178 | 0.383 | 0 | 1 | 41,024 |
| PROP3 | 0.173 | 0.378 | 0 | 1 | 41,024 |
| PROP4 | 0.173 | 0.379 | 0 | 1 | 41,024 |
| PROP5 | 0.174 | 0.379 | 0 | 1 | 41,024 |
| FINC2 | 0.200 | 0.400 | 0 | 1 | 41,024 |
| FINC3 | 0.204 | 0.403 | 0 | 1 | 41,024 |
| FINC4 | 0.206 | 0.404 | 0 | 1 | 41,024 |
| FINC5 | 0.203 | 0.402 | 0 | 1 | 41,024 |
| LINC2 | 0.199 | 0.400 | 0 | 1 | 41,024 |
| LINC3 | 0.205 | 0.403 | 0 | 1 | 41,024 |
| LINC4 | 0.207 | 0.405 | 0 | 1 | 41,024 |
| LINC5 | 0.204 | 0.403 | 0 | 1 | 41,024 |
| EDUC2 | 0.180 | 0.384 | 0 | 1 | 41,024 |
| EDUC3 | 0.406 | 0.491 | 0 | 1 | 41,024 |
| UNEMP | 0.024 | 0.152 | 0 | 1 | 41,024 |
| Y81 | 0.145 | 0.353 | 0 | 1 | 41,024 |
| Y82 | 0.162 | 0.368 | 0 | 1 | 41,024 |
| Y83 | 0.147 | 0.355 | 0 | 1 | 41,024 |
| Y84 | 0.160 | 0.366 | 0 | 1 | 41,024 |
| Y85 | 0.146 | 0.353 | 0 | 1 | 41,024 |
| Y86 | 0.105 | 0.307 | 0 | 1 | 41,024 |

income measures are converted to 1996 prices using the consumer price index. The two previous studies by Gerdtham *et al.* (1999) and Gerdtham and Johannesson (1999) used personal gross income as the income measure. Gerdtham *et al.* (1999) also used a dummy variable for if the person had a taxable net wealth. To be able to compare our results with these previous studies we carry out one analysis with personal gross income. In this analysis we also include a variable for the personal taxable net wealth (total taxable assets minus total liabilities).

A problem with using personal gross income is that it may be a poor reflection of private consumption for persons that are married/cohabitant. We are also interested in the disposable income rather than the gross pre tax income. In one analysis we therefore use disposable household income per adult person in the household. We thus assume that the household income is evenly divided between the spouses. In this analysis we also include the household taxable net wealth per adult person in the household.

The data recorded in the National Income Tax Statistics is the taxable net wealth that is used as the basis for the tax on wealth in Sweden. Due to the tax rules, not all assets are valued at the market value in the taxable net wealth measure. The measure thus systematically undervalues net wealth. The measure also depends on the tax rules at the time of the survey, which means that the values may not be strictly comparable between the different interview years. We therefore carry out an approximation of the net wealth at market value. To carry out this approximation we estimate the ratio between net wealth at market value and taxable net wealth for each interview year. We then multiply the taxable net wealth by this ratio for each person to get the net wealth of each person. As the measure of net wealth at market value we use the average value in an investigation about the average household net wealth at market value in the Swedish adult population in 1983, 1984, 1985 and 1988 (Statistics Sweden, 1990).[5] In one analysis, the annuity of household net wealth per adult person in the household is then added to the annual disposable household income per adult person in the household. The annuity is based on the average life-expectancy for men and women in different ages in Sweden and a 3 per cent discount rate (Statistics Sweden, 1998).

A problem with using the disposable income in a single year is that it may be an imperfect measure of the annual consumption. The income varies between years and individuals may borrow or save to even out the consumption between periods. In a sensitivity analysis, we therefore include an estimate of the annuity of the expected lifetime disposable income. The lifetime disposable income is estimated based on the percentage change in income with age in our sample. The percentage change in income with age is estimated separately for men and women and for the three education categories in our data set.[6] To estimate the lifetime income the average life-expectancy for men and women in Sweden is used (Statistics Sweden, 1998). A 3 per cent discount rate is used to estimate the lifetime disposable income in present value term. In one analysis, the annuity of the lifetime disposable income per adult person in the household is then added to the annuity of the household net wealth per adult person in the household.

In all analyses we use dummy variables rather than a continuous income variable to avoid making assumptions about the functional form. Income is divided into five groups of equal population size, and four dummy variables are included. In the analyses that includes net wealth as a separate variable, net wealth is also divided into five categories, and four dummy variables are included.[7] We expect the demand for health to increase with income and wealth.

Using income as an independent variable, introduces a potential endogeneity problem. According to the Grossman model health status affects labour income (through reducing sick time), and this leads to an endogeneity problem between income and health. Since workers in Sweden have paid sick-leave the endogeneity problem will, however, be reduced.

### Variables affecting the rate of depreciation in health

We include age as a variable that affects the rate of depreciation, since health status decreases with age. Rather than impose a functional form on the relationship between health and age, we again conservatively use four 0–1 dummies for age groups. Gender is also included in the model and is represented by a 0–1 dummy for male. The rate of depreciation is assumed to be higher for men, since they have a lower life-expectancy. We also include one dummy variable for if the individual is not married or cohabitant and one dummy variable for if the individual is currently unemployed. Both these variables are expected to increase the rate of depreciation.

We also include two dummy variables for immigration. The first dummy variable is a measure for first generation immigrants (persons born abroad whose parents are current or previous foreign citizens) and the second variable is a measure of second generation immigrants (persons born in Sweden whose parents are current or previous foreign citizens). Since the life-expectancy in Sweden is one of the highest in the world we expect immigrants to have a higher rate of depreciation of health (Statistics Sweden, 1998). We also include three dummy variables for the number of children in the household aged 0–18 years. It is important to control for the number of children since they reduce the consumption level of the adult persons in the household. The number of children may also have other effects on health status, through for instance increasing the incentives to stay healthy.

### Education

We include two dummies for the education of the individual. In the demand for health model education is assumed to increase the productivity of producing health (Grossman, 1972a,b). We thus expect the demand for health to increase with higher education.[8]

### Cohort effects

We include six dummy variables for the year of the interview to control for any cohort effects.

## Estimation methods

In estimating the demand-for-health model we have to take into account the fact that our health measure is an ordered response with three categories (0 = bad health, 1 = fair health, 2 = good health). An appropriate tool for analysing such ordered categorical data is the ordered probit model (for references see Amemiya, 1981; Cameron and Trivedi, 1986; Greene, 1993). Let $h_i^*$ be a continuous, latent variable which could be interpreted as representing the health of an individual on a continuous scale. We assume a linear dependence between the latent variable $h_i^*$ and $X_i$, $\beta$ and $\epsilon_i$:

$$h_i^* = \beta' X_i + \epsilon_i, \; \epsilon_i \sim N(0, \sigma^2).$$

The variable $h_i^*$ defines a variable $h_i$ which is related to the above mentioned categories in the following way:

$$h_1 = \begin{cases} 0 & \text{if } h_i^* \le \theta_0 \\ 1 & \text{if } \theta_0 \le h_i^* \le \theta_1 \\ 2 & \text{if } \theta_1 < h_i^* \end{cases}$$

where $\theta_i = 0,1$, are unobservable thresholds. Denoting the cumulative density function of the standard normal distribution as above ($\Phi$), it follows that the probabilities of an individual for each category are given by:

$$\text{Prob}[h_i = 0] = \Phi[\mu_0 - \alpha' X],$$

$$\text{Prob}[h_i = 1] = \Phi[\mu_1 - \alpha' X] - \Phi[\mu_0 - \alpha' X],$$

$$\text{Prob}[h_i = 2] = 1 - \Phi[\mu_1 - \alpha' X],$$

with $\alpha = \beta/\sigma$ and $\theta_j/\sigma = \mu_{j-1}$, 0, 1, i.e. note that only the ratios $\beta/\sigma$ and $\theta_j/\sigma$ are estimable (Greene, 1993). If the regression contains a constant term, the full set of coefficients is not identified. A common normalization is to set $\mu_0 = 0$ which means that the estimated coefficients $\mu_i$, i = 1 represent the differences in the respective thresholds: $\mu_i = \mu_i - \mu_{i-1}$ (Greene, 1995). Greene (1993) points out that the interpretation of the estimates is not straightforward. A positive estimate indicates that an increase in the respective variable shifts weight from category 0 into category 2, which means that the probability of category 2 increases and the probability of category 0 decreases.

## Estimation results

In Table 6.3 we report the ordered probit regression equations. Four regression equations are shown for the four different income measures used. The goodness of fit values (pseudo $R^2$) are about 0.18 in the four regression equations. In order to be able to interpret the size of the regression coefficients, we in Table 6.4 show the predicted probability of good health for each category of the dummy variables, at the mean level of all other explanatory variables.

Table 6.3 Ordered probit maximum likelihood estimation results: dependent variable: health (covariates included)[a]

| Covariate | Equation 1 | | Equation 2 | | Equation 3 | | Equation 4 | |
|---|---|---|---|---|---|---|---|---|
| | Coefficient | t-value | Coefficient | t-value | Coefficient | t-value | Coefficient | t-value |
| CONSTANT | 2.016*** | 59.902 | 1.896*** | 54.697 | 1.985*** | 60.279 | 1.890*** | 56.810 |
| MALE | −0.084*** | −5.503 | 0.059*** | 4.250 | 0.048*** | 3.470 | 0.039*** | 2.793 |
| AGE2 | −0.487*** | −22.753 | −0.502*** | −23.280 | −0.471*** | −22.116 | −0.355*** | −16.806 |
| AGE3 | −0.985*** | −42.361 | −0.986*** | −42.137 | −0.942*** | −41.781 | −0.831*** | −37.378 |
| AGE4 | −1.051*** | −39.413 | −1.048*** | −38.562 | −1.028*** | −40.773 | −0.094*** | −36.971 |
| AGE5 | −1.305*** | −39.480 | −1.303*** | −38.932 | −1.314*** | −42.174 | −1.221*** | −39.030 |
| CHILD2 | 0.080*** | 3.454 | 0.041* | 1.732 | 0.037 | 1.607 | 0.057*** | 2.477 |
| CHILD3 | 0.145*** | 5.722 | 0.090*** | 3.475 | 0.084*** | 3.278 | 0.103*** | 4.031 |
| CHILD4 | 0.175*** | 4.849 | 0.097*** | 2.657 | 0.084** | 2.309 | 0.102*** | 2.802 |
| IM2 | −0.392*** | −16.509 | −0.389*** | −16.394 | −0.417*** | −17.756 | −0.405*** | −17.182 |
| IM3 | −0.129 | −1.490 | −0.139 | −1.607 | −0.143* | −1.664 | −0.159* | −1.846 |
| SINGLE | −0.105*** | −6.558 | −0.096*** | −5.851 | −0.130*** | −8.191 | −0.133*** | −8.418 |
| PINC2 | −0.012 | −0.560 | — | | — | | — | |
| PINC3 | 0.103*** | 4.454 | — | | — | | — | |
| PINC4 | 0.261*** | 10.389 | — | | — | | — | |
| PINC5 | 0.444*** | 16.024 | — | | — | | — | |
| HINC2 | — | | 0.049** | 2.297 | — | | — | |
| HINC3 | — | | 0.159*** | 6.821 | — | | — | |
| HINC4 | — | | 0.256*** | 10.342 | — | | — | |
| HINC5 | — | | 0.400*** | 14.877 | — | | — | |
| FINC2 | — | | — | | 0.083*** | 3.970 | — | |
| FINC3 | — | | — | | 0.200*** | 9.066 | — | |

| | (1) | | (2) | | (3) | | (4) | |
|---|---|---|---|---|---|---|---|---|
| FINC4 | — | | — | | 0.279*** | 12.384 | — | |
| FINC5 | — | | — | | 0.455*** | 18.998 | — | |
| LINC2 | — | | — | | — | | 0.112*** | 5.504 |
| LINC3 | — | | — | | — | | 0.206*** | 9.611 |
| LINC4 | — | | — | | — | | 0.326*** | 14.411 |
| LINC5 | — | | — | | — | | 0.459*** | 19.210 |
| PPROP2 | 0.115*** | 5.342 | — | | — | | — | |
| PPROP3 | 0.166*** | 7.628 | — | | — | | — | |
| PPROP4 | 0.153*** | 7.042 | — | | — | | — | |
| PPROP5 | 0.193*** | 8.451 | — | | — | | — | |
| PROP2 | — | | 0.106*** | 4.944 | — | | — | |
| PROP3 | — | | 0.175*** | 7.983 | — | | — | |
| PROP4 | — | | 0.244*** | 10.971 | — | | — | |
| PROP5 | — | | 0.273*** | 12.141 | — | | — | |
| EDUC2 | 0.361*** | 15.409 | 0.388*** | 16.679 | 0.384*** | 16.535 | 0.392*** | 17.001 |
| EDUC3 | 0.139*** | 8.789 | 0.148*** | 9.366 | 0.146*** | 9.301 | 0.149*** | 9.492 |
| UNEMP | −0.127*** | −2.872 | −0.146*** | −3.315 | −0.166*** | −3.769 | −0.161*** | −3.663 |
| Y81 | 0.012 | 0.460 | 0.005 | 0.194 | 0.026 | 1.001 | 0.023 | 0.901 |
| Y82 | 0.092*** | 3.594 | 0.090*** | 3.499 | 0.114*** | 4.430 | 0.112*** | 4.370 |
| Y83 | 0.047* | 1.792 | 0.047* | 1.801 | 0.072*** | 2.763 | 0.072*** | 2.780 |
| Y84 | 0.061** | 2.358 | 0.061** | 2.367 | 0.083*** | 3.241 | 0.082*** | 3.188 |
| Y85 | 0.049* | 1.892 | 0.048* | 1.855 | 0.071*** | 2.742 | 0.068*** | 2.630 |
| Y86 | 0.037 | 1.297 | 0.040 | 1.397 | 0.064** | 2.252 | 0.062** | 2.187 |
| μ | 1.014 | 98.335 | 1.012 | 98.466 | 1.010 | 98.660 | 1.011 | 98.635 |
| Pseudo R² | 0.177 | | 0.176 | | 0.173 | | 0.174 | |

Note
a  *p < 0.10, **p < 0.05, ***p < 0.01.

*Table 6.4* Predicted probabilities of being in good health[a]

| Covariate | Equation 1 | Equation 2 | Equation 3 | Equation 4 |
|---|---|---|---|---|
| FEMALE | 0.7954 | 0.7745 | 0.7768 | 0.7774 |
| FEMALE | 0.7706 | 0.7917 | 0.7908 | 0.7887 |
| AGE1 | 0.9134 | 0.9140 | 0.9110 | 0.8978 |
| AGE2 | 0.8093 | 0.8060 | 0.8096 | 0.8196 |
| AGE3 | 0.6470 | 0.6479 | 0.6573 | 0.6693 |
| AGE4 | 0.6220 | 0.6246 | 0.6250 | 0.6299 |
| AGE5 | 0.5230 | 0.5250 | 0.5132 | 0.5193 |
| CHILD1 | 0.7699 | 0.7755 | 0.7768 | 0.7739 |
| CHILD2 | 0.7935 | 0.7875 | 0.7878 | 0.7908 |
| CHILD3 | 0.8115 | 0.8014 | 0.8010 | 0.8036 |
| CHILD4 | 0.8196 | 0.8034 | 0.8010 | 0.8033 |
| IM1 | 0.7927 | 0.7924 | 0.7938 | 0.7927 |
| IM2 | 0.6641 | 0.6648 | 0.6564 | 0.6595 |
| IM3 | 0.7538 | 0.7506 | 0.7506 | 0.7445 |
| NOT SINGLE | 0.7927 | 0.7917 | 0.7954 | 0.7950 |
| SINGLE | 0.7610 | 0.7632 | 0.7566 | 0.7550 |
| INCOME1 | 0.7313 | 0.7265 | 0.7167 | 0.7112 |
| INCOME2 | 0.7272 | 0.7425 | 0.7441 | 0.7482 |
| INCOME3 | 0.7642 | 0.7767 | 0.7803 | 0.7773 |
| INCOME4 | 0.8099 | 0.8045 | 0.8028 | 0.8114 |
| INCOME5 | 0.8558 | 0.8419 | 0.8480 | 0.8451 |
| PROPERTY1 | 0.7552 | 0.7402 | – | – |
| PROPERTY2 | 0.7898 | 0.7734 | – | – |
| PROPERTY3 | 0.8044 | 0.7936 | – | – |
| PROPERTY4 | 0.8007 | 0.8128 | – | – |
| PROPERTY5 | 0.8117 | 0.8203 | – | – |
| EDUC1 | 0.7460 | 0.7431 | 0.7442 | 0.7425 |
| EDUC2 | 0.8469 | 0.8510 | 0.8509 | 0.8516 |
| EDUC3 | 0.7884 | 0.7884 | 0.7890 | 0.7883 |
| NOT UNEMPLOYED | 0.7842 | 0.7841 | 0.7849 | 0.7841 |
| UNEMPLOYED | 0.7450 | 0.7391 | 0.7334 | 0.7341 |
| Y80 | 0.7700 | 0.7702 | 0.7648 | 0.7644 |
| Y81 | 0.7737 | 0.7717 | 0.7727 | 0.7715 |
| Y82 | 0.7972 | 0.7966 | 0.7983 | 0.7975 |
| Y83 | 0.7840 | 0.7842 | 0.7863 | 0.7861 |
| Y84 | 0.7880 | 0.7882 | 0.7895 | 0.7888 |
| Y85 | 0.7848 | 0.7846 | 0.7862 | 0.7849 |
| Y86 | 0.7812 | 0.7822 | 0.7841 | 0.7832 |

Note

a INCOME2–5 are PINC2–5, HINC2–5, FINC2–5, and LINC2–5 in equations 1, 2, 3, and 4, respectively. INCOME1 is the baseline income category in equations 1, 2, 3, and 4, respectively. PROPERTY2–5 are PPROP2–5 and PROP2–5 in equations 1 and 2, respectively. PROPERTY1 is the baseline category in equations 1 and 2, respectively.

The estimated effects of income on the demand for health are positive. The income dummy variables are positive and significant in all the four regression equations and the effect of income increases for every higher income category. The only exception to this is the second income dummy variable in the first regression equation that is negative and non-significant. The effect of income on the probability of being in good health is similar in the four regression equations and in equation 1 the estimated probability of being in good health increases from 0.73 in the lowest income category to 0.86 in the highest income category. The dummy variables for taxable net wealth are also positive and significant in equations 1 and 2 (net wealth is included in the income measure in the other two equations). In equation 1 the estimated probability of being in good health increases from 0.76 in the lowest wealth category to 0.81 in the highest wealth category.

The effect of male gender differs depending on the income measure. With personal income included, the effect of male gender is negative and significant. When instead the household income per adult person in the household is used, the effect of male gender is positive and significant. The predicted probability of good health is 0.77 for women and 0.79 for men in equation 2. As expected, age significantly decreases the demand for health. The effect of age is similar in all the four equations. In the first regression equation, the predicted probability of good health is 0.91 in the youngest age-group and 0.52 in the oldest age-group.

The dummy variables for the number of children are positive and significant in all the regression equations, with the exception of the dummy variable for one child in equation 3 that is not significant. In equation 1 the predicted probability of good health is 0.77 with no children and 0.82 with three or more children. The effect of the number of children is less in equations 2–4 when the income is based on household income rather than personal income. In equation 2, the predicted probability of good health is 0.78 with no children and 0.80 with three or more children.

The estimated effect of being single is, as expected, negatively significant. The effect of being single is similar in the four equations and in the first equation being single decreases the predicted probability of good health from 0.79 to 0.76. The estimated effect of unemployment is also negative and significant in all the four equations. In the first equation, unemployment decreases the predicted probability of good health from 0.78 to 0.74.

The dummy variable for first generation immigrants is significantly negative in all four regression equations. The dummy variable for second generation immigrants also has a negative sign in all the four regression equations, but it is only significant at the 10 per cent level in equations 3 and 4. In equation 1 the predicted probability of good health is 0.79 for non-immigrants, 0.75 for second generation immigrants, and 0.66 for first generation immigrants.

Education, as expected, has a positive effect on health in all the four regression equations, indicating that individuals with a higher education are more efficient producers of health. The predicted probability of being in good health is 0.85 for individuals with university education, 0.79 for individuals with high school education and 0.75 for individuals with less than high school education.

The cohort dummy variables are positive and significant for the years 1982, 1983, 1984, and 1985 in all the four regression equations, showing that the health status is higher in these cohorts than in the 1980 cohort. The 1986 cohort dummy variable is also positive and significant in equations 3 and 4.

## Discussion

Overall our results confirm the predictions of the demand-for-health model. The demand for health increased with income and education and decreased with age, unemployment, immigration and being single. The health status also increased with the number of children in the household. The effect of gender depended on the income measure included in the regression equation. With personal income included male gender had a significant negative effect on health status. If we instead used household income per adult person in the household male gender had a significant positive effect on health status. Which income measure proves most appropriate depends on if the household income is evenly divided between the spouses or divided according to their personal income level. It seems most reasonable to assume that the household income is evenly divided between the spouses. Using personal income will thus bias the coefficient for male gender towards a negative effect on health status, since personal income on average over-estimates the private consumption of men and underestimates the private consumption of women for men and women that are married/cohabiting. Our results for gender thus suggest that male gender has a positive effect on health status, which is unexpected since the life-expectancy is shorter for men than for women.

It is interesting to compare the results to our two previous studies based on Swedish data and a categorical health measure (Gerdtham *et al.*, 1999; Gerdtham and Johannesson, 1999). The following variables were included in all the studies: age, gender, personal income, education, unemployment, and being single. In all the studies, the demand for health increased significantly with income and education and decreased significantly with age and being single. Unemployment had a negative sign in the studies by Gerdtham *et al.* (1999) and Gerdtham and Johannesson (1999), but did not reach statistical significance. In this study, the negative effect of unemployment was statistically significant. This was probably due to the fact that the sample size was about ten times larger in this study, which leads to a greatly increased statistical power to detect significant differences. Male gender had a negative effect on health status in the study by Gerdtham *et al.* (1999) but was not significant. In the study by Gerdtham and Johannesson (1999), male gender had a significant negative effect on health status. Both previous studies included personal income and when personal income was included in our study male gender also had a significant negative effect. As noted above, however, this result seems to be an artefact of using personal income for persons that are married/cohabiting. Overall, the results are remarkably consistent between the three studies.

It is also interesting to compare our results to the recent studies by Wagstaff (1993), Nocera and Zweifel (1998), and Gerdtham *et al.* (1999). Wagstaff (1993) estimated demand-for-health equations with equivalent household pre-tax wage income, education, gender and age as explanatory variables based on data from the Danish Health Study. He estimated two equations in two separate age-groups (under and over 41 years). Age had the wrong sign (not significant) in the under-41s equation, but had the expected negative sign and was significant in the over-41s equation. Income and education had the expected signs in both equations, but income was not significant in the under-41s equation and education was not significant in the over-41s equation. Gender had no significant effect on health in either the under-41s equation or the over-41s equation. Our results for age, income and education are largely consistent with those of Wagstaff (1993) but provide stronger support for the demand-for-health model. Age, education and income were all significant with the expected signs in our estimations.

Nocera and Zweifel (1998) estimated demand-for-health equations based on two panel-data sets. The demand for health was estimated as a function of age, gender, education, wage rate, being single, smoking, overweight, and sporting activities. The effects of all variables were in the expected direction in the first data set, and most variables were significant. In the second data set the results were less consistent with the demand-for-health model, since the wage rate had a negative effect (not significant) on health and smoking had a positive effect on health (significant). Our results are similar to the results in the first data set used by Nocera and Zweifel (1998).

A difference between this study and the study by Gerdtham *et al.* (1999) is that the latter authors used a categorical health measure with five categories and we used a categorical health measure with three categories. So even though our dependent variable offers rather limited scope for variability in that it allows for only three different levels of health, it seems to work at least as well as the more sophisticated health measures used by Gerdtham *et al.* (1999) and others (Wagstaff, 1993; Nocera and Zweifel, 1998). A reason for this may be that having less categories reduces the random measurement noise in the health variable.

It is important to note some limitations of the study. One limitation concerns the fact that there may be some omitted variables, which affect the demand for health (e.g. the distance to health-care services, affecting the effective price of medical care). This could lead to omitted variable bias. Another limitation concerns causality. For some variables there could be problems with reversed causality, e.g. that the health status affects income and education rather than the other way round. If this is the case, the estimated effects of income and education will be biased, along with the effects of all other correlated regressors. Unfortunately, the lack of instruments precludes any formal tests of endogeneity. In further research, it would be interesting to use a panel-data set to be able to better control for omitted variables and reversed causality.

## Notes

1 It is, however, not an undisputed model. A key criticism of the model has been that it fails to take into account the uncertainty of the future health status and the uncertainty of the effects of investments in health production. For overviews of the criticisms of the Grossman model, see van Doorslaer (1987) and Zweifel and Breyer (1997).

2  These methods have been developed in the field of economic evaluation of health care to measure the quality weights to construct quality-adjusted life-years (Torrance, 1986).
3  A categorical health status measure was also used in the recent study by Nocera and Zweifel (1998).
4  In principle, the stock of health at time $t$ in the demand for health model depends on the level of the explanatory variables in all time periods and not only in period $t$ (Grossman, 1972a,b). Our analysis that is based on the level of the explanatory variables at one point in time can thus be interpreted as being based on the assumption that all the explanatory variables are constant over time. An exception to this is the age variable that will by definition vary over time.
5  The value of the household net wealth at market value was SEK 322,938 in 1996 prices. The ratio between this value and the taxable net wealth was: 1.83 in 1980, 1.32 in 1981, 1.35 in 1982, 1.32 in 1983, 1.45 in 1984, 1.47 in 1985, and 1.38 in 1986.
6  A regression equation of household disposable income per adult person in the household as a function of age and age-squared was used to estimate the percentage change in disposable income for each year until the age of 65 (the retirement age). After retirement, the annual income was assumed to be constant and to estimate the percentage change in income at retirement, we used the average income in the 65–69 years age-group in our data (for the gender and education category of the individual).
7  The net wealth was divided into four quartiles for persons with positive net wealth, and zero wealth was used as the baseline category.
8  An alternative hypothesis for why health status can be expected to be positively correlated with education is that the rate of time preference varies with education (Fuchs, 1982). According to this theory, both investments in education and investments in health will decrease with the rate of time preference. If this hypothesis holds, a positive regression coefficient for education does not indicate that more education leads to a better health status, but that a lower rate of time preference leads to a better health status.

# References

Amemiya, T. (1981) Qualitative response models: a survey. *Journal of Economic Literature* **19**, 481–536.

Cameron, C. and Trivedi, P. (1986) Econometric models based on count data: comparisons and applications of some estimators and tests. *Journal of Econometrics* **1**, 29–53.

Connelly, J.E., Philbrick, J.T., Smith, R., Kaiser, D.L. and Wymer, A. (1989) Health perceptions of primary care patients and the influence on health care utilization. *Medical Care* **27** (suppl.), 99–109.

Cropper, M.L. (1981) Measuring the benefits from reduced morbidity. *American Economic Review* **71**, 235–40.

Erbsland, M., Ried, W. and Ulrich, V. (1995) Health, health care, and the environment: econometric evidence from German micro data. *Health Economics* **4**, 169–182.

Fuchs, V.R. (1982) Time preference and health: an exploratory study. In *Economic Aspects of Health*, edited by V.R. Fuchs, pp. 93–120. University of Chicago Press, Chicago.

Gerdtham, U-G., Johannesson, M., Lundberg, L. and Isacson, D. (1999) The demand for health: results from new measures of health capital. *European Journal of Political Economy* **15**, 501–21.

Gerdtham, U-G., and Johannesson, M. (1999) New estimates of the demand for health: results based on a categorical health measure and Swedish micro data. *Social Science and Medicine* **49**, 1325–32.

Greene, W. (1993) *Econometric Analysis,* Second Edition. Macmillan Publishing Company, New York.

Greene, W. (1995) *LIMDEP™ Version 7.0 User's manual*. Econometric Software, Inc., New York.

Grossman, M. (1972a) *The Demand for Health: A Theoretical and Empirical Investigation*. NBER, New York.

Grossman, M. (1972b) On the concept of health capital and the demand for health. *Journal of Political Economy* **80**, 223–55.

Idler, E.L. and Kasl, S. (1991) Health perceptions and survival: do global evaluations of health status really predict mortality? *Journal of Gerontology* **46**, 555–65.

Kaplan, G.A. and Camacho, T. (1983) Perceived health and mortality: a nine-year follow-up of the human population laboratory cohort. *American Journal of Epidemiology* **117**, 292–304.

Leu, R.E. and Gerfin, M. (1992) Die Nachfrage nach Gesundheit – ein empirischer Test des Grossman-Modells (Demand for health – an empirical test of the Grossman model). In *Steuerungsprobleme im Gesundheitswesen*, edited by P. Oberender, pp. 61–78. Nomos, Baden-Baden.

Nocera, S. and Zweifel, P. (1998) The demand for health: an empirical test of the Grossman model using panel data. In *Health, the Medical Profession, and Regulation*, edited by P. Zweifel, pp. 35–49. Kluwer Academic Publishers, Dordrecht.

Statistics Sweden (1990). *Wealth Distribution of Families in 1975–1988*. Report Be 21 SSM 9002. Statistics Sweden, Stockholm.

Statistics Sweden (1997) *Living conditions and inequality in Sweden: a 20 year perspective 1975–1995*. Living conditions, Report 91, Statistics Sweden, Stockholm.

Statistics Sweden (1998) *Statistical yearbook of Sweden 1999*. Statistics Sweden, Stockholm.

Torrance, G.W. (1986) Measurement of health state utilities for economic appraisal: a review. *Journal of Health Economics* **5**, 1–30.

van Doorslaer, E.K.A. (1987) *Health, Knowledge and the Demand for Medical Care*. Van Gorcum, Assen/Maastricht.

Wagstaff, A. (1986) The demand for health: some new empirical evidence. *Journal of Health Economics* **5**, 195–233.

Wagstaff, A. (1993) The demand for health: an empirical reformulation of the Grossman model. *Health Economics* **2**, 189–98.

Wannamethee, G. and Shaper, A.G. (1991) Self-assessment of health status and mortality in middle-aged British men. *International Journal of Epidemiology* **20**, 239–45.

Zweifel, P. and Breyer, F. (1997) *Health Economics*. Oxford University Press, New York and Oxford.

# 7  Estimation of intangible benefits and costs of cancer screening with stated rank data

*Dorte Gyrd-Hansen and Jes Søgaard*

## Introduction

There is currently much focus on screening programmes such as screening for cervical cancer, breast cancer and colorectal cancer. Such programmes either have been introduced or are considered in many countries. Several cost-effectiveness studies have been published in the last decade (van der Maas *et al.*, 1989; Eddy, 1990; Koopmanschapf *et al.*, 1990a,b; de Koning *et al.*, 1991; Mushlin and Fintor, 1992; Gyrd-Hansen *et al.*, 1995, 1998; Wagner *et al.*, 1996). These studies have only to a small extent incorporated intangible benefits and costs, or perceived utility and disutility associated with cancer screening. How is the risk of a false positive screen test over lifetime traded off against the prospect of reduced disease specific mortality risk over lifetime – due to better survival prognosis at early diagnosis? The cost of increasing frequency of screening tests in terms of time costs and discomfort with the test and/or anxiety while waiting for the results of the screening test (Cohen and Henderson, 1988)? Do extra-attributive participation benefits exist (beyond mortality risk reduction) in terms of obtaining information (Berwick and Weinstein, 1985) and/or eliminating regret (Loomes and Sugden, 1982; Mooney and Lange, 1993)? Importance of such costs and benefits are widely recognized (Cairns and Shackley, 1993) and undoubtedly they influence health policy makers' decisions to introduce screening or not as well as individual decisions to participate if they are or become available.

The purpose of this chapter is to assess some intangible costs and benefits associated with participation in screening for colorectal cancer using the fecal occult blood test (H-II) or in mammography screening. The former is self-administered, whereas breast cancer screening involves a visit to a local mammography unit. If the screening test is positive, participants will be referred to diagnostic tests. In the case of colorectal cancer, a positive screening test is followed up by a colorectal examination, also called a colonoscopy. If a patient is suspected of having breast cancer, the introductory diagnostic test will entail a clinical mammography i.e. further x-rays, palpation and possibly a needle biopsy.

We interviewed a random sample of the Danish population at the age of 50 years to elicit their stated utility and disutility associated with participation, with cancer-specific mortality risk reduction, with risk of false positive test outcomes, and with the number of screening tests. We also included out-of-pocket payment as an attribute in order to obtain trade-offs between the other attributes and income losses or gains. We used an iterative discrete choice design, in which we effectively obtained a ranking for each interviewee between four screening options. One option is not to participate, the other three options are participation in screening programmes with different attribute values for risk reduction, false positive outcome, number of screening tests and out-of-pocket payment – all over remaining lifetime. We used the ordered logit model (Beggs *et al.*, 1981) to estimate parameters relating to the participation attribute values and to characteristics of the individual decision maker (household income, professional education, gender, and initial cancer mortality risk).

Research questions of this chapter include: (1) To test and quantify the strengths of preferences and measure willingness to pay for the attributes under study; (2) to test for differences between the two target cancers (breast and colorectal cancer) and between men and women; (3) to model income effects on trade-offs with income gains/losses, i.e. on the imputed willingness to pay; and (4) not least to obtain and report some experience with the applicability of this design and method to gather information about intangible benefits and costs of cancer screening programmes.

## Design and data

We use a variant of the conjoint analysis (discrete ranking modelling) with a stated preference design. The study population is the Danish population at 50 years of age. The age of 50 is the lower age limit considered in Danish screening policies for these two cancers. Representative and random samples of 255 women and 509 men and women were drawn for interviews about, respectively, mammography and colorectal cancer screening. The sampling was done in cooperation with the Danish Social Research Institute and their trained interviewers carried out the face-to-face, structured interviews, cf. Gyrd-Hansen and Søgaard, 2001.

As part of the interview, the interviewee was informed about the purpose of screening, the screening tests and subsequent diagnostic tests following positive screening test outcomes. The interviewee was then given a card describing four choices, see Table 7.1. The four choices were described with respect to four different attributes (see also Table 7.2):

1 Number of screening tests performed over the next 25 years (range: 0–25 tests).
2 The interviewee's risk of dying of the cancer (colorectal or breast cancer) over the next 30 years (range for colorectal cancer at low initial risk: 280 declining to a minimum of 217 per 10,000 with screening, and at high initial risk: 370 down to 295 per 10,000; range for breast cancer: 340 down to 210 per 10,000).
3 The interviewee's risk of being called in for an unnecessary diagnostic test (colonoscopy or clinical mammography) over the next 25 years (range for

*Table 7.1* Design of the choice cards

| Attribute | No participation | Programme 1 | Programme 2 | Programme 3 |
|---|---|---|---|---|
| $X = TEST$. Number of tests performed over lifetime | $x_0 = 0$ | $x_1 > 0$ | $x_2 = x_1$ | $x_3 > x_2$ or $x_3 = x_2$ |
| $Y = Y_0 - RED$. Cancer mortality risk over lifetime | $y_0 \%_{ooo}$[a] | $y_1 < y_0 \%_{ooo}$ | $y_2 < y_1 \%_{ooo}$ | $y_3 = y_2 \%_{ooo}$ |
| $Z = FP$. Risk of false positive over lifetime | $z_0 = 0$ | $z_1 > 0$ | $z_2 = z_1$ | $z_3 = z_2$ or $z_3 > z_2$ |
| $P = $ Out-of-pocket payment per test | $p_0 = 0$ | $p_1 = 0$ | $p_2 > 0$ | $p_3 = 0$ |

Note
a Initial cancer mortality risk is presented to the interviewee as $280 \%_{ooo}$ or $370 \%_{ooo}$ for colorectal cancer and $340 \%_{ooo}$ for breast cancer.

    colorectal cancer screening: 0–22 per cent, for mammography screening: 0–47 per cent).
4    The interviewee's out-of-pocket payment per test and in total over the next 25 years (range: 0–5000 DKK per test).

One option was not to participate. The other three options were participation in a programme (1, 2 or 3) with attribute values structured as shown in Table 7.1, and varying across the sample (see Table 7.2). Attribute values were designed pragmatically and not by systematic designs. Programme 1 had attribute values for number of tests, cancer mortality risk and false positive risk within a realistic range and out-of-pocket payment was always set to zero. Mortality risk reductions were estimated using the Walter–Day model (Day and Walter, 1984) and lead-time and sensitivity data on the tests (Tabar *et al.*, 1995 and Gyrd-Hansen *et al.*, 1997). False positivity risks were estimated from test specificity levels observed in randomized trials in Denmark (Kronborg *et al.*, 1996). Programmes 2 and 3 had higher effectiveness obtained with a more sensitive screening test but at an out-of-pocket price (programme 2), or as in programme 3 either at the cost of lower specificity or more frequent screening tests. For programme 2 the out-of-pocket price varied from 100 to 5000 DKK per test in order to include the 'top of the demand curve'.

When handed the choice card, the interviewee was asked four questions both to familiarize him or her with the information and to determine understanding: (1) Under which programme are you required to undergo most screening tests? (2) Which of the programmes save most lives? (3) Under which programme(s) is the risk of an unnecessary diagnostic test largest? (4) Which of the programmes requires an out-of-pocket payment? Interviewees unable to answer all four questions correctly were excluded from the data analysis.

*Table 7.2* Attribute values and other explanatory variables

| Label | Explanation and values used |
|---|---|
| TEST | Number of screening tests performed over lifetime (25 years):<br>CCS: 0, 5, 10, 14, 25<br>BCS: 0, 5, 10, 17, 25 |
| RED | Colorectal cancer *or* breast cancer mortality risk reduction out of 10,000 ($\%_{ooo}$) over lifetime (30 years):[a]<br>CCS (initial risk 280 $\%_{ooo}$): 0, 30, 45, 53, 63 $\%_{ooo}$<br>CCS (initial risk 370 $\%_{ooo}$): 0, 42, 52, 63, 75 $\%_{ooo}$<br>BCS (initial risk 340 $\%_{ooo}$): 0, 60, 90, 120, 130 $\%_{ooo}$ |
| FP | Risk of having one or more false positive screen test outcomes[b] over lifetime (25 years):<br>CCS: 0, 4, 10, 14, 22%<br>BCS: 0, 12, 23, 35, 47% |
| COST per TEST | Out of pocket expenditure: 0, 100, 500, 1000, 2000, 5000 DKK per test. Included as COST × TEST in units of 1000 DKK. |
| IR HIR | Initial risk of dying of colorectal cancer (or breast cancer), given to the interviewee. Included as HIR in dummy form in CCS sample only, HIR = 1 if IR = 370 $\%_{ooo}$, 0 otherwise. |
| PARTICIPATE | Dummy variable for participation in a screening programme in the regression analysis. |
| PAY | Dummy variable for an Out-of-Pocket Pay screening programme (COST > 0) |
| EDU | Professional education/training classification, None = 21.9%, Semi-skilled = 1.2%, Skilled = 38.7%, Short theoretical = 7.5%, Medium theoretical = 17.8%, Academic = 10.8%, Other = 1.2%. In the regression analysis entered in binary form (Some education = 1 (78.2%) versus None = 0 (21.9%)) |
| $Y$[c] | Monthly household income net of income taxes, reported in intervals of 5000 DKK, medium is 20,000–25,000 DKK, average is 22,330 DKK. Included in units of 1000 DKK. |

Notes
a The interviewees were given the absolute risk values at each programme and not the risk reduction as such, i.e. *IR + RED*.
b Stated to the interviewee as 'risk of being called in for an unnecessary diagnostic examination'.
c 43 interviewees did not report income. Their household income (Y (in 1000 DKK)) was estimated with $Y_i = 2.39 + 0.37 \times EDU_{j,i} + 0.84 \times EDU_{other\,i} + 2.0 \times CV$, where $EDU_{j,i}$ is Education level (0 = none, 1 = semi-skilled, 2 = skilled, 3,4,5 = short, medium or academic theoretical education; linear trend test, $F_{4,432} = 1.39$ (ns)), $EDU_{other\,i}$ is a dummy with 1's if education is other, and CV is a dummy with 1's if the interviewee is married or lives together with another adult (82%) and otherwise 0. Sex was tested but was insignificant (sizewise and statistically) in the income equation.

After these introductory questions, the interviewee was asked whether he or she wanted to participate in any of the three programmes presented to them. If the answer was 'yes', he or she was asked which one of the three possible programmes they would prefer, and next, which programme, if any, he or she would choose, should the initially preferred option turn out not to be available.

If the interviewee initially turned down the offer of screening, he or she was asked which programme was the least favourable and which was the most favourable of the screening programmes. Questions were asked such that a full or partial ranking of all alternatives could be deduced. Questions about motivation for choices were also asked but are not used in this analysis. Finally, the interviewee was asked about monthly household income net of tax and of professional education or formal training.

## The statistical model and hypotheses

The underlying model is a random utility model for person $i$'s utility from choice $j$ out of $J$ choices,

$$U_{ij} = V(w_i, x_{ij}) + \varepsilon_{ij}^* = V_{ij} + \varepsilon_{ij}^*, \qquad (7.1)$$

where $V_{ij}$ is the observable component of person $i$'s utility derived from the attributes $x_{ij}$ experienced by $i$ with the $j$'th choice and possibly interacting with personal characteristics of the person $i$ ($w_i$). $\varepsilon_{ij}^*$ is the – to the analyst – stochastic and unobservable component of $U_{ij}$. With ordinal ranking information we can determine the probability of a particular rank order, say $\Pr[U_{i1} > U_{i2} > \ldots > U_{iJ}]$, thereby exploit the additional information in rank rather than single choice data, and hence obtain more precise estimates. Pragmatic considerations limit the choice of probability distribution for $\varepsilon_{ij}^*$ to the independent and homoscedastic extreme value distribution. This leads to the ordered (conditional) logit model, in which the utility distribution of the higher ranking choices is independent of the ordering of the less favoured choices, Beggs *et al.*, 1981.

We also limit ourselves to a linear model for $V_{ij}$, i.e. $V_{ij} = Z_{ij}\beta$, where the $Z_{ij}$s are (possibly transformed) values of the choice attributes, choice constants and interaction between these and the $w_i$ values. The utility model is specified with gender and cancer specific parameters (subscript s),

$$
\begin{aligned}
U_{ijs} = {} & \beta_{1s} \cdot TEST_{ij} + \beta_{2s} \cdot FP_{ij}[ \times EDU_i] + \beta_{3s} \cdot RED_{ij} + \\
& \beta_{4s} \cdot COST_{ij} + \beta_{5s} \cdot COST_{ij} / \ln(Y_i) + \beta_{6s} \cdot PARTICIPATE_{ij} + \\
& \beta_{7s} \cdot PARTICIPATE_{ij} \times HIR_i + \beta_{8s} \cdot PARTICIPATE_{ij} \times EDU_i + \\
& \beta_{9s} \cdot PARTICIPATE_{ij} \times Y_i + \beta_{10s} \cdot PAY_{ij} + \beta_{11s} \cdot PAY_{ij} \times Y_i + \varepsilon_{ijs}.(7.2)
\end{aligned}
$$

where s denotes one of three sub-samples, s = fc denotes the female colorectal cancer screening sample (fCCS), s = mc denotes the male colorectal cancer screening sample (mCCS), and s = fb denotes the breast cancer screening (fBCS). $j$ is choice or programme ($j = 0,1,2,3$), and $i$ refers to the individual of the s'th sub-sample. The attribute variables are explained in Tables 7.1 and 7.2 and note that the payment variable (*COST*) enters as monetary price per test times, number of tests over lifetime, and is measured in 1000 DKK. *PARTICIPATE* is a dummy with 1's for any participation, and 0's otherwise.

*PAY* is a dummy with 1's for the pay programme ($j = 2$), and otherwise 0. Three person characteristics are included besides gender (for sample stratification), they are *EDU, HIR* and *Y. Y* is household net-income per month measured in units of 1000 DKK. *HIR* is a dummy coded with 1 for interviewees who were requested to make choices and rankings on the assumptions that they had high initial colorectal cancer mortality risk (370 out of 10,000) and 0 for interviewees who were requested to assume low initial risks (280). *EDU* is a professional education dummy coded with 1 if the interviewee reports any formal professional training, and otherwise 0. $\varepsilon_{ijs}$ is $\varepsilon_{ij}^*$ plus measurement and specification errors. The 32 $\beta$-parameters (10 $\times$ 3 + 2) are the ordered logit coefficients to be estimated and tested.

The utility associated with participation is expected to decrease with number of screen tests ($\beta_{1s} < 0$) (Cohen and Henderson, 1988), to decrease with risk of false positivity risks ($\beta_{2s} < 0$) (anxiety and process disutility), and to increase with risk reduction ($\beta_{3s} > 0$). We expect $\partial U/\partial COST < 0$ but diminishing with income and hence both $\beta_{4s} \leq 0$ and $\beta_{5s} < 0$. The term $COST_{ij}/\ln(Y_i)$ is included to test whether disutility with out-of-pocket expenditure (and hence WTP(A) for changes in *TEST, FP* and *RED*) is log-linearly related to household income; it is proportionally so if $\beta_{4s} = 0$. *PARTICIPATE* is included to pick up extra-attributive (dis)utility associated with screening participation; $\beta_{6s} > 0$ if information or regret benefits are present and outweigh other possible negative extra-attributive benefits of screening participation; there are theoretical arguments that participation benefits increase with higher initial risks (Jones-Lee, 1974; Weinstein *et al.*, 1980) but also empirical evidence for the opposite (Persson *et al.*, 1995; Smith and Desvouges, 1987), i.e. $\beta_{7s} < / > 0$. Based on observed participation rates in Denmark and other countries (Farrands *et al.*, 1983; Macrae *et al.*, 1986) we expect participation benefits to increase with socio-economic status, hence $\beta_{8s} > 0$ and $\beta_{9s} > 0$. *PAY* is included to pick up disutility with out-of-pocket payment independent on the level of payment, i.e. fundamental opposition to direct payment for health services ($\beta_{10s} < 0$), which we expect may diminish with household income ($\beta_{11s} > 0$).

Little is known about screening utility differences for different cancer screening programmes and between men and women. This specification is designed to measure and test such differences. Intangible costs and benefits from colorectal cancer screening may differ for men and women because women are more familiar with screening tests from other programmes. In Denmark, as in many other countries, there has been considerable focus in the media on mammography screening compared to colorectal cancer screening, and both the screening tests and the diagnostic procedures do differ.

The analytical reference option is the non-participation option, which means that utility associated with this alternative is set to zero. The utility associated with participation in a screening programme is a function of the risk reduction and other attributes, which in a simple additive utility function can be presented as

$$dU = \sum_{a=1}^{A} \frac{\partial U}{\partial x_a} dx_a,$$

where $A$ is the number of attributes $x$, $dx_a$ is the change in attribute values by participation, and $\partial U/\partial x_a$ is the marginal utility of attribute a to be estimated as the ordered logit parameters or functions thereof.

Setting $dU = 0$ we obtain indifference curves and we can calculate trade-offs or marginal rates of substitution between pairs of attributes, e.g. between risk reduction and out-of-pocket payment, i.e. $\text{WTP}_{RED} = (\beta_3/-(\beta_4 + \beta_5/\ln Y))$, or between risk reduction and risk of a false positive test outcome $(\beta_3/-\beta_2)$ to be used to weigh programme sensitivity against programme specificity at a given test technology.

We use backward stepwise regression to reduce the model (2) with 32 parameters. The down-testing is governed by the following five criteria:

1    Only one-degree restrictions are imposed.
2    Restrictions can be (a) zero-restriction on a coefficient or (b) an equality restriction on a regressor across two samples (it must be the same regressor).
3    The least significant restriction is imposed, and only this, at each step.
4    No a priori information is used, neither in the form of one-sided $p$-values for some restrictions, e.g. the *RED*-coefficient must be positive, nor in the form of regressors with forced entry status.
5    Down-testing stops when the least significant coefficient has a nominal $p$-value of at least 0.01 such as to obtain a real significance level at about 0.05 (Lovel, 1983).

We used the Newton–Raphson of LIMDEP 7.0 for all estimations, – the typical LIMDEP command is shown in Table 7.6.

## Results

### Preliminaries

A total of 509 50-year old men and women were randomly selected for the colorectal cancer screening interview. 21 could not be contacted, 39 declined to be interviewed and 28 were incapable of responding, resulting in a participation rate of 83 per cent. Of the 421 remaining interviewees 93 were excluded because they did not understand the information about the choices or because they ranked inconsistently. The effective CCS estimation sample therefore was 328 interviewees, 179 women and 149 men. From the 179 women we obtained full ranking of all four alternatives from 166 women and partial ranking (only three or two alternatives) from 13 women. For the 149 men the numbers were 134 full rankings and 15 partial rankings.

For the breast cancer interview 255 50-year old women were randomly selected. Of these 207 were successfully interviewed (81 per cent), 23 did not wish to participate, 13 individuals were incapable of responding, and 12 could not be contacted. 52 interviewees were excluded due to indication of poor understanding of the options or inconsistent ranking. The effective BCS estimation sample was 155 interviewees, from whom we had full ranking from 147 and partial ranking from 8 women.

Monthly household income was reported in 5000 DKK intervals from <5000 DKK per month up to 35,000–40,000 DKK per month and >40,000 DKK per month. The approximate mean household income was 22,330 DKK, and the median income was about 20,000 DKK per month, cf. Table 7.2. 106 (22 per cent) of the estimation sample had no professional education, 6 (1 per cent) had semi-skilled training, 187 (39 per cent) had skilled training, 36 (7½ per cent) had a short (<2 years) theoretical education, 86 (18 per cent) had a medium long (2–4 years) theoretical education ('college'), 52 (11 per cent) a long (>4 years) theoretical education ('university'), and 10 (1 per cent) reported 'another' professional education.

Table 7.3 presents observed rankings by cancer and gender. Only 13 per cent of the women in the breast cancer sample (fBCS) rank non-participation higher than participation, as compared to 31 per cent women and 38 per cent men in the colorectal cancer samples ($p < 0.01$). Conversely, more women in the fBCS sample rank non-participation lowest compared to the fCCS (60 per cent versus 36 per cent), and more women in the fBCS sample than in the fCCS rank programme 3 highest (59 per cent versus 41 per cent).

*Table 7.3* Ranking of options by cancer and gender. Frequencies (*n*) and proportions (*pr.*)[a]

| Option | R = 1 (highest) | | R = 2 | | R = 3 | | R = 4 | |
|---|---|---|---|---|---|---|---|---|
| | *n* | *pr.* | *n* | *pr.* | *n* | *pr.* | *n* | *pr.* |
| *Female colorectal cancer sample (fCCS) ranking distribution* | | | | | | | | |
| Not participate (0) | 56 | .31 | 10 | .06 | 54 | .31 | 59 | .36 |
| Programme 1 | 28 | .16 | 71 | .40 | 59 | .34 | 17 | .10 |
| Programme 2 | 22 | .12 | 36 | .20 | 32 | .18 | 82 | .49 |
| Programme 3 | 73 | .41 | 62 | .35 | 29 | .17 | 8 | .05 |
| Total | 179 | | 179 | | 174 | | 166 | |
| *Male colorectal cancer sample (mCCS) ranking distribution* | | | | | | | | |
| Not participate (0) | 56 | .38 | 3 | .02[c] | 33 | .23 | 57 | .43 |
| Programme 1 | 24 | .16 | 63 | .42 | 44 | .31 | 14 | .10 |
| Programme 2 | 23 | .15 | 25 | .17 | 40 | .28[b] | 54 | .40 |
| Programme 3 | 46 | .31[c] | 58 | .39 | 25 | .18 | 9 | .07 |
| Total | 149 | | 149 | | 142 | | 134 | |
| *Female breast cancer sample (fBCS) ranking distribution* | | | | | | | | |
| Not participate (0) | 20 | .13[a] | 8 | .05 | 36 | .24 | 88 | .60[a] |
| Programme 1 | 23 | .15 | 63 | .41 | 55 | .36 | 11 | .08 |
| Programme 2 | 21 | .14 | 44 | .28[c] | 49 | .32[a] | 37 | .25[a] |
| Programme 3 | 91 | .59[a] | 40 | .26[c] | 13 | .09[b] | 11 | .08 |
| Total | 155 | | 155 | | 153 | | 147 | |

Note

Difference of proportion tests, fCCS versus mCCS and fCCS versus fBCS. Two sided *z*-tests, a: $p < 0.01$, b: $p < 0.05$, c: $p < 0.10$.

### Regression results

The thirty-two parameter estimates of the unrestricted version of equation (7.2) are presented in Table 7.4. During the estimations we found the slope coefficients with *FP* to be insignificant unless we excluded the 22 per cent interviewees with no professional education, i.e. including *FP* only in interaction with *EDU*. Hence, throughout, our results with respect to false positivity refer only to those 78 per cent of the sample with some professional education. Several of the parameter estimates in Table 7.4 are both small and statistically insignificant, and clearly the results are statistically too inefficient to allow detailed interpretation. They serve as the starting point for (1) tests of equality of parameters by gender and cancer (Table 7.5), and (2) a starting point for down-testing to a more parsimonious model (Table 7.6).

Table 7.4 exposes considerable differences in parameter estimates, in particular between the male sample and the two female samples. The *COST*-parameters appear more different than they are, at medium income of DKK 20,000 the marginal disutility of out-of-pocket is 0.015 in both female samples, and 0.020 in the male sample, but it varies differently with income. The male equation has several parameter estimates contrary to expectations, but they are all statistically insignificant.

Differences between samples are more systematically reported in Table 7.5. First, we tested equality between samples for the parameters one by one with

*Table 7.4* Ordered logit models of utility of screening using stated ranks. By gender and cancer

| Regressor | Colorectal female n = 179 | | Colorectal male n = 149 | | Breast cancer females n = 155 | |
|---|---|---|---|---|---|---|
| | $\hat{\beta}_{f.c}$ | p-val | $\hat{\beta}_{m.c}$ | p-val | $\hat{\beta}_{f.b}$ | p-val |
| TEST | −.016 | .4476 | .010 | .6324 | −.048 | .0116 |
| FP * EDU | −.065 | .0033 | .030 | .2235 | −.055 | .0000 |
| RED | .045 | .0010 | −.001 | .9841 | .034 | .0000 |
| COST | −.069 | .0096 | .028 | .5975 | −.004 | .9272 |
| COST/ln(Y) | .162 | .0320 | −.148 | .3753 | −.033 | .8047 |
| PARTICIPATE | −1.34 | .0195 | .987 | .1699 | −1.86 | .0017 |
| ×HIR[a] | −.966 | .0000 | −.317 | .1443 | na | na |
| ×EDU | .812 | .0049 | .144 | .6880 | .637 | .0667 |
| ×Y | .010 | .3174 | −.032 | .0043 | .055 | .0000 |
| PAY | −2.60 | .0000 | −.642 | .2827 | −1.36 | .0213 |
| ×Y | .055 | .0091 | −.010 | .6414 | −.006 | .8071 |
| LL-values | LL($\beta_{f.c}$) = −483.819 | | LL($\beta_{m.c}$) = −412.700 | | LL($\beta_{f.b}$) = −387.421 | |
| | (all three samples) LL($\beta_{all}$) = −1283.940 (n = 483) | | | | | |

Note

a This regressor (*Participation × High Initial Risk*) only active for colorectal samples.

*Table 7.5* Tests of equality of parameters by gender and cancer in ordered logit models of utility of screening using stated ranks

| Regressor | Cross-sample equality by parameter $\beta_{fc,k} = \beta_{mc,k} = \beta_{fb,k}$, $k = 1,11$ | | Cross-sample equality all parameters $\beta_{fc} = \beta_{mc} = \beta_{fb}$ | |
|---|---|---|---|---|
| | $X^2(2)$ | p-val | $\hat{\beta}$ | p-val |
| TEST | 3.09 | .2132 | −.008 | .3729 |
| FP * EDU | 7.68 | .0215 | −.037 | .0000 |
| RED | 5.06 | .0798 | .023 | .0000 |
| COST | 3.70 | .1573 | −.027 | .1815 |
| COST/ln(Y) | 4.11 | .1281 | .028 | .6356 |
| PARTICIPATE | 8.37 | .0152 | −.519 | .0240 |
| ×HIR[a] | 2.55 | .1114 | −.557 | .0000 |
| ×EDU | 1.15 | .5616 | .515 | .0012 |
| ×Y | 9.96 | .0069 | .010 | .0988 |
| PAY | 6.76 | .0341 | −1.43 | .0000 |
| ×Y | 5.03 | .0808 | .021 | .0893 |

$$LL(\beta_*) = -1300.69$$

$H_o$ Equality of parameter vectors, chi-squared tests with p-values

| | | |
|---|---|---|
| $\beta_{fc} = \beta_{mc}$ | $X^2(11)$ | 17.6 (0.0908) |
| $\beta_{fc} = \beta_{fb}$ | $X^2(10)$ | 14.8 (0.1391) |
| $\beta_{fc} = \beta_{mc} = \beta_{fb}$ | $X^2(21)$ | 33.5 (0.0410) |

Note

a This regressor (*Participation × High Initial Risk*) only active for colorectal samples.

*Table 7.6* Reduced ordered logit model for the three sub-samples combined[a,b]

| Regressor | | $\hat{\beta}^*$ | a.s.e. | $\hat{\beta}^*$/a.s.e | p-value |
|---|---|---|---|---|---|
| $X_1$ | FP × EDU | −.0246 | .0047 | −5.19 | .0000 |
| $X_2$ | RED | .0220 | .0017 | 13.17 | .0000 |
| $X_3$ | COST/ln(Y) | −.0543 | .0112 | −4.84 | .0000 |
| $X_4$ | PART[c] × BCS | −1.3418 | .2565 | −5.23 | .0000 |
| $X_5$ | PART × CCS × HIR | −.5737 | .1051 | −5.46 | .0000 |
| $X_6$ | PART × BCS × Y | .0506 | .0091 | 5.54 | .0000 |
| $X_7$ | PAY | −.8879 | .1162 | −7.64 | .0000 |

Notes

a $n = 483$; $LL(\hat{\beta}^*) = -1302.366$, joint significance of deleted coefficients, $X^2(25) = 36.9$, $p = 0.0596$.

b LIMDEP command is *DISC; LHS = RANG,ALTNUM; CHOICES = $A_0$, $A_1$, $A_2$, $A_3$; RHS = $X_1$, $X_2$, $X_3$, $X_4$, $X_5$, $X_6$, $X_7$; RANKS$*.

c *PART* is short for *PARTICIPATE*.

chi-squared test statistics – allowing all the other parameters to vary between the samples. In 6 out of the 11 coefficients we detect differences at least at the 10 per cent level including the *FP×EDU* and the *RED* coefficients, and mainly due to differences in the male sample. Secondly, we tested the hypothesis that all three vectors of parameters were equal – and estimated the eleven parameters subject to this restriction (right part of Table 7.5). This restriction was rejected, $X^2(21) = 33.5, p < 0.05$, bottom of Table 7.5, and again mainly due to differences in the male samples compared to the other two. Thirdly, we designed the down-testing of equation (7.2) such as to allow for differences in parameter values across the three samples. However, the down-testing procedure resulted in a reduced ordered logit model with differences only between the two cancer samples, and only associated with the *PARTICIPATE* variable (Table 7.6). Although some differences may have been suppressed due to the fact that the down-testing used $p < 0.01$ as a criterion for non-exclusion we conclude that the utility functions for males and females are the same and that they differ between the two cancer samples only with respect to the extra-attributive characteristics.

Table 7.6 presents the main results of estimation. The attribute Number of tests over life time was nominally significant in the fBCS sample but dropped out in the downward testing. The other three attributes, *FP, RED,* and *COST* show the expected signs and are statistically significant, although for *PF* only for the 78 per cent of the sample with some professional education. Extra-attributive participation utility is, unexpectedly, negative in the CCS samples for high-risk individuals and zero for low-risk individuals, and in the BCS sample negative for low-income individuals and positive for high-income individuals. Payment requirements generate as expected disutility. Goodness-of-fit is moderate. A cross-tabulation of observed and predicted ranks showed that we only predict 43 per cent of the ranks correctly, and their correlation coefficient is 0.44, and the mean error is 1.18 (Table 7.7).

We use the results in Table 7.6 to calculate rates of substitution in Table 7.8. The marginal rate of substitution for specificity versus sensitivity is about 1.12, i.e. on average an interviewee would accept an increase of false positivity over 25 years of 1 percentage point against a lifetime decrease in mortality risk of 1.12 out of 10,000, or one statistical death to 90 statistical false positive experiences. We are not aware of similar trade of estimates in the literature and have no comparison.

*Table 7.7* Goodness of fit statistics for reduced ordered logit model (cross-tabulation of predicted and observed ranks)

| Predicted rank | Observed ranks | | | | |
|---|---|---|---|---|---|
| | *R = 1* | *R = 2* | *R = 3* | *R = 4* | *Total* |
| *R = 1* | 214 | 171 | 67 | 31 | 483 |
| *R = 2* | 94 | 198 | 147 | 44 | 483 |
| *R = 3* | 114 | 72 | 157 | 126 | 469 |
| *R = 4* | 61 | 42 | 98 | 246 | 447 |
| Total | 483 | 483 | 469 | 447 | 1882 |

Notes
Summary GOF-statistics
Mean error                                               1.18
Correlation (predicted/observed ranks)      0.44
Proportion true predictions                       0.43

Table 7.8 Marginal rates of substitutions (MRS with respect to 'out-of-pocket payment' (willingness to pay interpretation))

| *At household income* (1000 DKK/month) | $\Delta RED = +1$ *(of 10,000 over lifetime)* ln Y[.0220/ .0543] | $\Delta FP = -1\%$ *(over lifetime)* EDU = 1 ln Y[.0246/ .0543] | *Participation per se, BCS* ln Y[(−1.3418 + .0506*Y)/ .0543] | *Participation per se, CCS* *if HIR = 1* lnY[2 .5737/ .0543] |
|---|---|---|---|---|
| 10 | 874 DKK | 970 DKK | −36,089 DKK | −22,261 DKK |
| 20 | 1136 DKK | 1262 DKK | −21,447 DKK | −28,962 DKK |
| 40 | 1399 DKK | 1554 DKK | 36,406 DKK | −35,665 DKK |

Note

$MRS_{FP(0/0), RED(0/000)} = -0.0246/0.0220 = -1.12(1\%FP \sim 1.12(0/000) RED)$.

Willingness to pay for increased mortality risk reduction and for false positive risk reduction increases log-linearly with income according to our model. At low household income levels, about 10,000 DKK per month, the WTP estimate for $\Delta RED = 1$ (out of 10,000) is 874 DKK, at median household income levels (20,000 DKK/month) it is 1136 DKK and at very high income levels (40,000 DKK/month) it is 1399 DKK. Using gender- and cancer-specific sample estimates we note that these WTP are 3 per cent lower in the BCS sample, 35 per cent higher in the CCS female sample, and 35 per cent lower in the CCS male sample, but the differences may be due to sampling errors. Willingness to pay for lowering risk of false positive screen test outcomes ($\Delta FP = -1$ per cent) is, at the same three income levels, 970, 1356, and 1554 DKK over lifetime – for persons with some professional education. These estimates may be too low for women because of the adverse influence from the male sample. Willingness to pay for lower FP-risk is 35 per cent higher in the BCS sample and 25 per cent higher in the CCS female sample.

The maximum out-of-pocket expenditure must be set as part of the design, and may be a critical parameter similar to contingent valuation designs. To estimate sensitivity of our results with respect to maximum out-of-pocket expenditure as a design parameter we re-estimated the reduced ordered logit of Table 7.6 with lower maximum out-of-pocket expenditure per test. The results of this sensitivity analysis are reported in Table 7.9. Deletion of the 106 interviewees faced with the maximum out-of-pocket expenditure of 5000 DKK per test (such that the maximum was now 2000 DKK per test) had dramatic impact on the slope of $COST/\ln(Y)$, from −0.0543 with max 5000 DKK to −0.1104 with max 2000, and WTP for *RED* drops by almost 50 per cent and for FP by 40 per cent. Further reduction in maximum out-of-pocket expenditure seems to have little impact.

## Discussion and conclusions

We used stated rankings of hypothetical cancer screening programmes to elicit the utility of screening participation and of four attributes (number of tests, mortality

*Table 7.9* Selected coefficient estimates and marginal rates of substitution at various levels of maximum out-of-pocket expenditure per test

|  | *Cost/test* ≤ 5000 | *Cost/test* ≤ 2000 | *Cost/test* ≤ 1000 |
|---|---|---|---|
| $n$ | 483 | 377 | 308 |
| $\beta_2$ (*FP* × *EDU*) | −0.0246 | −0.02966 | −0.03269 |
| $\beta_3$ (*RED*) | 0.02196 | 0.02360 | 0.02420 |
| $\beta_5$ (*COST*/ln(*Y*)) | −0.05432 | −0.1104 | −0.12563 |
| $MRS_{FP, RED}$ | −1.12 | −1.26 | −1.35 |
| $MRS_{RED, COST \mid Y=20,000}$ | 1210 DKK | 640 DKK | 577 DKK |
| $MRS_{FP, COST \mid Y=20,000}$ | 1358 DKK | 805 DKK | 779 DKK |

reduction, risk of false positive events, and out-of-pocket payment) of screening for respectively breast and colorectal cancer. We parameterized utility effects of these four screening attributes within the framework of a linear and additive specification of the random utility model, and used ordered logit regression to estimate the parameters. The specification also included effects of participation per se and of payment requirements per se as well as characteristics of the individuals, monthly household income, gender, professional education and for the colorectal cancer screening case hypothetical colorectal cancer mortality risk without screening.

We found utility from screening participation to be positively related to cancer mortality risk reduction, and negatively to out-of-pocket costs and for the 78 per cent of the sample with some professional education also to risks of false positive test outcomes, and to be unrelated to the number of screening tests over lifetime. Some differences were detected in the size of these effects for men and women and – for women – between the two cancer diseases. However, except for differences in extra-attributive participation benefits between the two screening programmes the differences were not large enough to survive the nominal 1 per cent test levels used in the statistical analysis. The implied willingness to pay for a cancer mortality risk reduction of 1 out of 10,000 is 1136 DKK at medium household income in the sample (about 20,000 DKK per month). The implied willingness to pay for a 1 percentage point reduction in risk of a false positive test outcome is 1262 DKK at medium household income. Willingness to pay for both attributes increases log-linearly with household income since the income-effect is related exclusively to the out-of-pocket cost factor. Both benefits as well as payment are distributed over a 25–30 years period. The marginal rate of substitution between false positive risk reductions and mortality risk reductions, i.e. between specificity and sensitivity, is about 90 to 1. Extra-attributive breast cancer screening participation benefits were negative, e.g. −21,500 DKK at median household income, but diminishing with income such as to become positive just above median household income. Colorectal cancer participation benefits were negative, and increasingly so with income, but only for individuals at high initial mortality risk. Except for participation benefits these results agree with our expectations.

The negative extra-attributive participation benefits do not necessarily contradict presence of information and regret benefits. These can be outweighed by other participation costs. The participation parameter is pretty much like a constant in a regression equation and as such it picks up mean effects of all excluded sources of screening benefits, e.g. anxiety costs may be related to the offer of screening as such rather than the frequency of tests. However, we have no explanation that colorectal cancer screening participation costs exist only for individuals at high and not at low initial risk.

Many methodological reservations should be taken into account in the interpretation of these results. Although 81 per cent of the sample were contacted and accepted the interview, we lost 20–25 per cent of the interviewees due to the heavy information load of the hypothetical choice setup, so effectively the participation rate is only 63 per cent. This threatens the representativeness of our estimation sample.

Applications of contingent valuation methods in health care have been criticized for poor dose–response sensitivity or the embedding effect, i.e. that the quantity of effects matters little for WTP. This appears to be less of a problem in conjoint analysis used here, where magnitudes of both mortality reduction and of false positivity had significant impact on utility. The implied WTP for the saving of a statistical life is about 11 millions DKK at median income which is a little less than was found for prevention of a statistical life in a Danish contingent valuation study in the context fatal traffic accidents (median WTP of 13.6 M DKK for an avoided statistical fatal injury, Kidholm, 1995). The implied WTP to avoid a false test outcome event is about 125,000 DKK. We have no comparison for this estimate. In other words, it takes 90 events of false test outcomes to outweigh one statistical life saved by screening.

Although our results may have some intuitive face validity and compare well with other Danish WTP estimates from another context, we maintain some reservations. The implied individual WTP for screening programmes is very high, apparently much higher than among Danish politicians who face the true budget constraints. Hypothetical bias in our WTP results is suggested by high sensitivity of the *COST*-coefficient in the utility function to the maximum out-of-pocket expenditure presented in the sample as was illustrated in Table 7.9. There is no reason to believe that WTP based on conjoint analysis is less susceptible to hypothetical bias than has been observed for other methods (Liljas and Blumenschein, 2000). These authors also survey various calibration methods suggested in the literature to come closer to the real WTP, and it seems there is some way to go before such methods reliably are ready.

The advantage of the conjoint analysis approach over the more direct WTP methods is that conjoint analysis provides other relevant information in terms of strengths of preferences that can encompass process – as well as outcome utility. These preference values may not easily translate to monetary benefit values due to hypothetical bias and other problems, but they may nevertheless be useful in policy analysis and decision making.

## Notes

This research was supported by grant #9901111 from the Danish Medical Research Council. We are grateful for comments from Bengt Liljas and other participants at the 19th Arne Ryde Symposium 'Individual decisions for Health', Lund 27–28 August 1999, and from two anonymous referees.

## References

Beggs, S., Cardell, S. and Hausman, J. (1981). Assessing the potential demand for electric cars. *Journal of Econometrics* 16: 1–19.

Berwick, D.M. and Weinstein, M.C. (1985). What do patients value? Willingness to pay for ultrasound in normal pregnancy. *Medical Care* 23: 881–93.

Cairns, J. and Shackley, P. (1993). Sometimes sensitive, seldom specific: a review of the economics of screening. *Health Economics* 2: 43–53.

Cohen, D.R. and Henderson, J.B. (1988). *Health, prevention and economics.* Oxford University Press, Oxford.

Day, N.E. and Walter, S.D. (1984). Simplified models for screening for chronic disease: estimation procedures for mass screening. *Biometrics* 40: 1–14.

de Koning, H.J., van Ineveld, B.M., van Oortmarrsen, G.J., de Haes, J.C.J.M., Collette, H.J.A., Hendriks, J.H.C. and van der Maas, P.J. (1991). Breast cancer screening and cost effectiveness; policy alternatives, quality of life considerations and the possible impact of uncertain factors. *International Journal of Cancer* 49: 531–7.

Eddy, D.M. (1990). Screening for cervical cancer. *Annals of Internal Medicine* 113: 373–84.

Farrands, P.A., Chamberlain, J. and Hardcastle, J.D. (1983). Factors affecting compliance with screening for colorectal cancer. In: Abstracts of invited and proffered papers. *British Journal of Cancer* 47: 559–60.

Gyrd-Hansen, D., Hølund, B. and Andersen, P. (1995). A cost-effectiveness analysis of cervical cancer screening: health policy implications. *Health Policy* 34: 35–51.

Gyrd-Hansen, D., Søgaard, J., and Kronborg, O. (1997). Analysis of screening data: colorectal cancer. *International Journal of Epidemiology* 26(6): 1172–81.

Gyrd-Hansen, D., Søgaard, J. and Kronborg, O. (1998). Colorectal cancer screening: efficiency and cost effectiveness. *Health Economics* 7: 9–20.

Gyrd-Hansen, D. and Søgaard, J. (2001). Analysing public preferences for cancer screening programmes. *Health Economics* 10: 617–34.

Jones-Lee, M.W. (1974). The value of changes in the probability of death or injury. *Journal of Political Economy* 82: 835–49.

Kidholm, K. (1995). Estimation af betalingsvilje for forebyggelse af personskader ved trafikulykker. Udgivelse i serien: Afhandlinger fra det samfundsvidenskabelige fakultet på Odense Universitet.

Koopmanschapf, M.A. *et al.* (1990a). Economic aspects of cervical cancer screening. *Social Science and Medicine* 30: 1081–7.

Koopmanschapf, M.A. *et al.* (1990b). Cervical cancer screening: attendance and cost-effectiveness. *International Journal of Cancer* 45: 410–15.

Kronborg, O., Fenger, C., Olsen, J. *et al.* (1996). A randomised study of screening for colorectal cancer with fecal occult blood test at Funen in Denmark. *The Lancet* 348: 1467–71.

Liljas, B. and Blumenschein, K. (2000). On hypothetical bias and calibration in cost-benefit studies. *Health Policy* 52: 53–70.

Loomes, G. and Sugden, R. (1982). Regret Theory: An alternative theory of rational choice under uncertainty. *The Economic Journal* 92: 805–24.

Lovell, M.C. (1983). Data mining, *The Review of Economics and Statistics*, LXV(1): 1–12.

Macrae, F.A., St. John, J.B., Ambikapathy, A., Sharpe, K. Garner, J.F. and the Ballarat General Practitioner Research Group (1986). Factors affecting compliance in colorectal cancer screening. Results of a study performed in Ballarat. *The Medical Journal of Australia* 144: 621–3.

Mooney, G. and Lange, M. (1993). Ante-natal screening: what constitutes 'benefit'? *Social Science and Medicine* 37: 873–8.

Mushlin, A.I. and Fintor, L. (1992). Is screening for breast cancer cost-effective? *Cancer* Supplement 69(7): 1957–62.

Persson, U., Lugner, A. and Svensson, M. (1995). Valuing the benefits of reducing the risk of non-fatal injuries using the willingness to pay approach. The Swedish experience. In: Schwab, N. and Soguel, N. (eds), *Contingent Valuation, Transport Safety and Value of Life*. Kluwer, Boston.

Smith, V.K. and Desvouges, W.H. (1987). An empirical analysis of the economic value of risk changes. *Journal of Political Economy* 95: 89–114.

Tabar, L., Fagerberg, G., Chen, H.H. *et al.* (1995). Efficacy of breast cancer by age. New results from the Swedish two-county trial. *Cancer* 75(10): 2507–17.

van der Maas, de Koning, H.J., van Ineveld, B.M. *et al.* (1989). The cost-effectiveness of breast cancer screening. *International Journal of Cancer* 43: 1055–60.

Wagner, J.L., Tunis, S., Brown, M., Ching, A. and Almeida R. (1996). Cost-effectiveness of colorectal cancer screening in average-risk adults. In: Young, G.P., Rozen, P. and Levin, B. (eds), *Prevention and Early Detection of Colorectal Cancer,* ch. 19. W.B. Saunders, London.

Weinstein, M.C., Shepard, D.S. and Pliskin, J.S. (1980). The economic value of changing mortality probabilities: a decision-theoretic approach. *Quarterly Journal of Economics* 94: 373–96.

# Part II

# Other agents' decisions for an individual's health

# 8    Expected utility theory and medical decision making

*Louis Eeckhoudt*

## Introduction

In 1975, S. Pauker and J. Kassirer (henceforth P.K.) published in the *New England Journal of Medicine* a very influential paper where they defined the 'treatment threshold' in the presence of a diagnostic risk.

The basic story of the paper is a simple and pretty realistic medical problem, because there is no perfect test available. A physician and/or his patient[1] must make the (irreversible) decision to treat or not to treat while there is only suspicion that a single (well-defined) illness might be present. This risk is characterized by the a priori probability of disease ($p$ with $0 < p < 1$). Given the medical benefits and costs of the potential treatment for the patient (benefits and costs are assumed to be known with certainty), P.K. describe the critical value of $p$ (i.e, the threshold) above which treatment becomes the best decision. Because the costs and benefits of the treatment are known with certainty while the risk relates to the true health state of the patient, we consider here – as P.K. did – a situation of 'diagnostic risk'.[2] Of course other assumptions corresponding to other medical situations would be possible (e.g. random costs and benefits of the treatment) but they will not be considered here for the sake of brevity.

Quite clearly P.K.'s paper is written in the spirit of the expected utility (E-U) model and it uses results known at the time. In this presentation, we discuss some extensions of P.K.'s analysis that can be made by using new concepts developed in the framework of the E-U theory.[3] These extensions rely mostly upon the notion of *prudence* developed by Kimball (1990) to analyse saving decisions and extended by Eeckhoudt–Kimball (1991) to insurance problems.

The chapter is organized as follows. First we describe the main ideas and results of P.K.'s paper for the case of a risk neutral decision maker. In the following section, we examine how risk aversion defined in a E-U framework affects the treatment threshold. Then we discuss background risks (comorbidity risks) and we show how the notion of prudence becomes important in this framework. The penultimate section extends the analysis to the case of the willingness to pay notion and we also quickly indicate how one would treat the case of therapeutic risks. Some conclusions end the chapter.

## P.K.'s model under risk neutrality

From the quick presentation of P.K.'s problem in the introduction one can formalize the D.M.'s choice by the following decision tree (D.T.):

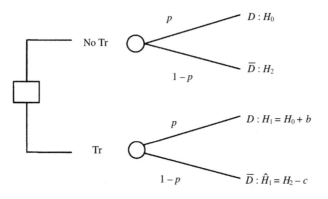

*Figure 8.1* The decision tree in the presence of diagnostic risks.

The consequence attached to the intersection between decisions [treatment (tr) or no treatment (no tr)] and states of the world [$D$ for disease and $\bar{D}$ for no disease] is a unidimensional variable denoted $H$ for health-stock. To make matters simple we interpret here $H$ as a number of remaining life years. In many cases[4] we have

$$H_0 < H_1 < \hat{H}_1 < H_2 \tag{8.1}$$

and $b$ stands for the (sure) benefit of a treatment correctly applied to a sick patient while $c$ is the (sure) detriment to health inflicted by treatment to a healthy patient.

Under risk neutrality $U(H) = H$ and treatment decision is the best one whenever

$$p[H_0 + b] + (1 - p)[H_2 - c] \geq pH_0 + (1 - p)H_2. \tag{8.2}$$

At the point of indifference (i.e when equality prevails in (8.2)) we obtain the value of the *treatment threshold* denoted $\hat{p}$. It is the a priori probability of disease that makes the two options (tr and no tr) equally attractive and it can easily be shown that

$$\hat{p} = \frac{c}{c + b}. \tag{8.3}$$

Whenever $p > \hat{p}$ (i.e. the likelihood of disease is sufficiently high) tr is quite naturally the best decision.

While P.K.'s model uses a decision variable of the '0–1' type we will sometimes consider an equivalent model where the decision variable – denoted y for
treatment intensity) – is continuous since this transformation makes the analysis
easier. The decision tree then sometimes reads as:

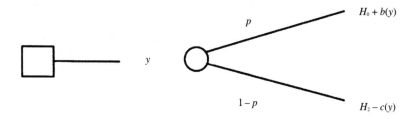

*Figure 8.2* A continuous treatment decision.

where $b(y)$ is increasing and concave in $y$ while $c(y)$ is increasing and convex.
Besides $b(0) = c(0) = 0$ and for all $y$: $H_0 + b(y) < H_2 - c(y)$.
   In this framework the risk neutral D.M. has to solve the following program:

$$\max_y p[H_0 + b(y)] + (1 - p)[H_2 - c(y)]. \tag{8.4}$$

The corresponding first-order condition (F.O.C) for an interior maximum is:

$$pb'(y) - (1 - p)c'(y) = 0, \tag{8.5}$$

while the second-order condition is automatically satisfied because of the concavity (convexity) of $b(y)$ $(c(y))$ function. The solution is denoted $y_N^*$.

## P.K.'s model under risk aversion

Once the solution is established under risk neutrality one can wonder how risk
aversion affects the decision to treat. Risk aversion is introduced by considering
an expected utility maximizer decision maker with a utility function $U(H)$ which
is increasing and concave in $H$ i.e. $U'(H) > 0$ and $U''(H) < 0$.
   In the '0–1' case à la P.K., the treatment threshold denoted $\hat{p}$ is obtained by
solving in $p$ the following equation:

$$pU(H_0 + b) + (1 - p)U(H_2 - c) = pU(H_0) + (1 - p)U(H_2), \tag{8.6}$$

yielding:

$$\hat{p} = \frac{U(H_2) - U(H_2 - c)}{[U(H_2) - U(H_2 - c)] + [U(H_0 + b) - U(H_0)]}. \tag{8.7}$$

By using the mean value theorem (see Appendix 1) one can show that

$$\hat{\hat{p}} < \hat{p}. \tag{8.8}$$

When the decision maker becomes risk averse, treatment is *more* often prefered to no treatment. This result comes as a surprise to many physicians because they have in mind (correctly) that 'treatments are risky'. This is true when one considers therapeutic hazards. However here both $b$ and $c$ are assumed to be known with certainty. The only source of risk in the present model is the diagnostic risk and vis à vis this risk, treatment is a risk reducing strategy. Indeed going back to Figure 8.1 it is obvious that the spread in outcomes is lower with the 'tr' branch than with the 'no tr' one because:

$$(H_2 - c) - (H_0 + b) < H_2 - H_0.$$

Since in a binary world with given probabilities the outcome spread is a good measure of the quantity of risk involved, it is clear that choosing 'tr' is risk reducing. Hence risk averse patients will tend to accept the treatment strategy even when its expected (average) outcome is negative.

The same kind of result emerges when one has a continuous decision variable. In this case, the optimization problem is:

$$\max_{y} pU(H_0 + b(y)) + (1 - p)U(H_2 - c(y)), \tag{8.9}$$

and the associated F.O.C. is:

$$pb'(y)U'(H_0 + b(y)) - (1 - p)c'(y)U'(H_2 - c(y)) = 0, \tag{8.10}$$

the solution of which being denoted $y_A^*$.

Now compare (8.10) with (8.5), the equivalent condition under risk neutrality. We see that the marginal benefit of treatment under risk neutrality ($pb'(y)$) is now multiplied by a number ($U'(H_0 + b(y))$) which – because of risk aversion – is higher than the one multiplying the marginal health cost of treatment (($1 - p)c'(y)$). Hence $y_A^*$ is surely higher than $y_N^*$: risk averse patients choose a higher treatment intensity than risk neutral ones. This result goes of course in the same direction as the one obtained for '0–1' decisions which indicates that treatment is more often used by risk averse patients than by risk neutral ones.

Now that we understand how risk aversion affects treatment decisions when only diagnostic risk is present, we are ready to examine the impact of background (comorbidity) risks.

## Background (comorbidity) risks

In our approach so far, the decision maker avails upon one instrument (treatment) to cope with a single risk.[5] However many other risks than the one which is managed are present and they can influence the treatment decision for the partly controllable risk. These exogenous risks are called 'background' and a good example in the medical field is given by 'comorbidity' risks.[6] Indeed if the patient does have the illness that is suspected and that is about to be treated, other more or less related conditions may or may not develop so that $H_0$ is no longer a given number but is indeed a random variable $\tilde{H}_0$. For the sake of simplicity and to concentrate on the main features we assume that:

$$\tilde{H}_0 = H_0 + \tilde{\varepsilon} \text{ with } E(\tilde{\varepsilon}) = 0. \tag{8.11}$$

If the patient is healthy, we assume that no side condition will prevail so that $H_2$ is not affected. The selection of the appropriate treatment intensity is now given by:

$$\max_y pE[U(H_0 + \tilde{\varepsilon} + b(y))] + (1 - p)U(H_2 - c(y)), \tag{8.12}$$

with first-order condition (F.O.C.):

$$pb'(y)E[U'(H_0 + \tilde{\varepsilon} + b(y))] - (1 - p)c'(y)[U'(H_2 - c(y))] = 0. \tag{8.13}$$

We want to compare (8.13) with (8.10), the optimality condition under risk aversion without background risk. Quite obviously, the optimal $y$ under background risk (denoted $y_c^{*}$)[7] exceed the one under risk aversion ($y_A^{*}$) if

$$E[U'(H_0 + \tilde{\varepsilon} + b(y))] > U'(H_0 + b(y)) \tag{8.14}$$

because the comorbidity risk affects the marginal benefit of $y$ without changing its cost. Since by assumption $E(\tilde{\varepsilon}) = 0$, it immediately follows from Jensen's inequality that (8.14) is satisfied whenever $U'$ is a convex function of $H$, that is when $U''' > 0$ (see Appendix 2 for a graphical illustration).

The condition $U''' > 0$ was termed 'prudence' by Kimball (1990). In a saving context it means that the decision maker saves more to pay when he faces uncertainty about his future income. In the medical context here, prudence means that the patient chooses a higher treatment intensity to compensate for the risk ($\tilde{\varepsilon}$) that surrounds his health state if sick. In fact the introduction of a new, uncontrollable risk ($\tilde{\varepsilon}$) induces a prudent patient to better control the risk he can manage, that is the diagnostic risk. Prudent patients have a tendency to substitute risks: if the comorbidity risk increases, the prudent patient reduces his diagnostic risk by increasing $y$. The 'imprudent' patient would do just the reverse and if $U''' = 0$, $y_c^{*}$ is insensitive to the presence of $\tilde{\varepsilon}$.

Kimball correctly insists that prudence should be distinguished from risk aversion. Risk aversion tells how much risk is *disliked* while prudence indicates how much the decision maker is willing to *act* when he has to face risk. While risk aversion is passive (it is a statement about preferences) prudence is an 'active' notion because it is concerned with the way in which risk alters current decisions. Finally observe that while $-U''/U'$ indicates the degree of (absolute) risk aversion, $-(U'''/U'')$ measures the intensity of the prudence motive. This result is easily obtained by applying to $U'$ the technique applied to $U$ by Arrow–Pratt to express absolute risk aversion.

Since the prudence coefficient – as well as that of absolute risk aversion – expresses, a behavioural attitude in the framework of the E-U model, experiments might be run to check whether $U'''$ is positive, negative or zero for decision makers who satisfy the E-U axioms.

Indeed for this purpose, one would have to specify to the interviewed person the values of $p$, $H_0$, $H_2$ and the $b(y)$ and $c(y)$ functions and ask him to choose a treatment intensity. Then one introduces risk around $H_0$ and one asks the interviewed person the new value he would select for $y$. The comparison between the new and old values of $y$ yields then information about the sign of the third derivative of the decision maker's utility function in the E-U model.

As is well known, once absolute risk aversion was defined, the assumption that is decreasing with wealth turned out to be powerful in economics and finance problems. In the same way as for risk aversion one may wonder how prudence changes with the stock of health.

To give an intuition about this question, let us consider that the background risk $\tilde{\varepsilon}$ now applies both to sick and healthy patients. It represents then all the other risks to life and it is independent of the diagnostic risk. In this case the patient's problem becomes:

$$\max_{y} pE[U(H_0 + \tilde{\varepsilon} + b(y))] + (1 - p)EU(H_2 + \tilde{\varepsilon}\, c(y)), \qquad (8.15)$$

yielding the F.O.C.

$$pb'(y)E[U'(H_0 + \tilde{\varepsilon} + b(y))] - (1 - p)c'(y)EU'(H_2 + \tilde{\varepsilon} - c(y))] = 0. \qquad (8.16)$$

We want to compare the solution of (8.16) denoted $\hat{y}$ again with that in (8.10) (that was denoted $y_A^*$). We first notice that (8.16) can be rewritten as

$$pb'(y)U'(H_0 + b(y) - \psi_0) - (1 - p)c'(y)U'(H_2 - c(y) - \psi_2) = 0, \qquad (8.17)$$

where $\psi_0$ and $\psi_2$ are the prudence premia associated with the $\tilde{\varepsilon}$ lottery evaluated at $H_0 + b(y)$ for $\psi_0$ and at $H_2 - c(y)$ for $\psi_2$.

If prudence is positive and decreasing in $H$, then $\psi_0$ exceeds $\psi_2$ and because of risk aversion (i.e. in this framework $U'$ decreasing in $H$) we obtain that the background risk increases more the marginal benefit of treatment $(pb'(y)U'(H_0 + b(y)))$ than its marginal cost $((1 - p)c'(y)U'(H_2 - c(y) - \psi_2))$. Hence under positive and decreasing prudence a background risk that is independent of the diagnostic risk leads to a higher treatment intensity. We thus obtain the same result as for the case where the background risk shows up only under $H_0$ but notice that we need one more assumption, namely that prudence is decreasing in $H$.[8]

## Another application: the value of an increased lifetime

While the role of the prudence concept was illustrated so far in a medical decision making framework with a unidimensional utility function, we now show that it is also relevant in other (more general) problems.

Start again from Figure 8.1 disregarding the 'tr' option so that the initial lottery faced by the individual is

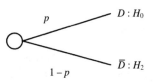

*Figure 8.3* The health lottery.

where $H_0$ and $H_2$ are numbers of life years.

Now let us wonder what the decision maker is willing to pay (WTP) to obtain with certainty (that is in each state of the world) $s$ more life years.[9]

To answer this question we now describe the decision maker's utility function by a two dimensional function:

$$U(W, H),$$

where $W$ stands for wealth.

As is standard in the literature on the value of a statistical life we assume

$$U_1 = \frac{\delta U}{\delta W} > 0, \quad U_{11} < 0$$

$$U_2 = \frac{\delta U}{\delta H} > 0, \quad U_{22} < 0$$

and $U_{12} \geq 0$, that is the marginal utility of wealth increases with health.

The WTP for $s$ additional life years received with certainty – which is denoted $M(s)$ – is obtained by solving:

$$pU(W_0 - M(s), H_0 + s) + (1 - p)U(W_0 - M(s), H_2 + s)$$
$$= pU(W_0, H_0) + (1 - p)U(W_0, H_2). \tag{8.18}$$

Keeping in mind that the right-hand side of (8.18) is constant, we obtain by differentiating (8.18) that:

$$\frac{dM(s)}{ds} = \frac{pU_2(W_0 - M(s), H_0 + s) + (1 - p)U_2(W_0 - M(s), H_2 + s)}{pU_1(W_0 - M(s), H_0 + s) + (1 - p)U_1(W_0 - M(s), H_2 + s)}. \tag{8.19}$$

As usual in the literature on the value of a statistical life we evaluate $dM(s)/ds$ at $s = 0$ so that (8.19) simplifies into:

$$\frac{dM(s)}{ds}\bigg|_{s=0} = \frac{pU_2(W_0, H_0) + (1-p)U_2(W_0, H_2)}{pU_1(W_0, H_0) + (1-p)U_1(W_0, H_2)}. \qquad (8.20)$$

Without surprise we obtain that the marginal rate of substitution between health and wealth is a ratio of (expected) marginal utilities. What is more interesting however is that the numerator measures the expected marginal utility of health at a given wealth level ($W_0$). Hence we can again use the prudence concept to obtain:

$$\frac{dM(s)}{ds}\bigg|_{s=0} = \frac{U_2(W_0, E(\tilde{H}) - \psi)}{pU_1(W_0, H_0) + (1-p)U_1(W_0, H_2)}. \qquad (8.21)$$

As a result we see that the monetary value of an increased life expectancy depends upon the decision maker's degree of prudence towards lotteries on health. In fact the greater his degree of prudence, the more value he puts on additional life years.

While prudence is relevant to look at the WTP concept, it is possible also to apply it in the framework of therapeutic hazards. In this case, it is known with certainty that the patient is sick but one does not know with certainty what the treatment outcome will be. The basic lottery then is:

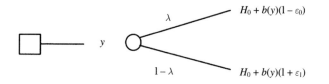

*Figure 8.4*  Therapeutic hazard where $\lambda$ is the probability of an adverse effect.

Introducing background risk on $H_0$ in this problem would also exhibit the prudence notion.

## Conclusions

In the early 80's expected utility theory was intensively used (implicitly or explicitly) as well in the medical decision making literature as in health economics. Since then many applications have been 'routinely' done while from time to time health economists and decision scientists showed interest for 'non E-U' models of choice. Recent publications by Wakker–Stiggelbout (1995), Treadwell–Lenert (1999) and Bayoumi–Redelmeier (2000) illustrate the growing impact of these new models in the field of medical decision making.

While I am convinced that these new models are both descriptively important and intellectually stimulating, one should not forget that progress has also been made since the 70's in the framework of the E-U model itself. To a wide extent these advances have concerned a better understanding of risk interrelationships. Thanks to the prudence concept and its recent extensions by Pratt–Zeckhauser (1987) or Gollier–Pratt (1996), we now have tools to examine how exogenous risks impact upon the management of endogenous ones. While prudence has already shown its usefulness in finance and economics problems, the purpose of this chapter was to show that it may also be relevant in medical decision making.

## Appendix 1

Using the mean value theorem we may write

$$U(H_2 - c) = U(H_2) - cU'(H_2 - \theta_c), \tag{8.22}$$

where $0 \leq \theta \leq 1$, and

$$U(H_2 + b) = U(H_0) + bU'(H_2 + \rho b),$$

where $0 \leq \rho \leq 1$.

Consequently (8.7) becomes:

$$\hat{p} = \frac{cU'(H_2 - \theta_c)}{cU'(H_2 - \theta_c) + bU'(H_0 + \rho b)},$$

so that

$$\frac{1}{\hat{p}} = 1 + \frac{bU'(H_0 + \rho b)}{cU'(H_2 - \theta_c)}. \tag{8.23}$$

Since from (8.3)

$$\frac{1}{\hat{p}} = 1 + \frac{b}{c},$$

and since risk aversion implies:

$$U'(H_2 + \rho b) > U'(H_2 - \theta_c),$$

it follows that

$$\frac{1}{\hat{p}} > \frac{1}{\hat{p}}$$

or

$$\hat{p} < \hat{p}.$$

Q.E.D.

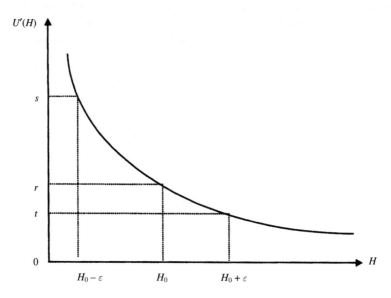

*Figure 8.5* The convex $U'(H)$ curve.

## Appendix 2

To show the relationship between prudence and the convexity of $U'$, let us draw in Figure 8.5 a curve for $U'$ that is convex in $H$, and to simplify matters let us assume that $\tilde{\varepsilon}$ is a binary and symmetric random variable.

Should $H_0$ be obtained with certainty, the corresponding level of $U'$ would be $r$. The introduction of a background risk creates two possible equally likely outcomes that yield respectively a marginal utility of $s$ (in case of bad luck) and of $t$ (in case of good luck). Hence because the outcomes are equally likely, expected marginal utility which is equal to $(1/2\ s) + (1/2)\ t$ exceeds $r$. Thus the convexity of $U'$ induces a prudent behaviour because it raises the marginal benefit of treatment and in this way leads to a higher treatment intensity.

## Notes

This chapter has benefited from discussions with H. Bleichrodt, D. Crainich, Ph. Godfroid and colleagues at CRESGE (Lille). Two referees' comments have also been quite useful to improve the text and clarify some points.

1  We will say for short the decision maker, assuming that the physician is a perfect agent for the patient.
2  Another risk that surrounds medical decisions is the 'therapeutic risk'. It corresponds to situations where the patient's state of health is known with certainty but where the effects of the treatment are random. The relationship between diagnostic and therapeutic risks is analysed in detail in Eeckhoudt (2002).

3 Of course, another potential extension is to apply non-E-U models to P.K.'s problem. See the conclusion for relevant references.

4 Although the ordering proposed in (8.1) is plausible, others are possible and cannot be rejected a priori. However their discussion would not add much to the results already obtained in the case that is more often observed.

5 In fact, in the 70s and 80s, this feature was also encountered in the economics and insurance literature. The consideration of background risks is recent also in these fields, since it was initiated by Kimball's paper in 1990.

6 For a first discussion of the impact of comorbidity risks, see Harris and Nease (1997).

7 The subscript $C$ stands for comorbidity.

8 To be technically complete we also need decreasing absolute risk aversion. Notice that non-negative prudence is necessary (but not sufficient) for decreasing absolute risk aversion.

9 The question is different from the one raised to find the value of a statistical life (VSL). There the concern is to obtain WTP for a change in the probability of a bad outcome.

# References

Bayoumi, A.M. and Redelmeier, D.A. (2000). 'Decision analysis with cumulative prospects theory', *Medical Decision Making* 20, 404–12.

Eeckhoudt, L. and Kimball, M.S. (1991). 'Background risk, prudence and the demand for insurance', in: Dionne, G. (ed.), *Contributions to Insurance Economics*, Kluwer Academic Publishers, Boston.

Eeckhoudt, L. (2002). *Risk and Medical Decision Making*, forthcoming, Kluwer Academic Publishers, Boston.

Gollier, C. and Pratt, J. (1996). 'Risk vulnerability and the tempering effect of background risk', *Econometrica* 64, 1109–24.

Harris, R.A. and Nease, R.F. Jr (1997). 'The importance of patient preferences for comorbidities in cost-effectiveness analyses', *Journal of Health Economics* 16(1), 113–19.

Kimball, M.S. (1990). 'Precautionary saving in the small and in the large', *Econometrica* 58, 53–73.

Pauker, S. and Kassirer, J. (1975). 'Therapeutic decision making: a cost-benefit analysis', *New England Journal of Medicine* 293, 229–34.

Pratt, J. and Zeckhauser, R. (1987). 'Proper risk aversion', *Econometrica* 55, 143–54.

Treadwell, J.R. and Lenert, L.A. (1999). 'Health value and prospect theory', *Medical Decision Making* 19, 344–52.

Wakker, P. and Stiggelbout, A. (1995). 'Explaining distorsion in utility elicitation through the rank-dependent model for risky choices', *Medical Decision Making* 15, 180–6.

# 9 Quality incentives under a capitation regime

## The role of patient expectations

*Hugh Gravelle and Giuliano Masiero*

### Introduction

The British National Health Service is a prominent example of a regulated capitated primary care system. Care is provided free of charge to patients. All patients must join the list of a general practitioner (GP) who is paid a tax-financed capitation fee for each registered patient. One rationale of a capitated system is to provide an incentive to GPs to compete via quality for additional patients. GPs can vary the quality of their service, for example increasing their surgery opening hours, employing more practice nurses to provide additional services, being more willing to make home visits, or keeping their medical knowledge up to date. Higher capitation fees make it more profitable to attract additional patients by raising the quality of the service provided.

Patients are unlikely to be very good judges of quality. The extensive literature on doctor–patient agency problems attests to the prevalence of the belief that patients are imperfectly informed about the quality of their doctors. However, it can be argued that many aspects of quality in primary care which may not be obvious when choosing a practice can be judged by patients once they have experienced them. Examples range from the interpersonal aspects of consultations to the ease of getting appointments or out of hours visits. Thus at least some aspects of the practice are experience goods.

But even if patients become better informed about their practice after experiencing its care, they face costs in switching to another GP. Their new GP will be initially less well informed about them than their current doctor. Medical records are an imperfect substitute for personal contact and are transferred with a significant delay. Thus in addition to the time and trouble involved in changing registrations, switching to another GP imposes costs in the form of a lower initial level of care *ceteris paribus*.

In this chapter we consider the extent to which imperfect patient information about quality and switching costs interact to blunt incentives to improve quality when capitation fees are increased. Our focus is on the extent to which different assumptions about the sophistication of patients leads to different conclusions about the power of the capitation system as a means of increasing quality. Given that patients are imperfect judges of quality when initially choosing a practice, we consider whether their awareness of this fact has implications for the effect of capitation fees on quality.

We compare the implications of three alternative assumptions about patient beliefs about the quality of GPs. In the first case patients are sophisticated. They know that their initial observations of quality may be mistaken and hence that they may wish to switch GPs when they learn more about the quality of the care provided by the GP they choose. The error distribution of patients is symmetrical in the sense that they are as likely to over estimate quality before experiencing care as to underestimate it. In the second case, patients still have unbiased expectations but they are myopic and do not realize that they may be making a mistake and wish to switch when they have experienced care. Finally, we consider the case in which patients are myopic and have biased expectations about quality.

In the next section we introduce a two-period model with overlapping generations of patients and derive the demand faced by GPs under our three assumptions about the sophistication of patients' quality expectations. In the following section, we examine the equilibrium quality of a publicly funded system in the three cases. We consider how quality is affected by patients' errors and switching costs and how quality responds to increases in the capitation fee. The penultimate section discusses welfare properties of the regulated market, derives the optimal capitation fee and examines the welfare implications of the different assumptions about patient expectations. Finally (p. 177) we present our conclusions.

## The model

We apply the standard horizontal product differentiation model to the market for primary care by incorporating switching costs and imperfect information about practice quality. Of the many switching cost models (Klemperer, 1995) ours is perhaps closest to the two-period model of Klemperer (1987). We have introduced additional features (endogenous product quality, experience goods[1]) but can make some simplifying assumptions to keep the model tractable. Because we examine a regulated market the price faced by firms (GPs) is fixed and constant over both periods, rather than endogenous and possibly varying over time. We also restrict attention to symmetric equilibria in which GPs follow identical policies.

At the beginning of the first period $n$ patients are located uniformly along a street of unit length. At the end of the period $\gamma^o n$ ($\gamma^o \in [0, 1]$) old patients leave the market and a new generation of young patients $\gamma^y n$ ($\gamma^y \in [0, 1]$) enters. At the end of the second period all patients leave and none enter.

We assume that preferences, costs, and technology are time invariant and such that the market is covered.[2] The *full coverage* assumption is adopted because we are interested in the efficiency of GPs' choice of quality. When the market is not fully covered reductions in quality could drive some patients from the market rather than to other GPs. It is well known (Spence, 1975) that quality and price are inefficient in such circumstances.[3] We wish to separate out the effects of switching costs on the quality of the experience good from other sources of inefficiency.

A practice is located at each end of the street and a patient's location between them determines his preference for the service characteristics. Patient distance $d \in [0, 1]$can be interpreted as a geographical distance or as the difference between the level of some horizontally differentiated service characteristic of the practice and the level which would maximize the utility of that particular patient. $td$ is the patient's disutility of being located at a distance $d$ from GP $A$ if he joins that practice. $t(1 - d)$ is the distance cost if he joins GP $B$. Patients are *ex ante* identical except for location and age.

GP $i$ provides a service of quality $q_i$. All patients would agree, if correctly informed, that the GP was providing a more valuable service if $q_i$ increased.[4]

### Errors and switching costs

Before joining a list a young patient has imperfect information about the quality of both practices and observes the quality provided by GP $i$ with an error $\tilde{e}_i$:

$$\tilde{q}_i = q_i + \tilde{e}_i. \tag{9.1}$$

An old patient has a perfect knowledge of the quality provided by the list he decided to join in the first period. He does not acquire any information about the quality of the other practice: he makes the same error about it as he did when young.

The errors which young patients make in observing practice quality are identically and independently distributed. To keep the analysis tractable we adopt a simple error structure and assume that the error made in observing the quality of practice $i$ by a patient is

$$\tilde{e}_i \in \{e_i, - e_i\}, \tag{9.2}$$

$$e_i = a_i + m_i q_i, \quad a_i \geq 0, \quad m_i \in [0, 1], \quad i = A, B. \tag{9.3}$$

The formulation allows for both purely additive ($a_i > 0$, $m_i = 0$) and multiplicative ($a_i = 0$, $m_i > 0$) errors as well as mixed types. Purely additive errors may be somewhat implausible since they imply that the range of perceived qualities does not vary with actual quality. The assumption is sometimes useful for generating unambiguous results.

The probability that the error is positive, so that observed quality is greater than true quality is $\pi = \Pr[\tilde{e}_i = e_i]$. With sophisticated patients (case 1) who know that their observations may be subject to error, we assume that the error distribution is symmetric: they are as likely to overestimate as to underestimate:

$$\pi = \Pr[\tilde{e}_i = e_i] = \Pr[\tilde{e}_i = -e_i] = 1/2.$$

Myopic or less sophisticated patients do not realize that they may make errors in assessing quality. In case 2 the myopic patients make unbiased estimates of quality and so $\pi = 1/2$. The third case has myopic patients who make biased estimates of quality. They may be optimistic ($\pi > 1/2$) or pessimistic ($\pi < 1/2$).

*Table 9.1* Notation

| | |
|---|---|
| $p$ | capitation fee |
| $d$ | patient's distance to GP $A$ |
| $t$ | cost per unit of distance |
| $q_i$ | quality of GP $i$ |
| $\tilde{q}_i = q_i + \tilde{e}_i$ | perceived quality of GP $i$ |
| $\tilde{e}_i \in \{e_i, -e_i\}$ | equiprobable errors of uninformed patients |
| $e_i = a_i + m_i q_i$ | error parameter |
| $S_i$ | cost to patient of switching to GP $i$ |
| $\delta_g^y, \delta_g$ | market segment of GP $A$ amongst first and second period young patients in group $g = 1, \ldots, 4$ |
| $\gamma^y$ | proportion of young patients entering in second period |
| $\gamma^o$ | proportion of old patients exiting in second period |
| $\delta_\gamma^{AB}$ | location of group $g$ patient who is indifferent between switching from GP $A$ to GP $B$ |
| $D_1^i$ | first period demand for GP $A$ |
| $D_2^i = D^{iy} + D^{io}$ | second period demand for GP $i$ |
| $V^i$ | expected discounted profit of GP $i$ |
| $\lambda$ | marginal deadweight loss from taxation |
| $\beta q_i^2$ | cost of quality |

An old patient who decides to change practices at the beginning of period 2 incurs a cost $s_i$ of switching to GP $i$ with $s_i < e_j$. The latter condition ensures that at least some patients will change their doctor in the second period. We assume that switching costs are exogenous and the same for both GPs: $s_A = s_B = s$. We also assume that the parameters in the error distributions are exogenous and the same for both GPs ($a_i = a$, $m_i = m$). We retain the distinguishing subscripts to aid derivation of results.[5]

In what follows in this section we derive the demand functions for GP $A$ and hence for GP $B$ for young and old consumers under the assumption that the differences between the qualities of the two GPs are sufficiently small. Using these demand functions we then show in the next section that there exists a Nash equilibrium in qualities in which the GPs do indeed choose the same quality.

### First-period demand

#### Case 1: sophisticated patients

We start by deriving demand in the first and second periods under the assumption that patients are sophisticated enough to realize that their observations of quality are subject to error. In the first period when all patients are young, a patient is located at a distance $d$ from GP $A$ and perceives benefits $r + \tilde{q}_A - td$ and $r + \tilde{q}_B - t(1 - d)$ from joining the list of GPs $A$ and $B$, compared with joining no list. Care is financed from taxation and practices do not charge prices to their patients.

Sophisticated young patients realize that their observations of quality $\hat{q}_i$ are subject to error and that they may wish to change GPs when they acquire better information about the GP chosen when young. The quality beliefs of young patients in the first period who have made their observations $\hat{q}_i$ of the quality of GP $i$ are summarized as

$$E_1\tilde{q}_i = q_i, \tag{9.4}$$

where $E_1$ denotes their expectation in period 1 given their observation of the quality of GP $i$.

In the second period, as old consumers, they have perfect quality information about GP $i$ they chose when young but no additional information about the other GP $j$. Their expectations are

$$E_{i2}\tilde{q}_i = q_i, \quad E_1E_{i2}\tilde{q}_i = E_1\hat{q}_i = \hat{q}_i, \tag{9.5}$$

$$E_{i2}\tilde{q}_j = \hat{q}_j, \quad E_1E_{i2}\tilde{q}_j = E_1\hat{q}_j = \hat{q}_j, \tag{9.6}$$

where $E_{i2}$ denotes the expectation in the second period of an old patient who chose GP $i$ when young.

The only new information a patient anticipates getting when old is the true quality of the GP chosen when young. He realizes that he may switch GPs in the second period but only if he receives unfavourable information about the GP chosen when young.[6] In the first period a young patient believes that if he chooses GP $A$ when young, he will switch to GP $B$ in the second period if he learns he has overestimated its quality when young and if[7]

$$E_1E_{A2}^u\tilde{q}_A - td = \hat{q}_a - e_A - td$$
$$< E_1E_{A2}^u\tilde{q}_B - t(1-d) - s_B$$
$$= \hat{q}_B - t(1-d) - s_B. \tag{9.7}$$

$E_1E_{A2}^u\tilde{q}_A$ is his belief at the first period, given his observation of quality in the first period, about second period quality net of distance costs, given that he will receive unfavourable information about GP $A$.

The inequality (9.7) establishes a critical distance $\hat{d}_1$

$$\hat{d}_1 = \frac{\hat{q}_A - \hat{q}_B + t - e_A + s_B}{2t} = \frac{\hat{z} - e_A + s_B}{2t}, \tag{9.8}$$

where $\hat{z} = \hat{q}_A - \hat{q}_B + t$. Patients who have $d \in [0, \hat{d}_1]$ believe they will not switch when old if they choose GP $A$ at the first period. They believe they will be with GP $A$ in both periods and get discounted expected utility from choosing GP $A$ of

$$\hat{q}_A - td + k_c\left[\frac{1}{2}(\hat{q}_A + e_A - td) + \frac{1}{2}(\hat{q}_A - e_A - td)\right] = (\hat{q}_A - td)(1 + k_c), \tag{9.9}$$

where $k_c \in [0, 1]$ is the one period discount factor for patients.

On the other hand, young patients with $d_i \in [\hat{d}, 1]$ believe that there is a probability 1/2 that they will get unfavourable information about GP *A* if they choose her when young, in which case they will be better off switching to GP *B* when old. They anticipate discounted expected utility from choosing GP *A* of

$$\hat{q}_A - td + k_c \left[ \frac{1}{2} (\hat{q}_A + e_A - td) + \frac{1}{2} [\hat{q}_B - t(1-d) - s_B] \right], \qquad (9.10)$$

which is the sum of expected utility from GP *A* in first period and the expected discounted utility in the second period given that they are equally likely to remain with GP *A* as to switch to GP *B*.

We proceed similarly with patients who choose GP *B* when young and define

$$\hat{d}_2 = \frac{\hat{z} + e_B - s_A}{2t} > \hat{d}_1. \qquad (9.11)$$

Patients who have $d \in [\hat{d}_2, 1]$ believe they will not switch when old if they choose GP *B* at first period. They believe they will get discounted expected utility from choosing GP *B* of

$$[\hat{q}_B - t(1 - d)](1 + k_c). \qquad (9.12)$$

Patients with $d \in [0, \hat{d}_2]$ believe they will switch to GP *A* with probability $\frac{1}{2}$ when old if they choose GP *B* when young. They anticipate discounted expected utility from choosing GP *B* of

$$\hat{q}_B - t(1 - d) + k_c \left[ \frac{1}{2} (\hat{q}_A - td - s_A) + \frac{1}{2} [\hat{q}_B + e_B - t(1 - d)] \right]. \qquad (9.13)$$

Using the expected discounted utilities from choosing GPs *A* and *B* we can now determine which patients choose which GP when young. From (9.11) patients with $d \in [0, d_1]$ do not believe they will switch if they choose GP *A*, in which case they will get (9.9), but they may switch if they choose GP *B*, in which case they will get (9.13). Hence they will choose GP *A* to GP *B* when young if and only if (9.9) exceeds (9.13). Since (9.9) is decreasing and (9.13) is increasing in *d*, all patients for whom

$$d \leq \hat{d}_1^o = \frac{1}{2t} \left[ \hat{z} - \frac{k_c}{2 + k_c} (e_B - s_A) \right]$$

prefer GP *A*. Similarly patients with $d \in [\hat{d}_2, 1]$, who do not believe they will switch from GP *B* if they choose it but may switch from GP *B*, will prefer GP *B* if and only if (9.12) exceeds (9.10) or

$$d > \hat{d}_2^o = \frac{1}{2t} \left[ \hat{z} + \frac{k_c}{2 + k_c} (e_A - s_B) \right].$$

Patients with $d \in [\hat{d}_1, \hat{d}_2]$ may switch to GP $B$ if they choose GP $A$ and vice versa. Using (9.10) and (9.13), they will choose GP $A$ if and only if

$$d \leq \frac{1}{2t}\left[\hat{z} + \frac{k_c}{2}(e_A - e_B + s_A - s_B)\right] = \frac{1}{2t}[\hat{z} + \omega] = \hat{\delta}, \qquad (9.14)$$

where $\omega = k_c(e_A - e_B + S_A + S_B)$. In the neighbourhood of symmetric equilibria where GPs follow identical policies $\hat{d}_1 < \hat{d}_1^o < \hat{\delta} < \hat{d}_2^o < \hat{d}_2$ and so all young patients with $d \in [0, \hat{\delta}]$ choose GP $A$ and all those with $d \in [\hat{\delta}, 1]$ choose GP $B$.

The realized values of the errors define four values of $\hat{\delta}$ and hence four groups of young patients. Since positive and negative errors are equiprobable each group is of size $n/4$. For example, group 1 are those who overestimate the quality of both GPs and their demand for GP $A$ is $n\delta_1/4$ where

$$\delta_1 = \frac{1}{2t}[z + e_A - e_B + \omega]$$

is the realization of $\hat{\delta}$ for patients who overestimate quality for both GPs.

Proceeding similarly for the other three groups we have Table 9.2. Making the appropriate substitutions for the error terms for the other patient groups, the total demand for GP $A$ in the first period is

$$D_1^A(q_A, q_B) = \sum_{g=1}^{4} \frac{n}{4}\delta_g = \frac{n}{2t}(z + \omega)$$

$$= \frac{n}{2t}\left[q_A - q_B + t + \frac{k_c}{2}(e_A - e_B + s_A - s_B)\right] \qquad (9.15)$$

GP $B$ has the remainder of the young patients: $D_1^B = n - D_1^A$.

*Table 9.2* Distances for young patients in period 1

| Groups | Errors | Distances | |
|---|---|---|---|
| 1 | $(e_A, e_B)$ | $\delta_1 =$ | $\dfrac{(z + e_A - e_B + \omega)}{2t}$ |
| 2 | $(e_A, -e_B)$ | $\delta_2 =$ | $\dfrac{(z + e_A + e_B + \omega)}{2t}$ |
| 3 | $(-e_A, e_B)$ | $\delta_3 =$ | $\dfrac{(z - e_A - e_B + \omega)}{2t}$ |
| 4 | $(-e_A, -e_B)$ | $\delta_4 =$ | $\dfrac{(z - e_A + e_B + \omega)}{2t}$ |

*Case 2: unsophisticated patients*

Unsophisticated young patients do not realize they may make mistakes and may wish to switch when old. They will prefer GP *A* to GP *B* if and only if

$$\hat{q}_A - td + k_c(\hat{q}_A - td) \geq \hat{q}_B - t(1 - d) + k_c[\hat{q}_B - t(1 - d)].$$

Equivalently, unsophisticated young consumers choose GP *A* if and only if

$$d \leq \hat{\delta}' = \frac{1}{2t}\hat{z}, \tag{9.16}$$

which also defines four groups of young consumers in terms of the realization of their errors and hence of $\hat{z}$. Note that the patient discount factor $k_c$ does not affect the choice of GP by unsophisticated patients. Comparing (9.14) and (9.16) we see that when $k_c = 0$ the decisions of sophisticated and myopic young consumers are identical given their observations of GP quality. The demand function of unsophisticated young patients is just (9.15) with $k_c = 0$ and hence $\omega = 0$. In what follows we will focus on the case of sophisticated young patients and note the implications of unsophisticated young patients by setting $k_c = 0$.

The demand function for young patients has two noteworthy features:

1   Changes in the error parameter $e_A$ for the GP affect his demand from young patients, despite the fact that the errors patients make in estimating GP quality have a zero mean and are symmetrical. The reason is that some patients know they will switch when they are old and take this into account when choosing their GP. From (9.13) we see that an increase in the error parameter $e_A$ increases the expected utility from GP *B* for those patients who overestimate GP *A* quality but reduces expected utility from GP *B* for those who underestimate GP *A* quality. Since these groups are of equal size the effect on demand from the changes in expected utility from GP *B* are offsetting. But now inspect (9.10). There are two types of effects on the expected utility from GP *A*. The first type is via expected net quality when young ($\hat{q}_A$) and again since equal numbers over- and underestimate quality the effects cancel. The second type is via the expected utility of those who remain with GP *A* when old. This must increase since such patients stay with the firm only if they get favourable information about it. Hence increases in $e_A$ increase the expected utility from choice of GP *A* and thus increase demand from young patients at the rate $\frac{1}{2}k_c$.

2   Increases in the costs of switching to GP *A* increase her first-period demand. The rationale is that patients realize that they may wish to switch to GP *A* when old if they choose GP *B* when young. An increase in the cost of switching to GP *A* increases the attractiveness of choosing GP *A* when young and thereby avoiding the cost of switching to it.

In the additive case, where the errors are exogenous, and in the equilibrium of the multiplicative case where qualities and therefore GPs' error distributions are

identical, young patients in groups 1 and 4 make offsetting errors. They choose
the same GP as they would if correctly informed. The errors for groups 2 and 3
are not offsetting. Some of the patients in these groups choose a different GP to
the one they would have chosen if correctly informed. We investigate the welfare
costs of such mistaken choices in the section on Welfare.

### Second-period demand

#### Demand from old patients

SOPHISTICATED PATIENTS

In the second period $\gamma^o n$ patients of the first period cohort leave the market and
$\gamma^y n$ new patients enter. The $(1 - \gamma^o)n$ old patients have improved information
about the quality of their chosen GP and must decide whether to switch GPs.

For example, consider old group 3 patients who overestimated the quality
of GP $B$ and underestimated the quality of GP $A$. Those who chose GP $B$ when
they were young in the first period now know that they will get $q_B - t(1 - d)$ if
they remain with GP $B$ and believe that they will have a benefit from GP $A$, net
of the cost of switching, of $q_A - e_A - s_A - td$. Only those old group 3 patients of
GP $B$ whose distance from GP $A$ is less than

$$\delta_3^{BA} = \frac{q_A - q_B + t - e_A - s_A}{2t} = \frac{z - e_A - s_A}{2t}$$

would be better off by switching to GP $A$. Since the old group 3 patients of GP $B$
have $d \in [\delta_3, 1]$, GP $A$ gains

$$S_3^{BA} = \max\left[ (1-\gamma^o)\frac{n}{4}(\delta_3^{BA}-\delta_3), \, 0 \right]$$

of GP $B$'s old group 3 patients.

Proceeding similarly for group 3 patients who chose GP $A$ when young
and for the other groups we get Table 9.3. Generally the number of group
$g = 1,\ldots, 4$ old patients of GP $A$ who switch to GP $B$ in the second period is
$S_g^{AB} = \max[(1-\gamma^o)\frac{n}{4}(\delta_g^{AB}-\delta_g), \, 0]$. Demand from old patients in period 2 is equal
to the number of patients who chose the GP in period 1 and did not leave
the market (the installed base $D_1^A$ times $(1-\gamma^o)$), plus those who switch in
($S^{BA} = \sum_g S_g^{BA}$) less those who switch out ($S^{AB} = \sum_g S_g^{AB}$).

Comparison of Tables 9.2 and 9.3 show that with equal switching costs and in
the neighbourhood of a symmetric equilibrium, where qualities and errors are the
same for both GPs, only members of groups 1 and 2, who overestimate GP $A$
quality, switch to GP $B$ and only members of groups 1 and 3, who overestimate
GP $B$ quality, switch to GP $A$. Patients in group 4 never switch to the other GP
because they revise their expectations of the quality of their chosen GP upward.

*Table 9.3* Distances for old patients in period 2

| Groups | Critical distance such that GP A is preferred by old patients of | |
| --- | --- | --- |
| | GP B | GP A |
| 1 | $\delta_1^{BA} = \dfrac{(z + e_A - s_A)}{2t}$ | $\delta_1^{AB} = \dfrac{(z - e_B + s_B)}{2t}$ |
| 2 | $\delta_2^{BA} = \dfrac{(z + e_A - s_A)}{2t}$ | $\delta_2^{AB} = \dfrac{(z + e_B + s_B)}{2t}$ |
| 3 | $\delta_3^{BA} = \dfrac{(z - e_A - s_A)}{2t}$ | $\delta_3^{AB} = \dfrac{(z - e_B + s_B)}{2t}$ |
| 4 | $\delta_4^{BA} = \dfrac{(z - e_A - s_A)}{2t}$ | $\delta_4^{AB} = \dfrac{(z + e_B + s_B)}{2t}$ |

In the neighbourhood of symmetric equilibria we have

$$S^{BA} = (1 - \gamma^o)\frac{n}{4t}(e_B - s_A - \omega), \tag{9.17}$$

$$S^{AB} = (1 - \gamma^o)\frac{n}{4t}(e_A - s_B + \omega); \tag{9.18}$$

and demand from old patients is

$$D^{Ao} = (1 - \gamma^o)D_1^A + S^{BA} - S^{AB}$$

$$= (1 - \gamma^o)\frac{n}{2t}\left[z + \frac{1}{2}(e_B - e_A + s_B - s_A)\right]. \tag{9.19}$$

GP $B$ gets the rest of the old patients.

The properties of $D^{Ao}$ are more intuitive than those of $D_1^A$:

(a) increases in the error parameter $e_A$ increase the number switching into the list of GP $B$

(b) increases in the cost of switching to GP $A$ reduce demand from old patients.

UNSOPHISTICATED PATIENTS

In the case where patients are unsophisticated and did not realize when young that they might switch when old, old patients know the quality of the GP chosen when young and have acquired no additional information about the other GP. They have the same information as if they were sophisticated. The critical distances at which they would be better off staying or switching are the same as if they were sophisticated patients and are given in Table 9.3. Their choices when young are different from those which would have been made by sophisticated patients and so the number of group $g = 1, \ldots, 4$ old patients of GP $A$ who switch to GP $B$ in the second period is $S_g^{AB} = \max[(1 - \gamma^o) \frac{n}{4t} (\delta_g^{AB} - \delta_g'), 0]$ where $\delta_g'$ is $\delta_g$ with $k_c = 0$. In the neighbourhood of symmetric equilibria where qualities are equal, the numbers of unsophisticated old patients who switch are

$$S_g^{'BA} = (1 - \gamma^o)\frac{n}{4t}(e_B - s_A), \tag{9.20}$$

$$S_g^{'AB} = (1 - \gamma^o)\frac{n}{4t}(e_A - s_B). \tag{9.21}$$

Adding and subtracting those switching from the number of patients who chose GP $A$ when young and who are still in the market $(1 - \gamma^o)D_1^A$ gives the demand from old unsophisticated patients

$$D^{'Ao} = (1 - \gamma^o)D_1^{'A} + S^{'BA} - S^{'AB}$$

$$= \frac{(1 - \gamma^o)n}{2t}z + (1 - \gamma^o)\frac{n}{4t}(e_B - s_A) - (1 - \gamma^o)\frac{n}{4t}(e_A - s_B)$$

$$= (1 - \gamma^o)\frac{n}{2t}\left[z + \frac{1}{2}(e_B - e_A + s_B - s_A)\right], \tag{9.22}$$

which is identical to the demand from old sophisticated patients. The degree of sophistication (captured by $k_c$) makes no difference to demand from old patients because the case of unsophisticated patients is equivalent to $k_c = 0$ and in the case of sophisticated patients the terms in $D_1^{'A}$ and $S^{'BA}$ and $S^{'AB}$ involving $k_c$ cancel.

*Demand from young patients in period 2*

The new young patients in period 2 know that they will stay in the market only for one period. A patient will choose GP $A$ rather than $B$ if and only if $q_A - td \geq q_B - t(1 - d)$. Of the patients whose realized errors are $(\hat{e}_A, \hat{e}_B)$, GP $A$ will get those whose distance from her is no more than

$$\delta(q_A, q_B, \hat{e}_A, \hat{e}_B) = \frac{\hat{q}_A - q_B + t}{2t} = \frac{z + \hat{e}_A - \hat{e}_B}{2t}, \tag{9.23}$$

and GP $B$ gets the remainder with $d \in [\delta(q_A, q_B, \hat{e}_A, \hat{e}_B), 1]$.

The realized values of the errors define four groups of young patients each of size $\gamma^y n/4$. Using (9.23) and making the appropriate substitutions for the error

*Table 9.4* Distances for young patients in period 2

| Groups | Errors | Distances |
|---|---|---|
| 1 | $(e_A, e_B)$ | $\delta_1^y = \frac{(z + e_A - e_B)}{2t}$ |
| 2 | $(e_A, -e_B)$ | $\delta_2^y = \frac{(z + e_A + e_B)}{2t}$ |
| 3 | $(-e_A, e_B)$ | $\delta_3^y = \frac{(z - e_A - e_B)}{2t}$ |
| 4 | $(-e_A, -e_B)$ | $\delta_4^y = \frac{(z - e_A + e_B)}{2t}$ |

terms for all the patients' groups (see Table 9.4), second period demand from young patients for GP $A$ is

$$D^{Ay} = \gamma^y \frac{n}{4} \sum_{g=1}^{4} \delta_g^y = \frac{n}{2t} \gamma^y z. \tag{9.24}$$

GP $B$ gets the remainder of the patients: $D^{By} = \gamma^y n - D^{Ay}$. Young patients in period 2 do not need to form expectations about quality next period since they exit the market at the end of period 2. Hence, in both cases 1 and 2 the demand from young patients in period 2 is given by (9.24).

Adding (9.19) to (9.24) gives the total second period demand for GP $A$ in the case of sophisticated patients:

$$D_2^A = D^{Ay} + D^{Ao} = \frac{n}{2t} \left[ \theta z + \frac{1}{2}(1 - \gamma^o)(e_B - e_A + s_B - s_A) \right], \tag{9.25}$$

where $\theta = 1 + \gamma^y - \gamma^o$. The demand for GP $B$ is just $D_2^B = n\theta - D_2^A$. Since $D'^{Ao} = D^{Ao}$ the second period demand in the case of unsophisticated consumers is also given by (9.25).

### Biased expectations

We next consider the demand in case 3 where patients are unsophisticated, so that they do not realize that they may make mistakes, and have biased expectations of quality in the sense that their probabilities of positive and negative errors are not equal: $E\tilde{e}_i = \pi e - (1 - \pi)e = (2\pi - 1)e \neq 0$. Consider first the demand by young patients in period 1. Since they are also unsophisticated and make the same size errors as the unsophisticated patients in case 2, the realizations of their observation errors yield four groups of patients who make the same choices as those in the same group in case 2. For example, those who overestimate the quality of GP $A$ and underestimate the quality of GP $B$ (group 2) will choose GP $A$ if their distance from GP $A$ is no more than $\delta_2 = (q_A - q_B + t + e_A + e_B)/2t$. The difference between cases 2 and 3 arises in the different numbers of patients in the four groups. For example, the proportion in group 2 is $\pi(1 - \pi)$ rather than 1/4.

Weighting the demands from each group appropriately and adding up, we have

$$D_1^A = \frac{n}{2t}[q_A - q_B + t + (e_A - e_B)(2\pi - 1)]. \tag{9.26}$$

When errors are multiplicative, GP $A$'s incentive to increase quality is increased or reduced by its effect on the errors made by patients, depending on whether patients are optimistic ($\pi > 1/2$) or pessimistic ($\pi < 1/2$).

Young patients in period 2 make exactly the same decisions conditional on their location and observations of quality as young unsophisticated patients in period 1. Hence the demand in period 2 from young patients for GP $A$ is

$$D_2^{Ay} = \gamma^y D_1^A.$$

Old patients in period 2 make exactly the same switching decisions as in case 2 given their information and location. Applying suitable weightings to the four groups of old patients we have

$$S^{AB} = S_1^{AB} + S_2^{AB} = \frac{n}{2t}\,\pi(1 - \gamma^o)(e_A - s_B),$$

$$S^{BA} = S_1^{BA} + S_2^{BA} = \frac{n}{2t}\,\pi(1 - \gamma^o)(e_B - s_A),$$

and

$$D^{Ao} = (1 - \gamma^o)D_1^A + S^{BA} - S^{AB}$$

$$= (1 - \gamma^o)\frac{n}{2t}\,[z + (e_B - e_A)(1 - \pi) + (s_B - s_A)\pi].$$

## Regulated market

### *Equilibrium quality*

In a regulated market, like the NHS, where the tax-financed capitation fee ($p$) per patient on the GP's list is set by the government and patients face a zero price for joining a practice list, quality is the only way in which GPs can compete for patients. The regulator cannot control quality directly and we are interested in the extent to which he can influence it indirectly via the regulated capitation fee.

GPs have identical cost functions and incur a constant unit cost per patient in each period of $c$. Practices make an investment in quality at a cost of $\beta q^2$ before the young patients in period 1 decide which practice to join. Practice quality is constant over the two periods and is an excludable public good in that its cost is independent of the number of practice patients. Examples are investment by the GP in a computer system for patient records or good practice facilities or in undergoing training (for example in minor surgery).

The discounted expected profit of GP $i$ is

$$V^i = (p - c)(D_1^i + k_f D_2^i) - \beta q_i^2 + \ell, \tag{9.27}$$

where $k_f \in [0, 1]$ is the discount factor on future earnings and $\ell$ is remuneration which does not vary with the number of patients.[8] We assume that $\ell$ is always large enough to ensure non-negative $V^i$ so that the GPs are always willing to participate. We first solve for the Nash equilibrium in case 1 with sophisticated patients and then derive the solution with unsophisticated patients in case 2 by setting the patient discount factor to zero. Case 3 with patients with biased expectations is solved separately.

Doctors take their competitor's choices as given and non-cooperatively maximize expected discounted profit by their investment in quality at the beginning of period 1. We consider only pure strategy Nash equilibria and, since the GPs have identical preferences, cost and demand functions, look for a symmetric solution. The obvious way to proceed is set the partial derivative of $V^i(q_i, q_j)$ with respect to $q_i$ equal to zero, impose $q_A = q_B$ and solve for the equilibrium quality $q^N$. Provided that $V^A(q^N, q^N) > V^A(q_A, q^N)$ for all $q_A \neq q^N$, and analogously for GP $B$, the procedure would yield the unique symmetric Nash equilibrium $q^N$. Unfortunately establishing that $V^A(q^N, q^N) > V^A(q_A, q^N)$ for all $q_A \neq q^N$, and analogously for GP $B$, is not straightforward despite the apparent simplicity of the demand functions and the convexity of cost in quality. The demand functions are piecewise linear in quality. The marginal revenue from quality is a step function with upward steps at points where the GP first becomes attractive to a particular group of patients by raising quality and downward steps where the GP attracts all the patients in a particular group.

In the Appendix we give a condition on the parameters which ensures that the marginal revenue function has only downward steps and the objective function of GP $A$ is concave in $q_A$. We show that it is always possible to find a combination of the parameters satisfying the condition.

Solving the first order condition on $V^i$, the symmetric Nash equilibrium quality is

$$q_A = q_B = q^N = \frac{n}{4\beta t} (p - c)\left(1 + k_f \phi + \frac{m}{2}k_c\right), \tag{9.28}$$

where $\phi = \gamma^y + (1 - \gamma^o)\left(1 - \frac{m}{2}\right)$.

### Comparative statics

The comparative static properties of the regulated equilibrium are straightforwardly derived from (9.28).

**Proposition 1**   *At the regulated equilibrium, quality is increasing in the proportion of patients who enter the market in the second period ($\gamma^y$), GPs and patients' discount factor ($k_f$ and $k_c$), and decreasing in the proportion of patients who leave the market after the first period ($\gamma^o$), the cost of quality ($\beta$) and distance costs ($t$). Additive errors ($a$) and switching costs ($s$) have no effect on quality.*

Switching costs ($s$) and additive errors ($a$) have no effect on equilibrium quality. They enter additively into GPs' demand functions and are equal for the two GPs and therefore offsetting. They do not interact with quality and do not affect the marginal revenue from quality changes and so have no effect on the profit maximizing quality.

Quality increases with the size of the total population of consumers, parameterized by $n$. The cost of quality is independent of the number of patients but marginal revenue from quality increases with $n$. When there are multiplicative errors equilibrium quality also depends on the mix of young and old patients since the demand from old patients depends on the error and the error increases with quality.

Suppose we fix the total size of the population in the second period by assuming that the inflow of young patients exactly offsets the outflow of old patients: $\gamma^y = \gamma^o$. Increases in proportion of young consumers in the patient population in period 2 (indicated by an equal increase in $\gamma^y$ and $\gamma^o$) lead to an increase in $\phi$ and thus to an increase in quality. The rationale is that demand from young consumers in period 2 is not affected by the size of the error but that from old consumers is reduced by increases in the error. Hence when the errors are multiplicative there is a increased incentive to raise quality, the smaller the proportion of second period patients who are old.

Quality is also lower the more consumers care about their distance from the practice i.e. the larger is their distance cost parameter $t$. A higher $t$ means that patients place more weight on location relative to quality when comparing practices, thereby reducing practices' incentives to compete via quality.

Patient misperceptions affect the equilibrium only if errors are multiplicative.

**Proposition 2**   *The equilibrium quality decreases with multiplicative errors ($m$) if and only if $k_c < (1 - \gamma^o)k_f$. An increase in the patient discount factor $k_c$ increases quality for any level of the capitation fee and multiplicative errors.*

When errors are multiplicative GPs take account of the effect of higher quality on the demand via the errors made by patients as well as the direct effect of higher quality in increasing demand. A larger error increases the demand from young consumers at the rate $nk_c/4t$ (see equation 9.15) but reduces demand next period from old consumers at the rate $(1 - \gamma^o)n/4t$. Since the GP firm discounts future demand at the rate $k_f$ it will benefit from larger errors only if $k_c < (1 - \gamma^o)k_f$.

In case 2 where patients are myopic ($k_c = 0$), multiplicative errors reduce the equilibrium quality for any given capitation fee. Quality is lower even though, on average, patients estimate quality correctly before they have joined a practice and can observe quality perfectly after experiencing it. The greater the error the more likely are old patients to switch to the other GP (see equation 9.19). Since higher quality leads to greater errors the gain to a GP from increasing quality is reduced.

### Equilibrium with biased expectations

The equilibrium quality when patients on average have biased expectations about quality is found by using the demand functions for young and old consumers above (p. 170). Proceeding in the same manner as for cases 1 and 2, the regulated equilibrium quality with myopic patients with biased expectations is

$$q^{Nb} = \frac{n(p - c)}{4\beta t}\{1 - (1 - 2\pi)m$$

$$+ k_f[(1 - \gamma^o + \gamma^y)(1 - m(1 - \pi)) + m\pi\gamma^y]\}, \tag{9.29}$$

which is identical to the solution with unbiased expectations and myopic patients when $\pi = 1/2$.

Inspection of (9.29) shows that when errors are additive, the equilibrium quality is the same in cases 1, 2 and 3: the nature of patient, expectations has no implication for the equilibrium quality. However in the more plausible case in which the error distribution does vary with quality, patients' expectations do affect the equilibrium quality. When errors are multiplicative, increase in $\pi$ increases quality: GPs have a greater incentive to invest in quality, the greater the degree of overestimation of quality. The rationale is that when patients over estimate quality a given increase in quality has a greater effect on average perceived quality and hence on demand.

Biased expectations make some of the clear predictions of cases 1 and 2 ambiguous. For example, multiplicative errors reduce quality when patients are pessimistic or unbiased ($\pi \leq 1/2$) but increase quality if patients are sufficiently optimistic. Thus the plausible suggestion that when patients are poor judges of quality firms have less incentive to supply it, may not be valid when patients are on balance optimistic in estimating quality.

### Incentive effects of capitation

We can use (9.28) and (9.29) to investigate arguments about the implications of imperfect information and switching costs on the ability of a regulator to influence quality by raising the capitation fee.

**Proposition 3** *Irrespective of patient expectations, increases in the capitation fee increase quality. The marginal effect of the capitation fee on equilibrium quality decreases with distance cost (t), the marginal cost of quality (β) and the proportion of patients leaving the market after the first period (γ⁰), increases with the size of the population (n), the provider and the patient discount factor*

($k_f$ and $k_c$), the proportion of new patients entering the market ($\gamma^y$), and is unaffected by additive errors and switching costs.

Increasing capitation fees to make patients more valuable for practices does indeed lead to higher quality even when patients also care about distance, are imperfect judges of quality and face costs in switching when they become better informed. However, the positive impact of the fee on quality is affected by distance costs so that a higher capitation fee is necessary for any required level of quality.

The nature of patient expectations also affects both the level of quality achieved for a given capitation fee and the marginal effect of the fee on quality.

**Proposition 4**   *The incentive effect of capitation fees on quality is greater with sophisticated than with myopic patients and with optimistic expectations than with pessimistic or unbiased expectations.*

## Welfare

Since the policy maker can alter the level of quality by varying the capitation fee we next turn to the question of how the welfare maximizing quality is affected by imperfect patient information and switching costs. The welfare function is

$$W = n(q - c)(1 + k\theta) - nT - 2\beta q^2 - \lambda[2\ell + pn(1 + k\theta)], \qquad (9.30)$$

where $T$ is the average patient distance and switching cost (to be derived shortly) and $\lambda$ is the marginal deadweight loss from the taxation required to finance payments to GPs. The social discount factor $k$ is assumed to be equal to the GP firm discount factor $k_f$.

Welfare is the sum of patients' surpluses and GPs' profits less the cost of taxes levied to finance payments to GPs. Equivalently, since any payments to doctors are exactly offset by payments by taxpayers, welfare is the sum of patients' willingness to pay for the quality of service received less their distance and switching costs, the costs of providing the service and of tax financing the payments to providers.

The welfare function is paternalistic in that welfare is assumed to depend on actual realized patient benefits, not on perceived benefits. It also implies that individuals are not considered the best judges of their own welfare because of their mistaken beliefs.

Since the equilibrium is symmetric, with GPs taking the same decisions and we are interested in regulation of those decisions, we evaluate the welfare function at $q_A = q_B = q$. The market is always covered so that every patient joins a list and the total gross benefit to young and old generations is $n(1 + k\theta)q$,[9] where $k$ is the social discount factor and $\theta = 1 - \gamma^o + \gamma^y$. As inspection of the demand functions above (pp. 159–70) shows, equilibrium demand is the same in all three cases, with each GP getting half the patients. Hence welfare does not depend, for given quality, on the nature of patient expectations and we can use the welfare function (9.30) for all three assumptions about patient expectations.

### Distance, error, and switching costs

Patients incur distance costs and some of them also incur switching costs. These costs differ with the errors made by patients and with their generation. Patients in group 1 overestimate the quality of both GPs. There are two subgroups defined by the GP chosen. When they are old and have acquired better information about the quality of their current GP some of them switch to the other GP in period 2. There are four subgroups of old group 1 patients defined by the GP chosen when young and whether the patient stays or switches to the other GP.

Patients in group 2 overestimate the quality of GP *A* and underestimate the quality of GP *B* when they are young. Their choice of practice defines five subgroups. There are two young subgroups of patients depending on whether they choose practice *A* or *B* in the first period. When they are old and have acquired information about the quality of the practice chosen those who chose GP *A* and overestimated her quality may decide to switch to GP *B*. Those who chose GP *B* never switch because they revise upward their beliefs about her quality. There are thus three old subgroups: those who stay with practice *A*, those who move to practice *B*, and those who stay with practice *B*. Similarly there are five subsets of young and old group 3 patients.

Group 4 patients underestimate the qualities of both GPs when young. Since they revise their beliefs about the quality of the chosen practice upward and do not change their beliefs about the quality of the other practice, none of them switch when old. There are two subgroups of young and old patients defined by their choice of practice.

The costs incurred by patients who are young in the first and second period are $nT^y$ and $n\gamma^y T^y$ respectively, where $T^y$ the average cost per young patient is[10]

$$T^y(e; t) = \left[ \frac{t}{4} + \frac{t}{2}\left(\frac{e}{t}\right)^2 4\pi(1-\pi) \right]. \tag{9.31}$$

The total costs for old patients are $n(1 - \gamma^o)T^o$, where

$$T^o(e; s; t) = \left[ \frac{t}{4} + \frac{\pi}{2t}(e^2 + s^2) + \frac{\pi}{t}(2e(1-\pi)-s)s \right]. \tag{9.32}$$

The first term inside the square brackets in each equation is the distance cost which would be incurred if there was perfect information: patients of each generation would choose correctly and would on average be located 1/4 units of distance away from their chosen practice and incur average distance costs of $t/4$.

The second terms are the welfare losses arising from poor information. Some patients choose the wrong GP and incur too great a distance cost. These mismatch costs increase with the errors made by patients. They also increase with the switching costs of old patients which prevent some old patients switching to a GP with smaller distance costs.

The third term in $T^o$ is the cost of switching: the proportion of old patients switching multiplied by the cost per switch.

The effect of biased expectations is perhaps counterintuitive: the costs of both young and old patients are on average smaller, the greater the bias in patients' expectations! Young patients in groups 1 and 4, who respectively over- and underestimate the quality of both GPs, choose the correct GP and incur no excess distance cost. Hence as $\pi$ tends to 1 or to 0 there are no mistakes in choice of GP by young patients and there are only distance costs for them. As $\pi$ tends to 0, no old patients will switch irrespective of their choice of GP when young and the old also only incur distance costs.

Adding up the costs of young and old patients gives the total per capita discounted distance, error and switching costs as

$$nT = n\{T^y + k[\gamma^y T^y + (1 - \gamma^o) + T^o]\}. \tag{9.33}$$

### Optimal quality

The regulator cannot observe quality directly but knows the equilibrium quality function $q^N(p, \cdot)$ or $q^{Nb}(p, \cdot)$ and chooses the capitation fee $p$ and the lump sum payment $\ell$ to maximize $W$ subject to the GP participation constraint $V^i(q^N, q^N) \geq 0, i = A, B$.

Setting up the Lagrangean $W + \phi V^i$ and solving the first-order conditions gives the optimal quality

$$q^* = \frac{2tn(1 + k\theta) - nm[a\psi + 4\pi(1 - \pi)sk(1 - \gamma^o)]}{(1 + \lambda)8\beta t + nm^2\psi}, \tag{9.34}$$

where $\psi = 8\pi(1 - \pi) + k[8\pi(1 - \pi)\gamma^y + 2\pi(1 - \gamma^o)]$. The optimal capitation fee is found by inverting (9.28) in cases 1 and 2 where expectations are unbiased ($\pi = 1/2$) and (9.29) in case 3 where expectations are biased ($\pi \neq 1/2$).

We see that when patient expectations are unbiased the level of the optimal fee is affected by patient expectations but the optimal quality is not. This is at first sight surprising since, for example, a higher level of the capitation fee is required to generate a given level of quality when patients are myopic (case 2) than when they are sophisticated (case 1) and there is a deadweight loss to raising additional tax revenue to finance the fee. The explanation is that the total demand met by each GP firm is not affected by quality (and hence not by the capitation fee) so that for any given quality the firm has a higher profit per unit when expectations imply a higher price to generate the required quality. Hence the higher capitation fee can be offset by a lower lump sum payment $\ell$ whilst still satisfying the participation constraint.

The degree of bias in patient expectations affects optimal quality via its effect on $\psi$. Notice that $\psi$ is greater at $\pi = 1$, than at $\pi = 0$, so that quality is greater when all patients are pessimistic about quality than when they are optimistic. The rationale is that when patients are optimistic they may switch when old whereas they will never switch if pessimistic. If errors are affected by quality ($m > 0$) then since mistakes are more costly with optimistic patients quality will be lower with extremely optimistic patients than with extremely pessimistic patients. The degree of bias also affects optimal quality via the amount of switching. This tends to reinforce its effects via $\psi$ since switching is maximized when expectations are unbiased.

Optimal quality is smaller, the more costly it is to produce (the greater is $\beta$) and the greater the marginal deadweight loss from the taxation required to finance its production. If errors are purely additive ($m = 0$) optimal quality is unaffected by the patient errors, distance costs or switching costs. However, in the more plausible case in which errors vary with the level of quality, the optimal quality is affected by imperfect information and switching costs.

**Proposition 5** *With unbiased expectations, optimal quality is unaffected by whether patients are sophisticated or myopic, but is reduced by multiplicative error. With biased expectations optimal quality is lower with extreme optimism ($\pi = 1$) than with extreme pessimism ($\pi = 0$) if there is multiplicative error. With multiplicative error quality is smaller the higher is switching cost and the smaller is distance cost whatever the nature of patient expectations.*

The marginal social benefit from an increase in quality depends on the gain to patients from increased quality and the marginal cost of producing extra quality. If patients' errors vary with quality, a third factor must be taken into account: increase in quality leads to larger errors and hence larger error costs. Hence, the greater the multiplicative error parameter $m$, the lower is socially optimal quality. Switching costs also reduce optimal quality when errors are multiplicative because when the error is greater more patients make costly switches. The negative effect of distance cost on optimal quality arises because quality becomes relatively less important to consumers in their choice of practice when distance cost is greater. Practices' incentives to increase quality are reduced and so is the error made by patients.

## Conclusions

In the market for primary care, patients improve their knowledge about the characteristic of the practice they join after experiencing its services. Patients make initial errors in judging quality and switching costs lock some of the mistaken patients into the wrong GP.

Regulation of the capitation fee received per patient can yield a welfare maximizing level of quality, despite the fact that patients are imperfect judges of quality and incur switching costs. In a system like the NHS where the price of care received by GPs is paid from taxation, errors and switching costs do have a real effect. They increase the cost to taxpayers of inducing a required level of quality and, when there is a deadweight loss from taxation, the socially optimal regulated quality is reduced.

Errors and switching costs also have direct welfare consequences. Errors lead some patients to choose the wrong practice. A reduction in the dispersion of the error distribution will make some patients better off and none worse off. Switching costs reduce the number of patients who switch when they revise their estimate of the quality of the GP they have chosen downward. Some of these patients would be better off as a result of switching because the other GP really does have higher quality. But some of them will be worse off because they over-estimate the quality of the other GP. Thus, although on average patients gain from a reduction in switching costs, some of them are made worse off.

The degree of sophistication of patients makes a difference both to the level of quality produced by firms facing a given capitation fee and to the incentive effects of increases in the fee. With more sophisticated consumers, who take account of the fact that they may wish to switch when they have experienced the quality of their chosen GP, quality is higher than when patients are myopic and do not realize that their perceptions of quality may be mistaken.

We have shown that the capitation fee is a valid instrument for raising quality levels even in the face of mistaken and unsophisticated consumers with biased perceptions of quality. This does not of course imply that the capitation fee should be the only instrument if policy makers wish to increase the quality of care. Nor should the quality of care consumed be the only consideration in choosing the capitation fee since the welfare of patients depends on whether they choose the right GP and whether they incur switching costs from changing their GP.

Policy makers can attempt to improve the accuracy of patient information, for example by collecting and publishing information on practice facilities. Such policies may lead to a direct increase in quality. They will also reduce the number of mismatched patients and the number who incur switching costs when they attempt to rectify their mistaken choices.[11]

## Appendix

*Concavity of the objective function.* When GP $A$ deviates from $q_A = q_B = q^N$ by choosing a lower level of quality, the first patients to be monopolized by GP $B$ will be the young patients in group 3 who underestimate the quality of GP $A$ and overestimate the quality of GP $B$ (compare critical distances for young and old patients in Tables 9.2–9.4 to see that none of the other groups of patients can be monopolized before young patients in group 3). To ensure that group 3 patients are never monopolized by GP $B$ even if GP $A$ chooses zero quality requires that $\delta_3 > 0$ at $q_A = 0$, $q_B = q^N$. Substituting from the definition of $\delta_3$ the condition is

$$0 < 0 - q^N + t - a - a - mq^N + \frac{k_c}{2}[a - a - mq^N]$$

$$= t - q^N\left[1 + m\left(1 + \frac{k_c}{2}\right)\right] - 2a,$$

and substituting the Nash equilibrium quality we get

$$0 < H = 4\beta t^2 - 8a\beta t - n(p - c)\left[1 + m\left(1 + \frac{k_c}{2}\right)\right]\left(1 + k_f\phi + \frac{m}{2}k_c\right).$$

$H$ is quadratic and convex in $t$ and so there always exists a positive $t$ for which the inequality is satisfied and $V^A(q, q^N)$ is concave in $q$ and similarly for $V^B$.

*Patients' distance and switching costs.* The average distance and switching costs of young and old patients in group 1 are

$$T_1^y = \pi^2 \left[ \int_0^{\delta_1} t\delta d\delta + \int_{\delta_1}^1 (1 - \delta)t d\delta \right]$$

and

$$T_1^o = \pi^2 \left[ \int_0^{\delta_1^{AB}} t\delta d\delta + \int_{\delta_1^{AB}}^{\delta_1} [(1 - \delta)t + s] d\delta \right.$$
$$\left. + \int_{\delta_1}^{\delta_1^{BA}} (t\delta + s) d\delta + \int_{\delta_1^{BA}}^1 [(1 - \delta)t d\delta \right].$$

$T_1^y$ is the distance costs of the two young subgroups of patients: those who choose GP *A* and those who choose GP *B*. Since in equilibrium the distances in Table 9.2 and 9.4 are identical, i.e. $\delta_g = \delta_g^y$, young patients subgroups are the same in both periods. $T_1^o$ defines the costs of the four old subgroups: those who stay with GP *A*, those who switch to GP *B* from GP *A*, those who switch to GP *A* from GP *B*, and those who stay with GP *B*.

The average costs of group 2 patients in each period are

$$T_2^y = \pi(1 - \pi)\left[ \int_0^{\delta_2} t\delta d\delta + \int_{\delta_2}^1 (1 - \delta)t d\delta \right]$$

and

$$T_2^o = \pi(1 - \pi)\left[ \int_0^{\delta_2^{AB}} t\delta d\delta + \int_{\delta_2^{AB}}^{\delta_2} [(1 - \delta)t + s] d\delta + \int_{\delta_2}^1 (1 - \delta)t d\delta \right].$$

Old patients either stay with the GP chosen when old (the first and third terms in $T_2^o$) or switch from GP *A* to GP *B* (the second term in $T_2^o$). Given the symmetry assumptions, the costs for group 3 patients who underestimate the quality of GP *A* and overestimate the quality of GP *B* is equal to the costs of group 2.

Total distance costs of young and old group 4 patients in each period who remain with the GP chosen when young are

$$T_4^y = T_4^o = (1 - \pi)^2 \left[ \int_0^{\delta_4} t\delta d\delta + \int_{\delta_4}^1 [(1 - \delta)t d\delta \right].$$

Using Tables 9.3 and 9.4, we evaluate the integrals to give the expressions for $T^y$ and $T^o$ given in the text.

## Notes

Support from the Department of Health to the NPCRDC is acknowledged. The views expressed are those of the authors and not necessarily those of the Department of Health. We are grateful for comments from Lise Rochaix and other participants in the 19th Arne Ryde Symposium in Lund and from referees.

1  In Schmalensee (1982) there are no direct costs of switching but consumers of an established good are deterred from switching to an entrant's objectively identical product because of uncertainty about its quality. The model does not address the issue of established firms competing in price and quality for the custom of cohorts of new consumers. Riorden (1986) adapts the Salop (1979) circular product differentiation model to allow for endogenous quality of experience goods but does not consider switching costs.

2  Full coverage is ensured by assuming that there is a utility from joining either practice of $r$ which is independent of the quality of the practice chosen and the patient's location. By making $r$ sufficiently large all patients will prefer to join some practice rather than none.

3  Gravelle (1999) shows, in the context of a Salop (1979) product differentiation model extended to allow for monopoly as well as monopolistic competition equilibria, that quality is efficient only if consumers preferences are weakly separable in distance costs, consumers have zero income elasticity of demand for quality, and firms costs are linear in quantity.

4  Vertical and horizontal product differentiation are examined in models with perfect consumer information in Wolinsky (1984), Economides (1993), and Gravelle (1999).

5  The welfare implications of endogenous information and switching costs are considered in a companion paper (Gravelle and Masiero, 2000), which assumes that patients are myopic and therefore has a simpler set of demand equations.

6  Although we restrict GPs to choose non-negative quality, we assume that patients believe that quality can be negative so that even if they observe negative quality they do not infer true quality.

7  We assume that patients do not switch GPs when old if they are indifferent between them and that they choose GP $A$ when young if they are indifferent between the two GPs.

8  In the NHS these include payments related to the age of the GP and the training status of the practice.

9  Patients get utility of $r + q$ from their practice (gross of distance costs) but since $r$ is constant and patients always join some list, we ignore it in the welfare analysis of quality levels.

10  The details of the derivation of the distance and switching costs for the various groups of young and old patients are in the Appendix.

11  We do not have space here to investigate such policies and the extent to which GPs will attempt to provide information to attract patients but the interested reader is referred to our companion paper (Gravelle and Masiero, 2000).

## References

Economides, N. (1993) 'Quality variations in the circular model of variety-differentiated products', *Regional Science and Urban Economics*, 23, 235–57.

Gravelle, H. (1999) 'Capitation contracts: access and quality', *Journal of Health Economics*, 18, 315–40.

Gravelle, H. and Masiero, G. (2000) 'Quality incentives with imperfect information and switching costs in a regulated market: capitation in general practice', *Journal of Health Economics*, 19, 1067–88.

Klemperer, P. (1987) 'The competitiveness of markets with switching costs', *RAND Journal of Economics*, 18, 138–50.

Klemperer, P. (1995) 'Competition when consumers have switching costs: an overview with applications to industrial organization, macroeconomics and international trade', *Review of Economic Studies*, 62, 515–39.

Riorden, M.H. (1986) 'Monopolistic competition with experience goods', *Quarterly Journal of Economics*, 101, 265–79.

Salop, S.C. (1979) 'Monopolistic competition with outside goods', *Bell Journal of Economics*, 10, 141–56.

Schmalensee, R. (1982) 'Product differentiation advantages of pioneering brands', *American Economic Review*, 72, 349–65.

Spence, M. (1975) 'Monopoly, quality, and regulation', *Bell Journal of Economics,* 6, 417–99.

Wolinsky, A. (1984) 'Product differentiation with imperfect information', *Review of Economic Studies*, 53–61.

# 10 The importance of micro-data for revealing income-motivated behaviour among GPs

*Tor Iversen and Hilde Lurås*

## Introduction

The interpretation of a positive relationship between the physician density in an area and the volume of medical care provision is a controversial issue. Some authors interpret the relationship as a support of income-motivated behaviour (induced demand) among physicians, while others emphasize the importance of patient-initiated services because of better accessibility to physicians. In this chapter we argue that micro-data describing whether a physician has obtained his optimal number of patients are essential for the detection of income-motivated behaviour among general practitioners (GPs). Our approach may be seen in relation to the literature review provided in Scott and Shiell (1997). They classify empirical studies of physicians' induced demand according to the kind of data that is used. The first period of research, during the 1970s, is characterized by studies using aggregate utilization data. In these studies the effect of demand creation is difficult to separate from the effect of better access. In the second period, the 1980s, studies often use service provision data at the individual physician level, mixed with aggregate area-level explanatory variables, such as physician density. These studies employ data with an hierarchical structure without taking the possible correlation between error terms into account. Scott and Shiell (1997) improve the methods of earlier studies by taking account of the hierarchical structure of data. They find a positive relationship between physician density and the volume of physician-initiated service provision measured by the probability of a follow-up visit.

The objective of this chapter is to take matters a step further, by arguing that micro-data describing whether a physician has obtained his optimal number of patients are required in the study of income-motivated behaviour among general practitioners. Macro-data on general practitioner density (GP-density) in an area are not likely to be useful because the effect of better access is often not distinguishable from physician-initiated services. In our approach the crucial distinction is between those GPs who provide care to their optimal number of patients and those who experience a shortage of patients. The second group is denoted rationed GPs. If rationed GPs provide a number of services to their patients that differ from their unconstrained colleagues, we conclude that their intensity of service provision deviates from their uncon-strained optimal volume.

Our argument is illustrated by a study that employs data from the Norwegian capitation experiment initiated by the central government in the early 1990s.[1] In Norway the municipalities are responsible for providing general medical services to its population. In the experiment each self-employed GP[2] took responsibility for a list of the municipality's residents. A GP's income consisted of a per capita component per listed person and a fee-per-item component.[3] The capitation fee was adjusted for a listed person's age and adjusted for whether the physician is a specialist in general medicine. The fee-per-item component from the National Insurance Scheme and from patient charges was paid according to a fixed fee schedule.[4] The fees depend, for instance, on the duration of a consultation and on whether certain types of examinations and laboratory tests are initiated during the consultation.[5]

All GPs in four municipalities participated in the experiment, and all inhabit-ants in these municipalities were listed by a GP. The list system then implies that both the number of patients and the distribution of patients according to age and gender at the individual practice level are public information. Previously, it was not known whether a 'number of consultations' provided during a certain period were given to a large or a small number of persons, and this made it difficult to compare GPs' practice styles.[6] If, for instance, two GPs provide the same number of services during one year, but GP *A* is responsible for twice as many patients as GP *B*, GP *B* has a more service-intensive practice style. However, when informa-tion on the number of patients on the list is not known, we might erroneously conclude that A and B have the same practice style.

In our data we also have *ex ante* information about the number of persons that each GP would like to have on his list stated at the beginning of the experiment. A GP's preferred list size reveals information about a physician's preferred practice style and his preferred workload. By comparing preferred list size *ex ante* and actual list size during the experimental period we can distinguish empirically between those GPs who experience a shortage of patients (rationing) and those who do not.

In the next section we summarize some results from previous work (Iversen and Lurås, 2000b) where we found that a shortage of patients is likely to imply a more service-intensive practice style among general practitioners. The data are described next, and the results from our empirical study after that. Concluding remarks end the chapter.

## Patient shortage and the intensity of service provision

In related work (Iversen and Lurås, 2000b) we have shown that a shortage of patients is likely to imply a more service-intensive practice style among general practitioners. Our point of departure is the observed variation in medical practice and its implication for the variation in the provision of health services. For instance, views among physicians may differ with respect to how often a patient with diabetes or a patient with hypertension should be called in for check-ups. Views may also differ on whether a GP who prescribes antibiotics to a patient should call in the patient for a follow-up consultation in one week or ask the patient to contact him if he feels worse. The intensity of service provision will on average be higher in the first case than in the second.

We argue that for many treatment choices there is an interval of health service provision where the marginal effect on health is not documented to be different from zero.[7] For our purpose, an interesting consequence of the lack of medical standards is that several practice profiles are all regarded as equally satisfactory from a professional point of view. A physician's practice style is simply defined as the optimal value of his decision variables, i.e. the number of patients and the number of services provided to each patient. His personal interests may influence the style of medicine he believes in. But since all feasible practice styles are assumed to have zero marginal effects on health, our approach implies that a patient's health is never balanced against the GP's income or leisure. This assumption simplifies the formal reasoning considerably, but is not critical for the argument. A relaxation of the assumption would imply that the effect of economic incentives is strengthened. In Iversen and Lurås (2000b), the maximization problem is analysed by means of concave programming. The GP's objective function has income and leisure as arguments, and there are three constraints:

1   working time and leisure add up to total time at disposal;
2   the number of services per patient are within the range of professionally acceptable practice styles; and
3   the number of patients are less or equal to the number who wish to be listed with the GP.

We assume a mixed capitation and fee-for-service payment system. If constraint (3) is ineffective, the problem then has a corner solution. If constraint (3) is effective, the GP experiences patient shortage and is said to be rationed. An interior solution as well as corner solutions are then possible. Since our focus in the present chapter is empirical issues, we present the main result without the formal argument and refer interested readers to Iversen and Lurås (2000b). In a mixed capitation and fee-for-service system, we find that:[8]

- A minimum volume of health services per patient is provided when patients are abundant.
- When a shortage of patients occurs, the volume of service provision per patient may exceed the minimum volume.

The intuition behind this result is straightforward: an increase in the level of service provision to existing patients has an opportunity cost because the time could have been used to provide services to additional patients. Since providing services to additional patients would also result in a capitation fee, providing services to additional patients is always more rewarding than increasing the service provision to patients already listed. When a shortage of patients occurs, increasing the list of patients is no longer an option. The volume of service provision per patient will then exceed the minimum if the marginal income of service provision per unit of time exceeds the marginal valuation of leisure. The more the rationing hurts (measured by the magnitude of the Lagrange-parameter in the maximization problem), the more service-intensive the practice style is likely to be.

Our model predicts that a GP experiencing a patient shortage has economic motives for a service-intensive practice style. An empirical test of this hypothesis requires micro-data on whether a GP in fact experiences a patient shortage. Macro-data on GP-density in an area[9] are not likely to be useful for this purpose for several reasons:

- The population in municipalities with a high GP-density may experience better access and hence, a lower threshold for patient-initiated contacts.
- GPs in high-density municipalities may over time develop a culture of a service-intensive practice style not because of economic motives but because they think patients are served better.
- Average GP-density does not take account of variation in patient constraints within a municipality. Even in municipalities with a high GP-density, individual GPs may experience a shortage of patients.

Hence, it is useful to distinguish between:

- variation in GP-density *between* municipalities and
- variation *within* a municipality, measured by micro-data on individual GPs' experiences of patient shortage.

We suggest that the first type of variation, the between-municipality variation, is useful for studying the effect of access on service provision. However the second type of variation, the intra-municipality variation, is essential for the study of whether service provision is motivated by the income it generates. The data we possess in this work are capable of distinguishing between these two types of variation.

## Description of the data

Data from the Norwegian capitation experiment are applied. Annual data on each physician's practice income were collected in 1994 and 1995. The total fee-for-service component consists of the payment from the National Insurance Scheme and from patient charges. This aggregate is used as an indicator of the total volume of services provided in a GP's practice during one year (INPERCAP). Data describing the composition of the fee-for-service component were collected in two representative periods of 14 days – one in March 1994 and one in March 1995.

Only physicians with more than 500 persons on the list and income data of sufficient quality were included.[10] Four physicians were excluded from the data set because they were outliers.[11] Our income data then consist of 218 observations.

The distribution of patients according to age and gender is expected to influence the volume of services provided. It is well known from various studies that females have more frequent consultations than men and that the elderly have more frequent consultations than younger (disregarding the infant age) people (Elstad, 1991). As an indicator of the patient load we used the female proportion of patients (PROPFEM) and the proportion of patients aged seventy and older (PROPOLD). These data were collected annually. Female physicians seem to have a practice style that differs from their male colleagues (Langwell, 1982). Kristiansen and Mooney (1993) found that on average female GPs had longer consultations than male GPs. In the analysis we take account of the physician's gender (FEMALE). All the GPs in our set of data are self-employed. Prior to the capitation experiment, however, some of the physicians were employed by the municipality on a fixed salary contract. It follows that they were unfamiliar with the fee schedule compared with their privately practising colleagues. In the transition period the income from fees may therefore underestimate their volume of service provision. We therefore introduced a dummy variable to account for the physician's employment status before the experiment (SALARIED).

Our prediction is that physicians who experience a shortage of patients have a more service-intensive practice style than their unconstrained colleagues. To account for differences in practice style between various groups of physicians, we included dummy variables in the analysis. Two dummy variables indicate whether GPs are rationed. Before the experiment started, all the participating GPs were asked to specify the number of persons they would like to have on their individual lists (PRELISTSIZE). It is important to note that a GP both takes account of his own characteristics, such as family situation and medical experience, and his own practice style when he expresses his preferred list size. For instance, one GP may wish to work ten hours a day, another prefers a part-time job, one prefers short consultations and yet another prefers to use considerable time on a patient during the consultation. It follows that the preferred number of persons on the list is likely to vary substantially between GPs. For each GP we compare preferred list size and actual list size and obtain an indicator of individual patient constraints.[12]

The dummy variable RATION_A is equal to one for those physicians who had a smaller list than they wanted in period one and experienced a net increase in the number of patients from period one to period two. The second dummy variable, RATION_B, is equal to one for those physicians who had a smaller list than they wanted in period one and experienced a constant or a declining number of patients from period one to period two. Our data then consist of three groups of

GPs according to rationing status: unrationed, lightly rationed (RATION_A) and strongly rationed (RATION_B) GPs. We predict that constrained GPs consider an increased number of patients in period two as a signal of a less severe constraint. Accordingly, it is optimal for them to have a less service-intensive practice style than their colleagues experiencing a shortage of patients in the first period and a constant or a declining list of patients in the second period. Hence, the effect of both light and strong rationing on service provision is expected to be positive, and the effect of strong rationing the more positive.

To account for the between-municipality differences in practice style following from variations in GP-density, medical culture among GPs and constraints contained in the GPs' contracts, we included three dummy variables for municipalities; MUNICIPALITY_2, MUNICIPALITY_3, and MUNICIPALITY_4. The number of inhabitants per GP is increasing in the designation of municipalities, i.e. the GP-density is highest in MUNICIPALITY_1 and lowest in MUNICIPALITY_4.

From Table 10.1 we see that the mean annual income from fees and patient charges per person listed for the whole sample of GPs was NOK 237. On average, 51 per cent of the persons on the individual lists were women and nearly 10 per cent were aged 70 and older. Thirty seven per cent of the physicians included were salaried community physicians prior to the experiment and 26 per cent of the physicians were female. During the 14 days of registration the GPs on average provided 0.07 consultations, 0.07 laboratory tests and used the duration-dependent fee 0.02 times per listed person. Calculated on an annual basis (multiplied by 26), our figures correspond to 1.9 consultations per person per year.

Almost 40 per cent of the GPs were lightly rationed and 26 per cent experienced strong rationing. Hence, almost 66 per cent of the physicians experienced a smaller list in period 1 than they preferred when the experiment was initiated. As seen from Table 10.1, the strongly rationed group annually earns NOK 50 more per listed person from the fee-for-service component than their unrationed colleagues. On average, both categories of rationed GPs provide more consultations, use the duration-dependent fee to a greater extent and provide more laboratory tests per listed person than their unconstrained colleagues.

Table 10.2 shows differences between the four municipalities according to the preferred and the actual number of patients. We notice the substantial difference between municipalities regarding the number of patients GPs would like to have on their list. A likely explanation is the variation in GP-density among the municipalities. For instance, in municipalities 3 and 4 the GP-density was quite low before the experiment started. Hence, each GP had to take care of a large number of patients. Their statements on preferred list size seem to correspond to what they were used to. We also note that in municipalities 2 and 3 the preferred list size is on average considerably longer than the actual list size, while in municipality 4 the actual list size is larger than the preferred. This difference is also reflected in the average values of the rationing variables; nearly 80 per cent of the GPs in municipality 3, and only 40 per cent of the GPs in municipality 4 did not achieve their preferred number of patients.

*Table 10.1* Descriptive statistics – mean (standard deviation) of the variables

| Variable | Definition | Unrationed (76 GPs) | Lightly rationed (86 GPs) | Strongly rationed (56 GPs) | All GPs (218 GPs) |
|---|---|---|---|---|---|
| INPERCAP | Annual income from fees and patient charges per listed person in NOK | NOK 211 (NOK 63) | NOK 245 (NOK 69) | NOK 262 (NOK 83) | NOK 237 (NOK 73) |
| DURATION[a] | The number of consultations per listed person where a GP uses the duration-dependent fee | 0.016 (0.015) | 0.027 (0.021) | 0.029 (0.023) | 0.024 (0.02) |
| LABS[a] | The number of laboratory tests per listed person | 0.06 (0.04) | 0.062 (0.051) | 0.09 (0.063) | 0.069 (0.053) |
| CONSULTS[a] | The number of consultations per listed person | 0.062 (0.033) | 0.07 (0.041) | 0.08 (0.041) | 0.07 (0.039) |
| PRELIST-SIZE | A GP's statement of preferred list size before the capitation experiment started | 1698 (461) | 1931 (409) | 1961 (400) | 1858 (440) |
| LISTSIZE | The actual number of persons on a GP's individual list | 1869 (427) | 1546 (365) | 1757 (435) | 1713 (428) |
| PROPOLD | The proportion of persons aged 70 and older on the list | 0.082 (0.059) | 0.094 (0.045) | 0.119 (0.071) | 0.096 (0.059) |
| PROPFEM | The proportion of females on the list | 0.535 (0.109) | 0.471 (0.11) | 0.52 (0.091) | 0.506 (0.108) |
| FEMALE | A dummy variable equal to one if the physician is a female | 0.368 | 0.14 | 0.286 | 0.257 |
| SALARIED | A dummy variable equal to one if the physician was a salaried community physician prior to the experiment | 0.395 | 0.279 | 0.464 | 0.367 |

Note
a For these variables we have observations of 183 GPs during two periods of 14 days.

*Table 10.2* Descriptive statistics – mean and standard deviation (in parentheses) – according to municipalities

| | Municipality 1 | Municipality 2 | Municipality 3 | Municipality 4 |
|---|---|---|---|---|
| Prelistsize | 1383 (450) | 1610 (412) | 1944 (404) | 1820 (455) |
| Listsize | 1353 (460) | 1475 (697) | 1717 (308) | 1840 (469) |
| Lightly rationed | 33% | 50% | 49% | 16% |
| Strongly rationed | 33% | 8% | 28% | 24% |

## Estimation and results

Data on GPs' service provision are observed in two periods and each GP belongs to a specific municipality.[13] Our data therefore have both a panel data structure and a hierarchical structure. We take account of the hierarchical structure of the data by introducing dummies for municipalities. Because it is reasonable to believe that each GP has a certain practice style related to his personality, his experience, the organization of his practice, etc. we assume dependence between the observations in period one and period two for each GP. In the estimation this dependence can be considered either by means of a fixed effects model (introducing a dummy for every GP minus one) or a random effects model. We assume a random effects model and test whether this is a valid assumption:

$$y_{it} = a_i + bx_{it} + v_{it} \ (i = 1, 2, \ldots, 109; \ t = 1, 2)$$

$$a_i = a + u_i$$

$$v_{it} = IID(0, \sigma^2) \tag{10.1}$$

$$u_i = IID(0, \sigma_u^2)$$

$$\text{cov}(v_{it}, u_i) = 0.$$

Equation (10.1) is a regression model with a random intercept, and with coefficients a and b being fixed. $y_{it}$ is the dependent variable with a subscript indicating observation number $t$ of GP number $i$ and $x_{it}$ is a vector of independent variables with a similar subscript. $u_i$ is the random individual effect and $v_{it}$ is the remainder. The two random components are assumed to be independent of each other, each one being i.i.d. with zero mean and with variance respectively $\sigma_u^2$ and $\sigma^2$.

Table 10.3 shows the results from the estimation of two models: model A includes municipality dummies only, while model B includes rationing dummies as well as municipality dummies. From the Hausman test we see that the random effects model is not rejected. We remember that the GP-density is highest in municipality 1 and lowest in municipality 4. From the coefficients of model A we see the effects of all municipality dummies are negative and the absolute value of the effect increases with the number of inhabitants per GP. Only the effect of the municipality with the highest number of inhabitants per GP is statistically significant at the five per cent level. A GP in municipality 4 is expected to have about NOK 79 lower income from fees per person listed than a GP in municipality 1. The municipality dummies of model B are of about the same magnitude as of model A. Also in model B only the effect of municipality 4 is statistically significant. From the coefficients of RATION_A and RATION_B we see that a patient shortage is expected to increase the income from fees per listed person. Only the effect of RATION_B is statistically significant at the five per cent level. GPs experiencing strong rationing are expected to generate NOK 38 more from fees per listed patient than their unrationed colleagues.

*Table 10.3* The estimated effect of a shortage of patients on income per person listed
(INPERCAP) (*p*-values in parentheses)

|  | Model A | Model B |
|---|---|---|
| CONSTANT | 225.0 (0.000) | 210.1 (0.000) |
| PROPOLD | 286.6 (0.020) | 211.0 (0.101) |
| PROPFEM | 65.2 (0.426) | 82.7 (0.320) |
| FEMALE | −17.4 (0.447) | −20.1 (0.369) |
| SALARIED | 6.7 (0.639) | 1.3 (0.927) |
| RATION_A[a] |  | 23.3 (0.108) |
| RATION_B |  | 38.4 (0.015) |
| MUNICIPALITY_2 | −29.7 (0.350) | −27.0 (0.385) |
| MUNICIPALITY_3 | −41.1 (0.139) | −47.4 (0.081) |
| MUNICIPALITY_4 | −78.7 (0.008) | −76.2 (0.009) |
| Number of observations | 218 | 218 |
| Adjusted R² | 0.16 | 0.19 |
| Hausman test | CHISQ(2) = 1.9723 p-value = 0.3730 | CHISQ(2) = 2.2041 p-value = 0.3322 |

Note
a As explained in the text, RATION_A is the group of lightly rationed GPs and RATION_B the
group of strongly rationed GPs.

The effects of the municipality dummies are of the same magnitude and significance in the two models. These effects reflect municipality characteristics, with access to GPs – expressed by GP-density – as the most important one. We found a positive and statistically significant effect of a patient shortage when we included micro-data on GPs' rationing status in the analysis. This result supports the hypothesis that service provision among GPs is income-motivated. That the municipality effects were only slightly changed when micro-data on rationing were included is in accordance with our hypothesis: income-motivated behaviour stems from patient shortage experienced by the individual GP. The effect of a patient shortage is independent of the aggregate GP-density in a municipality. Our main point then follows: micro-data are necessary to detect income-motivated behaviour among GPs.

## Concluding remarks

The objective of this chapter is to argue that micro-data are fundamental for the study of income-motivated behaviour among general practitioners. We have argued that a GP who experiences a shortage of patients in a mixed capitation and fee-for-service payment system is likely to have a more service-intensive practice style than his unconstrained colleagues. If he cannot have his optimal number of patients, a second best is to increase the number of services per patient if the income per time unit of providing services is greater than the marginal valuation of leisure.

An empirical test of this income-generating hypothesis requires micro-data on whether a GP in fact experiences a patient shortage. Macro-data on GP-density in an area are not likely to be useful because the effect of better access is often not distinguishable from the effect of physician-initiated services.

For the purpose of empirical studies, a capitation system is attractive since each GP's number of patients is known from administrative data. Since we in this study also have access to individual GPs' statements of their preferred number of patients, we are able to distinguish between the GPs who experience a shortage of patients and the GPs who have achieved their optimal number of patients, i.e. patient constraints on individual GP level. We introduced municipality dummies to account for the differences in GP-density and other area-specific characteristics.

The results of the estimation show that the effect of a patient shortage (strong rationing) on a GP's income from fees per patient is positive and statistically significant. Furthermore, we find that only the municipality with the lowest GP-density has a negative and statistically significant effect. If GP-density data only had been available, we might erroneously have concluded that income-motivated behaviour among GPs is not detected. The reason is that with aggregate data we miss the intra-municipality variation in the actual number of patients relative to the preferred number among GPs.

This point is further illustrated in Table 10.4. Table 10.4 displays a quantitative picture of the municipality effect and the patient shortage effect calculated by means of the estimated coefficients of model B and the mean composition of patients with regard to age and gender. Non-significant effects are also included.

We see from Table 10.4 that the municipality effect reduces the income from fees per listed person as the GP-density is reduced. We also see that the income per listed person increases, as rationing becomes more severe. But even if he is strongly rationed, a GP in municipality 3 or municipality 4 is expected to have a lower income per listed person than an unrationed GP in municipality 1. But he has a higher income per patient than the unrationed colleagues in his own municipality had. This variation is not accounted for when aggregate data are employed.

Several critical points could be raised against our approach and the data we employ. For instance, one could claim that the municipality dummies should be replaced by the GP-density to account for variation in municipality-specific access to GPs. In fact, we have run this alternative regression and found a positive,

*Table 10.4* Expected income from fee-for-service per listed person according to rationing status and municipality, parameters from Table 10.3, model B

|  | *Unrationed* | *Lightly rationed* | *Strongly rationed* |
|---|---|---|---|
| Municipality 1 | 272 NOK | 296 NOK | 311 NOK |
| Municipality 2 | 245 NOK | 269 NOK | 284 NOK |
| Municipality 3 | 225 NOK | 248 NOK | 263 NOK |
| Municipality 4 | 196 NOK | 219 NOK | 234 NOK |

but non-significant effect of GP-density on the volume of services delivered to each patient. Since the variation in GP-density becomes rather small with only four municipalities involved, we chose to present the results with municipality dummies. In addition, dummies also capture other municipality-specific characteristics not accounted for by the GP-density.

One could argue that the effect we find of a patient shortage stems from the fact that we do not distinguish between those GPs who have obtained their preferred number of patients and those who have more than their preferred number. From Table 10.1 we see that among the unrationed the average list size is greater than the average preferred number. We therefore split the unrationed group into two parts and introduced a dummy variable equal to one for those GPs who had more than 100 patients in excess of the preferred number. True enough, the effect of this variable has a negative sign, but the effect is far from statistically significant.[14]

One could also question the validity of the variable describing a GP's preferred number of patients, since the value of this variable is reported by the GP himself. However, we cannot see that there is an incentive for a systematically biased report. By overstating the true number a GP runs the risk of a less than optimal amount of leisure, while underreporting the true number may result in a smaller than optimal income.

A GP may have some possibilities for regulating his own workload by referring patients to treatment by a specialist. Referrals are not included in this chapter. In a related paper (Iversen and Lurås, 2000a) we found an increase in the referral rate in one of the municipalities after the capitation system was introduced. We found, however, no statistically significant effect of whether a GP is rationed or not.

Finally, our concepts of light and strong rationing are essentially dynamic concepts requiring dynamic modelling. Rationed GPs may have different strategies for increasing the size of the list relative to increasing the intensity of treatment, depending on the cost compared with the benefit of alternative strategies. These dynamic aspects will be addressed in our future research.

## Notes

The authors are grateful to Björn Lindgren, discussant Kristian Bolin, other participants at the 19th Arne Ryde Symposium, Lund, 27–28 August 1999 and two referees for helpful comments. Remaining errors are our own responsibility. Financial support from the Norwegian Ministry of Health and Social Affairs and the Research Council of Norway is acknowledged.

1 The system with capitation in general practice has long since been established in countries like Denmark, the Netherlands and the UK.
2 In the system before the capitation trial most GPs were self-employed contract physicians while the rest were municipal employees on a fixed salary. All GPs except two became privately employed when the trial was initiated. These two are omitted from the data set without any danger of selection bias from an empirical point of view.
3 Compared with the payment system of the contract physicians prior to the experiment, the municipal grant and some fees were replaced by the capitation component.

4 The sizes of the different fees are decided in centralised negotiations between the Norwegian Medical Association and the state.

5 About 50 per cent of the income of an average practice is expected to come from the capitation component, and about 50 per cent from the fee-per-item part.

6 In this article we interpret a GP's practice style in a quantitative way, i.e. the number of services given to a person during a certain period.

7 In health economics literature this interval is often referred to as 'flat of the curve medicine', see for instance Enthoven (1980).

8 In Iversen and Lurås (2000b) we have two types of health services and hence, an additional effect of the relative fees. Since the focus of the present paper is different, we simplify to a general health service without loss of important points.

9 In the Norwegian context we can use GP-density in the municipality as an indicator of GP-density in the area. The reason is that patients are listed by doctors in the municipality, and to a lesser extent visit doctors outside the municipality.

10 We suspect that GPs with small lists work part-time as a GP and may not be representative in the way they perform their work.

11 Their registered income per listed patient differed substantially between 1994 and 1995 while the list of patients was quite stable. We therefore suspect that an extraordinary time lag between service provision and income registration occurred in one of the years.

12 The absolute size of the lists and the reason why the size varies between GPs are not an issue in this study.

13 In the annual income data there are 218 observations of 109 different GPs from 4 municipalities.

14 The magnitude of the effect of strong rationing is slightly smaller than in our original analysis, but statistically significant at the 2 per cent level.

# References

Elstad, J.I. (1991) Flere leger, større bruk? Artikler om bruk av allmennlegetjenester, INAS-Rapport 1991: 11. Institutt for sosialforskning, Oslo.

Enthoven, A.S. (1980) *Health Plan: The Only Practical Solution to the Soaring Cost of Medical Care*. Addison-Wesley, Reading, Mass.

Iversen, T. and Lurås, H. (2000a) The effect of capitation on GPs' referral decisions, *Health Economics* 9, 199–210.

Iversen, T. and Lurås, H. (2000b) Economic motives and professional norms: The case of general medical practice, *Journal of Economic Behavior and Organization* 43, 447–70.

Kristiansen, I.S. and Mooney, G. (1993) The general practitioner's use of time: Is it influenced by the remuneration system? *Social Science and Medicine* 3, 393–9.

Langwell, K.M. (1982) Factors affecting the incomes of men and women physicians: Further explorations, *The Journal of Human Resources* 17, 261–76.

Scott, A. and Shiell, A. (1997) Analysing the effect of competition on general practitioners' behaviour using a multilevel modelling framework, *Health Economics* 6, 577–88.

# 11 The production and regulation of insurance

## Limiting opportunism in proprietary and non-proprietary organizations

*Tomas Philipson and George Zanjani*

## Introduction

It is often argued that the existence of nonprofit and consumer-owned enterprises arises from asymmetric information and incentive conflicts between producers and consumers. When quality is unobservable and costly to monitor, alternatives to proprietary ownership may be desirable if they can be utilized to limit opportunistic behaviour by producers (see, for examples, Hansmann, 1996; Weisbrod, 1988).

Because of a relatively long gap between payment and product delivery, the insurance product is thought to be especially vulnerable to opportunistic actions that jeopardize company solvency. That is, producers are tempted to take actions that increase profits but threaten product quality by making it less likely that the firm will be able to meet its obligations. Such behaviour may take a variety of forms. For example, companies controlled by shareholders might speculate with the company's assets, neglect costly risk management activities, or even distribute excessive amounts to shareholders through dividends. Nonprofit and mutual firms, however, are not affected by a profit motive. Nonprofits cannot distribute profits to owners, and the owners of mutuals are the consumers themselves. Because of this, management is argued to act in the interest of the policyholder, safeguarding the company's solvency.[1]

Thus, non-proprietary organizations would seem to have significant advantages in the production of insurance, especially for contracts where the gap between payment and final delivery is long, such as life insurance, long-term care insurance, renewable health insurance, and workers' compensation insurance. Yet, non-proprietary firms are the minority players in all major segments of the US insurance industry and do not appear to have market shares that vary across markets in a manner that would support this theory. In 1997, mutuals had a market share of roughly 35 per cent in both the property–casualty and life–health industries, and nonprofits accounted for about 35 per cent of Human Maintenance Organization (HMO) premiums.[2] Furthermore, coexistence of stock and non-proprietary firms has persisted throughout US history (see, for example, Zanjani, 2000), spanning a variety of different economic situations and regulatory regimes.

In order to understand the presence and growing importance of proprietary insurance production, we must understand how stock firms are able to compete with nonprofit and mutual firms in controlling opportunism. It has been argued that proprietary firms dominate the non-traditional forms of production in productive efficiency,[3] but it is not clear how proprietary firms compete in containing opportunistic behaviour. Understanding how they do this is key to understanding the preference among organizational forms shown by consumers, as well as whether non-traditional forms should receive preferential treatment from the public sector.

This chapter argues that the advantage of nonprofit forms in limiting opportunistic behaviour has been exaggerated. We show that, under some conditions, the cost of limiting agency problems is unaffected by the choice of organizational form. This neutrality result stems from the fact that there are perfect substitutes for non-proprietary ownership in controlling opportunism. Proprietary insurance firms may mitigate or eliminate agency problems by posting a bond (see Becker and Stigler, 1974). This bond is naturally interpreted as the surplus held by an insurance producer that is available for policyholders if results turn out unfavourably. If the costs associated with posting the bond are small, insurance firms will be able to overcome agency problems without submitting to the disadvantages of nonprofit or mutual structure. The choice between organizational forms, then, can only be understood in the context of the costs and benefits of this type of bonding.

This chapter builds on the work of Philipson and Zanjani (1998) by emphasizing the importance of solvency concerns in insurance production. These concerns have received much less attention in the literature than asymmetric information problems. In particular, the opportunistic behaviour by insurance producers that is often stressed arises from the incompleteness of the contract and concerns various aspects of claims-handling, such as the quality or amount of medical care delivered in the case of health insurance. While such opportunism may be important, it offers little to explain the prevalence of the non-proprietary form in life insurance, where the contingencies are clearly specified and producers have little discretion in handling claims. Furthermore, public involvement in the life, health, and property–casualty insurance markets is largely in the monitoring and regulation of company solvency, not claims-handling. Thus, it seems likely that solvency, and opportunism with respect to solvency, is important for understanding the organizational forms chosen in insurance markets and the production of insurance in general.

The chapter may be outlined as follows. The next section starts by demonstrating the equivalence between public enforcement of bonding in for-profit insurance production and enforcement of nondistribution constraints in nonprofit production. This can be regarded as bearing similarity to Hansmann's notion[4] that regulated stock firms are an alternative to mutual companies. The following section extends the analysis to a more general form of moral hazard. Here it is demonstrated that the holding of surplus can be a solution to opportunism, even without the direct involvement of regulation. In so doing, it helps to explain why the surplus bonding activity of stock insurers has historically been much higher than that of mutual insurers, both before and after the advent of regulation. Concluding remarks (p. 204) end the chapter.

## The neutrality of organizational form in insurance production

In this section, we analyse a special type of opportunism – premature distribution of funds to shareholders. We show that, conditional on a given scale and price, the different organizational forms face the same costs for reducing agency problems when stock firms can post a bond. Therefore, for any price and scale, there will be no advantage to changing organizational form. This simple set-up serves to illustrate the basic ideas before we address more sophisticated types of moral hazard.

The opportunity for exploitative behaviour arises because of the long-term nature of the insurance contract. Revenues are collected far in advance of the time losses are realized. This creates the risk that the insurance company will distribute portions of the premiums to shareholders before losses are realized, thereby threatening the solvency of the company. In its most extreme form, this problem could lead to the complete collapse of trade. That is, if shareholders were unrestrained in their ability to effect distributions of company funds, nothing would be left for the policyholders. Those responsible for carrying out the risk-sharing would not be trusted to do so, and no trade would occur in equilibrium. Because the liability of the insurance company is limited to available assets, policyholders will not be able to collect on claims if there are no funds left in the company. The long delay between payment and delivery that is unique to insurance makes it tempting, and indeed rational, for shareholders to 'take the money and run'.

However, it may be possible for stock firms to control this opportunistic behaviour. A possible solution is to post a bond that would be used to pay claims if the firm misbehaves. In other words, when revenues are insufficient to cover claims, the bond is used to pay the policyholders. Of course, it would be necessary for · this bond to be safe from shareholders. Solvency regulations, in terms of requiring company deposits and surplus, enable, and sometimes even *force*, this type of bonding. In essence, the insurance company acts as a borrower that needs to put up collateral in the form of surplus.

Let revenue be made up of the price times quantity $py$. Assume for now that there is no aggregate risk; claims $c$ are deterministic[5] due to a large scale. Suppose the owners can choose to consume $x$ units of the revenue before the claims occur. This makes the firm insolvent whenever the revenue less the consumption of shareholders does not cover claims

$$py - x \leq c.$$

Naturally, in the absence of any restraints, the shareholders would choose to consume all premiums: $x = py$.

These agency problems would be reduced or eliminated by nonprofit and mutual status. Nonprofits face a nondistribution constraint that limits the consumption of the firm's owners and managers, as in $x \leq x_0$. For a nonprofit, the nondistribution constraint guarantees solvency whenever this limited distribution leaves sufficient funds to cover costs:

$$py - x_0 \geq c.$$

A mutual company faces no conflict between owners and consumers, since it is owned by its consumers. Early distribution of revenues would not be in the interest of the consumers, who would be the recipients of such a distribution. Hence, the limit on distribution, $x_0$, for mutuals can be set equal to zero.

However, the for-profit firm may be able to solve the agency issue by alternative means. Consider when the shareholders post a surplus bond of size $s$ that consumers may access if the firm becomes insolvent. For the sake of illustrating the main ideas involved, imagine that this surplus is posted with a public regulator so that shareholders would not have access to it once posted.[6] If the surplus is not needed to cover the claims of the insured, the surplus is simply returned to the shareholders. Consider when the firm is fully bonded in the sense that the surplus covers claims costs $s \geq c$. This bonding eliminates the incentive to engage in opportunistic consumption of revenues, since shareholders simply lose the portion of the bond necessary to cover any shortfall when revenue minus consumption is insufficient to cover claims ($py - x < c$). Thus, when surplus covers the claims costs, shareholders are discouraged from engaging in opportunistic behaviour; they consume only the profits, since consumption beyond this point simply leads to losses of surplus on a dollar-for-dollar basis:

$$s > c \Rightarrow x^* = py - c.$$

In other words, with sufficient bonding, shareholders are not tempted to access funds held for claims liabilities. The surplus serves as a commitment device and is never used in equilibrium. In essence, the surplus in this setting is collateral that enables the insurance producer to commit to hold premium revenues from policyholders on consignment.

To illustrate the importance of surplus in actual insurance markets, we use data from *A.M. Best's Aggregates and Averages*. Table 11.1 below displays the total surplus held by HMOs, life–health insurers, and property–casualty insurers. The table displays sizes of annual premiums, claims, and surplus for 1997. The important point is that insurers in each of these industries hold significant financial

*Table 11.1* Premiums, benefits, and surplus in 1997 ($ billion)

| Industry | Premiums | Benefits | Surplus |
|---|---|---|---|
| Property–casualty | 267 | 168 | 256 |
| Life–health | 398 | 340 | 155 |
| HMO | 119 | 107 | 106 |

assets *in excess* of what is needed to pay claims. This is in spite of the fact that income from these assets is subjected to double-taxation: surplus appears to be necessary for policyholder security. (This will become more apparent when uncertainty is introduced in the later sections.)

What are the benefits associated with bonding, as in a for-profit firm, relative to those associated with the nondistribution constraint, as in a nonprofit or mutual firm? They are equivalent in the sense that both the nondistribution constraint and the surplus fund can be used to eliminate opportunism. The basic difference between these two substitutes stems from the fact that a nondistribution constraint and benevolent ownership attack rent-seeking directly, while surplus capitalization limits it indirectly.[7] At first glance, it may appear that for-profit bonding entails larger costs than the mechanisms used by mutuals and nonprofits, since shareholders must be compensated for the opportunity cost of their funds. This is not necessarily true; if the surplus funds are invested while being used as collateral, there may be no costs associated with the posting of the bond. Under these conditions, the benefits and costs associated with for-profit and nonprofit/mutual production are identical. In this sense, the two organizational forms are equivalent in their ability to control opportunism.

The agency solutions used by both forms are fully feasible only under public monitoring and enforcement. This is reflected in the behaviour of the public sector in actual insurance markets. Indeed, the main form of insurance regulation is the public monitoring and enforcement of capitalization requirements. This is the proprietary analogue of the nondistribution constraints of mutual and nonprofit firms, which also must be enforced.

### *The neutrality of organizational form when surplus funds may be used*

The previous section shows that when the average claim is certain and capital is not costly to hold, bonding and organizational form are perfect substitutes in limiting agency costs. This occurred because surplus was never used in equilibrium. However, this section shows that the argument generalizes to the case where insolvency may occur in equilibrium due to aggregate uncertainty in claims. Though often ignored in economic analysis, this uncertainty is prevalent in actual markets. For example, both correlation in claims across consumers and decreasing returns to the production of in-kind benefits could lead to aggregate uncertainty at the company or industry levels.

Consider the case where the total claims $c$ are distributed according to the cdf $F(c)$. When claims are uncertain, solvency of the insurance company becomes an important aspect of product quality. Policyholders will be concerned about the ability of any insurance firm to withstand unfavourable claims outcomes. The quality of the insurance product can thus be expressed as a function of the resources that are available to pay claims. These resources amount to revenues plus surplus, minus the consumption of owners or managers. Hence we write quality as an increasing function of these financial resources: $q(py + s - x)$. Note that, in this example, there is a one-to-one relationship between product quality and the likelihood that the company will be able to meet its obligations.[8] The probability of solvency can simply be expressed as the likelihood that claims will not exceed resources:

$$P(c \leq py + s - x) = \int_0^{py+s-x} dF(c),$$

which is an increasing function of $py + s - x$. Clearly, quality falls in shareholder consumption $q_x \leq 0$, but rises in surplus $q_s \geq 0$. Note here that surplus and nondistribution constraints are substitutes in the production of solvency. Nonprofit and mutual firms may be regarded as having a constraint on owner consumption $x_0$, but it is evident that reductions in consumption $x$ are equivalent to increases in surplus $s$.

Shareholder consumption is determined as the solution to:

$$\max_x \left\{ x + \left[ py - x - \int_0^{py+s-x} c \, dF(c) \right] \right\} \# \max_x \left\{ py - \int_0^{py+s-x} c \, dF(c) \right\}$$

(11.1)

subject to

$$x \leq py. \tag{11.2}$$

Shareholders will evidently choose to consume as much as possible ($x^* = py$), unless surplus is set so high as to cover the 'worst case scenario' for the realization of claims.[9] If this is the case, shareholders will be indifferent between consuming and not consuming.

Now consider when insurance producers limit agency costs by means of nonprofit or mutual status. As before, this is assumed to entail a nondistribution constraint so that $x \leq x_0$. Hence, constraint (11.2) can be rewritten as:

$$x \leq x_0 < py.$$

The imposition of this constraint implies that quality will always be higher (at least in the weak sense) in nonprofit and mutual firms for a given surplus and price level. Quality evidently falls as the nondistribution constraint is relaxed:

$$\frac{\partial q(py + s - x_0)}{\partial x_0} \leq 0.$$

However, the important message is that, if surplus can be raised without cost, the stock firm will always be able to match or improve on the quality offered by a nonprofit firm. Since surplus and reduced consumption are perfect substitutes in the production of solvency, a stock firm can always achieve an arbitrarily high level of quality simply by posting a sufficiently large bond. As was the case before, the two forms are equivalent in the sense that any level of solvency generated by a nondistribution constraint can be replicated by a for-profit insurer that posts an appropriate amount of surplus. In this way, the solvency induced by a nondistribution constraint can be just as easily produced through surplus posting by for-profit producers.

The development to this point relies on the public enforcement of both the nondistribution constraint on nonprofits and the bonding of for-profits, which echoes Hansmann's arguments about the 'enabling' effects of regulation (Hansmann, 1996). Yet, even after considering regulation, there are significant differences in the bonding activity of stock and mutual insurers. Some of this is due to regulatory requirements: some states vary surplus and deposit requirements according to organizational form. However, such variations are usually not substantial, and firms usually hold surplus well in excess of the amounts required by law: it seems likely that much of the difference in bonding reflects voluntary behaviour on the part of insurers. As an example, small stock firms have historically had much higher levels of capitalization than their mutual counterparts (see Spectator Company, 1911), even before deposit requirements were present (Zanjani, 2000).

These facts suggest that surplus capital was and is being used by firms to deliver security to policyholders in a sense not directly linked to regulation and, furthermore, that surplus bonding is more important for proprietary firms than for non-proprietary ones. In the next section, we show that surplus bonding is important even if owners are effectively barred from premature consumption. If there are risk management activities that are important for company solvency but not perfectly observable by the public or by regulators, surplus capital can be used both as a commitment device and even as a substitute for such activities.

## The neutrality of organizational form under endogenous risk

The previous section considered a specific example of moral hazard that involved the premature distribution of funds to shareholders. In this section, we consider the more general case of opportunistic behaviour, in which the company neglects its fiduciary responsibility by sacrificing company solvency for profits. This neglect may take more subtle forms than the direct distribution of funds to shareholders. For example, the company may engage in excessive speculation with assets or may neglect prudent (but costly) risk management that would enhance company solvency. Such behaviour is not easy for regulators to monitor directly.

In this section, the analysis is extended to the case when the aggregate risk facing the firm is partially controlled by the firm – as opposed to being determined exogenously. There is indeed substantial uncertainty in the claims experienced by an insurance company. However, the amount of uncertainty is, to some extent, under the control of the insurance company. Through careful underwriting and other risk management activities, an insurance company may reduce the degree of fluctuation in claims costs. Herein lies the divergence between owner and consumer interests in the insurance firm under endogenous claims risk. At the margin, the incentive to control liabilities through underwriting and other forms of risk management may be smaller for the shareholder-owned enterprise than the consumer-owned enterprise. Shareholders may not care about company risk per se, while consumers will.

As we saw in the previous section, one approach for a stock firm is to post a surplus bond that would be available to policyholders in the event that results turned out unfavourably. When claims are endogenous, surplus serves an additional function. With larger surplus, the firm's owners have more to lose if the firm goes bankrupt. Hence, the incentives of firm owners may become more closely aligned with those of policyholders, if risk management and underwriting involve reductions in mean claim costs as well as reductions in risk. However, it retains its role as a *substitute* method for producing solvency. Nonprofit and mutual enterprises may have an advantage in being able to commit to risk management activities, but proprietary firms have superior access to the capital market. By holding larger amounts of surplus, stock firms are able to provide an equivalent level of security for policyholders, even without engaging in the same level of risk management as non-proprietary firms.

To consider endogenous risk formally, let the distribution of claims be represented by the density function $f(c, r)$ (cdf $F(c, r)$), where $r$ is a level of risk management. Note that this is simply the density function from the previous section, but we have added an argument to account for the fact that the distribution may be affected by risk management. Greater levels of risk management may reduce the mean and the dispersion in the claim distribution. Risk management is only one part of the solvency picture, however. As was argued in the previous section, solvency is also determined by the funds the company has available to meet claims. This is simply the revenue $py$ plus the surplus $s$, as before. However, instead of a subtraction for shareholder consumption, we deduct the amount spent on risk management $r$. Hence, the amount of resources available for claims payment and the level of risk management jointly determine the probability of solvency as in:

$$q(py + s - r, r). \tag{11.3}$$

Quality captures both the likelihood and severity of default. It is increasing in both of its arguments. Consumer preferences for insurance can thus be defined over price and quality as in $U(p, q)$, where $U$ is decreasing in price but increasing in quality.

Since nonprofits cannot distribute profits to owners, and consumers are the residual claimants in mutuals, it is often argued that non-proprietary organizations will behave optimally from the perspective of policyholders. Given this assumption, a price, and a surplus level, the non-proprietary firm will choose risk management so as to maximize the welfare of policyholders:

$$\max_{r} \{U(p, q(py + s - r, r))\}. \tag{11.4}$$

This leads to the following optimality condition:

$$q_1 = q_2.$$

In other words, the marginal benefit associated with risk management must be balanced with its marginal cost. When price and surplus are fixed, both the marginal benefit and cost are measured in terms of the impact on quality.[10] That is, the direct benefit of risk management on quality is weighed against the indirect cost of risk management – resources that could be used to pay claims are consumed by this activity.

This contrasts with the case of a proprietary firm, which will choose risk management so as to maximize profits:

$$\max_r \left\{ py - r - \int_0^{py+s-r} cf(c, r)dc \right\}. \tag{11.5}$$

The first term in the maximand represents revenues collected, as before. The second term is expenditure on risk management. The last term is expected payments to policyholders. Thus, profit maximization will entail balancing marginal expenditure on risk management with any marginal benefits associated with changes in expected payments to policyholders. That is, risk management expenditure affects profit directly and also indirectly through its impact on the claims distribution. Formally, the first-order condition for the optimal choice of $r$ is given by:

$$-1 - \int_0^{py+s-r} cf_r \, dc + (py + s - r)f(py + s - r, r) = 0.$$

The first term represents the marginal cost of risk management, while the last two terms represent the marginal changes in expected payments to policyholders. These latter effects arise from changes in the claim distribution and changes in the resources available to pay (some are consumed by risk management). Needless to say, the solution to (11.5) is likely to be different from the solution to (11.4). The profit-maximizing manager does not care about quality per se: he/she only underwrites to the extent that the resources consumed by risk management at the margin equal to the marginal savings in claim costs. In fact, if risk management were a pure risk-reducing activity, with no impact on the mean claim cost, a profit-maximizing firm might have no interest in this activity.

Thus, for a given price and surplus level, non-proprietary firms have an advantage over stock firms. The alignment of owner with consumer incentives eliminates the moral hazard problem: proper levels of risk management will be chosen with due concern for solvency. Proprietary firms, on the other hand, are not able to commit to protecting consumer interests through risk management. When this activity cannot be verified and is only known after the fact, the stock firm will engage in opportunistic behaviour.

### Surplus as a substitute for risk management

Risk management is not the only way a firm can produce solvency. On the contrary, as indicated in (11.3), an alternative way of producing quality is to provide a large 'cushion' against unexpected losses. That is, a firm that offers greater claims-paying resources, $py + s - r$, offers greater quality. The advantage of stock firms, then, lies in their access to capital markets. Mutual and nonprofit firms are unable to issue equity; their capital base can only be built through contributions by consumers and benefactors. For a given capital and surplus, the non-proprietary form will always have an advantage in production, due to superior incentives in risk management. However, the mutual firm may be unable to obtain the level of capitalization that can be achieved by a stock firm.

To see this more clearly, define the optimal risk management functions implied by (11.4) and (11.5) by $r^p(p, s)$ (for proprietary firms) and $r^m(p, s)$ (for non-proprietary firms). These functions imply quality frontiers for the two types of organizations: $q^p(p^y + s - r^p(p, s), r^p(p, s))$ and $q^m(p^y + s - r^m(p, s), r^m(p, s))$. These are shown in Figure 11.1. Note that the mutual/nonprofit frontier lies above the proprietary frontier, implying an advantage for these forms at any surplus level. However, if the non-proprietary firm were unable to raise surplus above a certain level ($s^*$ in the figure), the stock firm would have a productive advantage at higher quality levels (above $q^*$ in the figure).

Surplus is a substitute for risk management. There is a trade-off between the superior incentives offered by the non-proprietary form and the superior capital market access offered by the stock form. The main idea here is that stock firms can achieve the same quality levels as non-proprietary firms in the insurance industry by posting surplus. This surplus affects quality directly, through the provision of additional claims-paying resources. It may also affect quality indirectly by improving incentives for risk management.

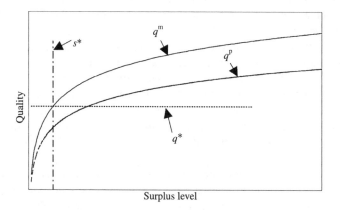

*Figure 11.1*   Quality frontiers for proprietary and non-proprietary firms.

### Neutrality of organizational form under endogenous risk

We have demonstrated that surplus can be used as a substitute for risk management in the production of solvency. In fact, if there is no cost associated with
surplus, then it could be argued that it is in fact *superior* to risk management in
producing solvency. If there is no cost associated with the holding of surplus
capital in insurance companies, there is no need to expend resources in risk
management: any claims fluctuation can be absorbed by the surplus. In this case,
mutuals enjoy no advantage over stock firms and would in fact be inferior.

However, raising capital will generally not be costless for insurance companies. Investment in financial assets through an insurance company will be
subjected to double-taxation; furthermore, regulations may dictate that funds be
invested in suboptimal assets. Investors may also demand additional returns for
exposing capital to risk, depending on how this risk relates to other types of risk
in the capital market. This means that insurance must be priced to yield an appropriate rate of return on invested capital, and this price will reflect the premium
demanded for risk-bearing and illiquidity by investors.

If the return on insurance capital varies, we can expect changes in the rate of
return demanded to have an effect on the relative attractiveness of the non-
proprietary form of organization. If capital is cheap, we expect consumers to substitute toward the stock form of organization, as this form is a heavy user of capital
as an input in solvency production. If capital is expensive, we should expect consumers to substitute toward alternative forms of organization – forms that are
more efficient users of capital, but cannot raise large amounts. Zanjani (2000) has
found evidence consistent with this substitution effect: mutual firms have been
relatively popular in the US during times of financial distress, such as the 1840s,
1870s, and the Great Depression.

## Concluding remarks

This chapter argued that the advantages of non-proprietary organizations in insurance production may have been exaggerated. Standard arguments about nonprofit
and mutual production imply that such firms should produce higher quality insurance than for-profit firms. We showed that this reasoning is too simplistic: there
are close substitutes for an organizational change in limiting agency costs.
Specifically, we show that the ability of proprietary firms to limit agency costs
through bonding enables these firms to produce insurance of quality comparable
to that produced by nonprofit and mutual forms. This may well help to explain
the dominance of the for-profit firm and its continuing growth in market share.
This bonding is observed in practice through the surplus held by firms and
through solvency regulations.

The empirical content of the nonprofit advantages has recently been developed
and put to a test. Philipson (2001) has argued that a testable implication of the
efficiency gains from nonprofit production is that their output should sell at a premium relative to for-profit firms when they coexist. That is, if nonprofits are more

successful at limiting agency costs than for-profits, consumers would shun the latter if it were more expensive. He presents evidence that seems inconsistent with the presence of a premium for nonprofits in the US long-term care market in the 1980s and 1990s. One interpretation of the absence of such a premium is that for-profit firms may be able to limit agency problems through alternative mechanisms.

Our result regarding the equivalence of organizational form in solvency production should not be interpreted to imply that there are no differences between non-proprietary and for-profit forms of production. The coexistence of the two forms presumably reflects different comparative advantages.[11] For example, nonprofit and small mutual enterprises receive favourable income tax treatment, while for-profit firms have better access to the capital market and may have advantages in achieving productive efficiency. However, our analysis does represent a step toward understanding why nonprofit and mutual forms do not dominate the industry. Furthermore, it should be noted that departure from the static setting used in this chapter will not necessarily reverse this conclusion: a dynamic setting might prove to be even more favourable to the stock form, as it would introduce the possibility of using a reputational mechanism as yet another alternative for mitigating opportunism.

We have offered a framework for thinking about the differences between the two forms and how the relative preference for the two forms has changed over time. In particular, substitution between the two forms will be driven by changes in the costs associated with bonding: we interpret the trend toward the proprietary firm as substitution toward bonding, which is relatively cheap in an era of well-developed financial markets. This prediction offers an important area for future empirical research.

## Notes

We thank Richard Epstein, Fredrik Andersson, two anonymous referees, and seminar participants at The University of Chicago, the 10th Annual Health Economics Conference at Berkeley, and the 1999 Arne Ryde Symposium for helpful comments and discussions.

1 See Hansmann (1996) and Mayers and Smith (1981) for the detailed versions of this argument.
2 Source: A.M. Best. The 'life–health' industry is defined according to the conventions used by A.M. Best.
3 However, the evidence on this has generally shown little in the way of significant differences. See, for example, Sloan (1997, 2000) on hospitals.
4 Hansmann (1996, p. 271).
5 Obviously, when costs are certain, consumers and producers should be able to write enforceable contracts on those costs, rendering suspect the notion of premature distribution. We use this assumption to illustrate the main ideas and then extend the analysis to the case of uncertain costs.
6 Deposit requirements for insurance companies in the US date to the nineteenth century.
7 In addition, retaining the stock form of organization may preserve productive incentives. We have abstracted from these differences here.
8 Quality will also depend on the characteristics of the claim distribution (and, hence, the *severity* of insolvency when it occurs). This has been ignored here, as the distribution is taken to be fixed.

9  Formally, this means that the support of *f*(.) is a subset of the interval [0, *s*].
10  For a comprehensive treatment of risk management in a model of solvency production, where price and surplus are not fixed, see Philipson and Zanjani (1998).
11  There is, of course, a large literature stressing the advantages of different organizational forms, although their comparative advantages have been analysed less. See, for example, Becker and Sloan (1985), Easley and O'Hara (1982), Gertler (1989), James and Rose-Ackerman (1986), Newhouse (1970), Pauly and Redisch (1973), and Weisbrod (1988).

# References

Becker, E. and Sloan, F. (1985), 'Hospital Ownership and Preference'. *Economic Inquiry* 23, 21–36.

Becker, G. and Stigler, G. (1974), 'Law Enforcement, Malfeasance, and Compensation of Enforcers'. *Journal of Legal Studies* 3, 1–18.

Easley, D. and O'Hara, M. (1982), 'The Economic Role of The Non-Profit Firm'. *Rand Journal of Economics* 14, 531–40.

Gertler, P. (1989), 'Subsidies, Quality, and the Regulation of Nursing Homes'. *Journal of Public Economics* 39, 33–53.

Hansmann, H. (1996), *The Ownership of Enterprise*. Cambridge and London: The Belknap Press of Harvard University Press.

James, E. and Rose-Ackerman, S. (1986), *The Nonprofit Enterprise in Market Economics*. New York: Harwood Academic Publishers.

Mayers, D. and Smith, C.W. (1981), 'Contractual Provisions, Organizational Structure, and Conflict Control in Insurance Markets'. *Journal of Business* 54, 407–34.

Newhouse, J. (1970), 'Towards a Theory Of Non-Profit Institutions: an Economic Model of a Hospital'. *American Economic Review* 60, 64–74.

Pauly, M. and Redisch, M. (1973), 'The Non-Profit Hospitals as a Physician Cooperative'. *American Economic Review* 63, 87–100.

Philipson, T. (2001), 'Asymmetric Information and the Not-for-Profit Sector: Does Its Output Sell at a Premium?' In: Cutler, D. (ed.), *The Changing Hospital Industry*. Chicago: University of Chicago Press.

Philipson, T. and Zanjani, G. (1998), *A Theory of the Production and Regulation of Insurance*. Mimeo, University of Chicago.

Sloan, F. (1997), 'How Do Non-Profit and Profit Hospitals Differ?' In: Cutler, D. (ed.), *Non-Profit Hospitals*, Chicago: University of Chicago Press.

Sloan, F. (2000), 'Not-for-Profit Ownership and Hospital Behavior'. In: Culyer, A.J. and Newhouse, J.P. (eds), *Handbook of Health Economics*, Amsterdam: Elsevier.

Spectator Company (1911), *Life Insurance History: 1843–1910*. New York and Chicago: The Spectator Company.

Weisbrod, B. (1988), *The Non-Profit Economy*, Cambridge: Harvard University Press.

Zanjani, G. (2000), *Essays on Capital and Risk in Insurance Production*. University of Chicago (Ph.D. dissertation).

# 12 Patching up the physician–patient relationship

## Insurers versus governments as complementary agents

*Peter Zweifel, Hansjörg Lehmann, and Lukas Steinmann*

## Introduction

The health care sector is characterized by a great deal of delegation of authority. In particular, the patient as the ultimate consumer of health care services frequently delegates decision making with respect to several dimensions to the physician in charge, such as the timing of the treatment, the procedures to be followed, the provider of some components of care, and the location of treatment. Delegation of authority occurs because the physician has superior knowledge of the health effects these choices have. However, the question then arises of how the physician can be made to choose in the best interest of his or her patient. Clearly, the same problem exists whenever asymmetry of information forces delegation of authority. The generic solution to the problem is principal–agent modelling, whose main result states that the agent may be controlled through the judicious choice of a payment scheme (Holmström, 1979).

Devising an optimal payment scheme typically requires information about the relationship between the likelihood of observing some outcome and the agent's unobserved effort. In the case of health, the patient as the principal may often rely on subjective measures, while the physician as the agent typically describes outcome in clinical terms. Once there was disagreement about the outcome, however, the likelihood of observing some outcome is not defined. This failure creates demand for what shall be called a complementary agent, whose task could be to provide the necessary information.[1] This line of thought points to models in which a monitoring agent indicates to the principal the type of agent he is dealing with, thus rendering the information interpretable (see e.g. Tirole, 1986). However, upon reflection one notices that in health care, complementary agents that merely provide information hardly exist. For example, governments (which might provide the lacking information) typically establish the payment scheme as well when stepping in as a complementary agent. Accordingly, this chapter revolves around the choice of a complementary agent in role of designer of incentives rather than provider of information in health care.

There are several actors that in principle qualify as designers of payment schemes (or negotiators) in health care.[2] An important aspect of the choice is the relative amount of transaction costs involved. These costs tend to be high when a separate contract has to be written and enforced whose only purpose is to enlist the complementary agent's help in developing a fee schedule for use with (a group of) physicians or hospitals. However, transaction costs will be much less if some contractual relationship already exists. For example, given that an individual already has health insurance, it is a minor addition to state that physician services shall be paid according to fees agreed upon by the insurer and the contracting physician group (or medical association, as the case may be). A similar argument holds for the employer. Given that a labour contract already exists, the employer can add the negotiation of health care as a fringe benefit. Finally, citizens of a democratic country have a contract-like arrangement with politicians to the extent that politicians running for office promise certain services in return for the tax revenue received. Since the physician–patient relationship appears to exhibit market failure, politicians arguably qualify as complementary agents that mitigate this failure.

In this chapter, only two of these possible complementary agents will be retained for analysis, being the most prominent ones: private insurers and governments. Indeed, health care systems by and large fall into these two categories. In one, competing insurers negotiate with physician groups (or medical associations in countries where antitrust legislation permits them to act as negotiators). The other camp is characterized by tax finance of health care (social security may be treated as a government-run scheme financed by a payroll tax). There, the government is responsible for the design of the payment scheme.

It is to be expected that the outcome of the interaction between the complementary agent and the suppliers of health care differs depending on the negotiator. Consumers can compare and value these outcomes, resulting in a preference for one of the two complementary agents. In direct democracies, this preference is reflected in the outcome of a popular referendum concerning health legislation. In representative democracies, individuals can vote in favour of delegates who commit to opt for the preferred alternative in parliament. Since a delegate stands for many other issues apart from health, the link between individual choices and the type of health care system is far more tenuous in this case.

The plan of this chapter is as follows. The next section is devoted to a literature review. In the following section, a simple model of negotiating complementary agents and their counterparts is derived, containing an objective function for a representative consumer. Likewise, objective functions for a physician group, an insurer, and the politicians making up the government are posited and reaction functions derived. These results permit the determination of sets of Nash equilibria in the respective interactions, to be modeled as non-cooperative games. After that, these outcomes are compared qualitatively in order to state the conditions under which the consumer prefers one equilibrium over the other, implying that he or she opts in favour of the complementary agent involved in that game.

The following section is devoted to some simple comparative-static investigations. One change in the environment has been an increased intensity of competition between physicians, caused by a marked increase of their supply in combination with some pro-competitive legislation. Another disturbance is technological change in medicine. Both may well affect the evaluation by the consumer, possibly creating demand for a change in the structuring of the health care system. Conclusions and an outlook on issues that require additional research end the chapter.

## Review of the literature

This section is devoted to two topics. First, the basic finding of principal–agent theory is reviewed, viz. the characterization of an optimal payment function in the presence of asymmetric information. When applied to the physician–patient relationship, the conclusion is that a patient is unlikely to be able to identify such a payment function. This leads to the second topic, viz. a description of the task of a complementary agent. Here, it will be found that this task will not be the provision of information but rather that of designing a payment scheme, which constitutes the motivation for the remainder of this chapter.

### *Principal–agent theory applied to physician–patient relationship*

The problems associated with the principal–agent relationship stem from a persistent asymmetry of information: the principal charges an agent with the execution of a task, but monitoring the agent's activity is impossible or exceedingly costly (Levinthal, 1988; Zweifel and Breyer, 1997, ch. 8). To the extent that his activity has an opportunity cost, the agent has an incentive to shirk. This cannot be easily detected because the outcome of the interaction, while depending on agent's effort, is stochastic. The objective for the principal (the potential patient in the present context) then is to devise a payment function $p^*(\theta)$ that must satisfy two constraints in view of the principal's inability to monitor the agent's effort. First, payment has to be high enough to make the agent (the physician in the present context) enter the contract. This is the so-called participation constraint, denoted by the Lagrangian multiplier $\lambda$ below. Second, payment needs to be designed in a way to counteract moral hazard on the part of the agent, which emanates from the fact that his or her effort has an opportunity cost (importantly in the guise of leisure time for a physician). This consideration results in the so-called incentive compatibility constraint, denoted by the Lagrangian multiplier $\mu$. The outcome of the transaction is assumed to be observable by the principal and to be expressed in money units (this is the money equivalent $\theta$ of the resulting health status in the present context, see below). Then, the optimal division of the payout $\theta$ is given by (see, e.g., Levinthal, 1988):

$$\frac{u'^P[\theta - p^*(\theta)]}{u'^A[p^*(\theta)]} = \lambda + \mu \frac{\dfrac{\partial f(\theta|a^*)}{\partial a}}{f(\theta|a^*)} = \lambda + \mu E, \tag{12.1}$$

with   $E = \dfrac{\partial f(\theta|a^*)/\partial a}{f(\theta|a^*)}.$

On the left-hand side (LHS), the patient's marginal utility derived from the net benefit from the transaction $u'^P[\theta - p^*(\theta)]$ is pitted against the physician's marginal utility derived from the payment $u'^A[p^*(\theta)]$. Given risk aversion of both parties $[u''(\cdot) < 0]$, the higher this ratio, the smaller the patient's share of the benefit.

The objective determinants of the ratio on the LHS appear on the right-hand side (RHS) of equation (12.1). First, the participation constraint must be satisfied. Second, the physician as the agent must also be remunerated according to his stochastic effectiveness $\partial f(\theta|a^*)/(\partial a)$, i.e. the probability mass that is shifted towards more favourable outcomes in response to a variation of his or her effort $a$.

The problems with the physician–patient relationship in the light of principal–agent theory can be illustrated with the help of equation (12.1).[2]

1   *Valuation of the outcome in monetary terms.* This point relates to the LHS of (12.1). Conceptually, assigning a money value $\theta$ to a health outcome is not a problem. One would have to proceed in two steps. First, use of the expected utility calculus permits to determine the marginal willingness to pay for an increased probability of living in a given health status (rather than dying). In a second step, an indifference relation may be constructed, e.g. between living in that given health status and living less time in a better health status (the outcome of the transaction with the physician). Empirically, however, estimates of willingness to pay for an increased probability of survival (step 1) already differ by an order of magnitude (Viscusi, 1992). The likely reason for these discrepancies lies with the dependence of $u'^p$ on the initial state of health envisaged. But how should a prospective patient devise a fee schedule that is valid under all circumstances if his willingness to pay (and hence marginal utility $u'^p$) varies importantly across states?

2   *Observability of outcome.* The basic presumption is that $\theta$ is observable by both parties. However, the physician typically describes a health outcome in terms of clinical parameters, which may not always correspond with what enters into the patient's utility function. This goes a long way towards precluding the identification of an optimal payment function $p^*(\theta)$. In particular, the problem is to identify the stochastic efficiency parameter in this situation. Given that both effort $a$ and $\theta$ are unobservable, reflected by fallible indicators at best, there are severe problems of identification (Jöreskog and Goldberger, 1975). But even if identification could be ascertained, there is still the issue of insufficient sample size. Those medical interventions where physician effort is relevant at the margin do not occur often during one's

lifetime. One might argue, as does Rochaix (1989) that some patients do know best medical practice from consulting agents. However, as noted by Mooney and Ryan (1993), conceptions of best medical practice vary so widely among physicians that this solution may well fail.

3   *Lack of knowledge about the Lagrangian multipliers.* With regard to $\lambda$, it is again the physician rather than the patient who can gauge how binding the participation constraint is. By overstating the utility of his next best alternative available, the physician may increase the marginal value of a constraint relaxation in the eyes of the patient, hence increase $\lambda$ and payment. More generally, physicians may be of different types. Those with an ethical orientation derive less utility from alternatives outside the contract, causing $\lambda$ to be lower. One might invoke the relevation principle from contract theory to argue that the physician will announce his true type, thus obviating problems of untrue representation. However, it should be noted that the relevation principle requires the principal to already have committed to the optimal payment scheme (Laffont and Tirole, 1993, Appendix A.1.2 to ch. 1). Such a commitment can only occur if the patient is able to identify the optimal payment function.

Turning to $\mu$, one notes similar problems. The relevant constraint states that the physician chooses optimal effort as to balance expected marginal revenue and marginal cost. A physician with an ethical orientation may well complement his marginal revenue by marginal utility derived from helping patients. Quite likely, this would also mean that a marginal violation of this constraint should have less deleterious consequences on the patient's utility, thus causing $\mu$ to be lower. The marginal cost of effort is also ambiguous, at least if the physician is an independent worker. In that event, it reflects the marginal rate of substitution of labour income for leisure, which again depends on his or her ethics.

**Conclusion 1**: Lack of stability, observability and identification of crucial parameters in condition (12.1) make it unlikely for the patient as the principal to identify the optimal payment function for physician services.

### The task of the complementary agent

Conclusion 1 points to a market failure of the informational type. Hence, the remedy seems to be a complementary agent providing the missing information.[3] Such agents have been accommodated in principal–agent theory by introducing hierarchical structure. In Bohn (1987), e.g., workers as ultimate agents are supervised by several managers who evaluate the signals coming from the workers. With additional effort, they can increase the likelihood that these signals are correct. The question now becomes of how to pay these information-producing (complementary) agents and how to structure the information flow optimally.

In Demski and Sappington (1987), the complementary agent can actually mis-report the type of the ultimate agent. This raises important issues with regard to possible coalitions between the supervisor and the agents and its implications for the payment of agents (Tirole, 1986). More recently, the possibility of an agent signaling in a way such that the supervisor's incentive to always report an agent to be high-cost have been studied. Under some circumstances, the optimal response of the principal may then be to throw out the supervisor altogether (Frascatore, 1998). This raises the more general question as to the circumstances under which it is profitable for the principal to hire a supervisor at all. Macho-Stadler and Pérez-Castrillo (1991) posit a principal who could himself undertake monitoring efforts as well, which however are non-verifiable. Thus, he is subject to moral hazard very much like the agent, resulting in a situation of double moral hazard. By overcoming his lack of commitment by an enforceable contract with the supervisor, the principal reaches a higher expected payoff for himself. The optimal degree of delegation of monitoring turns out to be complete. However, this result importantly hinges on the assumption that principal and supervisor share the same utility function with no risk aversion.

While these developments of principal–agent theory yield important insights into the structure of an organization, they do not appear to be of very great relevance to the analysis of the health-care sector. They limit the task of the com-plementary agent to provide some information, typically of the kind, 'the agent is of a favourable type' or 'the agent has spent great effort'. While this information would certainly help the consumer to identify the optimal payment function, it is not what is observed in reality. Institutions that merely provide information are rare in health care (Blomquist, 1991). Rather, the complementary agent typically takes over the design of the payment function himself.

It would be interesting to know the reasons that have prevented information-generating institutions from springing up in health care. One could interpret this as evidence of market failure; alternatively, there may be efficiency reasons for it.

The market failure argument notes that although physicians themselves could very well observe effort on the part of their colleagues, there is no medical specialty devoted to evaluation and quality assurance. This may be due to the dominant role of professional associations in health care. One way to further the interests of their members is for these associations to limit the flow of information, rendering consumer search less effective and thus reducing the pressure of competition (Zweifel and Eichenberger, 1992).

The other explanation is an efficiency argument. As shown convincingly by Ma and McGuire (1997), incentives acting on patients and incentives acting on physicians must be analysed jointly for the determination of optimal health insurance. Thus, merely providing the information about actual effort or the physician's marginal stochastic efficiency (in keeping with equation (12.1)) falls short of full optimization.

Finally, principal–agent theory assumes that once a principal has identified the optimal payment scheme, he can also implement it at no cost. However, setting up a contract and monitoring its execution can be associated with a great deal of transaction cost. For a physician, these are in the main the opportunity costs of his time, which tend to be quite high. But these costs may be considerable for the patient as well. According to equation (12.1) above, the optimal sharing rule depends on the condition considered. On the LHS of the equation, the marginal utility of wealth of the patient $u'^p$ is bound to vary with the condition, and on the RHS, stochastic efficiency $E$ varies according to the condition treated. Implementing condition-specific payment schemes would put a substantial burden on the patient.

Therefore, both the physician as the agent and the patient as the principal have an interest in delegating the implementation of the payment scheme to some third party. This third party, while possibly collecting information, negotiates a payment scheme. This may be an employer (especially in the United States), a private insurer, a social insurer, or the government. The partner in the game may be a group of physicians or a medical association, which has some degree of control over the quantity of medical services offered, in particular through restricting access to the market for medical services. Outside the United States with its very stringent antitrust law, medical associations are involved in actual negotiation with health insurers or their associations, a social security administration, or the government over medical fees.

At this juncture, it is necessary to characterize the type of game to be used in the following. While the interaction between the complementary agent and the providers of medical care will often be referred to as negotiation, it is not reminiscent of labour disputes with their strike threat. Medical associations do not have the control over the behaviour of their members that a union has. Physician strikes are a rare phenomenon; rather, payment schemes, quantities of services provided, and quality levels all evolve rather smoothly over time. Thus, it may be not too unrealistic to represent the interaction of the complementary agent with the suppliers of health care as a (static) Nash game.

**Conclusion 2**: Viewed from the perspective of principal–agent theory, the prominent task of a complementary agent serving the principal is the collection and transmission of information. Once the costs of implementing an optimal payment scheme are taken into account, the task of a complementary agent becomes one of negotiating a payment scheme.

Therefore, this is the choice situation of the consumer to be studied. There are several complementary agents that offer themselves as negotiators. This could be an employer, a competing health insurer, a social health insurer, or the government itself. In the following, only a private insurer and the government will be analysed. These are the two polar cases because employers typically limit their involvement as complementary agents in health care. Rather, they act as a purchaser of health insurance on behalf of their employees, leaving the implementation of a payment scheme to the insurer. On the other hand, social insurance usually relies on the government in two ways. First, tax revenue is used to finance its deficit and a surplus is incorporated in the public budget. Second, social insurers should fall back on the government as arbiter negotiations fail. In all, then, it is sufficient to focus on the private insurer (*INS* henceforth) and the government (*GOV*) as the two complementary agents between which the consumer has to choose.

On the side of the physicians (*MA*), the choice would be whether to delegate the fee-setting to the medical association at all. For simplicity, however, the cost of implementation of fee schedules is assumed high enough to cause physicians to delegate this task to the medical association or a group representative.

## A simple model of negotiating complementary agents and their counterparts

### The consumer

The consumer chooses the complementary agent for negotiation in the light of a utility function. This raises the issue of state-dependent utility payoffs, conditional on a healthy and a sick state. To keep the argument as simple as possible, however, assume that the probability of the sick state $\pi$ does not depend on the choice of complementary agent and that there is no cost sharing in the event of illness in either system. Also, note that the transaction costs associated with the two competing negotiators are comparable. Formally, let $P \cdot M + F$ be the health care expenditure (price $P$ will be split up into two components later), $F$ any capitation payment, $M$ medical services, $\rho \approx 0.3$ the loading for administrative expense, moral hazard, and profit charged by the insurer (*INS*), and $\gamma = 0.3$ the loss due to inefficiencies caused by raising the tax $T$ to finance health-care expenditure (HCE) by the government (*GOV*) (Laffont and Tirole, 1993, p. 38; Ballard *et al.*, 1985). The equality of the two loadings ($\rho = \gamma$) implies

$$R = \pi (1 + \rho)(P \cdot M + F)_{INS} \gtrless \pi(1 + \gamma)(P \cdot M + F)_{GOV} = T$$

$$\Leftrightarrow (P \cdot M + F)_{INS} \gtrless (P \cdot M + F)_{GOV}. \tag{12.2}$$

This means that the difference in performance between complementary agents must show in the price, quantity, any capitation paid, and the implied quality of medical care. Moreover, only the state of ill health needs to be considered in the evaluation by the consumer.

Given that he is ill, the consumer presumably values the quality of medical care $Q$, the amount of medical care $M$ received, and consumer goods available, $X$. Depending on the system, he seeks to maximize the utility function

$$C(Q, M, X),$$

subject to the following constraints:

$$X + R(\cdot, P) = Y, \, \partial R / \partial P > 0 \, (INS) \tag{12.3}$$

and

$$X + T(\cdot, P) = Y, \, \partial T / \partial P > 0 \, (GOV). \tag{12.4}$$

The constraints say that with the price of consumer goods normalized to unity, consumption expenditure and the insurance premium (tax payment, respectively) must add up to income $Y$, which is exogenously given. Now constraints (12.3) and (12.4) show that regardless of choice of system, optimally attainable utility $C^*$ depends negatively on $P$ (capitation payments $F$, designed to keep the systems running, will be disregarded in the following). A simple representation of $C^*$ is

$$C^* = C\left(X, \frac{Q \cdot M}{P}\right).$$
(12.5)

In order to be able to disregard income effects (which would make derivatives $C_Q$ and $C_M$ depend on the level of $X$), additive separability is imposed on this function. This permits to focus the analysis and discussion on the health-related second argument of equation (12.5), with the objective of determining equilibrium $Q/P$ and $M/P$ ratios, with $P = p + s(Q)Q$ (see below).

As to the particular form of the second argument of the utility function (12.5), the following may be noted. First, the derivative of its second argument w.r.t. $P$ increases (in absolute value) with $M$, which is in accordance with equation (12.2). Moreover, quality acts like a multiplier of the quantity of medical care $M$ available, and price like a deflator. Thus, the utility function is homogeneous of degree zero in price and quality, a specification that is in keeping with Lancaster's (1966) new demand theory. Finally, the consumer trades off quality against quantity in preference because $(dQ/dM)_{\overline{dC}=0} = -Q/M$, which corresponds to a well-behaved convex indifference curve.[4] Thus, the function (12.5) will be used for evaluating the outcomes of negotiation.

### Physician group objectives and reaction functions

Following standard formulations in the health economics literature (e.g. Selden, 1990), physicians are assumed to pursue two types of objectives. One derives from professional ethics, reflecting a concern for the patient's health. The other objective is the generation of income and profit. Self-selection mechanisms could result in the absence of the ethical component in the aggregate utility function of the medical association. Moreover, the ranking of alternatives may be inconsistent after aggregation in view of Arrow's impossibility theorem (Arrow, 1951). Nevertheless, the ethical component is assumed to be present in the aggregate objective function $U$ of the physician group (or medical association, respectively). It is expressed by a utility function (in monetary units, with $U' > 0$, $U'' < 0$), according to which physicians value the amount of effective care given to patients, with effective care reflected by the product $Q \cdot M$. Thus, doubling the quality of medical care has the same effect as doubling its quantity. The physicians constituting the medical association come close to being agents of the patients, except that contrary to equation (12.4), total payment does not enter their ethical concerns:

$$\underset{M,\,Q}{\text{Max}} \quad U(Q \cdot M) + F + [p + s(Q)Q]M - c(Q, M).$$
(12.6)

On the financial side, revenue consists of three components. The capitation $F$ is designed to satisfy the participation constraint, $p$ symbolizes the fee-for-service component, whereas the quality surcharge $s(Q)$ (with $s' > 0$, $s'' < 0$) derives from attempts on the part of the negotiator to make quality verifiable. Indeed, in the United States payments related to quality may account for up to 30 per cent of a physician group's income (Luft, 1996). Cost depends both on the quality ($Q$) and the quantity ($M$) of health care services produced, with $c_Q$, $c_M$, $c_{QQ}$, $c_{MM}$, $c_{QM} > 0$.

The first thing to check is whether the payment scheme defined in equation (12.6) has the expected effects. This can be determined through comparative static analysis. The first-order condition w.r.t. $Q$ reads, after dividing through by $M > 0$,

$$\partial C/\partial Q = U'(Q \cdot M) + s_Q(Q) \cdot Q + s(Q) - c_Q(Q, M)/M = 0. \qquad (12.7)$$

Condition (12.7) points to the fact that the cost $c_Q$ of additional quality need not be fully remunerated by the surcharge $s$ if ethical concerns are relevant at the margin.

The first-order condition for an interior maximum w.r.t. $M$ (assuming quantity to be determined by physicians rather than consumers) is given by

$$\partial C/\partial M = U'(Q \cdot M) \cdot Q + p + s(Q) \cdot Q - c_M(Q, M) = 0. \qquad (12.8)$$

Condition (12.8) is the standard result that ethical concerns should cause physicians to give up income. While payment $p$ for $M$ must fall short of unit cost, the capitation $F$ can be used to satisfy the break-even constraint. Since $F$ does not affect medical decisions w.r.t. quality and quantity, it is disregarded in what follows (although it could conceivably take on different values under the two alternatives).

To find out whether the quality surcharge $s$ does guarantee higher quality, let the complementary agent (*INS* or *GOV*) increase this surcharge by $d\sigma$ (an exogenous shift parameter) for a given quality level. For the optimality conditions (12.7) and (12.8) to be preserved, the following comparative static conditions must hold:

$$\partial C/\partial Q: U''(QdM + MdQ) + [s_{QQ}Q + s_Q]dQ + s_Q d\sigma$$

$$+s_{Q\sigma}Qd\sigma + s_\sigma d\sigma - c_{QQ}/M \cdot dQ - [c_{QM}/M - c_Q/M^2]dM = 0 \qquad (12.9)$$

$$\partial C/\partial M: U''(QdM + MdQ) \cdot Q + U'dQ + [s_Q Q + s]dQ$$

$$+ s_\sigma Qd\sigma - c_{MQ}dQ - c_{MM}dM = 0. \qquad (12.10)$$

Writing this in matrix form, one has

$$\begin{bmatrix} U''QM + U' + s_Q Q + s - c_{MQ} & U''Q^2 - c_{MM} \\ U''M + s_{QQ}Q + 2s_Q - \dfrac{c_{QQ}}{M} & U''Q - \dfrac{c_{QM}}{M} + \dfrac{c_Q}{M^2} \end{bmatrix} \begin{bmatrix} dQ \\ dM \end{bmatrix} = \begin{bmatrix} -s_\sigma \\ -s_\sigma - s_{Q\sigma}Q \end{bmatrix} d\sigma.$$

$$(12.11)$$

Let $D$ denote the determinant of the matrix on the LHS of the system (12.11). Assuming sufficient conditions for a maximum to be satisfied, this matrix must be negative definite, implying $D > 0$. Applying Cramer's rule yields for the quality response[5]

$$MA: \frac{dQ}{d\sigma} = \frac{1}{D} \begin{vmatrix} -Q & U''Q^2 - c_{MM} \\ -1 & U''Q - \dfrac{c_{QM}}{M} + \dfrac{c_Q}{M^2} \end{vmatrix} \tag{12.12}$$

$$\sim \left[ c_{QM} \frac{Q}{M} + c_Q \frac{Q}{M^2} - c_{MM} \right] \begin{cases} < 0 \text{ if } Q \text{ low.} \\ > 0 \text{ and increasing in } Q \text{ if } Q \text{ high.} \end{cases}$$

Thus, the effect of increasing the quality surcharge serves to encourage quality on the part of the physician, provided that quality is high [strengthening the incentive, see equation (12.6)]. However, it may prove counterproductive precisely when the quality-to-quantity ratio is small, i.e. when an improvement in quality is most needed.

Now for $\sigma$ to qualify as a payment parameter for the insurer or government it should also have a favourable effect on quantity. Solving the system (12.11) for $dM$ yields[6]

$$MA: \frac{dM}{d\sigma} = \frac{1}{D} \begin{vmatrix} U''QM + U' + s_Q Q + s - c_{MQ} & -Q \\ U''M + s_{QQ}Q + 2s_Q - \dfrac{c_{QQ}}{M} & -1 \end{vmatrix} \tag{12.13}$$

$$\sim \left[ -U' - s + c_{MQ} + s_{QQ}Q^2 + s_Q Q - c_{QQ}\frac{Q}{M} \right] \begin{cases} < 0 \text{ and decreasing in } M \text{ if } M \text{ small} \\ > 0 \text{ and decreasing in } M \text{ if } M \text{ large} \\ \text{and } \left| \dfrac{s_Q}{s_{QQ}} \right| \gg Q. \end{cases}$$

Thus, a surcharge for quality may prove counterproductive with regard to the quantity of medical care produced, unless it provides a strong incentive (increase $s_Q$ very large compared to rate of change $s_{QQ} < 0$ and the cost of quality is distributed over many units of service [$M$ large]).

**Conclusion 3**: Within the framework of the *MA* model adopted, a quality surcharge, while conditionally evoking higher quality, tends to have a negative effect on the quantity of medical services.

The traditional fee-for-service payment for medical services regardless of quality (parameter $p$; shift parameter $\pi$ and $\partial p/\partial \pi = 1$ without loss of generality), also has some unexpected features. Writing the comparative static conditions immediately in matrix form, one obtains

$$
\begin{bmatrix} U''QM + U' + s_Q Q + s - c_{MQ} & U''Q^2 - c_{MM} \\ U''M + s_{QQ}Q + 2s_Q - \dfrac{c_{QQ}}{M} & U''Q - \dfrac{c_{QM}}{M} + \dfrac{c_Q}{M^2} \end{bmatrix} \begin{bmatrix} dQ \\ dM \end{bmatrix} = \begin{bmatrix} -1 \\ 0 \end{bmatrix} d\pi,
$$

$$(12.14)$$

and solving for quality, one obtains

$$
MA: \frac{dQ}{d\pi} = \frac{1}{D} \begin{vmatrix} -1 & U''Q^2 - c_{MM} \\ 0 & U''Q - \dfrac{c_{QM}}{M} + \dfrac{c_Q}{M^2} \end{vmatrix}
$$

$$
\sim \left[ -U''Q + \frac{c_{QM}}{M} - \frac{c_Q}{M^2} \right] \begin{cases} < 0 \text{ if } M \text{ low.} \\ > 0 \text{ if } Q \text{ high.} \end{cases}
$$

$$(12.15)$$

Thus, stepping up the fee-for-service component may have the favourable side effect of increasing quality, especially if physicians indeed have an ethical orientation ($U'' < 0$).

Solving system (12.14) for $dM$ to obtain the quantity response, one has

$$
MA: \frac{dM}{d\pi} = \frac{1}{D} \begin{vmatrix} U''QM + U' + s_Q Q + s - c_{MQ} & -1 \\ U''M + s_{QQ}Q + 2s_Q - \dfrac{c_{QQ}}{M} & 0 \end{vmatrix}
$$

$$(12.16)$$

$$
\sim \left[ -U''M + s_{QQ}Q + 2s_Q - \frac{c_{QQ}}{M} \right] \begin{cases} < 0 \text{ if } M \text{ small.} \\ < 0 \text{ if } M \text{ or } Q \text{ large.} \end{cases}
$$

Here, an ethical orientation makes a negative quantity response more likely, especially if coupled with a high quality of medical service provided (since $s_{QQ} < 0$). Moreover, the quantity response is negative both for small and large values of $M$ and ambiguous for intermediate values.

**Conclusion 4**:   Within the framework of the *MA* model adopted, an increase in the traditional fee-for-service component of physician payment may cause quality of treatment to increase. However, the quantity of medical care is predicted to decrease under many quality–quantity combinations.

Intuitively, given that the higher fee level causes the quality level of treatment to increase, the cost of additional quantity can be supported only if the initial level of costly quality is low. A similar quality–quantity trade-off was found by Feldman and Sloan (1988).

In all, the quantity surcharge $d\tau$ cannot be expected to cause responses that will be deemed satisfactory by the negotiator (*INS* or *GOV*). Therefore, only the quality component will be retained for further analysis, with changes in the total fee $dP$ equivalent to a change $d\sigma$. The predicted responses are[7]

$$\frac{dQ}{dP} \begin{cases} <0 \text{ if } Q \text{ low.} \\ >0 \text{ and increasing in } Q \text{ if } Q \text{ high [equation (12.12)].} \end{cases}$$

*MA*:

$$\frac{dM}{dP} < 0 \text{ and decreasing in } M \text{ if } M \text{ small [equation (12.13)].}$$

(12.17)

**Conclusion 5**: Within the framework of this *MA* model, the complementary agent will conditionally be able to call forth higher quality but not quantity by increasing the quality surcharge in the fee paid.

### Insurer objectives and reaction functions

Insurers are assumed to act under monopolistic competition with differentiated products. This means that the premium of a representative insurer is not exogenous but depends on the characteristics of the product offered. An insurer under the pressure of competition must comply with consumer preferences. Thus, it will know that the willingness to pay of the insured increases in quality and quantity of medical care but decreases in the price of medical care $P$ because the premium contains a larger surcharge in absolute terms for administration and profit when $P$ and with it HCE increases [see equation (12.1)]. For simplicity, the argument of the function determining the attainable premium $R$ has the same multiplicative form as the consumer's utility function. From this, the value of claims given by HCE is deducted (neglecting the loading for administrative expense for simplicity), resulting in

$$\underset{P}{\text{Max }} R\left(\frac{Q \cdot M}{P}\right) - P \cdot M, \quad \text{with } R' > 0, \quad s.t. \ P \geq \overline{P} \text{ (see below).} \tag{12.18}$$

Thus, the insurer, while reflecting rather closely the interests of his client, is not a perfect agent because it views HCE (given by $P{\cdot}M$) negatively, contrary to the insured, who prefers more $M$ to less.

With $P$ as the only control variable, the first-order condition for a maximum reads

$$R'\left(\frac{Q \cdot M}{P}\right) \cdot \left(\frac{Q \cdot M}{-P^2}\right) - M < 0. \tag{12.19}$$

This is a boundary optimum because the insurer seeks to attain the minimum payment, which is zero. But with $P = 0$, physician services of acceptable quality would not be available; therefore, there must be a lower bound $\overline{P}$.

This optimum may now be disturbed in two ways. On the one hand, the physician group may decide to change the quality level of the treatment ($dQ$); on the other, they may decide to provide more or less quantity of services ($dM$). However, there is no reason why the constraint $P \geq \overline{P}$ in (12.18) should become nonbinding due to these changes. Since $P = \overline{P}$ before and after the change, the responses are simply

$$INS: \frac{dP}{dQ} = 0 \text{ and} \tag{12.20}$$

$$INS: \frac{dP}{dM} = 0. \tag{12.21}$$

**Conclusion 6**: To the extent that the lower bound on payment is binding, the competitive insurer's payment responses to increased quality and quantity are zero.

### Government objectives and reaction functions

In a democratic society, government must gain votes to come to or remain in power. In the following we neglect the possibility that a government enjoys such a wide margin in popularity that it loses interest in additional votes. Votes come from two sources in the present context. One are the providers of medical care who judge government performance in terms of their economic well-being.[8] Strictly speaking, this is given by their utility function (12.6); however, the government in its negotiating role cannot be held responsible for the cost of running a medical practice (which may well depend, e.g., on tax parameters under the control of government). The other source of votes are consumers, who judge the government according to quality, quantity, and price of medical care.[9] Through its payment policy, the government thus seeks to maximize support according to the following function

$$\text{Max}_P \ S(P \cdot M) + V\left(\frac{Q \cdot M}{P}\right), \tag{12.22}$$

with $S' > 0, \quad S'' < 0, \quad V' > 0, \quad V'' < 0.$

This additive formulation seems to neglect the fact that there are few physicians but many consumers. However, what counts is the marginal contribution of the two groups in terms of votes in response to a change in the physician fee level ($S'$ and $V'$). On this score physicians may easily beat consumers, who are far less organized. The necessary condition for an interior optimum is (after division through $M$)

$$S'(P \cdot M) + V'\left(\frac{Q \cdot M}{P}\right) \cdot \frac{Q}{-P^2} = 0. \tag{12.23}$$

Thus, setting the fee high attracts votes from the suppliers but turns away the consumers. When this condition is disturbed by an increase in the quality of medical services performed by the physicians $dQ$, the reaction function becomes

$$S'' \cdot M \cdot dP + V'' \cdot \frac{M}{P} dQ \cdot \frac{Q}{-P^2} + \frac{V'}{-P^2} dQ +$$

$$V'' \cdot \frac{Q \cdot M}{-P^2} dP \cdot \frac{Q}{-P^2} + V' \frac{2Q}{-P^3} dP = 0, \tag{12.24}$$

which can be solved to read

$$\frac{dP}{dQ} = \frac{V'' \dfrac{Q \cdot M}{P^3} + V' \dfrac{1}{P^2}}{S''M + V'' \dfrac{Q^2 M}{P^4} - 2V' \dfrac{Q}{P^3}}. \tag{12.25}$$

For ease of interpretation, numerator and denominator are multiplied by $P^3$ to yield

$$GOV: \quad \frac{dP}{dQ} = \frac{V''Q \cdot M + V'P}{S''M \cdot P^3 + V''Q^2M/P - 2V'Q} \quad \begin{cases} > 0 \text{ for } P \text{ small.} \\ = 0 \text{ for } P \text{ large.} \end{cases} \tag{12.26}$$

Thus, while the slope of this function cannot be determined in general, with $P$ small, the terms in $V''$ become dominant in the numerator and the denominator, causing the reaction function to have positive slope. Conversely, letting $P$ go towards large values makes the term involving $S''$ dominant, resulting in $dP/dQ = 0$.

Finally, the government's reaction function in response to a change in quantity $dM$ needs to be established. The condition to be satisfied reads

$$S''(dP \cdot M + P \cdot dM) + V''\left(\frac{Q}{P} dM \cdot \frac{Q}{-P^2} + \frac{Q \cdot M}{-P^2} dP \cdot \frac{Q}{-P^2}\right)$$

$$+ V' \frac{2Q}{-P^3} dP = 0. \tag{12.27}$$

This can be solved to yield

$$\frac{dP}{dM} = \frac{-S''P + V'' \dfrac{Q^2}{P^3}}{S''M + V'' \dfrac{Q^2 M}{P^4} - 2V' \dfrac{Q}{P^3}}. \tag{12.28}$$

Again multiplying through by $P^3$, one has

$$GOV: \frac{dP}{dM} = \frac{-S''P^4 + V''Q^2}{S''MP^3 + V''Q^2M/P - 2V'Q} \quad \begin{cases} > 0 \text{ for } P \text{ small.} \\ < 0 \text{ for } P \text{ large.} \end{cases} \quad (12.29)$$

When $P$ becomes small, the result is $dP/dM > 0$ because the terms involving $V''$ dominate. Conversely, with $P$ large, the first terms in the numerator and denominator dominate, resulting in $dP/dM < 0$.

It is interesting to see that in the case of a low fee level, the terms reflecting voter interests (involving $V''$) point in the direction of honouring better quality with increased payment.

**Conclusion 7**: The reaction function of a democratic government seeking to maximize votes is convex from below with regard to quality of services. It is first increasing with respect to quantity of treatment but becomes decreasing at very high price.

## Evaluation from the consumer's point of view

In this section, the location of the Nash solutions is determined graphically. This alternative avoids the parametrization of the objective functions and tedious algebra. Panel (a) of Figure 12.1 shows the outcomes in $(P, Q)$-space. Beginning with the medical association (*MA*), result (12.17) says that their reaction function should be decreasing at first and then increasing, with the slope of the function increasing in $Q$. Moreover, there must be a fee level $\overline{P}$ below which the members of the physician group cannot continue to practice. Thus, the *MA* reaction function starts at some point $A$ on the *INS* reaction function and is convex from below.

Under competition, the health insurer considered cannot leave any rents to the physicians and has its reaction function at $\overline{P}$. According to equation (12.20), it runs vertical from $\overline{P}$. This means that point $A$ is the Nash equilibrium of the *INS–MA* game.

With regard to the government, equation (12.26) also implies a reaction function that is increasing and becomes asymptotically vertical. It must run above that of *MA*, because otherwise the government would offer a greater payment for quality than physicians demand. One equilibrium of the *GOV–MA* game could conceivably be at point $A$, coinciding with that of the *INS–MA* alternative. The other equilibrium must be a point of tangency such as $B$.

Compared to point $A$ of Figure 12.1, point $B$ is characterized by a higher fee level but also a higher quality level. The higher the quality level that the insurer may achieve (point $A$), the less likely ceteris paribus will the additional fee buy an improvement over the *INS* price–quality ratio. In Figure 12.1, a case is shown where equilibrium $A$ is preferred by the consumer over equilibrium $B$ for a given quantity of services $M$ ($OA$ runs steeper than $OB$).

**Conclusion 8**:   The *GOV* alternative can achieve a better quality–price ratio than the *INS* alternative. However, this would have to occur at a high fee level and becomes less likely, the higher the quality level that is achieved in the *INS* alternative.

Turning to the (*P, M*)-space depicted in panel (b) of Figure 12.1, it may be noted that any *MA* reaction function again originates at the fee level $\bar{P}$. The *INS* reaction function again runs vertical at $\bar{P}$, in keeping with equation (12.21). Since a competitive insurer cannot leave any rents to the physician group, the origins of *MA* reaction functions along *INS* must be Nash equilibria of the *INS–MA* game. Their location can be determined by the following argument.

The reaction function of the government has a positive slope at $P = \bar{P}$ but changes to negative slope for high *P*, according to equation (12.29). For high

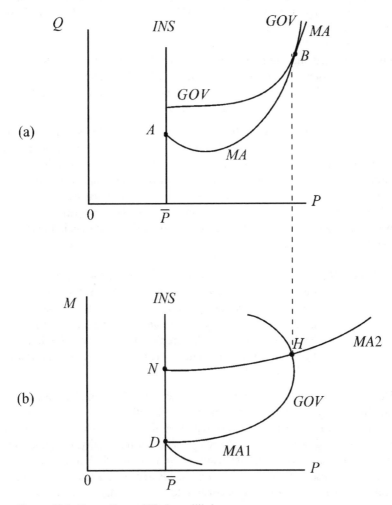

*Figure 12.1* Comparison of Nash equilibria.

values of *M*, however, its slope is undetermined. Since for a given value of *P*, the government rationally demands at least as much *M* as the medical association is willing to offer, the *MA* reaction function must be below the *GOV* function. Moreover, according to (12.17), it has negative slope for low *M*. One possibility thus is *MA1*, with *D* the Nash equilibrium for both insurers and the government. However, *MA2* (e.g. with positive slope for large *M*) is admissible as well, resulting, e.g., in point *H* as a *GOV–MA* equilibrium. Note that for high *P* the upper branch of the *GOV* function obtains so the government does ask for a larger quantity of medical care than physicians are prepared to deliver. Also, equilibrium point *H* must imply the same fee level as does equilibrium *B* of panel (a). However, whichever the *MA* reaction function, *GOV–MA* equilibria will be on the *GOV* locus, while *INS–MA* equilibria are on the *INS* locus. Since the *M/P* ratio is lower along the *GOV* reaction function than along the *INS* reaction function, with the only exception of the endpoint *D*, the *M/P* ratio of the *INS–MA* game must be more favourable on expectation.

**Conclusion 9**:   At the minimum fee level, the *INS* alternative elicits the same quantity of medical services as the *GOV* alternative. The *GOV* alternative may result in a higher fee level, in which case its quantity–price ratio is less favourable.

In view of conclusions 8 and 9, the final evaluation by the consumer must be somewhat ambiguous. At the minimum fee level achieved by a competitive insurer, government cannot come up with a higher quality or quantity than the insurer. Certainly, at a high fee level, the government may achieve a more favourable quality–price ratio than the insurer, ultimately because its objectives are less adversarial to *MA* interests than those of the (competitive!) insurer. However, this results in a less favourable quantity–price ratio than in the *INS–MA* game, at least on average.

**Conclusion 10**:   As an alternative to the minimum viable fee level as one outcome of both the *INS–MA* and *GOV–MA* game, the government can come up with an outcome that possibly has a better quality–price ratio but an inferior quantity–price ratio. Thus, the insurer is the predicted choice of complementary agent unless the outcome of the *GOV–MA* game attains a very high quality level.

Before concluding this section, it may be worthwhile to emphasize that these results hold only for the case of competitive health insurers. For example, if they have tax privileges that increase with health care expenditure, their incentive to push fees down to $\overline{P}$ is weakened. As another possibility, the government may step in as an arbiter of last resort should the fee level proposed by the insurer come close to $\overline{P}$. In this situation, the insurer must take the government's objective function into account, according to which some fee level $P > \overline{P}$ may be optimal.

## Changes in the environment and their consequences

In the recent past, two major changes affecting health care sectors have taken place. First, physician densities have been on the increase in most industrial countries. Since medical associations have not been able to enrol the entirety of this increase, a competitive fringe has been building. The second change is continuing technological change in medicine mainly of the product innovation type. This means that a given level of quality can be reached at reduced cost. These two changes will be considered in turn.

### *Increased intensity of competition*

The easiest way to represent the competitive fringe in the framework of the present model is to let the minimum payment $\overline{P}$ decrease to $\overline{P}'$. For simplicity, assume that the reaction functions merely shift towards the origin, without their shape being changed. In panel (a) of Figure 12.2, the high-quality *GOV–MA* equilibrium moves from *B* to *B'*, while the *INS–MA* equilibrium moves from *A* to *A'*. Clearly, the quality–price ratio increases in both games; however, the increase is more marked in the *INS* alternative (which may coincide with the *GOV–MA* equilibrium, see text before conclusion 8).

Panel (b) of Figure 12.2 displays the move to a new equilibrium in $(P, M)$-space. If point *D* was the original equilibrium for both *INS* and *GOV*, the shift to *D'* affects both *M/P* ratios in the same way. The transition from *H* to *H'* goes along with an improvement of the *M/P* ratio. As before, these new reaction functions originate on the *INS* reaction function. Thus, the Nash equilibria of the *INS-MA* game are points such as *N'* or *D'*. Equilibria on *INS'* indicate an improvement of *M/P* ratios relative to the initial equilibria on *INS*. By way of contrast, provided the slope of the *GOV* reaction function is locally stable some equilibria on *GOV'* have even less favourable *M/P* ratios than their initial counterparts on *GOV*. These findings lead to

**Conclusion 11**: The rise of a competitive fringe tends to favour insurers over government as complementary agents on behalf of consumers because both the quality–price and the quantity–price ratio increase in the *INS* alternative whereas the quality–price ratio may decrease in the *GOV* alternative.

### *Technological change in medicine*

In general terms, technological change can result in process and product innovation. In the case of the former, the characteristics of the product and hence the willingness to pay of the consumer are unchanged. However, the cost of production goes down, thanks to the innovation. In the case of a product innovation, quality improves and willingness to pay for the product increases. In medical care, technological change is directed towards improved outcomes of treatment; it therefore typically gives rise to product innovation. This is the case considered in

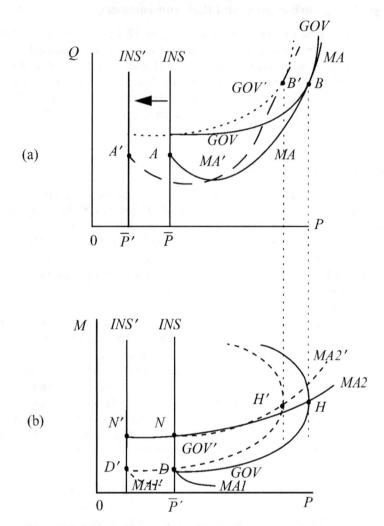

*Figure 12.2* Effects of a competitive fringe.

the following. In the present model, technological change lowers the derivatives $\{c_Q, c_{QQ}, c_{QM}\}$ of the cost function $c(Q, M)$, viz. the marginal cost of quality and its rate of increase.

Starting again with the *MA* reaction function with regard to quality, equation (12.15) shows a change in $c_{QM}$ to be more important than a change in $c_{QQ}$ of equal magnitude. Therefore, technological change serves to decrease the absolute value of the slope of the *MA* quality reaction function as long as it is falling but to increase it when it is rising [see the shift to *MA* $(d\bar{e})$ in panel (a) of Figure 12.3, with $d\bar{e}$ symbolizing the efficiency improvement through the reduction of $\{c_Q, c_{QQ}, c_{QM}\}$].

By way of contrast, none of these parameters appear in equation (12.16), which describes quantity adjustment. However, there is an unambiguous influence through the determinant $D$, which appears on the LHS of equation (12.14). Indeed, the following partial derivatives can be established:

$$\frac{\partial D}{\partial c_Q} = \frac{1}{M^2} \underbrace{(U''QM + U' + s_Q Q + s - c_{QM})}_{(-)} < 0,$$

(since $D$ is negative definite)

$$\frac{\partial D}{\partial c_{QQ}} = \frac{1}{M} \underbrace{(U''Q^2 - c_{MM})}_{(-)} > 0, \tag{12.30}$$

and

$$\frac{\partial D}{\partial c_{QM}} = \frac{c_{QM}}{M} \underbrace{(U''QM + U' + s_Q Q + s - c_{QM})}_{(-)} > 0$$

(since $D$ is negative definite).

The total effect on the determinant $D$ of an efficiency increase can be found by summing the three partial effects. One finds that $\partial D/\partial \bar{e} > 0$ for $M$ large but $\partial D/\partial \bar{e} < 0$ for $M$ small. This implies, in view of equation (12.13),

$$\left| \frac{dM}{dP} \right| \overline{de} < \left| \frac{dM}{dP} \right| \quad \text{if} \quad M \text{ large}$$

$$\left| \frac{dM}{dP} \right| \overline{de} > \left| \frac{dM}{dP} \right| \quad \text{if} \quad M \text{ small.} \tag{12.31}$$

Accordingly, the $MA$ $(d\bar{e})$ functions run as shown in panel (b) of Figure 12.3. The $INS$ reaction functions are unaffected. The same holds true of the $GOV$ reaction functions since the government is not held responsible for the cost of medical practice by assumption.

In panel (a) of Figure 12.3, the $GOV$–$MA$ equilibrium moves from $B$ to $B'$. In panel (b) of Figure 12.3, it may remain at point $D$ or shift from point $H$ to $H'$, with $H'$ implying the same fee level as $B'$ of panel (a).

In sum, to the extent that insurers under the pressure of competition continue to go for the minimum fee level, they do not participate in the benefits of

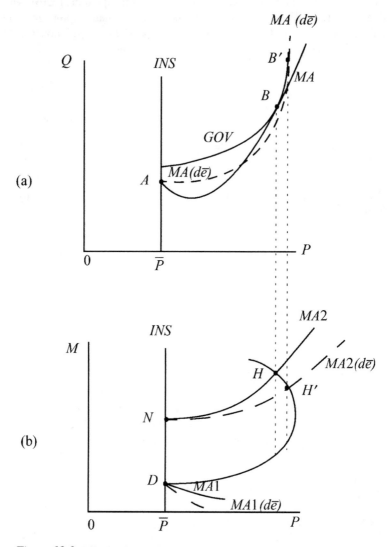

*Figure 12.3* Effects of technological change in medicine.

technological change in medicine. The Nash equilibria continue to lie on the *INS* reaction (such as *D*, *N*). If the government is in charge, there will be an increase in quality but not necessarily quantity, associated with an increase in the fee level, however. Technological change in medicine thus permits a quality increase under the *GOV* alternative, with ambiguous implications for both the ($Q/P$) and the ($M/P$)-ratios. Thus, it is not clear that overall performance ($M \cdot Q/P$) under the *GOV* alternative improves relative to the *INS* alternative.

**Conclusion 12**: With a competitive insurer acting as complementary agent, technological change in medicine may not result in an increased quality level; in return, the fee level will remain at a minimum. In the government-run alternative, quality will increase but quantity may fall, with uncertain implications for overall performance.

Therefore, it is not clear that technological change resulting in product innovation will cause consumers to switch from the *GOV–MA* to the *INS–MA* game. The quality increase under the *GOV–MA* alternative contrasts favourably with the constancy under the *INS–MA* alternative. But then, the *INS–MA* game as modeled here avoids the fee increase that is induced by technological change in medicine with the government as the negotiator.

## Discussion and conclusion

This chapter started from the observation that the physician–patient relationship is one of imperfect agency mainly because the information requirements on the patient as the principal are excessive (Conclusion 1). While much of the literature in this field has revolved about the behaviour of an intermediary that provides signals to the principal, the solution in the health care sector appears to be a different one. Prospective patients delegate the establishment of a payment scheme to a complementary agent (Conclusion 2). For this reason, the emphasis of this chapter has been on the Nash equilibria that can be expected when the payment scheme is devised by an insurer (*INS*) and by the government (*GOV*), respectively (Conclusions 3 to 5).

It was found that these two complementary agents have different objectives, which makes them react in different ways to the behaviour of their counterpart, thought of as a physician group or medical association (*MA*). The consumer's choice of complementary agent is based on a performance indicator that comprises the quantity and quality of medical services on the one hand and the fee level to be paid on the other.

Assuming competition, the insurer is predicted to go for the minimum fee level that is still compatible with a positive amount of medical services (Conclusion 6). Governments may achieve the same equilibrium, but there are other equilibria, characterized by a higher fee level, not necessariliy associated with a higher quality–price ratio but a lower quantity–price ratio (at least on expectation) than the *INS–MA* alternative (Conclusions 7 to 10).

The two systems were exposed to two exogenous shocks in order to find out whether consumer choice of the complementary agent might change in a systematic way. The first change considered was an increased physician density resulting in additional supply of services beyond the control of the medical association. Since the insurer can now push for a lower minimum viable fee level, it can offer consumers both an improved quality–price and quantity–price ratio. These effects are not guaranteed if the initial *GOV–MA* equilibrium entails a higher than the minimum feasible fee level. Thus, increased competition between physicians may cause voters to switch their preference for complementary agent from the government to competitive insurers (Conclusion 11).

The consequences of technological change in medicine are somewhat different from those of the competitive fringe under the *INS–MA* alternative. A possible increase in quality is not achieved because of lack of additional payment. In the *GOV–MA* alternative, the government profits from a higher quality–price ratio at the risk of a less favourable quantity–price ratio. In all, technological change has an ambiguous effect on overall performance of the government as the complementary agent compared to the insurer, where it remains unchanged (Conclusion 12).

Some of the preceding statements appear incompatible with the reality of present-day health care systems. In particular, the implication that governments as complementary agents may come up with a higher fee level than the insurance alternative (see Figure 12.1) is hardly acceptable at first sight. However, it should be recalled that insurers are assumed to be exposed to perfect competition. In most industrial countries, they were subject to product and price regulation well into the 1990s (until 1994 in most member countries of the European Union). Until recently, there was therefore little pressure on them to maximize their profits, causing the present model formulation to become relevant in the future only. Once this pressure makes itself felt, however, there will be a concern about quality of treatment, a concern that is voiced in the context of insurance deregulation already today.

There are many unresolved issues in this first attempt at describing health care systems with reference to negotiating complementary agents. First, the model assumes that the complementary agents can judge quality at least on average. With more and more indicators of quality becoming available, this may not be too much of a problem. However, the complementary agent must be able to communicate quality to the consumer, who then opts for one or the other of the agents. Here, the government may use quite different measures (such as physician density) whereas a private insurer may emphasize more amenity-type features.

An important issue worth exploring is Stackelberg leadership. Such leadership presupposes low cost of organization, permitting the negotiator to tie the members of the organization to a negotiated outcome. In the case of the medical association, this would mean that a quality level and a quantity of medical services provided can be enforced with some precision. This is not very likely, neither for a medical association nor a competitive insurer.[10] The one party that may have this opportunity is the government. However, there is little evidence that governments can muster the political clout to assume this role; rather, they seem to accept medical associations as negotiators on equal terms.[11]

The argument thus far focused on the delivery of services. This makes the performance comparison partial in that by assumption the two systems have identical cost of operation once the total fee level $P$ is given. With private insurers exposed to limited competition, it is quite possible that their loading $\rho$ [see equation (12.2)] exceeds the inefficiency loading $\gamma$ of the government. That latter parameter differs between governments too; in a representative democracy, tax resistance may be higher, resulting in a higher value of $\gamma$, than in a direct democracy where voters also decide about the use of their tax contribution (Pommerehne and Zweifel, 1991). In particular, to the extent that voters prefer tax revenue to be spent on health rather than defense (say), more expenditure on health may go along with reduced tax resistance. This may tip the balance in favour of the government as the complementary agent, who is able to offer medical care of a given quality at a lower total opportunity cost than the insurer.

It must also be noted that the preceding development was entirely couched in terms of efficiency. Working with the concept of a representative consumer, the model necessarily is silent about the equity implications of the two alternatives. An individual who is concerned about equality of access to medical care may well hesitate to opt for a private insurer as complementary agent because the resulting combination of values $\{Q, M, P\}$ might put the required premium easily out of reach for many citizens. Of course, the problem could be remedied by paying out targeted premium subsidies to the poor. The efficiency loss caused by this redistribution would however have to be added to the loading $\rho$ of the private insurer, making it less attractive as a complementary agent.

In sum, many factors that are not captured in this very simple model of choice of complementary agent in health care enter the picture, and several of them seem to favour the government rather than a competitive insurer. Increased competition among physicians as modeled tends to help the competitive insurers, while the implications of product innovation in medicine are uncertain. However, there is one change exogenous to the health care sector that tends to give the insurance solution a competitive edge. As long as information and income levels continue to rise, variety and choice will be increasingly valued. Now a multitude of insurers will come up with differing $\{Q, M, P\}$ combinations among which consumers can choose. A government, being one negotiating body, will typically come up with one equilibrium.

However, in view of the difficulties encountered in deriving unambiguous predictions regarding overall performance, it at the very least becomes understandable why consumers and voters are slow to exchange one complementary agent for another and hesitant to bear the concomitant cost of adjusting to a different type of health care system.

## Notes

The authors gratefully acknowledge comments and criticisms by Thomas Philipson (Chicago), other participants of the Arne Ryde Symposium and four anonymous referees.

1 This would result in consumer empowerment (Gafni, 1998); conversely, the physician cannot be a perfect agent to begin with unless fully informed by the patient (physician empowerment, cf. Williams, 1988).
2 One particular problem with the application of principal–agent theory to the physician–patient relationship is that the physician as the agent may pursue nonfinancial objectives as well. However, professional ethics could be accommodated simply by noting that they cause the pursuit of financial incentives to be fraught with opportunity costs. Thus, a marginal violation of either the participation or the

incentive compatibility constraint would entail a reduced adjustment of optimal effort on the part of the physicians, with the consequence that the Lagrange multipliers $\lambda$ and $\mu$ take on lower values. This means that problem No. 3 described in the text is mitigated to some extent.

3 Of course, a physician acting as a perfect agent would provide the necessary information herself (Gafni, 1998).

4 There are of course other alternatives; see e.g. Ma and McGuire (1997).

5 Note that since $s_\sigma(=\partial s/\partial\sigma)=1$ without loss of generality, $s_{\sigma Q}(=\partial^2 s/\partial Q\partial\sigma)=0$.

6 'Increasing' and 'decreasing' refer to the absolute value of the slope.

7 The case $\left|\dfrac{s_Q}{s_{QQ}}\right|\gg Q$ in equation (12.13), possibly resulting in $\dfrac{dM}{dP}>0$, is considered extreme and therefore disregarded in the following.

8 The importance of the medical profession as opinion leader is described in Feldstein (1996).

9 Traditional popularity functions of governments contain indicators of macroeconomic performance such as the change of real per capita income, the unemployment rate, and the inflation rate (Schneider, 1978). However, Schneider (1986) presents evidence suggesting that social transfers (which overlaps in part with public health care expenditure) contributes to government popularity as importantly as unemployment.

10 However, with the advent of the Dekker reforms in the Netherlands and the new Law on Health Insurance in Switzerland, insurers under the pressure of competition begin to play a more active role, but it is still questionable that they are sufficiently pre-emptive to qualify for Stackelberg leadership. Examining all these subcases clearly would result in a paper of excessive length.

11 The model case is the UK National Health Service (NHS), of course. However, even in the case of the NHS, there is little systematic evidence on this issue. Again, examining this subcase clearly would result in a paper of excessive length.

# References

Arrow, K.J. (1951), *Social Choice and Individual Values*, New York: Wiley.

Ballard, C., Shoven, J. and Whalley, J. (1985), General equilibrium computations of the marginal welfare costs of taxes in the United States, in: *American Economic Review*, 75, 128–38.

Blomquist, A. (1991), The doctor as double agent: information assymetry, health insurance, and medical care, in *Journal of Health Economics*, 10, 411–32.

Bohn, H. (1987), Monitoring multiple agents, in: *Journal of Economic Behavior and Organization*, 8, 279–305.

Demski, J.S. and Sappington, D.E.M. (1987), Hierarchical regulatory control, in: *Rand Journal of Economics*, 18(3), Autumn, 369–83.

Feldman, R. and Sloan, F. (1988), Competition among physicians, revisited, in: *Journal of Health Politics, Policy and Law*, 13, 239–61.

Feldstein, P.J. (1996), *The Politics of Health Legislation, An Economic Perspective*, 2nd ed., Chicago: Health Administration Press.

Frascatore, M.R. (1998), Collusion in a three-tier hierarchy: credible beliefs and pure self-interest, in: *Journal of Economic Behavior and Organization*, 34, 459–75.

Gafni, A. (1998), The physician encounter: the physician as perfect agent for the patient versus the informed treatment decision making model, in: *Social Science and Medicine*, 47(3), 332–5.

Holmström, B. (1979), Moral hazard and observability, in: *Bell Journal of Economics*, 101(1), Spring, 74–91.

Jöreskog, K.G. and Goldberger, A.S. (1975), Estimation of a model with multiple indicators and multiple causes of a single latent variable, in: *Journal of the American Statistical Association*, 70/351, September, 631–9.

Laffont, J.-J. and Tirole, J. (1993), *A Theory of Incentives in Procurement and Regulation*, Cambridge MA: MIT Press.

Lancaster, K. (1966), A new approach to consumer theory, in: *Journal of Political Economy*, 74, 132–57.

Levinthal, D. (1988), A survey of agency models of organizations, in: *Journal of Economic Behavior and Organization*, 9, 153–85.

Luft, H.S. (1996), Modifying managed competition to address cost and quality, in: *Health Affairs*, 15(1), 23–38.

Ma, C.A. and McGuire, T.G. (1997), Optimal health insurance and provider payment, in: *American Economic Review*, 87(4), September, 685–704.

Macho-Stadler, I. and Pérez-Castrillo, J.D. (1991), Double risque moral et délégation, in: *Recherches économiques de Louvain*, 57(3), 277–96.

Mooney, G. and Ryan, M. (1993), Agency in health care: getting beyond first principles, in: *Journal of Health Economics*, 12, 125–35.

Pommerehne, W.W. and Zweifel, P. (1991), Success of a tax amnesty: at the polls, for the fisc?, in: *Public Choice*, 72, 131–65.

Rochaix, L. (1989), Information asymmetry and search in the market for physicians' services, in: *Journal of Health Economics*, 8, 53–84.

Schneider, F. (1978), *Politisch-ökonomische Modelle, Ein theoretischer und empirischer Ansatz*, Hain: Königstein.

Schneider, F. (1986), The influence of political institutions on social security policies: a public choice view, in: J.-M. von der Schulenburg (ed.), *Essays in Social Security Economics*, Berlin: Springer, 13–31.

Selden, T.M. (1990), A model of capitation, in: *Journal of Health Economics*, 9(4), 379–409.

Tirole, J. (1986), Hierarchies and bureaucracies: on the role of collusion in organizations, in: *Journal of Law, Economics, and Organization*, 2(2), 181–214.

Viscusi, W.K. (1992), *Fatal Tradeoffs. Public and Private Responsibilities for Risk*, New York: Oxford University Press.

Williams, H.A. (1988), Priority setting in public and private health care, A guide through the methodological jungle, in: *Journal of Health Economics*, 7, 173–83.

Zweifel, P. and Breyer, F. (1997), *Health Economics*. New York: Oxford University Press.

Zweifel, P. and Eichenberger, R.E. (1992), The political economy of corporatism in medicine: self-regulation or cartel management? in: *Journal of Regulatory Economics*, 4, 89–108.

# 13 Recruiting health care rationers

## Individual versus collective choice

*Mark V. Pauly*

## Introduction

In order to protect people against the random risk of high medical services expenditures, health insurance of some form is appropriately furnished in all modern societies. However, because of the existence of moral hazard caused by insurance, it is almost equally inevitable that some method will be chosen to limit the quantity of care to an amount less than the provider would recommend and the patient would accept if the care were free of monetary cost at the point of use. Some moderate amount of limitation is provided by retaining some user money price, but in almost all cases the bulk of the burden of limitation is placed on the supply side – through rules, provider incentives, or characteristics of access, care is rationed.

While rationing is inevitable and therefore predictable, there are two things which vary greatly and which are unpredictable – how strictly care will be rationed and (a logically prior issue) what persons or institutions will act as the citizen's agent in deciding on the amount of rationing. The amount of health care people ultimately consume depends on a combination of their own decisions and those of others. Sometimes, the supply or rationing constraint imposed by others is binding, while at other times the person's own demand limits the quantity he or she will get.

There are two ways a person can choose the agent who will ration the care under health insurance: individually or collectively. The individual choice is expressed through markets. The collective choice is expressed through the political process. Which method is likely to be selected by different populations in different settings? In this chapter I will explore some theories about the choice of institutional arrangements, and apply those theories, in an informal way, to variations in institutions across countries. I will also, with some trepidation, use this model to comment on the much-discussed question of equity in the allocation of resources to medical services.

In the idealized and intuitive form of the individual market, each buyer confronts a choice among a set of 'managed care' insurance plans which differ in terms of the method and the outcomes of their rationing processes (Hall, 1997; Enthoven, 1988). Some plans ration strictly, either by setting administrative limits or by offering financial incentives to providers to induce them to supply relatively small amounts of care for a given illness; other plans have fewer rules and pay higher fees. Premiums vary depending on the rationing choices made. The person then chooses the plan whose rationing rule or expected rationed outcome comes closest to the one he or she most prefers, given the premium charged. Preference here primarily refers to maximization of expected utility. If there are a relatively large number of different plans, premiums should be bid down close to expected cost, and each person should be able to choose a plan with an outcome close to his or her ideal.

Intrinsically and essentially, the person choosing insurances in the private market is operating behind a veil of ignorance. While she/he may know something about a personal risk distribution, future illness levels are still uncertain; the probabilities of different states of the world will need to be taken into account. People in unregulated competitive private markets at the same level of risk will pay the same premium for a given level of coverage, but may pay different premiums at different levels of risk.

The collective choice model differs from the competitive market in two important ways. First, premiums will be collected as taxes or as statutory premium payments; these payments will tend to increase with total income or wage income. Second, the process by which the collective choice is made is a political process which will choose a single plan with a single level of rationing (in a sense to be defined). There is no fully accepted model of the political choice process or of political equilibrium; here I will therefore usually use a median voter model. The choice of plan rules and policies (whatever they turn out to be) will be made behind a veil of (partial) ignorance.

How closely political choices approximate the veil of ignorance model frequently referenced in discourses on equity depends in part on the period over which the insurance coverage is assumed to be fixed. The longer the policy period over which the choice persists, the closer the protection approximates a constitutional choice. There is no intrinsic reason why the period should differ between market and collective choice. Tax institutions do seem to change slowly, but national health system budgets are subject to change every year.

If there are no income effects on the demand for medical care (or the demand for health), the ideal or efficient quantity under either arrangement is easy to identify. It is the quantity the person would demand without insurance; this is the quantity at which the marginal expected benefit from more care equals its marginal expected cost. As DeMeza (1983) noted some time ago, if there are income effects and/or a state-dependent utility function (the net effect of higher expected utility and insurance-based transfers to the low health state), the ideal quantity with insurance can differ from that without insurance. The ideal quantity with insurance will generally be somewhat larger.[1]

Figure 13.1 provides an example I will use throughout the chapter. Each person is assumed to be at risk for three states. The person might be healthy or might have one of two possible illness states, 'mild' with demand curve $D_M$ and 'severe' with demand curve $D_S$, with associated probabilities $p_M$ and $p_S$. (The probability of being healthy is $(1 - p_M - p_S)$.) The optimal rate of use of care in each state

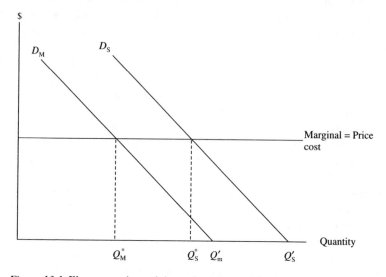

*Figure 13.1* Illness severity and the optimal demand for medical care.

(ignoring income effects associated with effects on utility from risk reduction and whatever tax or premium is levied) are the quantities $Q_M^*$ and $Q_S^*$. (With income effects, optimal quantities $Q_M^*$ and $Q_S^*$ could be larger than those indicated in the diagram.) Before the illness state is known, the representative person would most prefer the insurance arrangement which would provide these quantities. Once illness strikes, of course, because of moral hazard, the sick person would prefer the quantities $Q_M'$ and $Q_S'$ if he or she were fully insured.

Probably individuals care about (and may differ in their concern for) both the final quantity of care received and the 'hassle cost' associated with supply-side limits. For instance, if use of a medical specialist requires a prior visit to a primary care gatekeeper physician, people may differ in terms of how great a cost or bother that visit is. Such differences will lead to preferences for different types of rationing, different expected quantities, and different average costs.

The final and most important conceptual question is whether the manager(s) of the insurance plan(s) will have the ability and the desire to act as perfect agents of the consumer. Will they in fact deliver $Q_M^*$ and $Q_S^*$ at minimum cost? Given the information available to the insurer, it would appear that managers in the competitive market model will try to get as close as they can to the ideal. (They will not generally be able to be exact since they will not perfectly observe the health state.) It is competition among plans, not (necessarily) the direct incentives plans offer to their managers or their physicians, which brings about this outcome (although a plan is likely to get closer to the ideal outcome if it structures its incentives to make choice of that level optimal for its providers). In short, behind the veil of ignorance about what illness state will occur, competitive markets (with consumers informed about the amount of care delivered conditional on illness state) should come close to the optimum. If they fail to approximate it, the reason will be imperfect information.

What about the alternative of a single collectively chosen plan? The government agency is a nonprofit monopolist. While we cannot easily characterize the outcome, we can be reasonably sure that it will differ from the ideal (Leu, 1986). Again, if consumer/voters had perfect knowledge, they could still compel political agents to do the right thing. However, the absence of a benchmark – the absence, in a word, of competition – will make this harder to accomplish.

While the final objective is, at least in part, the same in either setting, the actual outcome may differ. Because of this possibility, different societies may, at a logically prior 'constitutional stage', choose different methods for deciding on the process of limiting the use of medical care. Some methods may fit some populations with some characteristics but not others. In this chapter I want to explore the expected variations in choices under differing assumptions about the characteristics of populations.

It is worth noting, as Reinhardt (1999) has remarked, that virtually all the devices American private managed care insurers use to control cost are also used by (and have been copied from) collectively chosen health systems. Capitation, gatekeeper providers, reference pricing, limits on hospital stay, and freedom from litigation all have characterized government insurance plans. The levels of use and health outcomes achieved also appear comparable (give the differences in input prices). The difference between privately and collectively chosen insurance plans is not based on the methods to control spending, but on the target or intended level of usage. Even here, the main difference is not the levels of use – there are US HMOs (Health Maintenance Organization) that can achieve the same level of real spending per capita as in Canada – but rather the variation permitted, in a private market, relative to the greater uniformity in a single payer system.

### Constitutional choice

The key question I want to address is what level of rationing a population would choose, if the choice were made behind a veil of ignorance in which voters' future health states and also future incomes and tastes are not known with certainty. I first examine this question by considering a series of simple examples.

### Case 1: World of identicals

Here we apply the standard public choice model with a single representative individual to the choice of method for determining or limiting the amount of care. I assume all persons are equally risk averse, with the same tastes for medical care and method of rationing, with the same income, and with the same prior risk of illness. I also assume initially that there are no marginal externalities at the level of rationing that will be chosen; neither additional care for contagious disease nor additional care that relieves suffering is valued at the margin by non-users.[2]

In this case individual or collective choice should yield the same outcome. If a market with competitive plans existed, the sole offering that would persist in competitive equilibrium would be the plan that provides the ideal level and type of rationing preferred by the representative individual. This result assumes, of course, that collective choice and management would be equally efficient as market behaviour with competing firms. From the earlier discussion, efficiency might fail to be achieved if either (a) the choice is collective but public managers are not efficient or (b) the market is used but it is not highly competitive.

If, in contrast, there were externalities at the margin, this population would be likely to employ subsidies or mandates to reduce the level of rationing below what individuals would choose privately. Such collective action to increase consumption would probably be preferred to voluntary charity or voluntary coordination which would suffer from the free rider problem. Given appropriate structure, such a proposal could command unanimous, current period approval.

### Case 2: Differing tastes

Next we assume that citizens are identical in income, risk aversion, and risk level, but that they have differing preferences over the amount of medical care they seek and the type of limitation they prefer. Those who value health highly and dislike 'hassle' will seek an insurance plan with only mild limits on use and cost, whereas those who value other goods more than health at the margin will prefer a strict plan. We could represent two levels of 'taste' as in Figure 13.2 with the pairs of demand curves $D_M$ and $D'_M$ and $D_S$ and $D'_S$.

The market solution in this simple example is clear. There will be two plans, with the 'prime plan' delivering more care in each illness state than the other plan. However, the prime plan will have a higher premium.

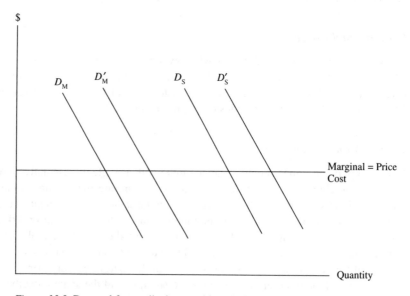

*Figure 13.2* Demand for medical care with variation in tastes.

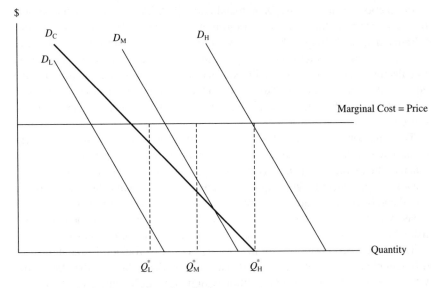

*Figure 13.3* Optimal quantities of medical care.

The challenges faced by collective choice of rationing limits, even if government managers are perfect agents, are twofold: (1) *information* on variations in citizen values must be obtained, and (2) the political choice mechanism must *accommodate* that variation. Collective choice works best (in the sense of accommodating to preferences) when only one plan level, uniform for all, is appropriately optimal; it has a difficult time accommodating significant differences in demands.

What if externalities were present? Figure 13.3 illustrates. The demand curves $D_L$, $D_M$, and $D_H$ are the expected or average demands for care (conditional on illness level) for people with low, medium, and high tastes for health care or health. We represent the existence of externalities by a community demand curve such as $D_C$; this curve measures, at any quantity for a given individual, the *summed* marginal valuations of all others in the community of additional consumption by that person. In the diagram, the optimal quantities for each 'taste type' are obtained by adding vertically each person's demand curve to the community demand curve, with the optimal quantities becoming $Q_L^*$, $Q_M^*$, and $Q_H^*$. ($Q_H^*$ does not differ from that person's private choice because, as drawn, the marginal externality is zero at the level of private choice.)

Adding externalities obviously causes the quantities to be closer together than in the private equilibrium, but they still differ. *How* close together they become depends in part on the slope of the community demand curve. If it were perfectly inelastic, the optimal quantity for everyone would be a single amount which could be chosen collectively. In addition, the intercept of the $D_C$ demand curve obviously matters; if it were far to the left, marginal externalities would be zero for most persons, and the case for the market would be stronger.

In practice, what does the $D_C$ demand curve look like? This has been studied by comparing public subsidy programmes (Medicaid) across US states (Grannemann and Pauly, 1982; Holahan *et al.*, 1994). The demand curve displays a price elasticity for total benefits (depending on the specification) of about 0.78. I conjecture, in the (nearly) equal incomes case for a developed country, that the community demand curve is likely to be to the left of the great bulk of individual demand curves. If so, there is relatively little role for collective intervention in this case.

This situation of varying tastes would seem to present a strong case for a market. Collective choice will have difficulty in accommodating the variation in demands, whereas the market will generally be able to do so, and do so in a way that should not raise great concerns about equity. The greater the variation in tastes, the greater the theoretical advantage of market arrangements over collective choice. A measure of variation in tastes is therefore an empirical fact that can help to establish whether or not collective choice is to be preferred to market choice.

The market equilibrium is not necessarily perfectly efficient. If the number of different plans that can be accommodated in any market is limited, then the model will be one of monopolistic competition with product differentiation, which does not necessarily yield the optimal mix of product varieties. While we cannot be precise, it is, nevertheless, likely that even an inefficient mix will be superior to a single plan option if there is more than a negligible amount of variation in demand.

### Case 3: Variation in income

Now let us assume that individuals have the possibility of varying incomes, and let us continue to assume no externalities at the level of rationing chosen by the lowest income person. For the moment, assume also that income effects on demand are zero, so that the desired or ideal health care rationing level at any premium is actually the same for all persons at all income levels. However, if the collectively chosen plan is financed by taxes that vary directly with income, the plan generosity desired by each voter could well decline as income rises. What level will be chosen? If we adopt a median voter model, we conclude that the chosen level will be that preferred by the person with median income at the tax price that person faces. If the distribution of income is skewed so that the median income is below the mean income, the level chosen will exceed the 'ideal' plan that equates marginal cost and marginal benefits. At the quasi-constitutional stage, one might then expect this inefficient outcome to be noted, and preference to shift toward market arrangements.

To the extent that the generosity of health insurance is a normal good – which is surely true over some range – things may differ. The person with the median income faces a below-average tax price, but also desires less insurance than average. The quantity will be less than the ideal *uniform* level if the income elasticity of demand for insured care is greater than the income elasticity of the tax system. The outcome under collective choice may still be inefficient, but the direction of the inefficiency is ambiguous. However, if there are income effects, the optimal quantities for each person will differ.

Would we then expect collective provision to be chosen in this situation? The expected utility for a person who has the population-level probability of having any given level of income would be lowered by collective provision unless the income redistribution associated with collective choice is felt to be of value to a risk averse person. Even in the latter case, it would generally be preferable to redistribute income explicitly, rather than use health insurance financing as the way to do so. The reason, of course, is that redistributive taxation for health care financing leads to inefficient collective choice of quantity. In the model thus far, health insurance is a private good, so it is publicly provided only imperfectly.

However, it is often assumed that, in the constitutional state, any income-related inequality of health care use is undesirable, and should be overridden – even if doing so would mean that lower income people are receiving health care which is worth less to them than the equivalent amount of money income.

This observation brings us to the heart of one of the most controversial questions in the normative and positive economics of health care. The conventional welfare economics solution to the general welfare choice problem is based on Musgrave's (1958) model of 'branches'. The distributional branch of the government, using constitutional rules, or whatever process that society has chosen to determine the distribution of income, implements the desired set of taxes and transfers of money income. The consequent distribution of income can be regarded as 'ideal'. The allocation branch then determines which collectively chosen goods are to be provided at what levels, using the marginal-cost-equals-marginal-benefit rule. In a more rigorously specified model, the two 'branches' actually operate simultaneously, rather than sequentially, but this causes no serious analytical problem.

A much-more-debated question is whether this model, which uses the Pareto criterion conditional on some ideal initial distribution of income, is the appropriate one to use for health care. I will turn to this issue in more detail later. For the present, the main conclusion is that under the Musgrave model a post-redistribution market solution for health care rationing will approximate the ideal choice if no externalities are present and if the post-redistribution income distribution is regarded as ideal. If, in contrast, it is felt that redistribution has been suboptimal, then greater equalization of medical care, possibly up to a near-uniform level, may be warranted. Compared to the given demand variation due to taste, that due to income variation can in principle be changed by changing the distribution of income. However, the question of why one would expect (behind the veil of ignorance) that the after-transfer distribution of income will be other than ideal is a difficult one, which will be discussed further below.

If externalities exist in an important way at the margin, taxes and subsidies to medical care to deal with those externalities will, when financed by appropriate (Lindahl) taxes, be strongly supported by voters at all income levels. High-income people will be willing to pay taxes to subsidize the health care consumption of lower income persons either because they wish to avoid the consequences of untreated contagious disease or (probably more importantly) because they care about others' consumption for altruistic reasons.

Here again, however, if the community demand curve is not perfectly inelastic, the resulting outcome will be one with consumption that is more equal than in the unsubsidized market but definitely not uniform. (Relabel the demand curves in Figure 13.3 to represent low, medium, and high incomes.) A market, but one with income-related or means-tested subsidies, will lead to an efficient solution. Note also that, in contrast to the identical-incomes case, increasing the quantities of the low users by taxing the high users further *reduces* the inequality of income spendable on other things. Moreover, the community demand curve is more likely to affect many demanders.

Is there then a case for some collective intervention if inequality in health care use is driven primarily by post-transfer inequality in income? The case for uniform collective choice (as opposed to a system of uniform subsidies that lead to non-uniform outcomes) depends as before on the slope or elasticity of the community demand curve. If the community feels that there is some unique quantity of care or associated rationing mechanism at which the marginal benefit falls precipitously to zero, the case for collective choice is strongest.

### Model 4: Identical tastes, identical incomes, unequal risk

Now we suppose that people will differ, at some points in time, in their expected expenses over the next period of insurance coverage. If market insurance is sold on a single-period basis, premiums per period will reflect the expected expense in that period. This makes the premium across time periods a random variable, something risk averse people would prefer to avoid. It may also be regarded as inequitable for a high-risk person to pay a higher premium, although this feeling may depend on the reason for the high risk. Higher risk due to smoking or alcohol abuse, or just to old age, is not for the most part random and may not be regarded as a source of unfairness, whereas the change in risk associated with an illness that spans more than one period (a chronic condition) would be regarded as unfair.

Collective choice will make taxes independent of risk. If the demand for insurance depends on risk (e.g. if high risks prefer less aggressive efforts at cost containment), there will be a trade-off – no risk of premium variation, but not exactly the right level of coverage. Nevertheless, this appears to be a strong case for collective provision compared to market provision.

However, there may be some alternative market arrangements which can reduce (though probably not eliminate) the kind of added risk we have been discussing. It has been shown that there exist several methods for selling multi-period insurance that can prevent the kind of premium risk just discussed (Cochrane, 1995; Pauly *et al.*, 1995). Neither method is perfect in theory – one requires that the risk level be established objectively, and the other compels people to precommit to an insurer for future periods, with the possibility of lock-in.

Some improvements are possible. Lock-in need not be a problem if the insurance contract can specify benefits accurately. (Paradoxically, lock-in will be a greater problem the more aggressively is care managed.) Variation from year to year in premiums may largely average out on a lifetime basis. Finally, if the level of risk can be measured, transfers can be made to high risks, but a competitive market is still allowed to function.

There is no perfect solution to this model. It appears to require a mix of collective and individual institutions, but I believe it is still possible to preserve individual choice. Of course, in this model with identical tastes there is less to be gained from allowing that choice than if tastes varied as well.

## What theory tells us

To sum up to this point: when individuals are identical, markets and collective choice are, in general, equivalent. Markets only work better in such cases than collective choice of the agents who ration if markets can be approximately competitive and/or if governments have difficulty in motivating their agents. In situations where markets cannot be competitive (because of low population density) collective choice will definitely be better. (If consumers are and will remain poorly informed, neither markets nor democracies populated by ignorant consumers will work well.)

What if people differ in characteristics that are strongly related to their desired level of rationing? The general principle is that greater demand variation leads to a preferences for markets. Comparing competitive market choice with collective choice (with not-too-imperfect agents):

1  If the primary variation in individually desired rationing is due to substantial variation in tastes, the preference for markets is strongest.
2  If the primary variation is due to substantial variation in income, the preference for markets may be somewhat weaker, but only if the income distribution that drives demand variation is regarded as less than ideal.
3  If the primary variation is due to substantial variation in prior risk, collective choice may be better than single-period markets. However, multi-period markets can exist which can solve this problem.

In what follows, I wish to consider two variations on these simple models, before turning to some empirical conjectures: (1) What really is equity when income varies? (2) Are hybrid or mixed models better? I then consider some applications of this model.

## Equity and allocation

The first issue goes back to Musgrave's distinction among branches. If the distributional branch, in performing its job, decides to permit some people to end up with substantially less income than others, and if, as a result of strong income effects, lower income people would in a market seek plans that ration more strictly, is this an ideal outcome?[3] Of course, the answer depends on what one means by 'ideal'. There is at present considerable confusion among analysts about the answer to this question, and animosity generated by the confusion.

Let us begin by going back to first principles. The conventional welfare economics solution is to assume that a set of societal welfare weights comes into existence to settle the distributional question. The reason for this assumption is not that there is evidence that such weights exist, but rather that they *need* to exist if the model is to be closed. To perform this task, most discussions in this area assume that welfare levels can and must be compared. Somehow different levels and distributions of welfare must be compared. There are three potential ways of doing so. One way is by recourse to some ethical model or ethical principle. For instance, one might adopt Rawls' maximin principle, or some other ethicist's definition of distributive justice. The second method, suggested most strongly by Culyer (1991), is to elicit weights or values from some public sector decision-maker, already in place, who is to determine what to do. Some cabinet secretary or minister of health, or perhaps the head of some commission, would play this role. The third method is to have recourse to what 'the public' thinks, although the precise method by which these thoughts are to be extracted and the justification for that method are often obscure. Moreover, any method of elicitation would fall prey to the problems with voting and preference revelation mechanisms. Public opinion polls of some sort, or informal reference to what everyone is said to believe, often provide the data here, although more recent efforts have used surveys or focus groups involving samples of citizens to respond to hypothetical questions about which allocation they would prefer.

The problem is that, without some additional criteria, any one of these methods is as good as any other. Part of the confusion in the literature is caused by fluctuating between a set of predetermined ethical principles as a guide to justice, on the one hand, and judgement or conjecture about the choices of a government official, community, or society deciding these issues in some poorly specified political process on the other. The discussion is by turns vaguely positive or subliminally normative, but dilemmas remain: if a particular distribution of income fit perfectly with some ethical theory – but citizens would never support politicians who supported this theory – the relevance of the ethical standard is called into question. But if some set of citizens should choose by majority rule to deny income altogether to some subgroup, based (say) on ethnicity or appearance, few analysts would advocate that choice as being a proper representation of the social welfare function.

This problem is difficult enough when it comes to the distribution of money income; it becomes even more complex if we allow for a second decision, after the first has been made, about health care services. Sometimes some people do seem to feel that the distribution of medical care is more important than, or in addition to, the distribution of generalized purchasing power – but should these feelings count any more than the discriminatory feelings most would reject? Indeed, having set out his 'branches' model, Musgrave himself created the category of 'merit-wants' to apply to things like public spending on medical care. The inconsistency of the merit-want concept with the rest of his framework has been noted (McLure, 1968), but the 'merit-want' label continues to be used.

What about some person or society that tolerates some income inequality but professes to recoil at the inequality in use of health care that would be generated by a distribution of income it finds acceptable? Is such a set of preferences, in the constitutional state, logically consistent or legitimate? In some of the literature, the answer to this question is provided by definition: since we are health economists, we should only worry about equity in health care, and assume that the importance of 'other things' is fully captured by a predetermined public or societal budget for health care. I would not take so parochial a view, either for myself or for my fellow citizens; there is more to life than health.

Perhaps because of this broader perspective, I conclude that there is no definitive solution to this dilemma. In the spirit of my discussion to this point, I believe it is useful to ask what choices ordinary people (not health economists) might make behind a veil of ignorance. So we begin with the collective choice issue. If persons were not sure what income level they would achieve, but had to specify now a process for determining the collective choice about rationing of care, what would they choose? (We will ignore for the moment the question of whether this choice will be a political equilibrium once the veil is lifted.)

There are two considerations. First, a person could think of what level of rationing he would want at a given income level, and what he would want to pay – all constrained by the requirement that the total amount of payments equals the total cost. If the level of taxes used for redistribution had already been chosen to be consistent with social welfare maximization and appropriate work incentives, there would be no reason to choose to finance health insurance with additional income-transferring taxes. Then, given those levels of income, the optimal choice would be to select the level of coverage that a person with a particular income level would choose. In the state in which the person had below-average income, for example, it would not be helpful to mandate more generous coverage, since the person would have to pay the additional cost, and would prefer the money to the health care.

If we think of the pattern of optimal purchases conditional on the distribution of income selected to be ideal, there might nevertheless be altruistic externalities at the margin once the veil of ignorance is lifted. That is, the low-income person might voluntarily choose a level of rationing so restrictive that higher income persons would place positive values on additional consumption. The appropriate change would be higher levels of coverage for lower income people, paid for by higher taxes on higher income people (adjusted for any effects on work effort). This change would increase everyone's expected utility, because the upper income people would feel less guilty and the lower income people would receive more (marginally) useful care.

Is there a rationale for overriding, or going beyond, this altruistic equilibrium? Since different people will have different views both on the fair (or efficient) distribution of income and the proper amount of altruistic behaviour, we should still expect some people to propose greater levels of equalization of health care use. But they would just be expressing their personal preferences, not society's preferences.

Here is a helpful thought experiment. Think of the distribution of general purchasing power chosen behind the veil of ignorance. Let the amount of health care chosen by the average person with the lowest income be $H^*_{min}$. Would there be a rationale for increasing the quantity beyond this level? It seems unlikely that people behind the veil would want to require larger purchases paid for by the low-income person, since that would make the person in that state worse off. Would it then be desired to reduce the income of higher income persons yet further to subsidize this consumption? Would a person prefer to have a lower income in the 'lucky' high-income state in order to observe more health care than $H^*_{min}$? Beyond the altruism argument, it is difficult to see why.

There is, nevertheless, the possibility that persons behind the veil of ignorance might treat health care as something special. For example, health care (or health itself) may be accorded the roles of a 'primary good' in the Rawls' framework (even though Rawls himself did not mention health care as a primary good). If the typical person at one of the lower income levels (consistent with the social preference) would choose to obtain less than some target amount of this good, one might prefer to override such persons' preferences and force that person to consume more health care and less of other goods than would have been preferred. (Alternatively, and equivalently, redistributing the last dollar away from a high-income person would be desirable only if that dollar were spent entirely on health.) Of course, forcing the persons to obtain health care might mean less effort devoted to other primary goods, but presumably there is some optimal combination of primary and non-primary goods that differs from the person's utility-maximizing bundle (given their cost).

While all of this is tautologically possible, is it reasonable? What good might be satisfied by forcing consumption of a medical-care-rich but non-preferred bundle? The most common answer is suggested by Daniels' (1985) concept of justice as entitlement to the specific resources needed for the 'normal opportunity range', or a Sugden and Williams (1978) 'fair innings' notion of quality-adjusted years of survival.

However, there is a dilemma here: why would the lower income consumer not be choosing the expenditure pattern that maximizes the possibility of attaining the 'normal opportunity range'? If opportunity is so fundamental to human existence, how can consumers not value it? Conversely, if they do not value it, how do we know it is important? There is no obvious rationale for requiring people to choose greater opportunities than they would prefer.

Why should a person want to be compelled to give up other consumption for health care? There is the usual 'wine, women, and song' or frivolous consumption answer, but these value-laden judgements will not do. The real question is – the opportunity to do what? If I have enough income to buy a flu shot or a music CD, and I choose the CD because I like music more than I fear chills and fever, I may have traded more current-period 'normal species functioning' (of which music is surely a part) for a lower chance of normal functioning in the future. However, there must be more to the discussion than an argument over discount rates. I find little basis for overriding individual choices, at the constitutional stage. My presumption is that it is self-evaluated overall individual welfare, not any specific component of the consumption bundle, which is the object of the distributional judgement.

## Hybrid solutions

To this point we have been comparing use of the competitive market to allocate resources to medical care versus collective choice of the total quantity each person would get. The preceding discussion of altruism suggests that there might be superior alternatives. For instance, there might be collective choice of a subsidy to some or all persons to be used for their purchases in private markets.

However, if the desired level of rationing by a person is one ideally increased by a subsidy, why not just make the choice of a higher quantity (and the resulting distribution of disposable income) the proposed collective choice? In a transactions-cost-free world, this would be a solution that is at least as good. However, if it is difficult to vary levels of coverage in a full collective choice situation, the alternative policy of offering subsidies to which different people will respond in different ways may make sense.

The subsidy might take one of two broad forms: a minimum amount of free care, or a matching rate or subsidy to health insurance premiums. The 'minimum package' model generally would not be chosen, since it would only affect those who would otherwise choose less than the minimum package. If that is the case, there is then no need to provide this subsidy to those who would or do supplement, paying the full private price at the margin. The other strategy is to match individuals' premium payments at some subsidy rate (which probably will decline as income and other demand indicators rise). Figure 13.3 illustrates the concept of the ideal subsidy when others in the community have equal concern about every citizen. The ideal outcome is for people with stronger own-valuations to get more care, but at a lower subsidy rate. Whether that income-related subsidy takes the form of a payment that falls as income rises but is fixed at any income level, or whether it takes the form of open-ended matching (or some combination) is of relatively little importance. Open-ended matching does make it harder for competition to work.

To operate this subsidized arrangement, however, it is clear that markets will be preferred to a single collectively chosen method for limiting *total* care. There is a collectively chosen *policy*, but its effect on the amount of rationing varies across persons (in an equitable way). However, since the total amount desired will vary across individuals – whether they differ by taste, income, or risk – it is clear that some type of market arrangement is to be preferred.

However, clearly there are some kinds of mixed systems that would not be chosen. For instance, in US Medicare the addition of a private subsidy raises the cost of care under the public programme, and yet those who supplement pay the same premium at the margin for the base coverage as do those who do not. Alternatives are clearly important here.

## Some observations on cross-country comparisons

Do these ideas help to explain why different countries choose different mixes of market choice and collective choice of rationing? I think the answer is yes. Some developed countries rely heavily on markets. Some use only collective choice. Many allow a higher income minority of the population to use markets, but use collective choice for everyone else.

The US is the most prominent country relying heavily on markets, although some middle income Asian countries do so as well. The key question, based on the theory I have outlined, is whether there is more variation in tastes or 'acceptable' income within these countries than within others that opted for full or partial collective choice.

Is there any empirical basis for judging whether demand for care (and rationing), given income and risk, varies more in some settings than others? Surprisingly, there has been relatively little investigation of this crucial question. We do know that explicit measures of income and prior risk explain only a small portion, probably less then 25 per cent of the variation in spending across persons (Newhouse, 1989). How much of the remaining 75 per cent is due to cross-persons variations in illness incidence, how much due to variation in nonprice rationing, and how much due to variation in tastes is hard to say.

The evidence from American experience with managed care is also difficult to interpret. Enthoven's (1988) concept of a variety of plans explicitly differing by strength of supply-side controls seems not to have occurred in most markets. Instead, there has been a process of homogenization, with most plans now offering a wide network, with coverage (at an out-of-pocket cost) of out-of-network providers. There has been some recent variation in levels of out-of-pocket payments (now rising for the first time in decades).

However, the convergence may simply reflect the similarity of equilibrium product types in a Hotelling-type model. Since the number of plans in most markets is shrinking, the gravitation toward a single style might be expected. On the other hand, in the public Medicare programme for the elderly more different types of plans have been permitted, and some of them have emerged.

Here is the kind of empirical study that would test my hypothesis. Compare two countries that have chosen different methods for rationing (e.g. the US and Sweden). Estimate health services demand functions for the citizens of both countries controlling for illness level. The hypothesis would be confirmed if the variation in demand is higher for the US than for Sweden. (I did not yet perform this test because I know of no data that tells us what people in a collective constrained system (such as Sweden) *would* use if they were in an unrestricted market.)

Next we turn to equity, and we again ask about the empirical basis for assumptions about what 'society' desires in different countries. While there have been surveys and focus groups to ask what equity means (and, to a lesser extent, what respondents are willing to give up to get it), most analysts are more casual. Culyer and Wagstaff begin their 1993 article on equity and quality with the assertion that 'equity is widely acknowledged to be an important policy objective in the health care field'. To support this statement, they note that 'a concern over growing inequalities in access to health care in the US appears to have been responsible – at least in part – for the plethora of US reform proposals'. With the benefit of hindsight, I would make two comments. First, the reform debate in the US, insofar as it considered (and still considers) 'access' to be important, was less concerned with *equality* of access, than the *low level* of access of the uninsured (Buchanan, 1984).[4] More importantly, the political debate over reform resulted in rejection of proposals to improve access, along with the rest of the Clinton plan. Are we to judge from this that, in the US, equity should not be postulated as a goal? That would seem to be consistent with revealed (political) preference. Here is another example. Rice (1998) has argued that 'people feel worse off when they find themselves falling behind (in medical care use) relative to others', but then argues that corrective taxes are 'a political impossibility'? If the corrective action is politically impossible, in what sense do we know that the 'feelings' exist at the margin? If the people had the feelings, would not they make the action politically possible?

I do not think, based on empirical evidence, that one could reject the null hypothesis that additional equity in health care is currently not a policy objective in the US. I hasten to add that I personally do not endorse this view; I proposed reforms to improve access long before the Clinton debate (Pauly, 1971; Pauly *et al.*, 1991). However, given the political choice rules adopted, there is no evidence that there is unsatisfied demand for equity in the US. Some want more, but others do not, and these desires cancel.

If there is then no single universal specification of the ideal amount of equity, is there then any objective basis for establishing a given society's desires with regard to equity? In principle one could undertake a veil-of-ignorance experiment, asking people to imagine they could have any income. An interesting question is whether the method for allocation of resources to medical care chosen behind the veil-of-ignorance would differ from the quantities that would be voluntarily chosen for altruistic reasons after the veil is lifted. Our analysis suggests that the answer is generally negative.[5]

## Conclusion

The inevitable (and unenviable) task of rationing medical services requires an agent. Multiple agents can be selected in a heterogeneous market, or a single agent can be chosen politically. A key issue is the variation in preferences among citizens relative to the variation in risk or income. At present, we know little about these matters empirically, so perhaps one should be slow to judge another country's health care system.

## Notes

1 But it could be smaller if insurance coverage obviates the need to receive care that would allow one to recover quickly enough to work to pay off medical bills.
2 For a definition of marginal externalities, see Pauly (1971).

3 An interesting question is whether the strength of income effects might vary across populations. Based on data from U.S. States, this seems to be the case.
4 Indeed, in the recent debate over possible tax credits for the low-income uninsured, not only has the higher level of coverage and use by the average higher income person been of no concern, but the low levels of use by the uninsured who are not poor or near poor (slightly less than half of the uninsured) have not often been thought to be deserving of subsidy or attention.
5 Will envy affect matters? If envy is strong, lower income people are made worse off when higher income people consume. If the effect of envy of health care on welfare is large enough, people may choose to prevent unequal consumption in the constitutional stage, precisely because they prefer higher welfare in the low-income states. However, the level of envy would have to be so high as to have a profound effect on welfare for this motivation to be important. The evidence that people would restrict spending in the interest of equity is rather slim. It has never been important in the US, or in countries with a German-type system that allows the very well off to opt out of social insurance. Only Canada forbids people from spending their own income on health care and, even there, the prohibition is limited to covered services, not to equally important services like prescription drugs. I do not think that one can reject the hypothesis that, beyond a vague discomfort at the effects of spending by the well to do, the envy motive is too weak to affect behaviour.

# References

Buchanan, A. 'The Right to a Decent Minimum of Health Care'. *Philosophy and Public Affairs* 1984;13:55–78.

Cochrane, J. 'Time Consistent Health Insurance'. *Journal of Political Economy* 1995; 103(3):445–73.

Culyer, A.J. 'An Extra-Welfarist View of Health Economics.' World Health Economics Congress, Zurich, Switzerland, 1991.

Culyer, A.J. and Wagstaff, A. 'Equity and Equality in Health and Health Care'. *Journal of Health Economics* 1993;12:431–58.

Daniels, N. *Just Health Care*. Cambridge: Cambridge University Press, 1985.

DeMeza, D. 'Health Insurance and the Demand for Medical Care'. *Journal of Health Economics* 1983;2:47–54.

Enthoven, A. *Theory and Practice of Managed Competition in Health Care Finance*. Amsterdam: North Holland, 1988.

Grannemann, T. and Pauly, M. *Controlling Medicaid Costs*. Washington: AEI Press, 1982.

Hall, M. *Making Medical Spending Decisions*. Oxford and New York: Oxford University Press, 1997.

Holahan, J. *et al*. *Medicaid since 1980: Costs, Coverage, and the Shifting Alliance between the Federal Governement and the States*. Washington, DC: Urban Institute Press, 1994.

Leu, R. 'The Public–Private Mix and International Healthcare Costs'. In A. Culyer and B. Jönsson, eds., *Public and Private Health Services*. Oxford: Basil Blackwell, 1986.

McLure, C.E. Jr. 'Merit Wants: A Normatively Empty Box'. *Finanzarchiv*. Vol. 27, 1968.

Musgrave, R. *The Theory of Public Finance*. New York: McGraw-Hill, 1958.

Newhouse, J. 'Rate Adjusters for Medicare under Capitation'. *Health Care Financing Review*, Winter 1989;11(2):45–55.

Pauly, M.V. *Medical Care at Public Expense*. New York: Praeger Publishers, 1971.

Pauly, M.V., Danzon, P., Feldstein, P. and Hoff, J. 'A Plan for "Responsible National Health Insurance"'. *Health Affairs*, Spring 1991;10(1):5–25.

Pauly, M.V., Kunreuther, H. and Hirth, R. 'Guaranteed Renewability in Insurance'. *Journal of Risk and Uncertainty* 1995;10:143–56.

Reinhardt, U. 'Remarks on the publication of *Regulating Managed Care*'. Association for Health Services Research, Chicago, June 1999.

Rice, T. *The Economics of Health Reconsidered*. Ann Arbor: Health Administration Press, 1998.

Sugden, R. and Williams, A. *The Principles of Practical Cost-Benefit Analysis*. New York: Oxford University Press, 1978.

# Index

156 - 379 - 391

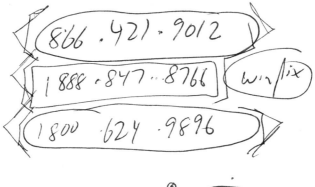

866 . 421 . 9012

1 888 . 847 . 8766     win/fix

1800 . 624 . 9896

108 . 336 . 431